CLASSICS OF WEST

VOLUME I

The Ancient World

THIRD EDITION

CLASSICS OF WESTERN THOUGHT

Under the General Editorship of
Thomas H. Greer
Michigan State University

I **The Ancient World** THIRD EDITION
Edited by
Stebelton H. Nulle
Michigan State University

II **Middle Ages, Renaissance,
and Reformation** THIRD EDITION
Edited by
Karl F. Thompson
Michigan State University

III **The Modern World** THIRD EDITION
Edited by
Charles Hirschfeld
Late of Richmond College,
The City University of New York
and
Edgar E. Knoebel
Michigan State University

IV **The Twentieth Century**
Edited by
Donald S. Gochberg
Michigan State University

CLASSICS OF
WESTERN
THOUGHT

VOLUME I

The Ancient World

THIRD EDITION

Edited by

Stebelton H. Nulle
Michigan State University

HARCOURT BRACE JOVANOVICH, PUBLISHERS
San Diego   New York   Chicago   Austin
London   Sydney   Toronto

ISBN: 0-15-507678-7

Library of Congress Catalog Card Number: 79-90089

Printed in the United States of America

Introduction to the Classics Series

Writings by the great minds of the Western tradition offer contemporary Westerners the best possible introduction to their humanistic heritage. To provide such an introduction, the editors of this series have brought together works that we consider classics of the Western tradition—of Western *thought,* in the broad sense. For the most part, these volumes of primary documents are intended for use in college-level courses in humanities or the history of civilization, normally in the company of a brief narrative text. One such text, designed especially for use with this series, is my *Brief History of Western Man,* Third Edition (Harcourt Brace Jovanovich, 1977).

The number and range of documents in Western civilization are, of course, enormous, and good reasons can always be advanced for choosing one work over another. We have sought works that are truly *classic,* that is to say, valuable both for their intrinsic merit and for having exerted a paramount influence on their own and later times—works that display judgment applied to observation as well as creative thought and literary skill. In deciding upon the length and quantity of selections, we have aimed to keep in balance two considerations: having each selection long enough to give a clear view of the author's ideas and, at the same time, offering selections from a substantial number of the foremost writers.

In previous years the Classics of Western Thought series has consisted of three volumes: *The Ancient World; Middle Ages, Renaissance, and Reformation;* and *The Modern World*—this third volume including documents of the last four centuries. Now a fourth volume, *The Twentieth Century,* has been added to the series. Containing writings from this century alone, it is suited especially for courses in contemporary history or humanities. As in the other volumes, each document of this collection is introduced by a brief account of the author's life, the author's role in shaping the Western tradition, and the significance of the particular work.

In preparing the present volumes, the editors have given careful attention to the suggestions of students and teachers who have read and taught from the series over the years. Our addition of a fourth volume is a response to these comments. Also in accordance with readers' suggestions, we have added to the first three volumes a number of selections that enrich and enliven their content, while deleting a few selections that were used infrequently. Most of the selections in the prior edition have been kept, however; and some of these works have been enhanced by means of new and improved translations. Finally, footnotes have been introduced throughout the volumes to explain parts of documents that might otherwise be obscure to some readers. As a result of these measures, we believe that both old and new readers of the series will find it an enjoyable aid in understanding and savoring the Western intellectual heritage.

Thomas H. Greer

Preface to the Third Edition

In this first volume of the Classics of Western Thought series is gathered some of the best thought and expression of the ancient Mediterranean world, spanning a period of more than a thousand years (from Homer to Augustine). Given the restricted number of selections, we can do little more than sample the cultural treasures of these earlier societies; for we are heirs to a legacy of unparalleled richness, whose sources are spread over the whole of classical antiquity.

First, we shall follow the Greeks in their search for rational answers to the problems of goodness and excellence, of truth and justice. Then we shall mark the Roman vision of a wider human concord, a community of humankind resting upon government and law. Justly the Romans could boast with the elder Pliny that the mission of Rome was "to give to humanity human culture, and in a word become for all peoples in the whole world their one and only country." Lastly, we shall witness the Judeo–Christian perception of God's oneness and the aspiration for a moral order in which the divine will is realized in the affairs of humanity.

To be sure, Hellenic culture was not without its irrational elements. But it was the moderation, harmony, and balance of the Greek classical ideal that spread throughout the Mediterranean world, finding expression in literature and the arts (what we now call the humanities), and (among a cultivated few at least) as a way of life. The Romans, adapting, interpreting, and extending Hellenic culture, also succeeded where Athens had failed, in giving humanity their own ideal of a universal human order, one that has never been forgotten.

But soon a feeling of profound malaise spread throughout the ancient world. A sense of failure and defeat and a realization of the imperfect nature of secular life led to an urgent search for supernatural meaning and guidance, and ultimately to the rise of Christianity. Gone was the Hellenic sense of the uniqueness of human beings—beings neither gods nor beasts; gone was the confidence in the potential excellence of all humanity; and gone was the bold reliance upon reason. Now there was a new religion based on revelations and expressed in rituals. The ideal of the Christian saint replaced the classical ideal of "the high-minded man," doing the utmost to fulfill latent human powers. The Middle Ages had arrived.

Despite the fluctuations of passing centuries, the ideals we identify with ancient Greece, Rome, and Judea were to live on in radically altered times. Today, in the thermonuclear age, they still offer answers to the perennial questions of value and meaning.

This new edition marks the first appearance of Homer in the volume, through selections from both *The Iliad* and *The Odyssey,* as well as the first appearance of Aristophanes, through his comedy *Lysistrata,* and of the Roman poet Ovid—all in fresh translations suited to contemporary readers. (The Epicurean philosopher Lucretius, though not a newcomer to the collection, is also represented by an engaging new translation.) Homer, although chronologically preclassical, foreshadows aspects of the classical ethos—masculine, aristocratic, enamored of old ways and forms. Aristophanes and Ovid are, on the other hand, associated with change—striking a modern note in claiming recognition for women in public affairs, or in private *affaires.*

The biblical selections in this edition are taken from a newer version of the Bible than the one used previously and include additional portions of the New Testament. In the latter may be seen ideas that, from the beginning of Christianity, set forth a radical challenge to the classical mind and manners.

Stebelton H. Nulle

Contents

Introduction to the Classics Series   v

Preface to the Third Edition   vii

1

Homer

The Iliad

*The earliest writings of Western civilization are the epic (heroic) poems of
Homer. Little is known about the author, and some scholars have even questioned whether the poems were in fact composed by one person. The time and
place of birth of the shadowy poet are also much in doubt; the Homeric
poems,* The Iliad *and* The Odyssey, *have been assigned varying dates,
ranging from the tenth to the seventh century* B.C. *In any case, the poems
certainly tell of a time that long preceded the writing, for the traditional date
of the fall of Troy, the event that ends one poem and begins the other, is
1184* B.C. *And whatever the facts of their creation, there is no doubt that
across the centuries, these poems have been read and admired like no others in
Western literature.*

*There are as many theories about the sources and composition of the epics
as about their authorship. The Iliad, the first of the two, is not so much the
tale of a war as the story of Achilles, its tragic hero, and the customs of his
age and class; indeed, the work might have properly been called the Achil-
leid. As the poem begins, nine years of war between the Achaeans (Greeks)
and Trojans have passed, and Troy (or Ilium) still stands. Helen, the
Achaean woman whose desertion of her husband, King Menelaus, for the
Trojan Paris is the cause of it all, still resides among the Trojans. So far, all
the Achaeans have to show for their efforts to recapture her are the spoils of
raids carried out in the region around the walled city. Nevertheless, as the
selection shows, the events of these raids have brought matters to a crisis by
inspiring the anger of Achilles toward his commander. His withdrawal from
the siege threatens to undo the Achaean cause; for, by all opinion (including
his own), he has excelled all others in battle and is indispensable to Achaean
hopes for victory.*

Homer, *The Iliad*, trans. E. V. Rieu (New York: Penguin Books, 1950), I, 23–39. ©
the Estate of E. V. Rieu, 1950. Reprinted by permission of Penguin Books Ltd.

As we read of the quarrel between the hero and King Agamemnon, brother to Menelaus and commander of the combined Achaean armies, we see Achilles' tragic flaw—imperious, unrelenting anger— which has led him to retire sullenly from battle. What follows, in the absence of his leadership, is a sharp reversal of fortunes for his comrades—and for him, worse still, the death of Patroclus, his dearest friend.

The narrative of The Iliad *is filled largely with descriptions of ups and downs in the long combat and of the part played in it all by the gods; but, perhaps more significantly, it also reveals the aristocratic interests and life-style of those Greeks who first heard the poem recited and of those who later were the first to read it. The climax of this epic work comes not with the pre-destined fall of Troy but with the struggle of Achilles to recover from his anger. It is through this personal victory, this restoration of the divine order, that the will of the gods and the moral sense of the ancient Greeks is confirmed.*

The epic poems of Homer have been many times translated from the original Greek and have been presented in several forms. One of the most charming and readable prose versions is that by the English scholar E. V. Rieu. The following selection from The Iliad *and the succeeding one from* The Odyssey *are taken from Rieu's translations.*

The Wrath of Achilles is my theme, that fatal wrath which, in fulfilment of the will of Zeus, brought the Achaeans [1] *so much suffering and sent the gallant souls of many noblemen to Hades, leaving their bodies as carrion for the dogs and passing birds. Let us begin, goddess of song, with the angry parting that took place between Agamemnon King of Men* [2] *and the great Achilles son of Peleus. Which of the gods was it that made them quarrel?*

It was Apollo, Son of Zeus and Leto, who started the feud, when he punished the King for his discourtesy to Chryses, his priest, by inflicting a deadly plague on his army and destroying his men. Chryses had come to the Achaean ships to recover his captured

---

[1] The ancient Greeks. Occasionally, Homer also refers to these warriors as Danaans (descendants of the legendary King Danaus).

[2] Agamemnon, king of Mycenae and the commander-in-chief of the expedition against Troy, was a kind of lord paramount or first among equals, for many other kings took part in the expedition.

daughter. He brought with him a generous ransom and carried the chaplet of the Archer-god Apollo on a golden staff in his hand. He appealed to the whole Achaean army, and most of all to its two commanders, the sons of Atreus.[3]

'My lords, and you Achaean men-at-arms; you hope to sack King Priam's city and get home in safety. May the gods that live on Olympus grant your wish—on this condition, that you show your reverence for the Archer-god Apollo Son of Zeus by accepting this ransom and releasing my daughter.'

The troops applauded. They wished to see the priest respected and the tempting ransom taken. But this was not at all to King Agamemnon's liking. He cautioned the man severely and rudely dismissed him.

'Old man,' he said, 'do not let me catch you loitering by the hollow ships to-day, nor coming back again, or you may find the god's staff and chaplet a very poor defence. Far from agreeing to set your daughter free, I intend her to grow old in Argos, in my house, a long way from her own country, working at the loom and sharing my bed. Off with you now, and do not provoke me if you want to save your skin.'

The old man trembled and obeyed him. He went off without a word along the shore of the sounding sea. But when he found himself alone he prayed fervently to King Apollo, Son of Leto of the Lovely Locks. 'Hear me, god of the Silver Bow, Protector of Chryse and holy Cilla, and Lord Supreme of Tenedos. Smintheus, if ever I built you a shrine that delighted you, if ever I burnt you the fat thighs of a bull or a goat, grant me this wish. Let the Danaans pay with your arrows for my tears.'

Phoebus Apollo heard his prayer and came down in fury from the heights of Olympus with his bow and covered quiver on his back. As he set out, the arrows clanged on the shoulder of the angry god; and his descent was like nightfall. He sat down opposite the ships and shot an arrow, with a dreadful twang from his silver bow. He attacked the mules first and the nimble dogs; then he aimed his sharp arrows at the men, and struck again and again. Day and night innumerable fires consumed the dead.

For nine days the god's arrows rained on the camp. On the tenth

---

[3] Agamemnon and his brother, Menelaus, king of Sparta. Homer's frequent reference to ancestry reflects a consciousness and pride of family among such warriors.

the troops were called to Assembly by order of Achilles—a measure that the white-armed goddess Here prompted him to take, in her concern for the Danaans whose destruction she was witnessing. When all had assembled and the gathering was complete, the great runner Achilles rose to address them:

'Agamemnon my lord, what with the fighting and the plague, I fear that our strength will soon be so reduced that any of us who are not dead by then will be forced to give up the struggle and sail for home. But could we not consult a prophet or priest, or even some interpreter of dreams—for dreams too are sent by Zeus—and find out from him why Phoebus Apollo is so angry with us? He may be offended at some broken vow or some failure in our rites. If so, he might accept a savoury offering of sheep or of full-grown goats and save us from the plague.'

Achilles sat down, and Calchas son of Thestor rose to his feet. As an augur,[4] Calchas had no rival in the camp. Past, present and future held no secrets from him; and it was his second sight, a gift he owed to Apollo, that had guided the Achaean fleet to Ilium. He was a loyal Argive, and it was in this spirit that he took the floor.

'Achilles,' he said, 'my royal lord, you have asked me to account for the Archer-King Apollo's wrath; and I will do so. But listen to me first. Will you swear to come forward and use all your eloquence and strength to protect me? I ask this of you, being well aware that I shall make an enemy of one whose authority is absolute among us and whose word is law to all Achaeans. A commoner is no match for a king whom he offends. Even if the king swallows his anger for the moment, he will nurse his grievance till the day when he can settle the account. Consider, then, whether you can guarantee my safety.'

'Dismiss your fears,' said the swift Achilles, 'and tell us anything you may have learnt from Heaven. For by Apollo Son of Zeus, the very god, Calchas, in whose name you reveal your oracles, I swear that as long as I am alive and in possession of my senses not a Danaan of them all, here by the hollow ships, shall hurt you, not even if the man you mean is Agamemnon, who bears the title of our overlord.'

At last the worthy seer plucked up his courage and spoke out. 'There is no question,' he said, 'of a broken vow or any shortcoming in our rites. The god is angry because Agamemnon insulted his

---

[4] A diviner of omens, considered invaluable by ancient armies.

priest, refusing to take the ransom and free his daughter. That is the reason for our present sufferings and for those to come. The Archer-King will not release us from this loathsome scourge till we give the bright-eyed lady back to her father, without recompense or ransom, and send holy offerings to Chryse. When that is done we might induce him to relent.'

Calchas sat down, and the noble son of Atreus, imperial Agamemnon, leapt up in anger. His heart was seething with black passion and his eyes were like points of flame. He rounded first on Calchas, full of menace.

'Prophet of evil,' he cried, 'never yet have you said a word to my advantage. It is always trouble that you revel in foretelling. Not once have you fulfilled a prophecy of something good—you have never even made one! And now you hold forth as the army's seer, telling the men that the Archer-god is persecuting them because I refused the ransom for the girl Chryseis, princely though it was. And why did I refuse? Because I chose to keep the girl and take her home. Indeed, I like her better than my consort, Clytaemnestra. She is quite as beautiful, and no less clever or skilful with her hands. Still, I am willing to give her up, if that appears the wiser course. It is my desire to see my people safe and sound, not perishing like this. But you must let me have another prize at once, or I shall be the only one of us with empty hands, a most improper thing. You can see for yourselves that the prize I was given is on its way elsewhere.'

The swift and excellent Achilles leapt to his feet. 'And where,' he asked, 'does your majesty propose that our gallant troops should find a fresh prize to satisfy your unexampled greed? I have yet to hear of any public fund we have laid by. The plunder we took from captured towns has been distributed, and it is more than we can ask of the men to reassemble that. No; give the girl back now, as the god demands, and we will make you triple, fourfold, compensation, if Zeus ever allows us to bring down the battlements of Troy.'

King Agamemnon took him up at once. 'You are a great man, Prince Achilles, but do not imagine you can trick me into that. I am not going to be outwitted or cajoled by you. "Give up the girl," you say, hoping, I presume, to keep your own prize safe. Do you expect me tamely to sit by while I am robbed? No; if the army is prepared to give me a fresh prize, chosen to suit my taste and to make up for my loss, I have no more to say. If not, I shall come and help myself to your prize, or that of Aias; or I shall walk off with Odysseus'.

And what an angry man I shall leave behind me! However, we can deal with all that later on. For the moment, let us run a black ship down into the friendly sea, give her a special crew, embark the animals for sacrifice, and put the girl herself, Chryseis of the lovely cheeks, on board. And let some Councillor of ours go as captain—Aias, Idomeneus, the excellent Odysseus, or yourself, my lord, the most redoubtable man we could choose—to offer the sacrifice and win us back Apollo's favour.'

Achilles the great runner gave him a black look. 'You shameless schemer,' he cried, 'always aiming at a profitable deal! How can you expect any of the men to give you loyal service when you send them on a raid or into battle? It was no quarrel with the Trojan spearmen that brought *me* here to fight. They have never done *me* any harm. They have never lifted cow or horse of mine, nor ravaged any crop that the deep soil of Phthia grows to feed her men; for the roaring seas and many a dark range of mountains lie between us. The truth is that we joined the expedition to please you; yes, you unconscionable cur, to get satisfaction from the Trojans for Menelaus and yourself—a fact which you utterly ignore.[5] And now comes this threat from you of all people to rob me of my prize, my hard-earned prize, which was a tribute from the ranks. It is not as though I am ever given as much as you when the Achaeans sack some thriving city of the Trojans. The heat and burden of the fighting fall on me, but when it comes to dealing out the loot, it is you that take the lion's share, leaving me to return exhausted from the field with something of my own, however small. So now I shall go back to Phthia. That is the best thing I can do—to sail home in my beaked ships. I see no point in staying here to be insulted while I pile up wealth and luxuries for you.'

'Take to your heels, by all means,' Agamemnon King of Men retorted, 'if you feel the urge to go. I am not begging you to stay on my account. There are others with me who will treat me with respect, and the Counsellor Zeus is first among them. Moreover, of all the princes here, you are the most disloyal to myself. To you, sedition, violence and fighting are the breath of life. What if you *are* a great soldier—who made you so but God? Go home now with your ships and your men-at-arms and rule the Myrmidons. I have no use

---

[5] It was Agamemnon who personally persuaded the Achaean princes to undertake a war to recover Helen, the wife of Menelaus.

for you: your anger leaves me cold. But mark my words. In the same way as Phoebus Apollo is robbing me of Chryseis, whom I propose to send off in my ship with my own crew, I am going to pay a visit to your hut and take away the beautiful Briseis, your prize, Achilles, to let you know that I am more powerful than you, and to teach others not to bandy words with me and openly defy their King.'

This cut Achilles to the quick. In his shaggy breast his heart was torn between two courses, whether to draw his sharp sword from his side, thrust his way through the crowd, and kill King Agamemnon, or to control himself and check the angry impulse. He was deep in this inward conflict, with his long sword half unsheathed, when Athene came down to him from heaven at the instance of the white-armed goddess Here, who loved the two lords equally and was fretting for them both. Athene stood behind him and seized him by his golden locks. No one but Achilles was aware of her; the rest saw nothing. He swung round in amazement, recognized Pallas Athene at once—so terrible was the brilliance of her eyes—and spoke out to her boldly: 'And why have you come here, Daughter of aegis-bearing[6] Zeus? Is it to witness the arrogance of my lord Agamemnon? I tell you bluntly—and I make no idle threats—that he stands to pay for this outrage with his life.'

'I came from heaven,' replied Athene of the Flashing Eyes, 'in the hope of bringing you to your senses. It was Here, goddess of the White Arms, that sent me down, loving the two of you as she does and fretting for you both. Come now, give up this strife and take your hand from your sword. Sting him with words instead, and tell him what you mean to do. Here is a prophecy for you—the day shall come when gifts three times as valuable as what you now have lost will be laid at your feet in payment for this outrage. Hold your hand, then, and be advised by us.'

'Lady,' replied Achilles the great runner, 'when you two goddesses command, a man must obey, however angry he may be. Better for him if he does. The man who listens to the gods is listened to by them.'

With that he checked his great hand on the silver hilt and drove the long sword back into its scabbard, in obedience to Athene, who then

---

[6] In Homer the aegis is a thundercloud; in the works of later writers it is a garment of Athene.

set out for Olympus and the palace of aegis-bearing Zeus, where she rejoined the other gods.

Not that Achilles was appeased. He rounded on Atreides[7] once again with bitter taunts. 'You drunken sot,' he cried, 'with the eyes of a dog and the courage of a doe! You never have the pluck to arm yourself and go into battle with the men or to join the other captains in an ambush—you would sooner die. It pays you better to stay in camp, filching the prizes of anyone that contradicts you, and flourishing at your people's cost because they are too feeble to resist—feeble indeed; or else, my lord, this act of brigandage would prove your last.

'But mark my words, for I am going to take a solemn oath. Look at this staff. Once cut from its stem in the hills, it can never put out leaves or twigs again. The billhook stripped it of its bark and foliage; it will sprout no more. Yet the men who in the name of Zeus safe-guard our laws, the Judges of our nation, hold it in their hands. By this I swear (and I could not choose a better token) that the day is coming when the Achaeans one and all will miss me sorely, and you in your despair will be powerless to help them as they fall in their hundreds to Hector killer of men. Then, you will tear your heart out in remorse for having treated the best man in the expedition with contempt.'

The son of Peleus finished, flung down the staff with its golden studs, and resumed his seat, leaving Atreides to thunder at him from the other side. But Nestor now leapt up, Nestor, that master of the courteous word, the clear-voiced orator from Pylos, whose speech ran sweeter than honey off his tongue. He had already seen two generations come to life, grow up, and die in sacred Pylos, and now he ruled the third. Filled with benevolent concern, he took the floor. 'This is indeed enough to make Achaea weep!' he said. 'How happy Priam and Priam's sons would be, how all the Trojans would rejoice, if they could hear of this rift between you two who are the leaders of the Danaans in policy and war. Listen to me. You are both my juniors. And what is more, I have mixed in the past with even better men than you and never failed to carry weight with them, the finest men I have ever seen or shall see, men like Peirithous and Dryas, Shepherd of the People, Caeneus, Exadius, the godlike Polyphemus and Aegeus' son, Theseus of heroic fame. They were the

---

[7] Son of Atreus: Agamemnon. The Atreidae were of a family famous in Greek legend.

strongest men that Earth has bred, the strongest men pitted against the strongest enemies, a savage, mountain-dwelling tribe whom they utterly destroyed. Those were the men whom I left my home in Pylos to join. I travelled far to meet them, at their own request. I played my independent part in their campaign. And they were men whom not a soul on earth to-day could face in battle. Still, they listened to what I said and followed my advice. You two must do the same; you will not lose by it. Agamemnon, forget the privilege of your rank, and do not rob him of the girl. The army gave her to him: let him keep his prize. And you, my lord Achilles, drop your contentious bearing to the King. Through the authority he derives from Zeus, a sceptred king has more than ordinary claims on our respect. You, with a goddess for Mother, may be the stronger of the two; yet Agamemnon is the better man, since he rules more people. My lord Atreides, be appeased. I, Nestor, beg you to relent towards Achilles, our mighty bulwark in the stress of battle.'

'My venerable lord, no one could cavil at what you say,' replied King Agamemnon. 'But this man wants to get the whip-hand here; he wants to lord it over all of us, to play the king, and to give us each our orders, though I know one who is not going to stand for that. What if the everlasting gods did make a spearman of him? Does that entitle him to use insulting language?'

Here the noble Achilles broke in on the King: 'A pretty nincompoop and craven I shall be called if I yield to you at every point, no matter what you say. Command the rest, not me. I have done with obedience to you. And here is another thing for you to ponder. I am not going to fight you or anybody else with my hands for this girl's sake. You gave her to me, and now you take her back. But of all else I have beside my good black ship, you shall not rob me of a single thing. Come now and try, so that the rest may see what happens. Your blood will soon be flowing in a dark stream down my spear.'

The two stood up, when the war of words was over, and dismissed the Assembly by the Achaean fleet. Achilles, with Patroclus and his men, made off to his trim ships and huts; while Atreides launched a fast vessel on the sea, chose twenty oarsmen to man her, and after embarking the cattle to be offered to the god, fetched Chryseis of the lovely cheeks and put her on board. The resourceful Odysseus went as captain, and when everyone was in, they set out along the highways of the sea.

Meanwhile Agamemnon made his people purify themselves by

bathing. When they had washed the filth from their bodies in the salt water, they offered a rich sacrifice of bulls and goats to Apollo on the shore of the unharvested sea; and savoury odours, mixed with the curling smoke, went up into the sky.

While his men were engaged on these duties in the camp, Agamemnon did not forget his quarrel with Achilles and the threat he had made to him at the meeting. He called Talthybius and Eurybates, his two heralds and obedient squires, and said to them: 'Go to the hut of Achilles son of Peleus, take the lady Briseis into your custody, and bring her here. If he refuses to let her go, I shall come in force to fetch her, which will be all the worse for him.'

He sent them off, and with his stern injunction in their ears, the two men made their unwilling way along the shore of the barren sea, till they reached the encampment and ships of the Myrmidons, where they found the prince himself sitting by his own black ship and hut. It gave Achilles no pleasure to see them. They came to a halt, too timid and abashed before the prince to address him and tell him what they wanted. But he knew without being told, and broke the silence. 'Heralds,' he said, 'ambassadors of Zeus and men, I welcome you. Come forward. My quarrel is not with you but with Agamemnon, who sent you here to fetch the girl Briseis. My lord Patroclus, will you bring the lady out and hand her over to these men? I shall count on them to be my witnesses before the happy gods, before mankind, before the brutal king himself, if the Achaeans ever need me again to save them from disaster. The man is raving mad. If he had ever learnt to look ahead, he would be wondering now how he is going to save his army when they are fighting by the ships.' Patroclus did as his friend had told him, brought out Briseis of the lovely cheeks from the hut, and gave her up to the two men, who made their way back along the line of ships with the unhappy girl.

Withdrawing from his men, Achilles wept. He sat down by himself on the shore of the grey sea, and looked across the watery wilderness. Then, stretching out his arms, he poured out prayers to his Mother.[8] 'Mother, since you, a goddess, gave me life, if only for a little while, surely Olympian Zeus the Thunderer owes me some

---

[8] Achilles' mother, Thetis, was a divine sea-nymph, a daughter of Nereus, the Old Man of the Sea. This appeal to her includes the first reference to the hero's tragically short lease on life.

measure of regard. But he pays me none. He has let me be flouted by imperial Agamemnon son of Atreus, who has robbed me of my prize and has her with him now.'

Achilles prayed and wept, and his Lady Mother heard him where she sat in the depths of the sea with her old Father. She rose swiftly from the grey water like a mist, came and sat by her weeping son, stroked him with her hand and spoke to him. 'My child,' she asked him, 'why these tears? What is it that has grieved you? Do not keep your sorrow to yourself, but tell me so that we may share it.'

Achilles of the swift feet sighed heavily. 'You know,' he said; 'and since you know, why should I tell you the whole story? We went to Thebe, Eëtion's sacred city; we sacked the place and brought back all our plunder, which the army shared out in the proper way, choosing Chryseis of the lovely cheeks as a special gift for Atreides. Presently Chryses, priest of the Archer-god Apollo, came to the ships of the bronze-clad Achaeans to set free his daughter, bringing a generous ransom and carrying the chaplet of the Archer Apollo on a golden staff in his hand. He importuned the whole Achaean army, but chiefly its two leaders, the Atreidae. The troops showed by their applause that they wished to see the priest respected and the tempting ransom taken. But this was not at all to Agamemnon's liking. He sent him packing, with a stern warning in his ears. So the old man went home in anger; but Apollo listened to his prayers, because he loved him dearly, and let his wicked arrows fly against the Argive army. The men fell thick and fast, for the god's shafts rained down on every part of our scattered camp. At last a seer who understood the Archer's will explained the matter to us. I rose at once and advised them to propitiate the god. This made Agamemnon furious. He leapt to his feet and threatened me. And now he has carried out his threats: the bright-eyed Achaeans are taking the girl to Chryse in a ship with offerings for the god, while the King's messengers have just gone from my hut with the other girl Briseis, whom the army gave to me.

'So now, if you have any power, protect your son. Go to Olympus, and if anything you have ever done or said has warmed the heart of Zeus, remind him of it as you pray to him. For instance, in my father's house I have often heard you proudly tell us how you alone among the gods saved Zeus the Darkener of the Skies from an inglorious fate, when some of the other Olympians—Here, Poseidon and Pallas Athene—had plotted to throw him into chains. You, goddess, went and saved him from that indignity. You quickly summoned to high Olympus the monster of the hundred arms whom the gods call Briareus, but mankind Aegaeon, a giant more powerful even than his father. He squatted by the Son of Cronos with such a show of force that the blessed gods slunk off in terror, leaving Zeus free.

'Sit by him now, clasp his knees, and remind him of that. Persuade him, if you can, to help the Trojans, to fling the Achaeans back on their ships, to pen them in against the sea and slaughter them. That would teach them to appreciate their King. That would make imperial Agamemnon son of Atreus realize what a fool he was to insult the noblest of them all.'

'My son, my son!' said Thetis, bursting into tears. 'Was it for this I nursed my ill-starred child? At least they might have left you carefree and at ease beside the ships, since Fate has given you so short a life, so little time. But it seems that you are not only doomed to an early death but to a miserable life. It was indeed an unlucky day when I brought you into the world. However, I will go to snow-capped Olympus to tell Zeus the Thunderer all this myself, and see whether I can move him. Meanwhile, stay by your gallant ships, keep up your feud with the Achaeans, and take no part in the fighting. Yesterday, I must tell you, Zeus left for Ocean Stream to join the worthy Ethiopians at a banquet, and all the gods went with him. But in twelve days' time he will be back on Olympus, and then you may rest assured that I shall go to his Bronze Palace, where I will throw myself at his feet. I am convinced that he will hear me.'

Thetis withdrew, leaving Achilles to his grief for the gentle lady whom they had forced him to give up. Meanwhile Odysseus and his men reached Chryse with the sacred offerings. When they had brought their craft into the deep waters of the port, they furled the sail and stowed it in the black ship's hold, dropped the mast neatly into its crutch by letting down the forestays, rowed her into her berth, cast anchor, made the hawsers fast, and jumped out on the beach. The cattle for the Archer-god were disembarked, and Chryseis stepped ashore from the seagoing ship. Odysseus of the nimble wits led the girl to the altar and gave her back to her father. 'Chryses,' he said, 'Agamemnon King of Men has ordered me to bring you your daughter and to make ceremonial offerings to Phoebus on the Danaans' behalf, in the hope of pacifying the Archer-King, who has struck their army a grievous blow.' Then he handed the lady over to her father, who welcomed his daughter with joy.

The offerings destined to do honour to the god were quickly set in place round the well-built altar. The men rinsed their hands and took up the sacrificial grains. Then Chryses lifted up his arms and prayed aloud for them: 'Hear me, God of the Silver Bow, Protector of Chryse and of holy Cilla, and Lord Supreme of Tenedos! My last petition found you kind indeed: you showed your regard for me and struck a mighty blow at the Achaean army. Now grant me a second wish and save the Danaans from their dreadful scourge.' Thus the old man prayed; and Phoebus Apollo heard him.

When they had made their petitions and scattered the grain, they first drew back the animals' heads, slit their throats and flayed them. Then they cut out slices from the thighs, wrapped them in folds of fat and laid raw meat above them. These pieces the old priest burnt on the faggots, while he sprinkled red wine over the flames and the young men gathered round him with five-pronged forks in their hands. When the thighs were burnt up and they had tasted the inner parts, they carved the rest into small pieces, pierced them with skewers, roasted them thoroughly, and drew them all off.

Their work done and the meal prepared, they fell to with a good will on the feast, in which all had equal shares. When their thirst and hunger were satisfied, the stewards filled the mixing-bowls to the brim with wine, and after first pouring out a few drops in each man's cup, served the whole company. And for the rest of the day these young Achaean warriors made music to appease the god, praising the Great Archer in a lovely song, to which Apollo listened with delight.

When the sun set and darkness fell, they lay down for sleep by the hawsers of their ship. But as soon as Dawn had lit the East with rosy hands, they set sail for the great Achaean camp, taking advantage of a breeze the Archer-god had sent them. They put up their mast and spread the white sail. The sail swelled out, struck full by the wind, and a dark wave hissed loudly round her stem as the vessel gathered way and sped through the choppy seas, forging ahead on her course. Thus they returned to the great Achaean camp, where they dragged their black ship high up on the mainland sands and underpinned her with long props. This done, they scattered to their several huts and ships.

Now all this time Achilles the great runner, the royal son of Peleus, had been sitting by his fast ships, nursing his anger. He not only kept away from the fighting but attended no meetings of the Assembly, where a man can win renown. He stayed where he was, eating his heart out and longing for the sound and fury of battle.

Eleven days went by, and at dawn on the twelfth the everlasting gods returned in full strength to Olympus, with Zeus at their head. Thetis, remembering her son's instructions, emerged in the morning from the depths of the sea, rose into the broad sky and reached Olympus. She found all-seeing Zeus sitting away from the rest on the topmost of Olympus' many peaks. She sank to the ground beside him, put her left arm round his knees, raised her right hand to touch his chin, and so made her petition to the Royal Son of Cronos. 'Father Zeus, if ever I have served you well among the gods, by word or deed, grant me a wish and show your favour to my son. He is already singled out for early death, and now Agamemnon King of Men has affronted him. He has stolen his prize and kept her for himself. Avenge my son, Olympian Judge, and let the Trojans have the upper hand till the Achaeans pay him due respect and make him full amends.'

The Marshaller of the Clouds made no reply to this. He sat in silence for a long time, with Thetis clinging to his knees as she had done throughout. At last she appealed to him once more: 'Promise me faithfully and bow your head, or else, since you have nothing to lose by doing so, refuse; and I shall know that there is no god who counts for less than I.'

Zeus the Cloud-gatherer was much perturbed. 'This is a sorry business!' he exclaimed. 'You will make me fall foul of Here, when she rails at me about it, as she will. Even as things are, she scolds me constantly before the other gods and accuses me of helping the Trojans in this war. However, leave me now, or she may notice us; and I will see the matter through. But first, to reassure you, I will bow my head—and the immortals recognize no surer pledge from me than that. When I promise with a nod, there can be no deceit, no turning back, no missing of the mark.'

Zeus, as he finished, bowed his sable brows. The ambrosial locks rolled forward from the immortal head of the King, and high Olympus shook.

The affair was settled, and the two now parted. Thetis swung down from glittering Olympus into the salt sea depths, while Zeus went to his own palace. There the whole company of gods rose from their chairs in deference to their Father. There was not one that dared to keep his seat as he approached; they all stood up to greet him.

Zeus sat down on his throne; and Here,[9] looking at him, knew at once that he and Thetis of the Silver Feet, the Daughter of the Old Man of the Sea, had hatched a plot between them. She rounded instantly on Zeus. 'What goddess,' she asked, 'has been scheming with you now, you arch-deceiver? How like you it is, when my back is turned, to settle things in your own furtive way. You never of your own accord confide in me.'

'Here,' the Father of men and gods replied, 'do not expect to learn all my decisions. You would find the knowledge hard to bear, although you are my Consort. What it is right for you to hear, no god or man shall know before you. But when I choose to take a step without referring to the gods, you are not to cross-examine me about it.'

'Dread Son of Cronos,' said the ox-eyed Queen, 'what are you suggesting now? Surely it never was my way to pester you with questions. I have always let you make your own decisions in perfect peace. But now I have a shrewd idea that you have been talked round by Thetis of the Silver Feet, the Daughter of the Old Man of the Sea. She sat with you this morning and clasped your knees. This makes me think that you have pledged your word to her to support Achilles and let the Achaeans be slaughtered at the ships.'

'Madam,' replied the Cloud-compeller, 'you think too much, and I can keep no secrets from you. But there is nothing you can *do*, except to turn my heart even more against you, which will be all the worse for yourself. If things are as you say, you may take it that my will is being done. Sit there in silence and be ruled by me, or all the gods in Olympus will not be strong enough to keep me off and save you from my unconquerable hands.'

This made the ox-eyed Queen of Heaven tremble, and curbing herself with an effort she sat still. Zeus had daunted all the other Heavenly Ones as well, and there was silence in his palace, till at last Hephaestus the great Artificer spoke up, in his anxiety to be of service to his Mother, white-armed Here. 'This is unbearable!' he exclaimed. 'A pretty pass we are coming to, with you two spoiling for a fight about mankind and setting the gods at loggerheads. How can a good dinner be enjoyed with so much trouble in the air? I do advise my Mother, who knows well enough what is best, to make her

---

[9]Here (more often spelled Hera) was Zeus' sister and queen consort. In this conference we see the gods beginning to take sides in the war.

peace with my dear Father, Zeus, or she may draw another reprimand from him and our dinner be entirely spoilt. What if the Olympian, the Lord of the Lightning Flash, the strongest god in Heaven, should feel disposed to blast us from our seats? No, Mother, you must humbly ask his pardon, and the Olympian will be gracious to us again.'

As he said this, Hephaestus hurried forward with a two-handled cup and put it in his Mother's hand. 'Mother,' he said, 'be patient and swallow your resentment, or I that love you may see you beaten, here in front of me. A sorry sight for me—but what could I do to help you? The Olympian is a hard god to pit oneself against. Why, once before when I was trying hard to save you, he seized me by the foot and hurled me from the threshold of Heaven. I flew all day, and as the sun sank I fell half-dead in Lemnos, where I was picked up and looked after by the Sintians.'

The white-armed goddess Here smiled at this, and took the beaker from her Son, still smiling. Hephaestus then went on to serve the rest in turn, beginning from the left, with sweet nectar which he drew from the mixing-bowl; and a fit of helpless laughter seized the happy gods as they watched him bustling up and down the hall.

So the feast went on, all day till sundown. Each of them had his equal share and they all ate with zest. There was music too, from a beautiful harp played by Apollo, and from the Muses,[10] who sang in turn delightfully. But when the bright lamp of the Sun had set, they all went home to bed in the separate houses that the great lame god Hephaestus had built for them with skilful hands. Olympian Zeus, Lord of the Lightning, also retired to the upper room where he usually slept, and settled down for the night, with Here of the Golden Throne beside him.

---

[10]Minor goddesses, nine in number, who encouraged and protected music, literature, and the arts.

2

Homer

The Odyssey

While The Iliad *was probably intended not only to amuse but to improve its audience,* The Odyssey *was no doubt intended to be sheer entertainment. It is the story of Odysseus, King of Ithaca and all-round man of action, who, after ten years of fighting alongside his fellow Achaean warriors in the siege of Troy, sets sail longingly for home and family, with a crew of faithful followers and a shipload of Trojan loot.*

But ten years are to pass before he sees his kingdom again. An astonishing series of perils and marvels delay his progress (so interestingly and to such an extent that any eventful and prolonged wandering is now called an "odyssey"). Several of these frustrating years are spent with the divine sea-nymph Calypso, who not only conceals him on her isle but wishes to marry him. When Odysseus, at last free to leave her, sets out again, he is soon driven toward the rocky coast of Scherie, the land of the Phaeacians, and nearly drowned. However, thanks to the goddess Athene, he swims safely ashore at a river mouth—naked, empty-handed, and unknown. It may be that, of all Odysseus' adventures, none is now more engaging than the one introduced here—partly because of its naturalism and humanity, but also for its glimpse of the life of women and their place in that far-off Hellenic world.

While the noble, much-enduring Odysseus, conquered by sleep and worn out by his exertions, lay resting there, Athene came to the

Homer, *The Odyssey*, trans. E. V. Rieu (New York: Penguin Books: 1977), VI, 102–11. © the Estate of E. V. Rieu, 1946. Reprinted by permission of Penguin Books Ltd.

country of the Phaeacians and entered their city. These Phaeacians had once lived in the broad lands of Hypereie, and been neighbours to the Cyclopes, a quarrelsome people, who took advantage of their greater strength to plague them, till the day when their king, Nausithous, made them migrate and settled them in Scherie,[1] far from the busy haunts of men. There he laid out the walls of a new city, built them houses, put up temples to the gods, and allotted the land for cultivation. But he had met his fate long since and gone to Hades' Halls;[2] and it was now the divinely-inspired Alcinous who ruled them. To his palace the bright-eyed goddess Athene made her way, still intent on her plans for King Odysseus' restoration.

The good King Alcinous had a young daughter called Nausicaa, tall and beautiful as a goddess. She was asleep now in her richly-furnished room, with two of her ladies, both blest with beauty by the Graces, lying by the door-posts, one on either side. The polished doors were closed; but Athene swept through like a breath of air to the girl's bed, leant over the head of it and spoke to her, disguising herself as the daughter of a ship's captain named Dymas, a woman of Nausicaa's own age and one of her bosom friends.

'Nausicaa,' said bright-eyed Athene, imitating her friend's voice, 'how did your mother come to have such a lazy daughter as you? Look at the lovely clothing you allow to lie about neglected, although you may soon be married and stand in need of beautiful clothes, not only to wear yourself but to provide for your bridegroom's party. It's this kind of thing that gives a girl a good name in the town, besides pleasing her father and her mother. Let us go and do some washing together the first thing in the morning. I offer to go with you and help, so that you can get yourself ready as soon as possible, for you certainly won't remain unmarried long. Why, every nobleman in the place wants you for his wife, you, a Phaeacian princess. Do ask your royal father in the morning to have a waggon made ready for you with a couple of mules. These waistbands and robes, and glossy wraps could go in it, and it would be much more comfortable for you yourself to drive than to go on foot, as it's a long way from the city to the washing-pools.'

When she had finished, Athene of the flashing eyes withdrew to

---

[1] The fabled Scherie has been identified by some as Kérkira (or Corfu), an island between Greece and the "heel" of Italy. Its inhabitants, the Phaeacians, were noted for enjoying lives of blissful tranquility.
[2] The underworld abode of dead souls.

Olympus, where people say the gods have made their everlasting home. Shaken by no wind, drenched by no showers, and invaded by no snows, it is set in a cloudless sea of limpid air with a white radiance playing over all. There the happy gods spend their delightful days, and there the Lady of the Bright Eyes went when she had explained her wishes to the girl.

Soon after, Dawn enthroned herself in the sky, and Nausicaa in her lovely gown awoke. She was amazed at her dream and set out at once through the palace to tell her father and her mother. She found them both in the house. Her mother was sitting at the hearth with her maids, spinning yarn stained with sea-purple; and she caught her father just as he was going out to join his princely colleagues at a conference to which he was called by the Phaeacian nobles. She went as close to him as she could and said:

'Father dear, I wonder if you could tell them to get me a big waggon with strong wheels, so that I can take all the fine clothes that I have lying dirty here to the river to wash? And indeed it is only decent for you yourself when you are discussing affairs of state with important people to have clean linen on your back. Then again, there are five sons of yours in the palace, two of them married, while three are merry bachelors who are always asking for clothes straight from the wash to wear at dances. It is I who have to think of all these things.'

She spoke in this way because she was too shy to mention her marriage to her father. But he understood her thoroughly and replied:

'I don't grudge you the mules, my child, or anything else. You may go; and the servants shall get you a fine big waggon with a hood to it.'

He called to his men and they set to work. While they prepared a smooth-running mule-cart outside the house, led the mules under the yoke, and harnessed them to the vehicle, Nausicaa fetched the gay clothing from the store-room. She then packed it in the polished waggon, while her mother filled a box with various kinds of appetizing provisions and dainties to go with them, and poured some wine into a goatskin bottle. The girl climbed into the cart and her mother handed her a golden flask of soft olive-oil, so that she and her maids could anoint themselves after bathing. And now Nausicaa took the whip and the glistening reins, and flicked the mules to make them go. There was a clatter of hooves, and then they stepped out bravely, taking the clothes and their mistress along. But as her maids followed and kept her company, she was not left to go alone.

In due course they reached the noble river with its never-failing pools, in which there was enough clear water always bubbling up and swirling by to clean the dirtiest clothes. Here they turned the mules loose from under the yoke and drove them along the eddying stream to graze on the sweet grass. Then they lifted the clothes by armfuls from the cart, dropped them into the dark water and trod them down briskly in the troughs, competing with each other in the work. When they had rinsed them till no dirt was left, they spread them out in a row along the sea-shore, just where the waves washed the shingle clean when they came tumbling up the beach. Next, after bathing and rubbing themselves with olive-oil, they took their meal at the riverside, waiting for the sunshine to dry the clothes. And presently, when mistress and maids had all enjoyed their food, they threw off their headgear and began playing with a ball, while Nausicaa of the white arms led them in their song. It was just such a scene as gladdens Leto's heart, when her Daughter, Artemis the Archeress, has come down from the mountain along the high ridge of Taygetus or Erymanthus[3] to chase the wild boar or the nimble deer, and the Nymphs[4] of the countryside join with her in the sport. They too are heaven-born, but Artemis overtops them all, and where all are beautiful there is no question which is she. So did this maiden princess stand out among her ladies.

When the time came for Nausicaa to set out for home after yoking the mules and folding up the clothes, the bright-eyed goddess Athene intervened once more and arranged for Odysseus to wake up and see this lovely girl who was to serve as his escort to the Phaeacian city. Accordingly, when the princess passed the ball to one of her maids, she missed her and dropped it instead into the deep and eddying current. At this they all gave a loud shriek. The good Odysseus awoke, and sitting up took counsel with himself.

'Alas!' he sighed. 'What country have I come to now? What people are there here? Some brutal tribe of lawless savages, or kindly and god-fearing folk? And what is this shrill echo in my ears, as though some girls were shrieking? Nymphs, I suppose—who haunt the

[3] Mountains in the Peloponnese (the southern portion of the Greek mainland).
[4] Minor female divinities. Being caught by these lovelies made men happily forget all else.

steep hill-tops, the springs of rivers, and the grassy meadows. Or am I within hail, by any chance, of human beings who can talk as I do? Well, I must go and use my own eyes to find out.'

So the gallant Odysseus crept out from under the bushes, after breaking off with his great hand a leafy bough from the thicket to conceal his naked manhood. Then he advanced on them like a mountain lion who sallies out, defying wind and rain in the pride of his power, with fire in his eyes, to hunt the oxen or the sheep, to stalk the roaming deer, or to be forced by hunger to besiege the very walls of the homestead and attack the pens. The same urgent need now constrained Odysseus, naked as he was, to bear down upon these gentle girls. Begrimed with salt he made a gruesome sight, and one look at him sent them scuttling in every direction along the jutting spits of sand. Alcinous' daughter was the only one to stand firm. Emboldened by Athene, who stopped her limbs from trembling, she checked herself and confronted him, while Odysseus considered whether he should throw his arms round the beautiful girl's knees and so make his prayer, or be content to keep his distance and beg her with all courtesy to give him clothing and direct him to the city. After some hesitation he decided that as the lady might take offence if he embraced her knees it would be better to keep his distance and politely plead his case. In the end, his address was not only disarming but full of subtlety:

'Mistress, I throw myself on your mercy. But are you some goddess or a mortal woman? If you are one of the gods who live in the sky, it is of Artemis, the Daughter of almighty Zeus, that your beauty, grace, and stature most remind me. But if you are one of us mortals who live on earth, then lucky indeed are your father and your gentle mother; lucky, your brothers too. How their hearts must glow with pleasure every time they see their darling join the dance! But he is the happiest of them all who with his wedding gifts can win you for his home. For never have I set eyes on such perfection in man or woman. I worship as I look. Only in Delos have I seen the like, a fresh young palm-tree shooting up by the altar of Apollo, when my travels took me there—with a fine army at my back, that time, though the expedition was doomed to end so fatally for me. I remember how long I stood spellbound at the sight, for no lovelier sapling ever sprang from the ground. And it is with just the same wonder and veneration that I look at you, my lady; with such awe, indeed, that I dare not clasp your knees, though my troubles are serious enough. Only yesterday, after nineteen days of it, I made my escape from the wine-dark sea. It took all that time for the waves and the tempestuous winds to carry me here from the island of Ogygia.[5] And now some god has flung me on this shore, no doubt to suffer more disasters here. For I have no hope that my troubles are coming to an end: the gods have plenty in store for me before that can be. Pity me, my queen. You are the first person I have met after all I have been through, and I do not know a soul in this city or this land. I beg you to direct me to the town and to give me some rag to put round myself, if only the wrapper you may have brought for your linen when you came. And in return may the gods grant you your heart's desire; may they give you a husband and a home, and the harmony that is so much to be desired, since there is nothing nobler or more admirable than when two people who see eye to eye keep house as man and wife, confounding their enemies and delighting their friends, as they themselves know better than anyone.'

'Sir,' said the white-armed Nausicaa, 'your manners prove that you are no rascal and no fool; and as for these ordeals of yours, they must have been sent you by Olympian Zeus, who follows his own will in dispensing happiness to people whatever their merits. You have no choice but to endure. But since you have come to our country and our city here, you certainly shall not want for clothing or anything else that an unfortunate outcast has the right to expect from those he approaches. I will show you to the town and tell you who we are. This country and the city you will see belong to the Phaeacians. I myself am the daughter of King Alcinous, who is the head and mainstay of our state.'

Here she turned and called out her orders to the gentlewomen in attendance: 'Stop, my maids. Where are you flying to at the sight of a man? Don't tell me you take him for an enemy, for there is no man on earth, nor ever will be, who would dare to set hostile feet on Phaeacian soil. The gods are too fond of us for that. Remote in this sea-beaten home of ours, we are the outposts of mankind and come in contact with no other people. The man you see is an unfortunate wanderer who has strayed here, and now commands our care, since all strangers and beggars come under the protection of Zeus, and the charity that is a trifle to us can be precious to others. Bestir your-

---

[5] A fancied island in the Ionian Sea, it was the home of Calypso, the sea nymph with whom Odysseus spent seven pleasant years.

selves, girls, provide our guest with food and drink, and bathe him in the river where there's shelter from the wind.'

The rebuke from their mistress checked the women's flight. They called halt to each other, and then found Odysseus a seat in the sheltered spot that the Princess Nausicaa had pointed out. On the ground beside him they laid a cloak and tunic for him to wear, and giving him some soft olive-oil in a golden flask they suggested that he should wash himself in the running stream. But the gallant Odysseus demurred.

'Ladies,' he said, 'be good enough to stand back over there and leave me to wash the brine myself from my shoulders and rub my body with olive-oil, to which it has long been a stranger. I am not going to take my bath with you looking on. I should be ashamed to stand naked in the presence of gentlewomen.'

At this the maids withdrew and told their young mistress what had occurred. Meanwhile Odysseus was cleaning himself with river-water of the salt that encrusted his back and his broad shoulders, and scrubbing his head free of the scurf left there by the barren brine. When he had thoroughly washed and rubbed himself with oil and had put on the clothes which the young girls had given him, Athene, Daughter of Zeus, made him seem taller and sturdier than ever and caused the bushy locks to hang from his head thick as the petals of the hyacinth in bloom. Just as a craftsman trained by Hephaestus and herself in the secrets of his art takes pains to put a graceful finish to his work by overlaying silver-ware with gold, she finished now by endowing his head and shoulders with an added beauty. When Odysseus retired to sit down by himself on the sea-shore, he was radiant with comeliness and grace. Nausicaa gazed at him in admiration and said to her fair attendants:

'Listen, my white-armed maids, while I tell you what I have been thinking. This man's arrival among the Phaeacians, who are so near the gods themselves, was not unpremeditated by the Olympian powers. For when first we met I thought he cut a sorry figure, but now he looks like the gods who live in heaven. That is the kind of man whom I could fancy for a husband, if he would settle here. I only hope that he will choose to stay. But come, girls, give the stranger something to eat and drink.'

Her maids at once carried out her orders and set food and drink before the stalwart Odysseus, who ate and drank with avidity, for it was a long time since he had tasted any food.

Meanwhile Nausicaa of the white arms had come to a decision. After folding up the clothing, she stowed it in her fine waggon, harnessed the sturdy mules, and herself climbed in. Then she called to Odysseus and gave him his instructions.

'Come, sir,' she said, 'it is time for you to make a move towards the city, so that I may direct you to my good father's house, where you can count on meeting all the Phaeacian nobility. But this is how you must manage—and I take you for a man of tact. So long as we are passing through the country and the farmers' lands, walk quickly with my maids behind the waggon and the mules, following my lead. But that will not do when we come to town.

'Our city is surrounded by high battlements; it has an excellent harbour on each side and is approached by a narrow causeway, where the curved ships are drawn up to the road and each owner has his separate slip. Here is the people's meeting-place, built up on either side of the fine temple of Poseidon with blocks of quarried stone bedded deeply in the ground. It is here too that the sailors attend to the rigging of the black ships, to their cables and their sails, and the smoothing of their oars. For the Phaeacians have no use for the bow and quiver, but spend their energy on masts and oars and on the graceful craft they love to sail across the foam-flecked seas.

'Now it is the possibility of unpleasant talk among these sailors that I wish to avoid. I am afraid they might give me a bad name, for there are plenty of vulgar fellows in the place, and I can well imagine one of the baser sort saying after he had seen us: "Who is this tall and handsome stranger Nausicaa has in tow? Where did she run across him? Her future husband no doubt! She must have rescued some shipwrecked foreigner who had strayed this way, since we have no neighbours of our own. Or perhaps some god has answered her importunate prayers and stooped from heaven to make her his for ever. And it is better so, better that she should venture out herself and find a husband from abroad. For she obviously despises her countrymen here, though so many of the best would like to marry her." That is how they will talk, and my good name would suffer. Indeed I should blame any girl who acted so, with her parents alive, running away from her friends to consort with men before she was properly married.

'So you, sir, had best take note of my directions, if you wish to make sure of being sent home by my father with the least possible delay. You will see near the path a fine poplar wood sacred to Athene, with a spring welling up in the middle and a meadow all round. That is where my father has his royal park and vegetable garden, within call of the city. Sit down there and wait awhile till we get into the town and reach my father's house. When you think we have had time to do so, go into the city yourself and ask for the palace of my father, King Alcinous. It is quite easy to recognize: any little child could show it you. For the houses of the rest are not built in anything like the style of Lord Alcinous' mansion. Directly you have passed through the courtyard and into the buildings, walk quickly through the great hall till you reach my mother, who generally sits in the firelight by the hearth, weaving yarn stained with sea-purple, and forming a delightful picture, with her chair against a pillar and her maids sitting behind. My father's throne is close to hers, and there he sits drinking his wine like a god. Slip past him and clasp my mother's knees if you wish to make certain of an early and happy return to your home, however far you may have strayed. For, once you have secured her sympathy, you may confidently expect to get back to your motherland and to walk once more into your own fine house and see your friends again.'

When she had finished, Nausicaa used her glistening whip on the mules, and they soon left the flowing river behind them, swinging along at a steady trot. But the princess kept them to a pace which allowed the maids and Odysseus to keep up with her on foot, and used her judgement in laying on the whip. As the sun was setting they reached the well-known grove that bore Athene's name. Here the good Odysseus sat down and proceeded to offer up a prayer to the Daughter of almighty Zeus.

'Listen to me, unsleeping child of Zeus who wears the aegis, and hear my prayer this time, though you turned a deaf ear to me the other day, when I was shipwrecked and the great Earthshaker broke me up. Grant that the Phaeacians may receive me with kindness and compassion.'

Pallas Athene heard his prayer but still refrained from appearing before him, out of deference to her Father's Brother,[6] who persisted in his rancour against the noble Odysseus till the very day when he reached his own land.

---

[6] Poseidon, the god of the sea, whom Odysseus had offended by blinding (in self-defense) his son Polyphemus, the one-eyed giant.

3

Sophocles

Oedipus Rex

Dramatic tragedy represents the chief literary achievement of Athens in the Golden Age and one of the noblest products of the human imagination. Its development was encouraged by the extraordinary awareness and maturity of outlook that characterized the Athenian populace in the sixth and fifth centuries B.C. Poets of genius found an audience of comparable taste and feeling, and those who wrote tragedies had a favorable climate in which to present both their interpretations of Hellenic traditions and ideals and their own insights into the nature of human life and destiny. Of these dramatists the three considered supreme were Aeschylus, Euripides, and Sophocles (ca. 496–406 B.C.).

Throughout his long life Sophocles had every advantage: aristocratic birth, wealth, good looks, success, and, above all, the inspiration of living in Athens during the Golden Age. Unfortunately, of the more than one hundred plays he wrote, only seven survive. The most famous of these, Oedipus Rex, dates from about 429 B.C. (the year of the statesman Pericles' death); it is regarded not only as his masterpiece but as one of the great tragedies of all time.

The story of this drama is drawn from a well-known Greek legend. As interpreted by Sophocles, it deals with mankind's relationship to the divine order. Since divine order and justice are considered identical, King Oedipus, who unintentionally broke the moral code guaranteed by the Olympian gods, is made to suffer horribly. Whether or not his punishment is just by human standards is irrelevant to the judgment of the gods. It is their will that humans should know themselves and thus realize their limitations. At the *end of the play, the blinded Oedipus, having come to know the moral code through suffering, emerges a wiser man, more aware of life's meaning than he ever was as a confident, proud ruler.*

This was not the private viewpoint of Sophocles alone. The sentiments of the Chorus, whose role was to comment upon and to express general opinion, showed that the belief that human beings should know themselves was part of the consciousness of the Athenian citizens. The miracle of Periclean Athens was based in part upon the corollary of this attitude: that each individual has the potential to face harsh realities, even the prospect of ultimate doom, with courage and dignity. Both the suffering of Oedipus—evoking the emotions of pity and terror—and his grandeur in adversity are both evidence of such potential and the essence of tragedy. This Greek attitude—awe and wonder at the uniqueness of human beings and their inherent moral stature—is also the essence of the philosophy known as humanism.

Characters

OEDIPUS, *king of Thebes*
A PRIEST
CREON, *brother-in-law of Oedipus*
CHORUS *of Theban elders*
TEIRESIAS, *a prophet*
JOCASTA, *sister of Creon, wife of Oedipus*
MESSENGER
SERVANT *of Laius, father of Oedipus*
SECOND MESSENGER
(*silent*) ANTIGONE *and* ISMENE, *daughters of Oedipus*

SCENE.   *Before the palace of Oedipus at Thebes. In front of the large central doors, an altar; and an altar near each of the two side doors. On the altar steps are seated suppliants—old men, youths, and young boys—dressed in white tunics and cloaks, their hair bound with white fillets. They have laid on the altars olive branches wreathed with wool-fillets.*

The old PRIEST OF ZEUS *stands alone facing the central doors of the palace. The doors open, and* OEDIPUS, *followed by two attendants who stand at either door, enters and looks about.*

OEDIPUS.   O children, last born stock of ancient Cadmus,[1]
What petitions are these you bring to me
With garlands on your suppliant olive branches?
The whole city teems with incense fumes,
Teems with prayers for healing and with groans.
Thinking it best, children, to hear all this
Not from some messenger, I came myself,
The world renowned and glorious Oedipus.
But tell me, aged priest, since you are fit
To speak before these men, how stand you here,
In fear or want? Tell me, as I desire
To do my all; hard hearted I would be
To feel no sympathy for such a prayer.
PRIEST.   O Oedipus, ruler of my land, you see
How old we are who stand in supplication
Before your altars here, some not yet strong
For lengthy flight, some heavy with age,
Priests, as I of Zeus, and choice young men.
The rest of the tribe sits with wreathed branches,
In market places, at Pallas'[2] two temples,
And at prophetic embers by the river.
The city, as you see, now shakes too greatly
And cannot raise her head out of the depths
Above the gory swell. She wastes in blight,
Blight on earth's fruitful blooms and grazing flocks,
And on the barren birth pangs of the women.
The fever god has fallen on the city,
And drives it, a most hated pestilence
Through whom the home of Cadmus is made empty.
Black Hades is enriched with wails and groans.
Not that we think you equal to the gods
These boys and I sit suppliant at your hearth,
But judging you first of men in the trials of life,
And in the human intercourse with spirits:—
You are the one who came to Cadmus' city
And freed us from the tribute which we paid

---

[1] The founder and first king of Thebes, an ancestor of Laius, the fifth king, and of Laius' son Oedipus, the sixth king; the citizens of Thebes were also considered Cadmus' descendants.
[2] Athena's. The goddess was often called Pallas Athena.

To the harsh-singing Sphinx.[3] And that you did
Knowing nothing else, unschooled by us.
But people say and think it was some god
That helped you to set our life upright.
Now Oedipus, most powerful of all,
We all are turned here toward you, we beseech you,
Find us some strength, whether from one of the gods
You hear an omen, or know one from a man.
For the experienced I see will best
Make good plans grow from evil circumstance.
Come, best of mortal men, raise up the state.
Come, prove your fame, since now this land of ours
Calls you savior for your previous zeal.
O never let our memory of your reign
Be that we first stood straight and later fell,
But to security raise up this state.
With favoring omen once you gave us luck;
Be now as good again; for if henceforth
You rule as now, you will be this country's king,
Better it is to rule men than a desert,
Since nothing is either ship or fortress tower
Bare of men who together dwell within.

OEDIPUS.   O piteous children, I am not ignorant
Of what you come desiring. Well I know
You are all sick, and in your sickness none
There is among you as sick as I,
For your pain comes to one man alone,
To him and to none other, but my soul
Groans for the state, for myself, and for you.
You do not wake a man who is sunk in sleep;
Know that already I have shed many tears,
And travelled many wandering roads of thought.
Well have I sought, and found one remedy;
And this I did: the son of Menoeceus,
Creon, my brother-in-law,[4] I sent away
Unto Apollo's Pythian halls[5] to find

---

[3] A monster, half woman and half lion, that had plagued the road to Thebes, putting a
riddle to all passersby and strangling any who could not solve it.
[4] Creon was Queen Jocasta's brother.
[5] The shrine of Apollo at Delphi, whose oracular priestess was called the Pythia.

What I might do or say to save the state.
The days are measured out that he is gone;
It troubles me how he fares. Longer than usual
He has been away, more than the fitting time.
But when he comes, then evil I shall be,
If all the god reveals I fail to do.

PRIEST.   You speak at the right time. These men just now
Signal to me that Creon is approaching.

OEDIPUS.   O Lord Apollo, grant that he may come
In saving fortune shining as in eye.

PRIEST.   Glad news he brings, it seems, or else his head
Would not be crowned with leafy, berried bay.

OEDIPUS.   We will soon know. He is close enough to hear.—
Prince, my kinsman, son of Menoeceus,
What oracle do you bring us from the god?

CREON.   A good one. For I say that even burdens
If they chance to turn out right, will all be well.

OEDIPUS.   Yet what is the oracle? Your present word
Makes me neither bold nor apprehensive.

CREON.   If you wish to hear in front of this crowd
I am ready to speak, or we can go within.

OEDIPUS.   Speak forth to all. The sorrow that I bear
Is greater for these men than for my life.

CREON.   May I tell you what I heard from the god?
Lord Phoebus[6] clearly bids us to drive out,
And not to leave uncured within this country,
A pollution we have nourished in our land.

OEDIPUS.   With what purgation? What kind of misfortune?

CREON.   Banish the man, or quit slaughter with slaughter
In cleansing, since this blood rains on the state.

OEDIPUS.   Who is this man whose fate the god reveals?

CREON.   Laius, my lord, was formerly the guide
Of this our land before you steered this city.

OEDIPUS.   I know him by hearsay, but I never saw him.

CREON.   Since he was slain, the god now plainly bids us
To punish his murderers, whoever they may be.

OEDIPUS.   Where are they on the earth? How shall we find
This indiscernible track of ancient guilt?

---

[6] An epithet (descriptive name) of Apollo.

CREON.   In this land, said Apollo. What is sought
    Can be apprehended; the unobserved escapes.
OEDIPUS.   Did Laius fall at home on this bloody end?
    Or in the fields, or in some foreign land?
CREON.   As a pilgrim, the god said, he left his tribe
    And once away from home, returned no more.
OEDIPUS.   Was there no messenger, no fellow wayfarer
    Who saw, from whom an inquirer might get aid?
CREON.   They are all dead, save one, who fled in fear
    And he knows only one thing sure to tell.
OEDIPUS.   What is that? We may learn many facts from one
    If we might take for hope a short beginning.
CREON.   Robbers, he said, met there and killed him
    Not by the strength of one, but many hands.
OEDIPUS.   How did the robber unless something from here
    Was at work with silver, reach this point of daring?
CREON.   These facts are all conjecture. Laius dead,
    There rose in evils no avenger for him.
OEDIPUS.   But when the king had fallen slain, what trouble
    Prevented you from finding all this out?
CREON.   The subtle-singing Sphinx made us let go
    What was unclear to search at our own feet.
OEDIPUS.   Well then, I will make this clear afresh
    From the start. Phoebus was right, you were right
    To take this present interest in the dead.
    Justly it is you see me as your ally
    Avenging alike this country and the god.
    Not for the sake of some distant friends,
    But for myself I will disperse this filth.
    Whoever it was who killed that man
    With the same hand may wish to do vengeance on me.
    And so assisting Laius I aid myself.
    But hurry quickly, children, stand up now
    From the altar steps, raising these suppliant boughs.
    Let someone gather Cadmus' people here
    To learn that I will do all, whether at last
    With Phoebus' help we are shown saved or fallen.
PRIEST.   Come, children, let us stand. We came here
    First for the sake of what this man proclaims.
    Phoebus it was who sent these prophecies
    And he will come to save us from the plague.

CHORUS.

O sweet-tongued voice of Zeus, in what spirit do you come
From Pytho rich in gold
To glorious Thebes? I am torn on the rack, dread shakes my fear-
ful mind,
Apollo of Delos, hail!
As I stand in awe of you, what need, either new
Do you bring to the full for me, or old in the turning times of
the year?
Tell me, O child of golden Hope, undying Voice!
First on you do I call, daughter of Zeus, undying Athene
And your sister who guards our land,
Artemis, seated upon the throne renowned of our circled Place,
And Phoebus who darts afar;
Shine forth to me, thrice warder-off of death;
If ever in time before when ruin rushed upon the state,
The flame of sorrow you drove beyond our bounds, come also
now.

O woe! Unnumbered that I bear
The sorrows are! My whole host is sick, nor is there a sword of
thought
To ward off pain. The growing fruits
Of glorious earth wax not, nor women
Withstand in childbirth shrieking pangs.
Life on life you may see, which, like the well-winged bird,
Faster than stubborn fire, speed
To the strand of the evening god.

Unnumbered of the city die.
Unpitied babies bearing death lie unmoaned on the ground.
Grey-haired mothers and young wives
From all sides at the altar's edge
Lift up a wail beseeching, for their mournful woes.
The prayer for healing shines blent with a grieving cry;
Wherefore, O golden daughter of Zeus,
Send us your succour with its beaming face.

Grant that fiery Ares,[7] who now with no brazen shield

---

[7] The god of war and destruction.

Flames round me in shouting attack
May turn his back in running flight from our land,
May be borne with fair wind
To Amphitrite's[8] great chamber
Or to the hostile port
Of the Thracian surge.
For even if night leaves any ill undone
It is brought to pass and comes to be in the day.
O Zeus who bear the fire
And rule the lightning's might,
Strike him beneath your thunderbolt with death![9]
O lord Apollo, would that you might come and scatter forth
Untamed darts from your twirling golden bow;
Bring succour from the plague; may the flashing
Beams come of Artemis,[10]
With which she glances through the Lycian hills.
Also on him I call whose hair is held in gold,
Who gives a name to this land,
Bacchus[11] of winy face, whom maidens hail!
Draw near with your flaming Maenad band[12]
And the aid of your gladsome torch
Against the plague, dishonoured among the gods.

OEDIPUS.   You pray; if for what you pray you would be willing
To hear and take my words, to nurse the plague,
You may get succour and relief from evils.
A stranger to this tale I now speak forth,
A stranger to the deed, for not alone
Could I have tracked it far without some clue,
But now that I am enrolled a citizen
Latest among the citizens of Thebes
To all you sons of Cadmus I proclaim
Whoever of you knows at what man's hand
Laius, the son of Labdacus, met his death,
I order him to tell me all, and even

---

[8] Amphitrite, a sea nymph, was the wife of Poseidon, god of the sea.
[9] The thunderbolt was the special symbol and instrument of Zeus.
[10] Twin sister of Apollo, goddess of the moon, and a huntress.
[11] Another name for Dionysos, god of wine and rebirth.
[12] The Maenads were female worshippers of Bacchus.

If he fears, to clear the charge and he will suffer
No injury, but leave the land unharmed.
If someone knows the murderer to be an alien
From foreign soil, let him not be silent;
I will give him a reward, my thanks besides.
But if you stay in silence and from fear
For self or friend thrust aside my command,
Hear now from me what I shall do for this;
I charge that none who dwell within this land
Whereof I hold the power and the throne
Give this man shelter whoever he may be,
Or speak to him, or share with him in prayer
Or sacrifice, or serve him lustral rites,
But drive him, all, out of your homes, for he
Is this pollution on us, as Apollo
Revealed to me just now in oracle.
I am therefore the ally of the god
And of the murdered man. And now I pray
That the murderer, whether he hides alone
Or with his partners, may, evil coward,
Wear out in luckless ills his wretched life.
I further pray, that, if at my own hearth
He dwells known to me in my own home,
I may suffer myself the curse I just now uttered.
And you I charge to bring all this to pass
For me, and for the god, and for our land
Which now lies fruitless, godless, and corrupt.
Even if Phoebus had not urged this affair,
Not rightly did you let it go unpurged
When one both noble and a king was murdered!
You should have sought it out. Since now I reign
Holding the power which he had held before me,
Having the selfsame wife and marriage bed—
And if his seed had not met barren fortune [13]
We should be linked by offspring from one mother;
But as it was, fate leapt upon his head.
Therefore in this, as if for my own father

---

[13] That is, if Laius had fathered children by his queen, Jocasta, now the wife of Oedipus.

I fight for him, and shall attempt all
Searching to seize the hand which shed that blood,
For Labdacus' son, before him Polydorus,
And ancient Cadmus, and Agenor of old.
And those who fail to do this, I pray the gods
May give them neither harvest from their earth
Nor children from their wives, but may they be
Destroyed by a fate like this one, or a worse.
You other Thebans, who cherish these commands,
May Justice, the ally of a righteous cause,
And all the gods be always on your side.

CHORUS.   By the oath you laid on me, my king, I speak.
I killed not Laius, nor can show who killed him.
Phoebus it was who sent this question to us,
And he should answer who has done the deed.

OEDIPUS.   Your words are just, but to compel the gods
In what they do not wish, no man can do.

CHORUS.   I would tell what seems to me our second course.

OEDIPUS.   If there is a third, fail not to tell it too.

CHORUS.   Lord Teiresias [14] I know, who sees this best
Like lord Apollo; in surveying this,
One might, my lord, find out from him most clearly.

OEDIPUS.   Even this I did not neglect; I have done it already.
At Creon's word I twice sent messengers.
It is a wonder he has been gone so long.

CHORUS.   And also there are rumors, faint and old.

OEDIPUS.   What are they? I must search out every tale.

CHORUS.   They say there were some travellers who killed him.

OEDIPUS.   So I have heard, but no one sees a witness.

CHORUS.   If his mind knows a particle of fear
He will not long withstand such curse as yours.

OEDIPUS.   He fears no speech who fears not such a deed.

CHORUS.   But here is the man who will convict the guilty.
Here are these men leading the divine prophet
In whom alone of men the truth is born.

OEDIPUS.   O you who ponder all, Teiresias,
Both what is taught and what cannot be spoken,
What is of heaven and what trod on the earth,

---

[14] A blind Theban seer and prophet. He appears often in Greek legends.

Even if you are blind, you know what plague
Clings to the state, and, master, you alone
We find as her protector and her saviour.
Apollo, if the messengers have not told you,
Answered our question, that release would come
From this disease only if we make sure
Of Laius' slayers and slay them in return
Or drive them out as exiles from the land.
But you now, grudge us neither voice of birds
Nor any way you have of prophecy.
Save yourself and the state; save me as well.
Save everything polluted by the dead.
We are in your hands; it is the noblest task
To help a man with all your means and powers.

TEIRESIAS.   Alas! Alas! How terrible to be wise,
Where it does the seer no good. Too well I know
And have forgot this, or would not have come here.

OEDIPUS.   What is this? How fainthearted you have come!

TEIRESIAS.   Let me go home; it is best for you to bear
Your burden, and I mine, if you will heed me.

OEDIPUS.   You speak what is lawless, and hateful to the state
Which raised you, when you deprive her of your answer.

TEIRESIAS.   And I see that your speech does not proceed
In season; I shall not undergo the same.

OEDIPUS.   Don't by the gods turn back when you are wise,
When all we suppliants lie prostrate before you.

TEIRESIAS.   And all unwise; I never shall reveal
My evils, so that I may not tell yours.

OEDIPUS.   What do you say? You know, but will not speak?
Would you betray us and destroy the state?

TEIRESIAS.   I will not hurt you or me. Why in vain
Do you probe this? You will not find out from me.

OEDIPUS.   Worst of evil men, you would enrage
A stone itself. Will you never speak,
But stay so untouched and so inconclusive?

TEIRESIAS.   You blame my anger and do not see that
With which you live in common, but upbraid me.

OEDIPUS.   Who would not be enraged to hear these words
By which you now dishonor this our city?

TEIRESIAS.   Of itself this will come, though I hide it in silence.

OEDIPUS.   Then you should tell me what it is will come.
TEIRESIAS.   I shall speak no more. If further you desire,
    Rage on in wildest anger of your soul.
OEDIPUS.   I shall omit nothing I understand
    I am so angry. Know that you seem to me
    Creator of the deed and worker too
    In all short of the slaughter; if you were not blind,
    I would say this crime was your work alone.
TEIRESIAS.   Really? Abide yourself by the decree
    You just proclaimed, I tell you! From this day
    Henceforth address neither these men nor me.
    You are the godless defiler of this land.
OEDIPUS.   You push so bold and taunting in your speech;
    And how do you think to get away with this?
TEIRESIAS.   I have got away. I nurse my strength in truth.
OEDIPUS.   Who taught you this? Not from your art you got it.
TEIRESIAS.   From you. You had me speak against my will.
OEDIPUS.   What word? Say again, so I may better learn.
TEIRESIAS.   Didn't you get it before? Or do you bait me?
OEDIPUS.   I don't remember it. Speak forth again.
TEIRESIAS.   You are the slayer whom you seek, I say.
OEDIPUS.   Not twice you speak such bitter words unpunished.
TEIRESIAS.   Shall I speak more to make you angrier still?
OEDIPUS.   Do what you will, your words will be in vain.
TEIRESIAS.   I say you have forgot that you are joined
    With those most dear to you in deepest shame
    And do not see where you are in sin.
OEDIPUS.   Do you think you will always say such things in joy?
TEIRESIAS.   Surely, if strength abides in what is true.
OEDIPUS.   It does, for all but you, this not for you
    Because your ears and mind and eyes are blind.
TEIRESIAS.   Wretched you are to make such taunts, for soon
    All men will cast the selfsame taunts on you.
OEDIPUS.   You live in entire night, could do no harm
    To me or any man who sees the day.
TEIRESIAS.   Not at my hands will it be your fate to fall.
    Apollo suffices, whose concern it is to do this.
OEDIPUS.   Are these devices yours, or are they Creon's?
TEIRESIAS.   Creon is not your trouble; you are yourself.
OEDIPUS.   O riches, empire, skill surpassing skill

In all the numerous rivalries of life,
How great a grudge there is stored up against you
If for this kingship, which the city gave,
Their gift, not my request, into my hands—
For this, the trusted Creon, my friend from the start
Desires to creep by stealth and cast me out
Taking a seer like this, a weaver of wiles,
A crooked swindler who has got his eyes
On gain alone, but in his art is blind.
Come, tell us, in what clearly are you a prophet?
How is it, when the weave-songed bitch was here
You uttered no salvation for these people?
Surely the riddle then could not be solved
By some chance comer; it needed prophecy.
You did not clarify that with birds
Or knowledge from a god; but when I came,
The ignorant Oedipus, I silenced her,
Not taught by birds, but winning by my wits,
Whom you are now attempting to depose,
Thinking to minister near Creon's throne.
I think that to your woe you and that plotter
Will purge the land, and if you were not old
Punishment would teach you what you plot.

CHORUS.   It seems to us, O Oedipus our king,
   Both this man's words and yours were said in anger.
   Such is not our need, but to find out
   How best we shall discharge Apollo's orders.

TEIRESIAS.   Even if you are king, the right to answer
   Should be free to all; of that I too am king.
   I live not as your slave, but as Apollo's.
   And not with Creon's wards shall I be counted.
   I say, since you have taunted even my blindness,
   You have eyes, but see not where in evil you are
   Nor where you dwell, nor whom you are living with.
   Do you know from whom you spring? And you forget
   You are an enemy to your own kin
   Both those beneath and those above the earth.
   Your mother's and father's curse, with double goad
   And dreaded foot shall drive you from this land.
   You who now see straight shall then be blind,

And there shall be no harbour for your cry
With which all Mount Cithaeron[15] soon shall ring,
When you have learned the wedding where you sailed
At home, into no port, by voyage fair.
A throng of other ills you do not know
Shall equal you to yourself and to your children.
Throw mud on this, on Creon, on my voice—
Yet there shall never be a mortal man
Eradicated more wretchedly than you.

OPEDIPUS.   Shall these unbearable words be heard from him?
Go to perdition! Hurry! Off, away,
Turn back again and from this house depart.

TEIRESIAS.   If you had not called me, I should not have come.

OEDIPUS.   I did not know that you would speak such folly
Or I would not soon have brought you to my house.

TEIRESIAS.   And such a fool I am, as it seems to you.
But to the parents who bore you I seem wise.

OEDIPUS.   What parents? Wait! What mortals gave me birth?

TEIRESIAS.   This day shall be your birth and your destruction.

OEDIPUS.   All things you say in riddles and unclear.

TEIRESIAS.   Are you not he who best can search this out?

OEDIPUS.   Mock, if you wish, the skill that made me great.

TEIRESIAS.   This is the very fortune that destroyed you.

OEDIPUS.   Well, if I saved the city, I do not care.

TEIRESIAS.   I am going now. You, boy, be my guide.

OEDIPUS.   Yes, let him guide you. Here you are in the way.
When you are gone you will give no more trouble.

TEIRESIAS.   I go when I have said what I came to say
Without fear of your frown; you cannot destroy me.
I say, the very man whom you long seek
With threats and announcements about Laius' murder—
This man is here. He seems an alien stranger,
But soon he shall be revealed of Theban birth,
Nor at this circumstance shall he be pleased.
He shall be blind who sees, shall be a beggar
Who now is rich, shall make his way abroad
Feeling the ground before him with a staff.
He shall be revealed at once as brother

---

[15] Mountain near Thebes.

And father to his own children, husband and son
To his mother, his father's kin and murderer.
Go in and ponder that. If I am wrong,
Say then that I know nothing of prophecy.

CHORUS.

Who is the man the Delphic rock said with oracular voice
Unspeakable crimes performed with his gory hands?
It is time for him now to speed
His foot in flight, more strong
Than horses swift as the storm.
For girt in arms upon him springs
With fire and lightning, Zeus' son
And behind him, terrible,
Come the unerring Fates.[16]

From snowy Parnassus[17] just now the word flashed clear
To track the obscure man by every way,
For he wanders under the wild
Forest, and into caves
And cliff rocks, like a bull,
Reft on his way, with care on care
Trying to shun the prophecy
Come from the earth's mid-navel,
But about him flutters the ever living doom.

Terrible, terrible things the wise bird-augur stirs.
I neither approve nor deny, at a loss for what to say,
I flutter in hopes and fears, see neither here nor ahead;
For what strife has lain
On Labdacus' sons or Polybus' that I have found ever before
Or now, whereby I may run for the sons of Labdacus
In sure proof against Oedipus' public fame
As avenger for dark death?

Zeus and Apollo surely understand and know
The affairs of mortal men, but that a mortal seer
Knows more than I, there is no proof. Though a man
May surpass a man in knowledge,

---

[16] The three goddesses responsible for punishment of crimes.
[17] A mountain overlooking the shrine of Apollo at Delphi.

Never shall I agree, till I see the word true, when men blame
    Oedipus,
For there came upon him once clear the winged maiden
And wise he was seen, by sure test sweet for the state.
So never shall my mind judge him evil guilt.

CREON.   Men of our city, I have heard dread words
    That Oedipus our king accuses me.
    I am here indignant. If in the present troubles
    He thinks that he has suffered at my hands
    One word or deed tending to injury
    I do not crave the long-spanned age of life
    To bear this rumor, for it is no simple wrong
    The damage of this accusation brings me;
    It brings the greatest, if I am called a traitor
    To you and my friends, a traitor to the state.
CHORUS.   Come now, for this reproach perhaps was forced
    By anger, rather than considered thought.
CREON.   And was the idea voiced that my advice
    Persuaded the prophet to give false accounts?
CHORUS.   Such was said. I know not to what intent.
CREON.   Was this accusation laid against me
    From straightforward eyes and straightforward mind?
CHORUS.   I do not know. I see not what my masters do;
    But here he is now, coming from the house.
OEDIPUS.   How dare you come here? Do you own a face
    So bold that you can come before my house
    When you are clearly the murderer of this man
    And manifestly pirate of my throne?
    Come, say before the gods, did you see in me
    A coward or a fool, that you plotted this?
    Or did you think I would not see your wiles
    Creeping upon me, or knowing, would not ward off?
    Surely your machination is absurd
    Without a crowd of friends to hunt a throne
    Which is captured only by wealth and many men.
CREON.   Do you know what you do? Hear answer to your charges
    On the other side. Judge only what you know.
OEDIPUS.   Your speech is clever, but I learn it ill
    Since I have found you harsh and grievous toward me.
CREON.   This very matter hear me first explain.

OEDIPUS.   Tell me not this one thing: you are not false.
CREON.   If you think stubbornness a good possession
   Apart from judgment, you do not think right.
OEDIPUS.   If you think you can do a kinsman evil
   Without the penalty, you have no sense.
CREON.   I agree with you. What you have said is just.
   Tell me what you say you have suffered from me.
OEDIPUS.   Did you, or did you not, advise my need
   Was summoning that prophet person here?
CREON.   And still is. I hold still the same opinion.
OEDIPUS.   How long a time now has it been since Laius—
CREON.   Performed what deed? I do not understand.
OEDIPUS.   —Disappeared to his ruin at deadly hands?
CREON.   Far in the past the count of years would run.
OEDIPUS.   Was this same seer at that time practising?
CREON.   As wise as now, and equally respected.
OEDIPUS.   At that time did he ever mention me?
CREON.   Never when I stood near enough to hear.
OEDIPUS.   But did you not make inquiry of the murder?
CREON.   We did, of course, and got no information.
OEDIPUS.   How is it that this seer did not utter this then?
CREON.   When I don't know, as now, I would keep still.
OEDIPUS.   This much you know full well, and so should speak:—
CREON.   What is that? If I know, I will not refuse.
OEDIPUS.   This: If he had not first conferred with you
   He never would have said that I killed Laius.
CREON.   If he says this, you know yourself, I think;
   I learn as much from you as you from me.
OEDIPUS.   Learn then: I never shall be found a slayer.
CREON.   What then, are you the husband of my sister?
OEDIPUS.   What you have asked is plain beyond denial.
CREON.   Do you rule this land with her in equal sway?
OEDIPUS.   All she desires she obtains from me.
CREON.   Am I with you two not an equal third?
OEDIPUS.   In just that do you prove a treacherous friend.
CREON.   No, if, like me, you reason with yourself.
   Consider this fact first: would any man
   Choose, do you think, to have his rule in fear
   Rather than doze unharmed with the same power?
   For my part I have never been desirous

Of being king instead of acting king.
Nor any other man has, wise and prudent.
For now I obtain all from you without fear.
If I were king, I would do much unwilling.
How then could kingship sweeter be for me
Than rule and power devoid of any pain?
I am not yet so much deceived to want
Goods besides those I profitably enjoy.
Now I am hailed and gladdened by all men.
Now those who want from you speak out to me,
Since all their chances' outcome dwells therein.
How then would I relinquish what I have
To get those gains? My mind runs not so bad.
I am prudent yet, no lover of such plots,
Nor would I ever endure others' treason.
And first as proof of this go on to Pytho;
See if I told you truly the oracle.
Next proof: see if I plotted with the seer;
If you find so at all, put me to death
With my vote for my guilt as well as yours.
Do not convict me just on unclear conjecture.
It is not right to think capriciously
The good are bad, nor that the bad are good.
It is the same to cast out a noble friend,
I say, as one's own life, which best he loves.
The facts, though, you will safely know in time,
Since time alone can show the just man just,
But you can know a criminal in one day.
CHORUS.   A cautious man would say he has spoken well.
O king, the quick to think are never sure.
OEDIPUS.   When the plotter, swift, approaches me in stealth
I too in counterplot must be as swift.
If I wait in repose, the plotter's ends
Are brought to pass and mine will then have erred.
CREON.   What do you want then? To cast me from the land?
OEDIPUS.   Least of all that. My wish is you should die,
Not flee to exemplify what envy is.
CREON.   Do you say this? Will you neither trust nor yield?
OEDIPUS.   [No, for I think that you deserve no trust.]
CREON.   You seem not wise to me.

OEDIPUS.   I am for me.

CREON.   You should be for me too.

OEDIPUS.   No, you are evil.

CREON.   Yes, if you understand nothing.

OEDIPUS.   Yet I must rule.

CREON.   Not when you rule badly.

OEDIPUS.   O city, city!

CREON.   It is my city too, not yours alone.

CHORUS.   Stop, princes. I see Jocasta coming
Out of the house at the right time for you.
With her you must settle the dispute at hand.

JOCASTA.   O wretched men, what unconsidered feud
Of tongues have you aroused? Are you not ashamed,
The state so sick, to stir up private ills?
Are you not going home? And you as well?
Will you turn a small pain into a great?

CREON.   My blood sister, Oedipus your husband
Claims he will judge against me two dread ills:
Thrust me from the fatherland or take and kill me.

OEDIPUS.   I will, my wife; I caught him in the act
Doing evil to my person with evil skill.

CREON.   Now may I not rejoice but die accursed
If ever I did any of what you accuse me.

JOCASTA.   O, by the gods, believe him, Oedipus.
First, in reverence for his oath to the gods,
Next, for my sake and theirs who stand before you.

CHORUS.   Hear my entreaty, lord. Consider and consent.

OEDIPUS.   What wish should I then grant?

CHORUS.   Respect the man, no fool before, who now in oath is
strong.

OEPIDUS.   You know what you desire?

CHORUS.   I know.

OEDIPUS.   Say what you mean.

CHORUS.   Your friend who has sworn do not dishonour
By casting guilt for dark report.

OEDIPUS.   Know well that when you ask this grant from me,
You ask my death or exile from the land.

CHORUS.   No, by the god foremost among the gods,
The Sun, may I perish by the utmost doom
Godless and friendless, if I have this in mind.

But ah, the withering earth wears down
My wretched soul, if to these ills
Of old are added ills from both of you.
OEDIPUS.   Then let him go, though surely I must die
Or be thrust dishonoured from this land by force.
Your grievous voice I pity, not that man's;
Wherever he may be, he will be hated.
CREON.   Sullen you are to yield, as you are heavy
When you exceed in wrath. Natures like these
Are justly sorest for themselves to bear.
OEDIPUS.   Will you not go and leave me?
CREON.   I am on my way.
You know me not, but these men see me just.
CHORUS.   O queen, why do you delay to bring this man indoors?
JOCASTA.   I want to learn what happened here.
CHORUS.   Unknown suspicion rose from talk, and the unjust devours.
JOCASTA.   In both of them?
CHORUS.   Just so.
JOCASTA.   What was the talk?
CHORUS.   Enough, enough! When the land is pained
It seems to me at this point we should stop.
OEDIPUS.   Do you see where you have come? Though your intent
Is good, you slacken off and blunt my heart.
CHORUS.   O lord, I have said not once alone,
Know that I clearly would be mad
And wandering in mind, to turn away
You who steered along the right,
When she was torn with trouble, our beloved state.
O may you now become in health her guide.
JOCASTA.   By the gods, lord, tell me on what account
You have set yourself in so great an anger.
OEDIPUS.   I shall tell you, wife; I respect you more than these men.
Because of Creon, since he has plotted against me.
JOCASTA.   Say clearly, if you can; how started the quarrel?
OEDIPUS.   He says that I stand as the murderer of Laius.
JOCASTA.   He knows himself, or learned from someone else?
OEDIPUS.   No, but he sent a rascal prophet here.
He keeps his own mouth clean in what concerns him.
JOCASTA.   Now free yourself of what you said, and listen.

Learn from me, no mortal man exists
Who knows prophetic art for your affairs,
And I shall briefly show you proof of this:
An oracle came once to Laius. I do not say
From Phoebus himself, but from his ministers
That his fate would be at his son's hand to die—
A child, who would be born from him and me.
And yet, as the rumour says, they were strangers,
Robbers who killed him where three highways meet.
But three days had not passed from the child's birth
When Laius pierced and tied together his ankles,
And cast him by others' hands on a pathless mountain.
Therein Apollo did not bring to pass
That the child murder his father, nor for Laius
The dread he feared, to die at his son's hand.
Such did prophetic oracles determine.
Pay no attention to them. For the god
Will easily make clear the need he seeks.

OEDIPUS.   What wandering of soul, what stirring of mind
Holds me, my wife, in what I have just heard!

JOCASTA.   What care has turned you back that you say this?

OEDIPUS.   I thought I heard you mention this, that Laius
Was slaughtered at the place where three highways meet.

JOCASTA.   That was the talk. The rumour has not ceased.

OEDIPUS.   Where is this place where such a sorrow was?

JOCASTA.   The country's name is Phocis. A split road
Leads to one place from Delphi and Daulia.

OEDIPUS.   And how much time has passed since these events?

JOCASTA.   The news was heralded in the city scarcely
A little while before you came to rule.

OEDIPUS.   O Zeus, what have you planned to do to me?

JOCASTA.   What passion is this in you, Oedipus?

OEDIPUS.   Don't ask me that yet. Tell me about Laius.
What did he look like? How old was he when murdered?

JOCASTA.   A tall man, with his hair just brushed with white.
His shape and form differed not far from yours.

OEDIPUS.   Alas! Alas! I think unwittingly
I have just laid dread curses on my head.

JOCASTA.   What are you saying? I shrink to behold you, lord.

OEDIPUS.   I am terribly afraid the seer can see.
That will be clearer if you say one thing more.

JOCASTA.   Though I shrink, if I know what you ask, I will answer.
OEDIPUS.   Did he set forth with few attendants then,
    Or many soldiers, since he was a king?
JOCASTA.   They were five altogether among them.
    One was a herald. One chariot bore Laius.
OEDIPUS.   Alas! All this is clear now. Tell me, my wife,
    Who was the man who told these stories to you?
JOCASTA.   One servant, who alone escaped, returned.
OEDIPUS.   Is he by chance now present in our house?
JOCASTA.   Not now. Right from the time when he returned
    To see you ruling and Laius dead,
    Touching my hand in suppliance, he implored me
    To send him to fields and to pastures of sheep
    That he might be farthest from the sight of this city.
    So I sent him away, since he was worthy
    For a slave, to bear a greater grant than this.
OEDIPUS.   How then could he return to us with speed?
JOCASTA.   It can be done. But why would you order this?
OEDIPUS.   O lady, I fear I have said too much.
    On this account I now desire to see him.
JOCASTA.   Then he shall come. But I myself deserve
    To learn what it is that troubles you, my lord.
OEDIPUS.   And you shall not be prevented, since my fears
    Have come to such a point. For who is closer
    That I may speak to in this fate than you?
    Polybus of Corinth was my father,
    My mother, Dorian Merope. I was held there
    Chief citizen of all, till such a fate
    Befell me—as it is, worthy of wonder,
    But surely not deserving my excitement.
    A man at a banquet overdrunk with wine
    Said in drink I was a false son [18] to my father.
    The weight I held that day I scarcely bore,
    But on the next day I went home and asked
    My father and mother of it. In bitter anger
    They took the reproach from him who had let it fly.
    I was pleased at their actions; nevertheless
    The rumour always rankled; and spread abroad.
    In secret from mother and father I set out

---

[18] That is, not born of his flesh.

Toward Delphi. Phoebus sent me away ungraced
In what I came for, but other wretched things
Terrible and grievous, he revealed in answer;
That I must wed my mother and produce
An unendurable race for men to see,
That I should kill the father who begot me.
When I heard this response, Corinth I fled
Henceforth to measure her land by stars alone.
I went where I should never see the disgrace
Of my evil oracles be brought to pass,
And on my journey to that place I came
At which you say this king had met his death.
My wife, I shall speak the truth to you. My way
Led to a place close by the triple road.
There a herald met me, and a man
Seated on colt-drawn chariot, as you said.
There both the guide and the old man himself
Thrust me with driving force out of the path.
And I in anger struck the one who pushed me,
The driver. Then the old man, when he saw me,
Watched when I passed, and from his chariot
Struck me full on the head with double goad.
I paid him back and more. From this very hand
A swift blow of my staff rolled him right out
Of the middle of his seat onto his back.
I killed them all. But if relationship
Existed between this stranger and Laius,
What man now is wretcheder than I?
What man is cursed by a more evil fate?
No stranger or citizen could now receive me
Within his home, or even speak to me,
But thrust me out; and no one but myself
Brought down these curses on my head.
The bed of the slain man I now defile
With hands that killed him. Am I evil by birth?
Am I not utterly vile if I must flee
And cannot see my family in my flight
Nor tread my homeland soil, or else be joined
In marriage to my mother, kill my father,
Polybus, who sired me and brought me up?

Would not a man judge right to say of me
That this was sent on me by some cruel spirit?
O never, holy reverence of the gods,
May I behold that day, but may I go
Away from mortal men, before I see
Such a stain of circumstance come to me.

CHORUS.   My lord, for us these facts are full of dread.
Until you hear the witness, stay in hope.

OEDIPUS.   And just so much is all I have of hope,
Only to wait until the shepherd comes.

JOCASTA.   What, then, do you desire to hear him speak?

OEDIPUS.   I will tell you, if his story is found to be
The same as yours, I would escape the sorrow.

JOCASTA.   What unusual word did you hear from me?

OEDIPUS.   You said he said that they were highway robbers
Who murdered him. Now, if he still says
The selfsame number, I could not have killed him,
Since one man does not equal many men.
But if he speaks of a single lonely traveller,
The scale of guilt now clearly falls to me.

JOCASTA.   However, know the word was set forth thus
And it is not in him now to take it back;
This tale the city heard, not I alone.
But if he diverges from his previous story,
Even then, my lord, he could not show Laius' murder
To have been fulfilled properly. Apollo
Said he would die at the hands of my own son.
Surely that wretched child could not have killed him,
But he himself met death some time before.
Therefore, in any prophecy henceforth
I would not look to this side or to that.

OEDIPUS.   Your thoughts ring true, but still let someone go
To summon the peasant. Do not neglect this.

JOCASTA.   I shall send without delay. But let us enter.
I would do nothing that did not please you.

CHORUS.

May fate come on me as I bear
Holy pureness in all word and deed,

For which the lofty striding laws [19] were set down,
Born through the heavenly air
Whereof the Olympian sky alone the father was;
No mortal spawn of mankind gave them birth,
Nor may oblivion ever lull them down;
Mighty in them the god is, and he does not age.

Pride breeds the tyrant.
Pride, once overfilled with many things in vain,
Neither in season nor fit for man,
Scaling the sheerest height
Hurls to a dire fate
Where no foothold is found.
I pray the god may never stop the rivalry
That works well for the state.
The god as my protector I shall never cease to hold.

But if a man goes forth haughty in word or deed
With no fear of the Right
Nor pious to the spirits' shrines,
May evil doom seize him
For his ill-fated pride,
If he does not fairly win his gain
Or works unholy deeds,
Or, in bold folly lays on the sacred profane hands.
For when such acts occur, what man may boast
Ever to ward off from his life darts of the gods?
If practices like these are in respect,
Why then must I dance the sacred dance?

Never again in worship shall I go
To Delphi, holy navel of the earth, [20]
Nor to the temple at Abae,
Nor to Olympia,
If these prophecies do not become
Examples for all men.
O Zeus, our king, if so you are rightly called,
Ruler of all things, may they not escape

---

[19] That is, the divine laws.
[20] The Greeks believed that Delphi was the center-point, or "navel," of the earth's surface.

You and your forever deathless power.
Men now hold light the fading oracles
Told about Laius long ago
And nowhere is Apollo clearly honored;
Things divine are going down to ruin.

JOCASTA.   Lords of this land, the thought has come to me
To visit the spirits' shrines, bearing in hand
These suppliant boughs and offerings of incense.
For Oedipus raises his soul too high
With all distresses; nor, as a sane man should,
Does he confirm the new by things of old,
But stands at the speaker's will if he speaks terrors.
And so, because my advice can do no more,
To you, Lycian Apollo—for you are nearest—
A suppliant, I have come here with these prayers,
That you may find some pure deliverance for us:
We all now shrink to see him struck in fear,
That man who is the pilot of our ship.
MESSENGER.   Strangers, could I learn from one of you
Where is the house of Oedipus the king?
Or best, if you know, say where he is himself.
CHORUS.   This is his house, stranger; he dwells inside;
This woman is the mother of his children.
MESSENGER.   May she be always blessed among the blest,
Since she is the fruitful wife of Oedipus.
JOCASTA.   So may you, stranger, also be. You deserve
As much for your graceful greeting. But tell me
What you have come to search for or to show.
MESSENGER.   Good news for your house and your husband, lady.
JOCASTA.   What is it then? And from whom have you come?
MESSENGER.   From Corinth. And the message I will tell
Will surely gladden you—and vex you, perhaps.
JOCASTA.   What is it? What is this double force it holds?
MESSENGER.   The men who dwell in the Isthmian country[21]
Have spoken to establish him their king.
JOCASTA.   What is that? Is not old Polybus still ruling?
MESSENGER.   Not he. For death now holds him in the tomb.

---

[21]Corinth, located on an isthmus, was the principal city of that area.

JOCASTA.   What do you say, old man? Is Polybus dead?
MESSENGER.   If I speak not the truth, I am ready to die.
JOCASTA.   O handmaid, go right away and tell your master
    The news. Where are you, prophecies of the gods?
    For this man Oedipus has trembled long,
    And shunned him lest he kill him. Now the man
    Is killed by fate and not by Oedipus.
OEDIPUS.   O Jocasta, my most beloved wife,
    Why have you sent for me within the house?
JOCASTA.   Listen to this man, and while you hear him, think
    To what have come Apollo's holy prophecies.
OEDIPUS.   Who is this man? Why would he speak to me?
JOCASTA.   From Corinth he has come, to announce that your father
    Polybus no longer lives, but is dead.
OEDIPUS.   What do you say, stranger? Tell me this yourself.
MESSENGER.   If I must first announce my message clearly,
    Know surely that the man is dead and gone.
OEDIPUS.   Did he die by treachery or chance disease?
MESSENGER.   A slight scale tilt can lull the old to rest.
OEDIPUS.   The poor man, it seems, died by disease.
MESSENGER.   And by the full measure of lengthy time.
OEDIPUS.   Alas, alas! Why then do any seek
    Pytho's prophetic art, my wife, or hear
    The shrieking birds on high, by whose report
    I was to slay my father? Now he lies
    Dead beneath the earth, and here am I
    Who have not touched the blade. Unless in longing
    For me he died, and in this sense was killed by me.
    Polybus has packed away these oracles
    In his rest in Hades.[22] They are now worth nothing.
JOCASTA.   Did I not tell you that some time ago?
OEDIPUS.   You did, but I was led astray by fear.
JOCASTA.   Henceforth put nothing of this on your heart.
OEDIPUS.   Why must I not still shrink from my mother's bed?
JOCASTA.   What should man fear, whose life is ruled by fate,
    For whom there is clear foreknowledge of nothing?
    It is best to live by chance, however you can.
    Be not afraid of marriage with your mother;

---

[22]The underworld realm of dead souls.

Already many mortals in their dreams
Have shared their mother's bed. But he who counts
This dream as nothing, easiest bears his life.

OEDIPUS.   All that you say would be indeed propitious,
If my mother were not alive. But since she is,
I still must shrink, however well you speak.

JOCASTA.   And yet your father's tomb is a great eye.

OEDIPUS.   A great eye indeed. But I fear her who lives.

MESSENGER.   Who is this woman that you are afraid of?

OEDIPUS.   Merope, old man, with whom Polybus lived.

MESSENGER.   What is it in her that moves you to fear?

OEDIPUS.   A dread oracle, stranger, sent by the god.

MESSENGER.   Can it be told, or must no other know?

OEDIPUS.   It surely can. Apollo told me once
That I must join in intercourse with my mother
And shed with my own hands my father's blood.
Because of this, long since I have kept far
Away from Corinth—and happily—but yet
It would be most sweet to see my parents' faces.

MESSENGER.   Was this your fear in shunning your own city?

OEDIPUS.   I wished, too, old man, not to slay my father.

MESSENGER.   Why then have I not freed you from this fear,
Since I have come with friendly mind, my lord?

OEDIPUS.   Yes, and take thanks from me, which you deserve.

MESSENGER.   And this is just the thing for which I came,
That when you got back home I might fare well.

OEDIPUS.   Never shall I go where my parents are.

MESSENGER.   My son, you clearly know not what you do.

OEDIPUS.   How is that, old man? By the gods, let me know.

MESSENGER.   If for these tales you shrink from going home.

OEDIPUS.   I tremble lest what Phoebus said comes true.

MESSENGER.   Lest you incur pollution from your parents?

OEDIPUS.   That is the thing, old man, that always haunts me.

MESSENGER.   Well, do you know that surely you fear nothing?

OEDIPUS.   How so? If I am the son of those who bore me.

MESSENGER.   Since Polybus was no relation to you.

OEDIPUS.   What do you say? Was Polybus not my father?

MESSENGER.   No more than this man here but just so much.

OEDIPUS.   How does he who begot me equal nothing?

MESSENGER.   That man was not your father, any more than I am.

OEDIPUS.   Well then, why was it he called me his son?

MESSENGER.   Long ago he got you as a gift from me.

OEDIPUS.   Though from another's hand, yet so much he loved me!

MESSENGER.   His previous childlessness led him to that.

OEDIPUS.   Had you bought or found me when you gave me to him?

MESSENGER.   I found you in Cithaeron's folds and glens.

OEDIPUS.   Why were you travelling in those regions?

MESSENGER.   I guarded there a flock of mountain sheep.

OEDIPUS.   Were you a shepherd, wandering for pay?

MESSENGER.   Yes, and your saviour too, child, at that time.

OEDIPUS.   What pain gripped me, that you took me in your arms?

MESSENGER.   The ankles of your feet will tell you that.

OEDIPUS.   Alas, why do you mention that old trouble?

MESSENGER.   I freed you when your ankles were pierced together.

OEDIPUS.   A terrible shame from my swaddling clothes I got.

MESSENGER.   Your very name[23] you got from this misfortune.

OEDIPUS.   By the gods, did my mother or father do it? Speak.

MESSENGER.   I know not. He who gave you knows better than I.

OEDIPUS.   You didn't find me, but took me from another?

MESSENGER.   That's right. Another shepherd gave you to me.

OEDIPUS.   Who was he? Can you tell me who he was?

MESSENGER.   Surely. He belonged to the household of Laius.

OEDIPUS.   The man who ruled this land once long ago?

MESSENGER.   Just so. He was a shepherd in that man's service.

OEDIPUS.   Is this man still alive, so I could see him?

MESSENGER.   You dwellers in this country should know best.

OEDIPUS.   Is there any one of you who stand before me
Who knows the shepherd of whom this man speaks?
If you have seen him in the fields or here,
Speak forth; the time has come to find this out.

CHORUS.   I think the man you seek is no one else
Than the shepherd you were so eager to see before.
Jocasta here might best inform us that.

OEDIPUS.   My wife, do you know the man we just ordered
To come here? Is it of him that this man speaks?

JOCASTA.   Why ask of whom he spoke? Think nothing of it.
Brood not in vain on what has just been said.

OEDIPUS.   It could not be that when I have got such clues,
I should not shed clear light upon my birth.

[23] Oedipus means, literally, "swollen foot."

JOCASTA.   Don't, by the gods, investigate this more
   If you care for your own life. I am sick enough.
OEDIPUS.   Take courage. Even if I am found a slave
   For three generations, your birth will not be base.
JOCASTA.   Still, I beseech you, hear me. Don't do this.
OEDIPUS.   I will hear of nothing but finding out the truth.
JOCASTA.   I know full well and tell you what is best.
OEDIPUS.   Well, then, this best, for some time now, has given me
      pain.
JOCASTA.   O ill-fated man, may you never know who you are.
OEDIPUS.   Will someone bring the shepherd to me here?
   And let this lady rejoice in her opulent birth.
JOCASTA.   Alas, alas, hapless man. I have this alone
   To tell you, and nothing else forevermore.
CHORUS.   O Oedipus, where has the woman gone
   In the rush of her wild grief? I am afraid
   Evil will break forth out of this silence.
OEDIPUS.   Let whatever will break forth. I plan to see
   The seed of my descent, however small.
   My wife, perhaps, because a noblewoman
   Looks down with shame upon my lowly birth.
   I would not be dishonoured to call myself
   The son of Fortune, giver of the good.
   She is my mother. The years, her other children,
   Have marked me sometimes small and sometimes great.
   Such was I born! I shall prove no other man,
   Nor shall I cease to search out my descent.

CHORUS.

   If I am a prophet and can know in mind,
   Cithaeron, by tomorrow's full moon
   You shall not fail, by mount Olympus,
   To find that Oedipus, as a native of your land,
   Shall honour you for nurse and mother.
   And to you we dance in choral song because you bring
   Fair gifts to him our king.
   Hail, Phoebus, may all this please you.

   Who, child, who bore you in the lengthy span of years?
   One close to Pan who roams the mountain woods,
   One of Apollo's bedfellows?

For all wild pastures in mountain glens to him are dear.
Was Hermes [24] your father, who Cyllene sways,
Or did Bacchus, dwelling on the mountain peaks,
Take you a foundling from some nymph
Of those by springs of Helicon, [25] with whom he sports the
      most?

OEDIPUS.   If I may guess, although I never met him,
   I think, elders, I see that shepherd coming
   Whom we have long sought, as in the measure
   Of lengthy age he accords with him we wait for.
   Besides, the men who lead him I recognize
   As servants of my house. You may perhaps
   Know better than I if you have seen him before.
CHORUS.   Be assured, I know him as a shepherd
   As trusted as any other in Laius' service.
OEDIPUS.   Stranger from Corinth, I will ask you first,
   Is this the man you said?
MESSENGER.   You are looking at him.
OEDIPUS.   You there, old man, look here and answer me
   What I shall ask you. Were you ever with Laius?
SERVANT.   I was a slave, not bought but reared at home.
OEDIPUS.   What work concerned you? What was your way of life?
SERVANT.   Most of my life I spent among the flocks.
OEDIPUS.   In what place most of all was your usual pasture?
SERVANT.   Sometimes Cithaeron, or the ground nearby.
OEDIPUS.   Do you know this man before you here at all?
SERVANT.   Doing what? And of what man do you speak?
OEDIPUS.   The one before you. Have you ever had congress with
   him?
SERVANT.   Not to say so at once from memory.
MESSENGER.   That is no wonder, master, but I shall remind him,
   Clearly, who knows me not; yet well I know
   That he knew once the region of Cithaeron.
   He with a double flock and I with one
   Dwelt there in company for three whole years
   During the six months' time from spring to fall.

---

[24] The divine messenger of the gods, born on Mount Cyllene.
[25] A mountain in central Greece, home of the sacred Muses and often associated with
   Bacchus.

When winter came, I drove into my fold
My flock, and he drove his to Laius' pens.
Do I speak right, or did it not happen so?

SERVANT.   You speak the truth, though it was long ago.

MESSENGER.   Come now, do you recall you gave me then
A child for me to rear as my own son?

SERVANT.   What is that? Why do you ask me this?

MESSENGER.   This is the man, my friend, who then was young.

SERVANT.   Go to destruction! Will you not be quiet?

OEDIPUS.   Come, scold him not, old man. These words of yours
Deserve a scolding more than this man's do.

SERVANT.   In what, most noble master, do I wrong?

OEDIPUS.   Not to tell of the child he asks about.

SERVANT.   He speaks in ignorance, he toils in vain.

OEDIPUS.   If you will not speak freely, you will under torture.

SERVANT.   Don't, by the gods, outrage an old man like me.

OEDIPUS.   Will someone quickly twist back this fellow's arms?

SERVANT.   Alas, what for? What do you want to know?

OEDIPUS.   Did you give this man the child of whom he asks?

SERVANT.   I did. Would I had perished on that day!

OEDIPUS.   You will come to that unless you tell the truth.

SERVANT.   I come to far greater ruin if I speak.

OEDIPUS.   This man, it seems, is trying to delay.

SERVANT.   Not I. I said before I gave it to him.

OEDIPUS.   Where did you get it? At home or from someone else?

SERVANT.   It was not mine. I got him from a man.

OEDIPUS.   Which of these citizens? Where did he live?

SERVANT.   O master, by the gods, ask me no more.

OEDIPUS.   You are done for if I ask you this again.

SERVANT.   Well then, he was born of the house of Laius.

OEDIPUS.   One of his slaves, or born of his own race?

SERVANT.   Alas, to speak I am on the brink of horror.

OEDIPUS.   And I to hear. But still it must be heard.

SERVANT.   Well, then, they say it was his child. Your wife
Who dwells within could best say how this stands.

OEDIPUS.   Was it she who gave him to you?

SERVANT.   Yes, my lord.

OEDIPUS.   For what intent?

SERVANT.   So I could put it away.

OEDIPUS.   When she bore him, the wretch.

SERVANT.   She feared bad oracles.

OEDIPUS.   What were they?

SERVANT.   They said he should kill his father.

OEDIPUS.   Why did you give him up to this old man?

SERVANT.   I pitied him, master, and thought he would take him
    away
    To another land, the one from which he came.
    But he saved him for greatest woe. If you are he
    Whom this man speaks of, you were born curst by fate.

OEDIPUS.   Alas, alas! All things are now come true.
    O light, for the last time now I look upon you;
    I am shown to be born from those I ought not to have been.
    I married the woman I should not have married,
    I killed the man whom I should not have killed.

CHORUS.

    Alas, generations of mortal men!
    How equal to nothing do I number you in life!
    Who, O who, is the man
    Who bears more of bliss
    Than just the seeming so,
    And then, like a waning sun, to fall away?
    When I know your example,
    Your guiding spirit, yours, wretched Oedipus,
    I call no mortal blest.

    He is the one, O Zeus,
    Who peerless shot his bow and won well-fated bliss,
    Who destroyed the hook-clawed maiden,
    The oracle-singing Sphinx,
    And stood a tower for our land from death;
    For this you are called our king,
    Oedipus, are highest-honoured here,
    And over great Thebes hold sway.

    And now who is more wretched for men to hear,
    Who so lives in wild plagues, who dwells in pains,
    In utter change of life?
    Alas for glorious Oedipus!
    The selfsame port of rest

Was gained by bridegroom father and his son,
How, O how did your father's furrows ever bear you, suffering
    man?
How have they endured silence for so long?

You are found out, unwilling, by all-seeing Time.
It judges your unmarried marriage where for long
Begetter and begot have been the same.
Alas, child of Laius,
Would I had never seen you.
As one who pours from his mouth a dirge I wail,
To speak the truth, through you I breathed new life,
And now through you I lulled my eye to sleep.

SECOND MESSENGER.   O men most honoured always of this land
    What deeds you shall hear, what shall you behold!
    What grief shall stir you up, if by your kinship
    You are still concerned for the house of Labdacus!
    I think neither Danube nor any other river
    Could wash this palace clean, so many ills
    Lie hidden there which now will come to light.
    They were done by will, not fate; and sorrows hurt
    The most when we ourselves appear to choose them.
CHORUS.   What we heard before causes no little sorrow.
    What can you say which adds to that a burden?
SECOND MESSENGER.   This is the fastest way to tell the tale;
    Hear it: Jocasta, your divine queen, is dead.
CHORUS.   O sorrowful woman! From what cause did she die?
SECOND MESSENGER.   By her own hand. The most painful of the ac-
    tion
    Occurred away, not for your eyes to see.
    But still, so far as I have memory
    You shall learn the sufferings of that wretched woman:
    How she passed on through the door enraged
    And rushed straight forward to her nuptial bed,
    Clutching her hair's ends with both her hands.
    Once inside the doors she shut herself in
    And called on Laius, who has long been dead,
    Having remembrance of their seed of old
    By which he died himself and left her a mother
    To bear an evil brood to his own son.

She moaned the bed on which by double curse
She bore husband to husband, children to child.
How thereafter she perished I do not know,
For Oedipus burst in on her with a shriek,
And because of him we could not see her woe.
We looked on him alone as he rushed around.
Pacing about, he asked us to give him a sword,
Asked where he might find the wife no wife,
A mother whose plowfield bore him and his children.
Some spirit was guiding him in his frenzy,
For none of the men who are close at hand did so.
With a horrible shout, as if led on by someone,
He leapt on the double doors, from their sockets
Broke hollow bolts aside, and dashed within.
There we beheld his wife hung by her neck
From twisted cords, swinging to and fro.
When he saw her, wretched man, he terribly groaned
And slackened the hanging noose. When the poor woman
Lay on the ground, what happened was dread to see.
He tore the golden brooch pins from her clothes,
And raised them up, and struck his own eyeballs,
Shouting such words as these "No more shall you
Behold the evils I have suffered and done.
Be dark from now on, since you saw before
What you should not, and knew not what you should."
Moaning such cries, not once but many times
He raised and struck his eyes. The bloody pupils
Bedewed his beard. The gore oozed not in drops,
But pured in a black shower, a hail of blood.
From both of them these woes have broken out,
Not for just one, but man and wife together.
The bliss of old that formerly prevailed
Was bliss indeed, but now upon this day
Lamentation, madness, death, and shame—
No evil that can be named is not at hand.

CHORUS.   Is the wretched man in any rest now from pain?
SECOND MESSENGER.   He shouts for someone to open up the doors
And show to all Cadmeans his father's slayer,
His mother's—I should not speak the unholy word.
He says he will hurl himself from the land, no more
To dwell cursed in the house by his own curse.

Yet he needs strength and someone who will guide him.
His sickness is too great to bear. He will show it to you
For the fastenings of the doors are opening up,
And such a spectacle you will soon behold
As would make even one who abhors it take pity.

CHORUS.   O terrible suffering for men to see,
Most terrible of all that I
Have ever come upon. O wretched man,
What madness overcame you, what springing daimon[26]
Greater than the greatest for men
Has caused your evil-daimoned fate?
Alas, alas, grievous one,
But I cannot bear to behold you, though I desire
To ask you much, much to find out,
Much to see,
You make me shudder so!

OEDIPUS.   Alas, alas, I am grieved!
Where on earth, so wretched, shall I go?
Where does my voice fly through the air,
O Fate, where have you bounded?

CHORUS.   To dreadful end, not to be heard or seen.

OEDIPUS.   O cloud of dark
That shrouds me off, has come to pass, unspeakable,
Invincible, that blows no favoring blast.
Woe,
O woe again, the goad that pierces me,
Of the sting of evil now, and memory of before.

CHORUS.   No wonder it is that among so many pains
You should both mourn and bear a double evil.

OEDIPUS.   Ah, friend,
You are my steadfast servant still,
You still remain to care for me, blind.
Alas! Alas!
You are not hid from me; I know you clearly,
And though in darkness, still I hear your voice.

CHORUS.   O dreadful doer, how did you so endure
To quench your eyes? What daimon drove you on?

---

[26] A spirit or devil.

OEDIPUS.   Apollo it was, Apollo, friends
    Who brought to pass these evil, evil woes of mine.
    The hand of no one struck my eyes but wretched me.
    For why should I see,
    When nothing sweet there is to see with sight?
CHORUS.   This is just as you say.
OEDIPUS.   What more is there for me to see,
    My friends, what to love,
    What joy to hear a greeting?
    Lead me at once away from here,
    Lead me away, friends, wretched as I am,
    Accursed, and hated most
    Of mortals to the gods.
CHORUS.   Wretched alike in mind and in your fortune,
    How I wish that I had never known you.

OEDIPUS.   May he perish, whoever freed me
    From fierce bonds on my feet,
    Snatched me from death and saved me, doing me no joy.
    For if then I had died, I should not be
    So great a grief to friends and to myself.
CHORUS.   This also is my wish.
OEDIPUS.   I would not have come to murder my father,
    Nor have been called among men
    The bridegroom of her from whom I was born.
    But as it is I am godless, child of unholiness,
    Wretched sire in common with my father.
    And if there is an evil older than evil left,
    It is the lot of Oedipus.
CHORUS.   I know not how I could give you good advice,
    For you would be better dead than living blind.

OEDIPUS.   That how things are was not done for the best—
    Teach me not this, or give me more advice.
    If I had sight, I know not with what eyes
    I could ever face my father among the dead,
    Or my wretched mother. What I have done to them
    Is too great for a noose to expiate.
    Do you think the sight of my children would be a joy
    For me to see, born as they were to me?

No, never for these eyes of mine to see.
Nor the city, nor the tower, nor the sacred
Statues of gods; of these I deprive myself,
Noblest among the Thebans, born and bred,
Now suffering everything. I tell you all
To exile me as impious, shown by the gods
Untouchable and of the race of Laius.
When I uncovered such a stain on me,
Could I look with steady eyes upon the people?
No, no! And if there were a way to block
The spring of hearing, I would not forbear
To lock up wholly this my wretched body.
I should be blind and deaf.—For it is sweet
When thought can dwell outside our evils.
Alas, Cithaeron, why did you shelter me?
Why did you not take and kill me at once, so I
Might never reveal to men whence I was born?
O Polybus, O Corinth, O my father's halls,
Ancient in fable, what an outer fairness,
A festering of evils, you raised in me.
For now I am evil found, and born of evil.
O the three paths! Alas the hidden glen,
The grove of oak, the narrow triple roads
That drank from my own hands my father's blood.
Do you remember any of the deeds
I did before you then on my way here
And what I after did? O wedlock, wedlock!
You gave me birth, and then spawned in return
Issue from the selfsame seed; you revealed
Father, brother, children, in blood relation,
The bride both wife and mother, and whatever
Actions are done most shameful among men.
But it is wrong to speak what is not good to do.
By the gods, hide me at once outside our land,
Or murder me, or hurl me in the sea
Where you shall never look on me again.
Come, venture to lay your hands on this wretched man.
Do it. Be not afraid. No mortal man
There is, except myself, to bear my evils.

CHORUS.   Here is Creon, just in time for what you ask

To work and to advise, for he alone
Is left in place of you to guard the land.

OEDIPUS.   Alas, what word, then, shall I tell this man?
What righteous ground of trust is clear in me,
As in the past in all I have done him evil?

CREON.   Oedipus, I have not come to laugh at you,
Nor to reproach you for your former wrongs.

(*To the attendants*)

If you defer no longer to mortal offspring,
Respect at least the all-nourishing flame
Of Apollo, lord of the sun. Fear to display
So great a pestilence, which neither earth
Nor holy rain nor light will well receive.
But you, conduct him to the house at once.
It is most pious for the kin alone
To hear and to behold the family sins.

OEDIPUS.   By the gods, since you have plucked me from my fear,
Most noble, facing this most vile man,
Hear me one word—I will speak for you, not me.

CREON.   What desire do you so persist to get?

OEDIPUS.   As soon as you can, hurl me from this land
To where no mortal man will ever greet me.

CREON.   I would do all this, be sure. But I want first
To find out from the god what must be done.

OEDIPUS.   His oracle, at least, is wholly clear;
Leave me to ruin, an impious parricide.

CREON.   Thus spake the oracle. Still, as we stand
It is better to find out sure what we should do.

OEDIPUS.   Will you inquire about so wretched a man?

CREON.   Yes. You will surely put trust in the god.

OEDIPUS.   I order you and beg you, give the woman
Now in the house such burial as you yourself
Would want. Do last rites justly for your kin.
But may this city never be condemned—
My father's realm—because I live within.
Let me live in the mountains where Cithaeron
Yonder has fame of me, which father and mother
When they were alive established as my tomb.
There I may die by those who sought to kill me.

And yet this much I know, neither a sickness
Nor anything else can kill me. I would not
Be saved from death, except for some dread evil.
Well, let my fate go wherever it may.
As for my sons, Creon, assume no trouble;
They are men and will have no difficulty
Of living wherever they may be.
O my poor grievous daughters, who never knew
Their dinner table set apart from me,
But always shared in everything I touched—
Take care of them for me, and first of all
Allow me to touch them and bemoan our ills.
Grant it, lord,
Grant it, noble. If with my hand I touch them
I would think I had them just as when I could see.

(*Creon's attendants bring in* ANTIGONE *and* ISMENE.)

What's that?
By the gods, can it be I hear my dear ones weeping?
And have you taken pity on me, Creon?
Have you had my darling children sent to me?
Do I speak right?
CREON.   You do. For it was I who brought them here,
Knowing this present joy your joy of old.
OEDIPUS.   May you fare well. For their coming may the spirit
That watches over you be better than mine.
My children, where are you? Come to me, come
Into your brother's hands, that brought about
Your father's eyes, once bright, to see like this.
Your father, children, who, seeing and knowing nothing,
Became a father whence he was got himself.
I weep also for you—I cannot see you—
To think of the bitter life in days to come
Which you will have to lead among mankind.
What citizens' gatherings will you approach?
What festivals attend, where you will not cry
When you go home, instead of gay rejoicing?
And when you arrive at marriageable age,
What man, my daughters, will there be to chance you,
Incurring such reproaches on his head,

Disgraceful to my children and to yours?
What evil will be absent, when your father
Killed his own father, sowed seed in her who bore him,
From whom he was born himself, and equally
Has fathered you whence he himself was born.
Such will be the reproaches. Who then will wed you?
My children, there is no one for you. Clearly
You must decay in barrenness, unwed.
Son of Menoeceus [27]—since you are alone
Left as a father to them, for we who produced them
Are both in ruin—see that you never let
These girls wander as beggars without husbands,
Let them not fall into such woes as mine.
But pity them, seeing how young they are
To be bereft of all except your aid.
Grant this, my noble friend, with a touch of your hand.
My children, if your minds were now mature,
I would give you much advice. But, pray this for me,
To live as the time allows, to find a life
Better than that your siring father had.

CREON.   You have wept enough here, come, and go inside the house.

OEDIPUS.   I must obey, though nothing sweet.

CREON.   All things are good in their time.

OEDIPUS.   Do you know in what way I go?

CREON.   Tell me, I'll know when I hear.

OEDIPUS.   Send me outside the land.

CREON.   You ask what the god will do.

OEDIPUS.   But to the gods I am hated.

CREON.   Still, it will soon be done.

OEDIPUS.   Then you agree?

CREON.   What I think not I would not say in vain.

OEDIPUS.   Now lead me away.

CREON.   Come then, but let the children go.

OEDIPUS.   Do not take them from me.

CREON.   Wish not to govern all,
    For what you ruled will not follow you through life.

CHORUS.   Dwellers in native Thebes, behold this Oedipus

---

[27] Creon, that is.

Who solved the famous riddle, was your mightiest man.
What citizen on his lot did not with envy gaze?
See to how great a surge of dread fate he has come!
So I would say a mortal man, while he is watching
To see the final day, can have no happiness
Till he pass the bound of life, nor be relieved of pain.

4

Herodotus
History

Dramatic tragedy was not the only humanistic endeavor that flourished during the Golden Age. The same century saw the emergence of history (that is, the written record of contemporary events—in prose) as a new way—epic poetry being the old—of preserving the deeds of mankind from oblivion; the name of the Muse of history, Clio, means "the celebrator." The appearance of history might be described as a result of the Greek spirit of inquiry, and as an attempt to do for mankind what the nature-philosophers had done for the physical world. But the immediate inspiration for the earliest surviving prose work of Western literature was patriotic: the great national effort of the Persian Wars (490–445 B.C.).

Herodotus (ca. 484–425 B.C.), called the "Father of History" (though he was not actually the first historian), was born at Halicarnassus in Caria—a Greek city chafing under Persian control. After an unsuccessful revolt on the part of the inhabitants, Herodotus went into exile; thereafter, although he loved Athens and made it his home, he spent much of his life wandering through the lands of the eastern Mediterranean.

It was during this time that he set out to record the great happenings of the Persian Wars. His main object was to depict the rival worlds of Greece and Persia as seen through a single mind; for this purpose he put together the reams of material he had gathered on his travels. This bold and original undertaking he called historiē *("researches"). Judged by modern historical standards, his* History *is defective in many ways; it is, however, a work of striking impartiality and tolerance, as the following excerpts suggest. Even in the patriotic saga of Thermopylae, Herodotus treats the Persian enemies and their culture with respect.*

Herodotus, *The History of Herodotus,* trans. George Rawlinson (London: Murray, 1880), I, 163–68, 205–208, 210, 212–14; 441–44, 509–13; IV, 162–71, 174–80.

Herodotus wrote his History *for recitation before a public audience, not to be read privately; for it was as a public teller of tales that he made his living. However skeptical he might have been about some of the particulars, the form of his work was determined by the need to keep the interest of the listening audience. As a consequence the work is full of fascinating stories, some of them drawn from the folklore of the Middle East—as are the two stories in this selection. Both stories are also examples of the moral sequence congenial to Greek tradition: prosperity-presumption-ruin.*

ACCOUNT OF THE GREEKS AT THERMOPYLAE

King Xerxes[1] pitched his camp in the region of Malis called Trachinia, while on their side the Greeks occupied the straits. These straits the Greeks in general call Thermopylae (the Hot Gates); but the natives, and those who dwell in the neighbourhood, call them Pylae (the Gates). Here then the two armies took their stand; the one master of all the region lying north of Trachis, the other of the country extending southward of that place to the verge of the continent.

The Greeks who at this spot awaited the coming of Xerxes were the following:—From Sparta, three hundred men-at-arms; from Arcadia, a thousand Tegeans and Mantineans, five hundred of each people; a hundred and twenty Orchomenians, from Orchomenus; and a thousand from other Arcadian cities; from Corinth, four hundred men; from Phlius, two hundred; and from Mycenae eighty. Such was the number from the Peloponnese.[2] There were also present, from Boeotia, seven hundred Thespians and four hundred Thebans.

Besides these troops, the Locrians of Opus and the Phocians had obeyed the call of their countrymen, and sent, the former all the force they had, the latter a thousand men. For envoys had gone from the Greeks at Thermopylae among the Locrians and Phocians, to call on them for assistance, and to say—"They were themselves but the vanguard of the host, sent to precede the main body, which might every day be expected to follow them. The sea was in good keeping,

[1] Xerxes, king of Persia from 485 to 465 B.C., invaded Greece in 480 B.C.
[2] The southern portion of Greece, connected to the north by the isthmus of Corinth.

watched by the Athenians, the Eginetans, and the rest of the fleet. There was no cause why they should fear; for after all the invader was not a god but a man; and there never had been, and never would be, a man who was not liable to misfortunes from the very day of his birth, and those misfortunes greater in proportion to his own greatness. The assailant therefore, being only a mortal, must needs fall from his glory." Thus urged, the Locrians and the Phocians had come with their troops to Trachis.

The various nations had each captains of their own under whom they served; but the one to whom all especially looked up, and who had the command of the entire force, was the Lacedaemonian,[3] Leonidas.

Leonidas had come to be king of Sparta quite unexpectedly.

Having two elder brothers, Cleomenes and Dorieus, he had no thought of ever mounting the throne. However, when Cleomenes died without male offspring, as Dorieus was likewise deceased, having perished in Sicily, the crown fell to Leonidas, who was older than Cleombrotus, the youngest of the sons of Anaxandridas, and, moreover, was married to the daughter of Cleomenes. He had now come to Thermopylae, accompanied by the three hundred men which the law assigned him, whom he had himself chosen from among the citizens, and who were all of them fathers with sons living. On his way he had taken the troops from Thebes, whose number I have already mentioned, and who were under the command of Leontiades the son of Eurymachus. The reason why he made a point of taking troops from Thebes, and Thebes only, was that the Thebans were strongly suspected of being well inclined to the Medes.[4] Leonidas therefore called on them to come with him to the war, wishing to see whether they would comply with his demand, or openly refuse, and disclaim the Greek alliance. They, however, though their wishes leant the other way, nevertheless sent the men.

The force with Leonidas was sent forward by the Spartans in advance of their main body, that the sight of them might encourage the allies to fight, and hinder them from going over to the Medes, as it was likely they might have done had they seen that Sparta was back-

---

[3] Another name for Spartan.
[4] The Medes and Persians were a joint force, and Herodotus often uses their names interchangeably.

ward. They intended presently, when they had celebrated the Car-
neian festival, which was what now kept them at home, to leave a
garrison in Sparta, and hasten in full force to join the army. The rest
of the allies also intended to act similarly; for it happened that the
Olympic festival fell exactly at this same period. None of them
looked to see the contest at Thermopylae decided so speedily; wherefore they were content to send forward a mere advanced guard. Such
accordingly were the intentions of the allies.

The Greek forces at Thermopylae, when the Persian army drew
near to the entrance of the pass, were seized with fear; and a council
was held to consider about a retreat. It was the wish of the Peloponnesians generally that the army should fall back upon the Peloponnese, and there guard the Isthmus. But Leonidas, who saw with
what indignation the Phocians and Locrians heard of this plan, gave
his voice for remaining where they were, while they sent envoys to
the several cities to ask for help, since they were too few to make a
stand against an army like that of the Medes.

While this debate was going on, Xerxes sent a mounted spy to observe the Greeks, and note how many they were, and see what they
were doing. He had heard, before he came out of Thessaly, that a
few men were assembled at this place, and that at their head were
certain Lacedaemonians, under Leonidas, a descendant of Hercules.
The horseman rode up to the camp, and looked about him, but did
not see the whole army; for such as were on the further side of the
wall (which had been rebuilt and was now carefully guarded) it was
not possible for him to behold; but he observed those on the outside,
who were encamped in front of the rampart. It chanced that at this
time the Lacedaemonians held the outer guard, and were seen by the
spy, some of them engaged in gymnastic exercises, other combing
their long hair. At this the spy greatly marvelled, but he counted
their number, and when he had taken accurate note of everything, he
rode back quietly; for no one pursued after him, nor paid any heed to
his visit. So he returned, and told Xerxes all that he had seen.

Upon this, Xerxes, who had no means of surmising the truth—
namely, that the Spartans were preparing to do or die manfully—but
thought it laughable that they should be engaged in such employments, sent and called to his presence Demaratus[5] the son of Ariston,
who still remained with the army. When he appeared, Xerxes told

[5] A Greek who supplied military intelligence to the Persians.

him all that he had heard, and questioned him concerning the news, since he was anxious to understand the meaning of such behaviour on the part of the Spartans. Then Demaratus said—

"I spake to thee, O King! concerning these men long since, when we had but just begun our march upon Greece; thou, however, didst only laugh at my words, when I told thee of all this, which I saw would come to pass. Earnestly do I struggle at all times to speak truth to thee, sire; and now listen to it once more. These men have come to dispute the pass with us; and it is for this that they are now making ready. 'Tis their custom, when they are about to hazard their lives, to adorn their heads with care. Be assured, however, that if thou canst subdue the men who are here and the Lacedaemonians who remain in Sparta, there is no other nation in all the world which will venture to lift a hand in their defence. Thou hast now to deal with the first kingdom and town in Greece, and with the bravest men."

Then Xerxes, to whom what Demaratus said seemed altogether to surpass belief, asked further, "How was it possible for so small an army to contend with his?"

"O King!" Demaratus answered, "let me be treated as a liar, if matters fall not out as I say."

But Xerxes was not persuaded any the more. Four whole days he suffered to go by, expecting that the Greeks would run away. When, however, he found on the fifth that they were not gone, thinking that their firm stand was mere impudence and recklessness, he grew wroth, and sent against them the Medes and Cissians,[6] with orders to take them alive and bring them into his presence. Then the Medes rushed forward and charged the Greeks, but fell in vast numbers; others however took the places of the slain, and would not be beaten off, though they suffered terrible losses. In this way, it became clear to all, and especially to the King, that though he had plenty of combatants, he had but very few warriors. The struggle, however, continued during the whole day.

Then the Medes, having met so rough a reception, withdrew from the fight; and their place was taken by the band of Persians under Hydarnes, whom the King called his "Immortals"; they, it was thought, would soon finish the business. But when they joined battle with the Greeks, 'twas with no better success than the Median de-

---

[6] Allies of the Persians.

tachment—things went much as before—the two armies fighting in a narrow space, and the barbarians using shorter spears than the Greeks, and having no advantage from their numbers. The Lacedae-monians fought in a way worthy of note, and showed themselves far more skillful in fight than their adversaries, often turning their backs, and making as though they were all flying away, on which the bar-barians would rush after them with much noise and shouting, when the Spartans at their approach would wheel round and face their pur-suers, in this way destroying vast numbers of the enemy. Some Spartans likewise fell in these encounters, but only a very few. At last the Persians, finding that all their efforts to gain the pass availed nothing, and that, whether they attacked by divisions or in any other way, it was to no purpose, withdrew to their own quarters.

During these assaults, it is said that Xerxes, who was watching the battle, thrice leaped from the throne on which he sat, in terror for his army.

Next day the combat was renewed, but with no better success on the part of the barbarians. The Greeks were so few that the barbar-ians hoped to find them disabled, by reason of their wounds, from offering any further resistance; and so they once more attacked them. But the Greeks were drawn up in detachments according to their cit-ies, and bore the brunt of the battle in turns,—all except the Pho-cians, who had been stationed on the mountain to guard the pathway. So, when the Persians found no difference between that day and the preceding, they again retired to their quarters.

Now, as the King was in a great strait, and knew not how he should deal with the emergency, Ephialtes, the son of Eurydêmus, a man of Malis, came to him and was admitted to a conference. Stirred by the hope of receiving a rich reward at the King's hands, he had come to tell him of the pathway which led across the mountain to Thermopylae; by which disclosure he brought destruction on the band of Greeks who had there withstood the barbarians.

• • •

The Greeks at Thermopylae received the first warning of the de-struction which the dawn would bring on them from the seer Megis-tias, who read their fate in the victims as he was sacrificing. After this, deserters came in and brought the news that the Persians were marching round by the hills; it was still night when the men arrived. Last of all, the scouts came running down from the heights and brought in the same accounts when the day was just beginning to break. Then the Greeks held a council to consider what they should do, and here opinions were divided: some were strong against quitting their post, while others contended to the contrary. So, when the council had broken up, part of the troops departed and went their ways homeward to their several states; part, however, resolved to remain and to stand by Leonidas to the last.

It is said that Leonidas himself sent away the troops who departed because he tendered their safety, but thought it unseemly that either he or his Spartans should quit the post which they had been especially sent to guard. For my own part, I incline to think that Leonidas gave the order, because he perceived the allies to be out of heart and unwilling to encounter the danger to which his own mind was made up. He therefore commanded them to retreat, but said that he himself could not draw back with honour; knowing that if he stayed glory awaited him and that Sparta in that case would not lose her prosperity. For when the Spartans, at the very beginning of the war, sent to consult the oracle concerning it, the answer which they received from the Pythoness[7] was, "that either Sparta must be overthrown by the barbarians or one of her kings must perish." . . .

The remembrance of this answer, I think, and the wish to secure the whole glory for the Spartans, caused Leonidas to send the allies away. . . .

So the allies, when Leonidas ordered them to retire, obeyed him and forthwith departed. Only the Thespians and the Thebans remained with the Spartans; and of these the Thebans were kept back by Leonidas as hostages, very much against their will. The Thespians, on the contrary, stayed entirely of their own accord, refusing to retreat, and declaring that they would not forsake Leonidas and his followers. So they abode with the Spartans and died with them. Their leader was Demophilus, the son of Diadromes.

At sunrise Xerxes made libations,[8] after which he waited until the time when the forum is wont to fill and then began his advance. Ephialtes had instructed him thus, as the descent of the mountain is much quicker and the distance much shorter than the way round the hills, and the ascent. So the barbarians under Xerxes began to draw nigh; and the Greeks under Leonidas, as they now went forth deter-

---

[7] The oracular priestess of Apollo at Delphi.
[8] Symbolic religious sacrifices.

mined to die, advanced much further than on previous days, until they reached the more open portion of the pass. Hitherto they had held their station within the wall and from this had gone forth to fight at the point where the pass was the narrowest. Now they joined battle beyond the defile and carried slaughter among the barbarians, who fell in heaps. Behind them the captains of the squadrons, armed with whips, urged their men forward with continual blows. Many were thrust into the sea, and there perished; a still greater number were trampled to death by their own soldiers. No one heeded the dying. For the Greeks, reckless of their own safety and desperate, since they knew that as the mountain had been crossed their destruction was nigh at hand, exerted themselves with the most furious valour against the barbarians.

By this time the spears of the greater numbers were all shivered, and with their swords they hewed down the ranks of the Persians; and here, as they strove, Leonidas fell fighting bravely, together with many other famous Spartans whose names I have taken care to learn on account of their great worthiness, as indeed I have those of all the three hundred. There fell too at the same time very many famous Persians: among them two sons of Darius. . . . Thus two brothers of Xerxes here fought and fell.

And now there arose a fierce struggle between the Persians and the Lacedaemonians over the body of Leonidas, in which the Greeks four times drove back the enemy, and at last by their great bravery succeeded in bearing off the body. This combat was scarcely ended when the Persians with Ephialtes approached; and the Greeks, informed that they drew nigh, made a change in the manner of their fighting. Drawing back into the narrowest part of the pass, and retreating even behind the cross wall, they posted themselves upon a hillock, where they stood all drawn up together in one close body, except only the Thebans. The hillock whereof I speak is at the entrance of the straits, where the stone lion stands which was set up in honour of Leonidas. Here they defended themselves to the last, such as still had swords using them, and the others resisting with their hands and teeth; till the barbarians, who in part had pulled down the wall and attacked them in front, in part had gone round and now encircled them upon every side, overwhelmed and buried the remnant which was left beneath showers of missile weapons.

Thus nobly did the whole body of Lacedaemonians and Thespians behave; but nevertheless one man is said to have distinguished himself above all the rest: to wit, Dieneces the Spartan. A speech which he made before the Greeks engaged the Medes remains on record. One of the Trachinians told him, "Such was the number of the barbarians that when they shot forth their arrows the sun would be darkened by their multitude," Dieneces, not at all frightened at these words, but making light of the Median numbers, answered, "Our Trachinian friend brings us excellent tidings. If the Medes darken the sun, we shall have our fight in the shade.". . .

The slain were buried where they fell; and in their honour, nor less in honour of those who died before Leonidas sent the allies away, an inscription was set up which said,

> "Here did four thousand men from Pelops' land
> Against three-hundred myriads bravely stand." [9]

This was in honour of all. Another was for the Spartans alone:

> "Go, stranger, and to Lacedaemon tell
> That here, obeying her orders we fell."

CROESUS-SOLON STORY

Croesus, king of Lydia (560–546 B.C.) made war in turn upon every Ionian and Aeolian state, bringing forward, where he could, a substantial ground of complaint; where such failed him, advancing some poor excuse.

In this way he made himself master of all the Greek cities in Asia, [10] and forced them to become his tributaries.

• • •

Croesus, afterwards, in the course of many years, brought under his sway almost all the nations to the west of the Halys. [11] The Lycians and Cilicians alone continued free; all the other tribes he reduced and held in subjection. . . .

When all these conquests had been added to the Lydian empire, and the prosperity of Sardis [12] was now at its height, there came

---

[9] Myriad is a unit of ten-thousand.
[10] That is, Asia Minor (modern Turkey).
[11] A river in the central region of Asia Minor.
[12] The capital of Lydia.

thither, one after another, all the sages of Greece living at the time, and among them Solon, the Athenian. He was on his travels, having left Athens to be absent ten years, under the pretence of wishing to see the world, but really to avoid being forced to repeal any of the laws which, at the request of the Athenians, he had made for them. Without his sanction the Athenians could not repeal them, as they had bound themselves under a heavy curse to be governed for ten years by the laws which should be imposed on them by Solon.

On this account, as well as to see the world, Solon set out upon his travels, in the course of which he went to Egypt to the court of Amasis, and also came on a visit to Croesus at Sardis. Croesus received him as his guest, and lodged him in the royal palace. On the third or fourth day after, he bade his servants conduct Solon over his treasuries, and show him all their greatness and magnificence. When he had seen them all, and, so far as time allowed, inspected them, Croesus addressed this question to him. "Stranger of Athens, we have heard much of thy wisdom and of thy travels through many lands, from love of knowledge and a wish to see the world. I am curious therefore to inquire of thee, whom, of all the men that thou hast seen, thou deemest the most happy?" This he asked because he thought himself the happiest of mortals: but Solon answered him without flattery, according to his true sentiments, "Tellus of Athens, sire." Full of astonishment at what he heard, Croesus demanded sharply, "And wherefore dost thou deem Tellus happiest?" To which the other replied, "First, because his country was flourishing in his days, and he himself had sons both beautiful and good, and he lived to see children born to each of them, and these children all grew up; and further because, after a life spent in what our people look upon as comfort, his end was surpassingly glorious. In a battle between the Athenians and their neighbours near Eleusis, he came to the assistance of his countrymen, routed the foe, and died upon the field most gallantly. The Athenians gave him a public funeral on the spot where he fell, and paid him the highest honours."

Thus did Solon admonish Croesus by the example of Tellus, enumerating the manifold particulars of his happiness. When he had ended, Croesus inquired a second time, who after Tellus seemed to him the happiest, expecting that at any rate, he would be given the second place. "Cleobis and Bito," Solon answered; "they were of Argive race; their fortune was enough for their wants, and they were besides endowed with so much bodily strength that they had both gained prizes at the Games. Also this tale is told of them:—There was a great festival in honour of the goddess Juno at Argos, to which their mother must needs be taken in a car. Now the oxen did not come home from the field in time: so the youths, fearful of being too late, put the yoke on their own necks, and themselves drew the car in which their mother rode. Five and forty furlongs did they draw her, and stopped before the temple. This deed of theirs was witnessed by the whole assembly of worshippers, and then their life closed in the best possible way. Herein, too, God showed forth most evidently, how much better a thing for man death is than life. For the Argive men, who stood around the car, extolled the vast strength of the youths; and the Argive women extolled the mother who was blessed with such a pair of sons; and the mother herself, overjoyed at the deed and at the praises it had won, standing straight before the image, besought the goddess to bestow on Cleobis and Bito, the sons who had so mightily honoured her, the highest blessing to which mortals can attain. Her prayer ended, they offered sacrifice and partook of the holy banquet, after which the two youths fell asleep in the temple. They never woke more, but so passed from the earth. The Argives, looking on them as among the best of men, caused statues of them to be made, which they gave to the shrine at Delphi."

When Solon had thus assigned these youths the second place, Croesus broke in angrily, "What, stranger of Athens, is my happiness, then, so utterly set at naught by thee, that thou dost not even put me on a level with private men?"

"Oh! Croesus," replied the other, "thou askedst a question concerning the condition of man, of one who knows that the power above us is full of jealousy, and fond of troubling our lot. A long life gives one to witness much, and experience much oneself, that one would not choose. Seventy years I regard as the limit of the life of man. In these seventy years are contained, without reckoning intercalary months, twenty-five thousand and two hundred days. Add an intercalary month to every other year, that the seasons may come round at the right time, and there will be, besides the seventy years, thirty-five such months, making an addition of one thousand and fifty days. The whole number of the days contained in the seventy years will thus be twenty-six thousand two hundred and fifty, whereof not one but will produce events unlike the rest. Hence man is wholly accident. For thyself, oh! Croesus, I see that thou art wonderfully rich, and art the lord of many nations; but with respect to that whereon thou questionest me, I have no answer to give, until I hear that thou hast closed thy life happily. For assuredly he who possesses great store of riches is no nearer happiness than he who has what suffices for his daily needs, unless it happens that luck attend upon him, and so he continue in the enjoyment of all his good things to the end of life. For many of the wealthiest men have been unfavoured of fortune, and many whose means were moderate have had excellent luck. Men of the former class excel those of the latter but in two respects; these last excel the former in many. The wealthy man is better able to content his desires, and to bear up against a sudden buffet of calamity. The other has less ability to withstand these evils (from which, however, his good luck keeps him clear), but he enjoys all these following blessings: he is whole of limb, a stranger to disease, free from misfortune, happy in his children, and comely to look upon. If, in addition to all this, he end his life well, he is of a truth the man of whom thou art in search, the man who may rightly be termed happy. Call him, however, until he die, not happy but fortunate. Scarcely, indeed, can any man unite all these advantages: as there is no country which contains within it all that it needs, but each, while it possesses some things, lacks others, and the best country is that which contains the most; so no single human being is complete in every respect—something is always lacking. He who unites the greatest number of advantages, and retaining them to the day of his death, then dies peaceably, that man alone, sire, is, in my judgment, entitled to bear the name of 'happy.' But in every matter it behooves us to mark well the end: for oftentimes God gives men a gleam of happiness, and then plunges them into ruin."

Such was the speech which Solon addressed to Croesus, a speech which brought him neither largess nor honour. The king saw him depart with much indifference, since he thought that a man must be an arrant fool who made no account of present good, but bade men always wait and mark the end.

After Solon had gone away a dreadful vengeance, sent of God, came upon Croesus, to punish him, it is likely, for deeming himself the happiest of men. First he had a dream in the night, which foreshowed him truly the evils that were about to befall him in the person of his son. For Croesus had two sons, one blasted by a natural defect, being deaf and dumb; the other, distinguished far above all his co-mates in every pursuit. The name of the last was Atys. It was this son concerning whom he dreamt a dream, that he would die by the blow of an iron weapon. When he woke, he considered earnestly with himself, and, greatly alarmed at the dream, instantly made his son take a wife; and whereas in former years the youth had been wont to command the Lydian forces in the field, he now would not suffer him to accompany them. All the spears and javelins, and weapons used in the wars, he removed out of the male apartments, and laid them in heaps in the chambers of the women, fearing lest perhaps one of the weapons that hung against the wall might fall and strike him.

Now it chanced that while he was making arrangements for the wedding, there came to Sardis a man under a misfortune, who had upon him the stain of blood. He was by race a Phrygian,[13] and belonged to the family of the king. Presenting himself at the palace of Croesus, he prayed to be admitted to purification according to the customs of the country.

• • •

Then the king sent for Adrastus, the Phrygian, and said to him, "Adrastus, when thou wert smitten with the rod of affliction—no reproach, my friend—I purified thee, and have taken thee to live with me in my palace, and have been at every charge. Now, therefore, it behooves thee to requite the good offices which thou hast received at my hands by consenting to go with my son on this hunting party, and to watch over him, if perchance you should be attacked upon the road by some band of daring robbers. Even apart from this, it were right for thee to go where thou mayest make thyself famous by noble deeds. They are the heritage of thy family, and thou too art so stalwart and strong."

Adrastus answered, "Except for thy request, oh! king, I would rather have kept away from this hunt; for methinks it ill beseems a man under a misfortune such as mine to consort with his happier compeers; and besides, I have no heart to it. On many grounds I had stayed behind; but, as thou urgest it, and I am bound to pleasure thee (for truly it does behoove me to requite thy good offices), I am content to do as thou wishest. For thy son, whom thou givest into my charge, be sure thou shalt receive him back safe and sound, so far as depends upon a guardian's carefulness."

[13] A native of Phrygia, a country in the central region of Asia Minor.

Thus assured, Croesus let them depart, accompanied by a band of picked youths, and well provided with dogs of chase. When they reached Olympus, they scattered in quest of the animal; he was soon found, and the hunters, drawing round him in a circle, hurled their weapons at him. Then the stranger, the man who had been purified of blood, whose name was Adrastus, he also hurled his spear at the boar, but missed his aim, and struck Atys. Thus was the son of Croesus slain by the point of an iron weapon, and the warning of the vision was fulfilled. Then one ran to Sardis to bear the tidings to the king, and he came and informed him of the combat and of the fate that had befallen his son.

If it was a heavy blow to the father to learn that his child was dead, it yet more strongly affected him to think that the very man whom he himself once purified had done the deed. In the violence of his grief he called aloud on Jupiter Catharsius, to be a witness of what he had suffered at the stranger's hands. Afterwards he invoked the same god as Jupiter Ephistius and Hetaereus—using the one term because he had unwittingly harboured in his house the man who had now slain his son; and the other, because the stranger, who had been sent as his child's guardian, had turned out his most cruel enemy.

Presently the Lydians arrived, bearing the body of the youth, and behind them followed the homicide. He took his stand in front of the corpse, and, stretching forth his hand to Croesus, delivered himself into his power with earnest entreaties that he would sacrifice him upon the body of his son—"his former misfortune was burthen enough; now that he had added to it a second, and had brought ruin on the man who purified him, he could not bear to live." Then Croesus, when he heard these words, was moved with pity towards Adrastus, notwithstanding the bitterness of his own calamity; and so he answered, "Enough, my friend; I have all the revenge that I require, since thou givest sentence of death against thyself. But in sooth it is not thou who hast injured me, except so far as thou hast unwittingly dealt the blow. Some god is the author of my misfortune, and I was forewarned of it a long time ago."

• • •

At the end of this time the grief of Croesus was interrupted by intelligence from abroad. He learnt that Cyrus, the son of Cambyses, had destroyed the empire of Astyages, the son of Cyaxares; and that the Persians were becoming daily more powerful. This led him to consider with himself whether it were possible to check the growing power of that people before it came to a head. With this design he resolved to make instant trial of the several oracles in Greece, and of the one in Libya. So he sent his messengers in different directions, some to Delphi, some to Abae in Phocis, and some to Dodôna; others to the oracle of Amphiaraüs; others to that of Trophonius; others, again, to Branchidae in Milesia. These were the Greek oracles which he consulted. To Libya he sent another embassy, to consult the oracle of Ammon. These messengers were sent to test the knowledge of the oracles, that, if they were found really to return true answers, he might send a second time, and inquire if he ought to attack the Persians.

The messengers who were despatched to make trial of the oracles were given the following instructions: they were to keep count of the days from the time of their leaving Sardis, and, reckoning from that date, on the hundredth day they were to consult the oracles, and to inquire of them what Croesus the son of Alyattes, king of Lydia, was doing at that moment. The answers given them were to be taken down in writing, and brought back to him. None of the replies remain on record except that of the oracle at Delphi. There, the moment that the Lydians entered the sanctuary, and before they put their questions, the Pythoness thus answered them in hexameter verse:—

> "I can count the sands, and I can measure the ocean;
> I have ears for the silent, and know what the dumb man meaneth;
> Lo! on my sense there striketh the smell of a shell-covered tortoise,
> Boiling now on the fire, with the flesh of a lamb, in a cauldron,—
> Brass is the vessel below, and brass the cover above it."

These words the Lydians wrote down at the mouth of the Pythoness as she prophesied, and then set off on their return to Sardis. When all the messengers had come back with the answers which they had received, Croesus undid the rolls, and read what was written in each. Only one approved itself to him, that of the Delphic oracle. This he had no sooner heard than he instantly made an act of adoration, and accepted it as true, declaring that the Delphic was the only really oracular shrine, the only one that had discovered in what way he was in fact employed. For on the departure of his messengers he had set himself to think what was most impossible for any one to conceive of his doing, and then, waiting till the day agreed on came, he acted as he had determined. He took a tortoise and a lamb, and cutting them in pieces with his own hands, boiled them both together in a brazen cauldron, covered over with a lid which was also of brass.

Such then was the answer returned to Croesus from Delphi. What the answer was which the Lydians who went to the shrine of Amphiaraüs and performed the customary rites, obtained of the oracle there, I have it not in my power to mention, for there is no record of it. All that is known is, that Croesus believed himself to have found there also an oracle which spoke the truth.

After this Croesus, having resolved to propitiate the Delphic god with a magnificent sacrifice, offered up three thousand of every kind of sacrificial beast, and besides made a huge pile, and placed upon it couches coated with silver and with gold, and golden goblets, and robes and vests of purple; all which he burnt in the hope of thereby making himself more secure of the favour of the god. Further he issued his orders to all the people of the land to offer a sacrifice according to their means. When the sacrifice was ended, the king melted down a vast quantity of gold, and ran it into ingots, making them six palms long, three palms broad, and one palm in thickness. The number of ingots was a hundred and seventeen, four being of refined gold, in weight two talents and a half, the others of pale gold, and in weight two talents. He also caused a statue of a lion to be made in refined gold, the weight of which was ten talents. At the time when the temple of Delphi was burnt to the ground, this lion fell from the ingots on which it was placed; it now stands in the Corinthian treasury, and weighs only six talents and a half, having lost three talents and a half by the fire.

On the completion of these works, Croesus sent them away to Delphi, and with them two bowls of an enormous size, one of gold, the other of silver, which used to stand, the latter upon the right, the former upon the left, as one entered the temple.

• • •

These were the offerings sent by Croesus to Delphi. To the shrine of Amphiaraüs, with whose valour and misfortune he was acquainted, he sent a shield entirely of gold, and a spear, also of solid gold, both head and shaft. They were still existing in my day at Thebes, laid up in the temple of Ismenian Apollo.

The messengers who had the charge of conveying these treasures to the shrines, received instructions to ask the oracles whether Croesus should go to war with the Persians, and if so, whether he should strengthen himself by the forces of an ally. Accordingly, when they had reached their destinations and presented the gifts, they proceeded to consult the oracles in the following terms:— "Croesus, king of Lydia and other countries, believing that these are the only real oracles in all the world, has sent you such presents as your discoveries deserved, and now inquires of you whether he shall go to war with the Persians, and if so, whether he shall strengthen himself by the forces of a confederate." Both the oracles agreed in the tenor of their reply, which was in each case a prophecy that if Croesus attacked the Persians, he would destroy a mighty empire, and a recommendation to him to look and see who were the most powerful of the Greeks, and to make alliance with them.

At the receipt of these oracular replies Croesus was overjoyed, and feeling sure now that he would destroy the empire of the Persians, he sent once more to Pytho, and presented to the Delphians, the number of whom he had ascertained, two gold staters [14] apiece. In return for this the Delphians granted to Croesus and the Lydians the privilege of precedency in consulting the oracle, exemption from all charges, the most honourable seat at the festivals, and the perpetual right of becoming at pleasure citizens of their town.

After sending these presents to the Delphians, Croesus a third time consulted the oracle, for having once proved its truthfulness, he wished to make constant use of it. The question whereto he now desired an answer was—"Whether his kingdom would be of long duration?" The following was the reply of the Pythoness:—

"Wait till the time shall come when a mule is monarch of Media;
Then, thou delicate Lydian, away to the pebbles of Hermus;
Haste, oh! haste thee away, nor blush to behave like a coward."

Of all the answers that had reached him, this pleased him far the best, for it seemed incredible that a mule should ever come to be king of the Medes, and so he concluded that the sovereignty would never depart from himself or his seed after him. Afterwards he turned his thoughts to the alliance which he had been recommended to contract, and sought to ascertain by inquiry which was the most powerful of the Grecian states. His inquiries pointed out to him two

[14] The stater was a unit of coinage.

states as pre-eminent above the rest. These were the Lacedaemonians and the Athenians, the former of Doric, the latter of Ionic blood.

● ● ●

He then disbanded the army—consisting of mercenary troops—which had been engaged with the Persians and had since accompanied him to his capital, and let them depart to their homes, never imagining that Cyrus, after a battle in which victory had been so evenly balanced, would venture to march upon Sardis.

While Croesus was still in this mind, all the suburbs of Sardis were found to swarm with snakes, on the appearance of which the horses left feeding in the pasture-grounds, and flocked to the suburbs to eat them. The king, who witnessed the unusual sight, regarded it very rightly as a prodigy. He therefore instantly sent messengers to the soothsayers of Telmessus, to consult them upon the matter. His messengers reached the city, and obtained from the Telmessians an explanation of what the prodigy portended, but fate did not allow them to inform their lord; for ere they entered Sardis on their return, Croesus was a prisoner. What the Telmessians had declared was, that Croesus must look for the entry of an army of foreign invaders into his country, and that when they came they would subdue the native inhabitants; since the snake, said they, is a child of earth, and the horse a warrior and a foreigner. Croesus was already a prisoner when the Telmessians thus answered his inquiry, but they had no knowledge of what was taking place at Sardis, or of the fate of the monarch.

Cyrus, however, when Croesus broke up so suddenly from his quarters after the battle at Pteria, conceiving that he had marched away with the intention of disbanding his army, considered a little, and soon saw that it was advisable for him to advance upon Sardis with all haste, before the Lydians could get their forces together a second time. Having thus determined, he lost no time in carrying out his plan. He marched forward with such speed that he was himself the first to announce his coming to the Lydian king. That monarch, placed in the utmost difficulty by the turn of events which had gone so entirely against all his calculations, nevertheless led out the Lydians to battle. In all Asia there was not at that time a braver or more warlike people. Their manner of fighting was on horseback; they carried long lances, and were clever in the management of their steeds.

The two armies met in the plain before Sardis.

• • •

The combat was long; but at last, after a great slaughter on both sides, the Lydians turned and fled. They were driven within their walls, and the Persians laid siege to Sardis.

Thus the siege began. Meanwhile Croesus, thinking that the place would hold out no inconsiderable time, sent off fresh heralds to his allies from the beleaguered town. His former messengers had been charged to bid them assemble at Sardis in the course of the fifth month; they whom he now sent were to say that he was already besieged, and to beseech them to come to his aid with all possible speed. Among his other allies Croesus did not omit to send to Lacedaemon.

It chanced, however, that the Spartans were themselves just at this time engaged in a quarrel with the Argives about a place called Thyrea. . . .

Although the Spartans were engaged with these matters when the herald arrived from Sardis to entreat them to come to the assistance of the besieged king, yet, notwithstanding, they instantly set to work to afford him help. They had completed their preparations, and the ships were just ready to start, when a second message informed them that the place had already fallen, and that Croesus was a prisoner. Deeply grieved at his misfortune, the Spartans ceased their efforts.

• • •

Thus was Sardis taken by the Persians, and Croesus himself fell into their hands, after having reigned fourteen years, and been besieged in his capital fourteen days; thus too did Croesus fulfil the oracle, which said that he should destroy a mighty empire,—by destroying his own. Then the Persians who had made Croesus prisoner brought him before Cyrus. Now a vast pile had been raised by his orders, and Croesus, laden with fetters, was placed upon it, and with him twice seven of the sons of the Lydians. I know not whether Cyrus was minded to make an offering of the first-fruits to some god or other, or whether he had vowed a vow and was performing it, or whether, as may well be, he had heard that Croesus was a holy man, and so wished to see if any of the heavenly powers would appear to save him from being burnt alive. However it might be, Cyrus was thus engaged, and Croesus was already on the pile, when it entered his mind in the depth of his woe that there was a divine warning in the words which had come to him from the lips of Solon, "No one while he lives is happy." When this thought smote him he fetched a long breath, and breaking his deep silence, groaned out aloud, thrice uttering the name of Solon. Cyrus caught the sounds, and bade the interpreters inquire of Croesus who it was he called on. They drew near and asked him, but he held his peace, and for a long time made no answer to their questionings, until at length, forced to say something, he exclaimed, "One I would give much to see converse with every monarch." Not knowing what he meant by this reply, the interpreters begged him to explain himself; and as they pressed for an answer, and grew to be troublesome, he told them how, a long time before, Solon, an Athenian, had come and seen all his splendour, and made light of it; and how whatever he had said to him had fallen out exactly as he foreshowed, although it was nothing that especially concerned him, but applied to all mankind alike, and most to those who seemed to themselves happy. Meanwhile, as he thus spoke, the pile was lighted, and the outer portion began to blaze. Then Cyrus, hearing from the interpreters what Croesus had said, relented, bethinking himself that he too was a man, and that it was a fellow-man, and one who had once been as blessed by fortune as himself, that he was burning alive; afraid, moreover, of retribution, and full of the thought that whatever is human is insecure. So he bade them quench the blazing fire as quickly as they could, and take down Croesus and the other Lydians, which they tried to do, but the flames were not to be mastered.

Then, the Lydians say that Croesus, perceiving by the efforts made to quench the fire that Cyrus had relented, and seeing also that all was in vain, and that the men could not get the fire under, called with a loud voice upon the god Apollo, and prayed him, if he had ever received at his hands any acceptable gift, to come to his aid, and deliver him from his present danger. As thus with tears he besought the god, suddenly, though up to that time the sky had been clear and the day without a breath of wind, dark clouds gathered, and the storm burst over their heads with rain of such violence, that the flames were speedily extinguished. Cyrus, convinced by this that Croesus was a good man and a favourite of heaven, asked him after he was taken off the pile, "Who it was that had persuaded him to lead an army into his country, and so become his foe rather than continue his friend?" to which Croesus made answer as follows:

"What I did, oh! king, was to thy advantage and to my own loss. If there be blame, it rests with the god of the Greeks, who encouraged me to begin the war. No one is so foolish as to prefer . . . war, in which, instead of sons burying their fathers, fathers bury their sons. But the gods willed it so."

Thus did Croesus speak. Cyrus then ordered his fetters to be taken off, and made him sit down near himself, and paid him much respect, looking upon him, as did also the courtiers, with a sort of wonder.

• • •

STORY OF THE RING OF POLYCRATES

While Cambyses [15] was carrying on this war in Egypt, the Lacedaemonians likewise sent a force to Samos against Polycrates, [16] the son of Aeaces, who had by insurrection made himself master of that island. At the outset he divided that state into three parts, and shared the kingdom with his brothers, Pantagnôtus and Syloson; but later, having killed the former and banished the latter, who was the younger of the two, he held the whole island. Hereupon he made a contract of friendship with Amasis, the Egyptian king, sending him gifts, and receiving from him others in return. In a little while his power so greatly increased, that the fame of it went abroad throughout Ionia and the rest of Greece. Wherever he turned his arms, success waited on him. He had a fleet of a hundred penteconters, [17] and bowmen to the number of a thousand. Herewith he plundered all, without distinction of friend or foe; for he argued that a friend was better pleased if you gave him back what you had taken from him, than if you spared him at the first. He captured many of the islands, and several towns upon the mainland. Among his other doings he overcame the Lesbians in a seafight, when they came with all their forces to the help of Miletus, and made a number of them prisoners. These persons, laden with fetters, dug the moat which surrounds the castle at Samos.

The exceeding good fortune of Polycrates did not escape the notice

---

[15] Cambyses, king of Persia from 528 to 522 B.C.
[16] Polycrates, ruler of the island of Samos from 535 to 522 B.C.
[17] War vessels.

of Amasis, who was much disturbed thereat. When therefore his successes continued increasing, Amasis wrote him the following letter, and sent it to Samos. "Amasis to Polycrates thus sayeth: It is a pleasure to hear of a friend and ally prospering; but thy exceeding prosperity does not cause me joy, forasmuch as I know that the gods are envious. My wish for myself, and for those whom I love, is, to be now successful, and now to meet with a check; thus passing through life amid alternate good and ill, rather than with perpetual good fortune. For never yet did I hear tell of any one succeeding in all his undertakings, who did not meet with calamity at last, and come to utter ruin. Now, therefore, give ear to my words, and meet thy good luck in this way: bethink thee which of all thy treasures thou valuest most and canst least bear to part with; take it, whatsoever it be, and throw it away, so that it may be sure never to come any more into the sight of man. Then, if thy good fortune be not thenceforth chequered with ill, save thyself from harm by again doing as I have counselled."

When Polycrates read this letter, and perceived that the advice of Amasis was good, he considered carefully with himself which of the treasures that he had in store it would grieve him most to lose. After much thought he made up his mind that it was a signet-ring which he was wont to wear, an emerald set in gold, the workmanship of Theodore, son of Têlecles, a Samian. So he determined to throw this away; and, manning a penteconter, he went on board, and bade the sailors put out into the open sea. When he was now a long way from the island, he took the ring from his finger, and, in the sight of all those who were on board, flung it into the deep. This done, he returned home, and gave vent to his sorrow.

Now it happened five or six days afterwards that a fisherman caught a fish so large and beautiful, that he thought it well deserved to be made a present of to the king. So he took it with him to the gate of the palace, and said that he wanted to see Polycrates. Then Polycrates allowed him to come in; and the fisherman gave him the fish with these words following—"Sir king, when I took this prize, I thought I would not carry it to market, though I am a poor man who live by my trade. I said to myself, it is worthy of Polycrates and his greatness; and so I brought it here to give it to you." This speech pleased the king, who thus spoke in reply:—"Thou didst right well, friend; and I am doubly indebted, both for the gift, and for the speech. Come now, and sup with me." So the fisherman went home, esteeming it a high honour that he had been asked to sup with the king. Meanwhile the servants, on cutting open the fish, found the signet of their master in its belly. No sooner did they see it than they seized upon it, and hastening to Polycrates with great joy, restored it to him, and told him in what way it had been found. The king, who saw something providential in the matter, forthwith wrote a letter to Amasis, telling him all that had happened, what he had himself done, and what had been the upshot—and despatched the letter to Egypt.

When Amasis had read the letter of Polycrates, he perceived that it does not belong to man to save his fellow-man from the fate which is in store for him; likewise he felt certain that Polycrates would end ill, as he prospered in everything, even finding what he had thrown away. So he sent a herald to Samos, and dissolved the contract of friendship. This he did, that when the great and heavy misfortune came, he might escape the grief which he would have felt if the sufferer had been his bond-friend.

About the time of Cambyses' last sickness, the following events happened. There was a certain Oroetes, a Persian, whom Cyrus had made governor of Sardis. This man conceived a most unholy wish. He had never suffered wrong or had an ill word from Polycrates the Samian—nay, he had not so much as seen him in all his life; yet, notwithstanding, he conceived the wish to seize him and put him to death. This wish, according to the account which the most part give, arose from what happened one day as he was sitting with another Perisian in the gate of the king's palace. The man's name was Mitrobates, and he was ruler of the satrapy of Dascyleium. He and Oroetes had been talking together, and from talking they fell to quarrelling and comparing their merits; whereupon Mitrobates said to Oroetes reproachfully, "Art thou worthy to be called a man, when, near as Samos lies to thy government, and easy as it is to conquer, thou hast omitted to bring it under the dominion of the king? Easy to conquer, said I? Why, a mere common citizen, with the help of fifteen men-at-arms, mastered the island, and is still king of it." Oroetes, they say, took this reproach greatly to heart; but, instead of seeking to revenge himself on the man by whom it was uttered, he conceived the desire of destroying Polycrates, since it was on Polycrates' account that the reproach had fallen on him.

Another less common version of the story is that Oroetes sent a herald to Samos to make a request, the nature of which is not stated; Polycrates was at the time reclining in the apartment of the males, and Anacreon the Teian was with him; when therefore the herald came forward to converse, Polycrates, either out of studied contempt for the power of Oroetes, or it may be merely by chance, was lying with his face turned away toward the wall; and so he lay all the time that the herald spake, and when he ended, did not even vouchsafe him a word.

Such are the two reasons alleged for the death of Polycrates; it is open to all to believe which they please. What is certain is, that Oroetes, while residing at Magnesia on the Maeander, sent a Lydian, by name Myrsus, the son of Gyges, with a message to Polycrates at Samos, well knowing what that monarch designed. For Polycrates entertained a design which no other Greek, so far as we know, ever formed before him, unless it were Minos the Cnossian, and those (if there were any such) who had the mastery of the Aegaean at an earlier time—Polycrates, I say, was the first of mere human birth who conceived the design of gaining the empire of the sea, and aspired to rule over Ionia and the islands. Knowing then that Polycrates was thus minded, Oroetes sent his message, which ran as follows:—

"Oroetes to Polycrates thus sayeth: I hear thou raisest thy thoughts high, but thy means are not equal to thy ambition. Listen then to my words, and learn how thou mayest at once serve thyself and preserve me. King Cambyses is bent on my destruction—of this I have warning from a sure hand. Come thou, therefore, and fetch me away, me and all my wealth—share my wealth with me, and then, so far as money can aid, thou mayest make thyself master of the whole of Greece. But if thou doubtest my wealth, send the trustiest of thy followers, and I will show my treasures to him."

Polycrates, when he heard this message, was full of joy, and straightway approved the terms; but, as money was what he chiefly desired, before stirring in the business he sent his secretary, Maeandrius, son of Maeandrius, a Samian, to look into the matter. This was the man who, not very long afterwards, made an offering at the temple of Juno of all the furniture which had adorned the male apartments in the palace of Polycrates, an offering well worth seeing. Oroetes, learning that one was coming to view his treasures, contrived as follows:—he filled eight great chests almost brimful of stones, and then covering over the stone with gold, corded the chests, and so held them in readiness. When Maeandrius arrived, he was shown this as Oroetes' treasure, and having seen it returned to Samos.

On hearing his account, Polycrates, notwithstanding many warnings given him by the soothsayers, and much dissuasion of his friends, made ready to go in person. Even the dream which visited his daughter failed to check him. She had dreamed that she saw her father hanging high in air, washed by Jove, and anointed by the sun. Having therefore thus dreamed, she used every effort to prevent her father from going; even as he went on board his penteconter crying after him with words of evil omen. Then Polycrates threatened her that, if he returned in safety, he would keep her unmarried many years. She answered, "Oh! that he might perform his threat; far better for her to remain long unmarried than to be bereft of her father!"

Polycrates, however, making light of all the counsel offered him, set sail and went to Oroetes. Many friends accompanied him; among the rest, Democêdes, the son of Calliphon, a native of Crotona, who was a physician, and the best skilled in his art of all men then living. Polycrates, on his arrival at Magnesia, perished miserably, in a way unworthy of his rank and of his lofty schemes. For, if we except the Syracusans, there has never been one of the Greek tyrants who was to be compared with Polycrates for magnificence. Oroetes, however, slew him in a mode which is not fit to be described, and then hung his dead body upon a cross. His Samian followers Oroetes let go free, bidding them thank him that they were allowed their liberty; the rest, who were in part slaves, in part free foreigners, he alike treated as his slaves by conquest. Then was the dream of the daughter of Polycrates fulfilled; for Polycrates, as he hung upon the cross, and rain fell on him, was washed by Jupiter; and he was anointed by the sun, when his own moisture overspread his body. And so the vast good fortune of Polycrates came at last to the end which Amasis the Egyptian king had prophesied in days gone by.

5

Thucydides
History of the Peloponnesian War

🔲

The Persian Wars, as recounted by Herodotus, were the prelude to Greek glory; the Peloponnesian War (431–404 B.C.), between Athens and Sparta, brought suffering and disaster to Greece. The task of recording and analyzing that bitter struggle of Greek against Greek fell to a younger historian, Thucydides (ca. 471–ca. 400 B.C.). Born in Athens to rank and wealth, Thucydides was elected a general in 432 B.C. and given command against the Spartans in the north Aegean. For allowing himself to be outmaneuvered by the enemy's best general, he was exiled and did not return to Athens until 404. He spent his years of exile recording the tragedy of his own times: the Peloponnesian War. Behind his narrative lay a special purpose. Why had Athens, with the fairest prospects of victory, been beaten? In essence, Thucydides' History is an analysis of the causes of the Athenian defeat; hence it has been well described as a study in the pathology of imperialism and war.

Thucydides' own reflections on issues and motives are found in the forty or more set speeches for which the History is famous. These speeches, which appear as direct quotations but were written by Thucydides, represent a familiar expository device in ancient literature; like the oration and the dialogue, they must be accounted for by the importance of the spoken word in Greek culture. Thucydides claimed that he "put into the mouth of the speaker the sentiments proper to the occasion, expressed as I thought he would be likely to express them." The most famous speech is by the great Athenian statesman, Pericles. His Funeral Oration, reprinted here, is a eulogy of Athens as the noblest product of human reason. Another famous pas-

Thucydides, *History of the Peloponnesian War*, trans. Benjamin Jowett (Boston: Lothrop, 1883), 115–24, 398–407.

sage included here is the Melian Dialogue, in which the monstrous realities of the conflict are stripped bare. To the question, "Why did Athens fall?" Thucydides answers that Periclean moderation had been abandoned for barbarous extremism.

Thucydides says he composed his History *as "a thing to possess and keep forever." It is accurate, impartial, and meditative, conveying a stark picture of the moral degeneration and disillusionment that result when the life of reason is sacrificed for wealth and power. There is in his writing none of the sentiment or supernaturalism which makes Herodotus entertaining, but lovers of his Olympian detachment and historical outlook have hailed Thucydides as the supreme historian of all time.*

During the same winter, in accordance with an old national custom, the funeral of those who first fell in this war was celebrated by the Athenians at the public charge. The ceremony is as follows: Three days before the celebration they erect a tent in which the bones of the dead are laid out, and every one brings to his own dead any offering which he pleases. At the time of the funeral the bones are placed in chests of cypress wood, which are conveyed on hearses; there is one chest for each tribe. They also carry a single empty litter decked with a pall for all whose bodies are missing, and cannot be recovered after the battle. The procession is accompanied by any one who chooses, whether citizen or stranger, and the female relatives of the deceased are present at the place of interment and make lamentation. The public sepulchre is situated in the most beautiful spot outside the walls; there they always bury those who fall in war; only after the battle of Marathon the dead, in recognition of their pre-eminent valor, were interred on the field. When the remains have been laid in the earth, some man of known ability and high reputation, chosen by the city, delivers a suitable oration over them; after which the people depart. Such is the manner of interment; and the ceremony was repeated from time to time throughout the war. Over those who were the first buried Pericles was chosen to speak. At the fitting moment he advanced from the sepulchre to a lofty stage, which had been erected in order that he might be heard as far as possible by the multitude, and spoke as follows:—

FUNERAL ORATION

"Most of those who have spoken here before me have commended the lawgiver who added this oration to our other funeral customs; it seemed to them a worthy thing that such an honor should be given at their burial to the dead who have fallen on the field of battle. But I should have preferred that, when men's deeds have been brave, they should be honored in deed only, and with such an honor as this public funeral, which you are now witnessing. Then the reputation of many would not have been imperilled on the eloquence or want of eloquence of one, and their virtues believed or not as he spoke well or ill. For it is difficult to say neither too little nor too much; and even moderation is apt not to give the impression of truthfulness. The friend of the dead who knows the facts is likely to think that the words of the speaker fall short of his knowledge and of his wishes; another who is not so well informed, when he hears of anything which surpasses his own powers, will be envious and will suspect exaggeration. Mankind are tolerant of the praises of others so long as each hearer thinks that he can do as well or nearly as well himself, but, when the speaker rises above him, jealousy is aroused and he begins to be incredulous. However, since our ancestors have set the seal of their approval upon the practice, I must obey, and to the utmost of my power shall endeavor to satisfy the wishes and beliefs of all who hear me.

"I will speak first of our ancestors, for it is right and becoming that now, when we are lamenting the dead, a tribute should be paid to their memory. There has never been a time when they did not inhabit this land, which by their valor they have handed down from generation to generation, and we have received from them a free state. But if they were worthy of praise, still more were our fathers, who added to their inheritance, and after many a struggle transmitted to us their sons this great empire. And we ourselves assembled here to-day, who are still most of us in the vigor of life, have chiefly done the work of improvement, and have richly endowed our city with all things, so that she is sufficient for herself both in peace and war. Of the military exploits by which our various possessions were acquired, or of the energy with which we or our fathers drove back the tide of war, Hellenic or Barbarian, I will not speak; for the tale would be long and is familiar to you. But before I praise the dead, I should like to point out by what principles of action we rose to power, and under what institutions and through what manner of life our empire became great. For I conceive that such thoughts are not unsuited to the occasion, and that this numerous assembly of citizens and strangers may profitably listen to them.

"Our form of government does not enter into rivalry with the institutions of others. We do not copy our neighbors, but are an example to them. It is true that we are called a democracy, for the administration is in the hands of the many and not of the few. But while the law secures equal justice to all alike in their private disputes, the claim of excellence is also recognized; and when a citizen is in any way distinguished, he is preferred to the public service, not as a matter of privilege, but as the reward of merit. Neither is poverty a bar, but a man may benefit his country whatever be the obscurity of his condition. There is no exclusiveness in our public life, and in our private intercourse we are not suspicious of one another, nor angry with our neighbor if he does what he likes; we do not put on sour looks at him which, though harmless, are not pleasant. While we are thus unconstrained in our private intercourse, a spirit of reverence pervades our public acts; we are prevented from doing wrong by respect for authority and for the laws, having an especial regard to those which are ordained for the protection of the injured as well as to those unwritten laws which bring upon the transgressor of them the reprobation of the general sentiment.

"And we have not forgotten to provide for our weary spirits many relaxations from toil; we have regular games and sacrifices throughout the year; at home the style of our life is refined; and the delight which we daily feel in all these things helps to banish melancholy. Because of the greatness of our city the fruits of the whole earth flow in upon us; so that we enjoy the goods of other countries as freely as of our own.

"Then, again, our military training is in many respects superior to that of our adversaries. Our city is thrown open to the world, and we never expel a foreigner or prevent him from seeing or learning anything of which the secret if revealed to an enemy might profit him. We rely not upon management or trickery, but upon our own hearts and hands. And in the matter of education, whereas they from early youth are always undergoing laborious exercises which are to make them brave, we live at ease, and yet are equally ready to face the perils which they face. And here is the proof. The Lacedaemonians[1] come into Attica not by themselves, but with their whole

---

[1] That is, the Spartans.

confederacy following; we go alone into a neighbor's country; and although our opponents are fighting for their homes and we on a foreign soil, we have seldom any difficulty in overcoming them. Our enemies have never yet felt our united strength; the care of a navy divides our attention, and on land we are obliged to send our own citizens everywhere. But they, if they meet and defeat a part of our army, are as proud as if they had routed us all, and when defeated they pretend to have been vanquished by us all.

"If then we prefer to meet danger with a light heart but without laborious training, and with a courage which is gained by habit and not enforced by law, are we not greatly the gainers? Since we do not anticipate the pain, although, when the hour comes, we can be as brave as those who never allow themselves to rest; and thus too our city is equally admirable in peace and in war. For we are lovers of the beautiful, yet simple in our tastes, and we cultivate the mind without loss of manliness. Wealth we employ, not for talk and ostentation, but when there is a real use for it. To avow poverty with us is no disgrace: the true disgrace is in doing nothing to avoid it. An Athenian citizen does not neglect the state because he takes care of his own household; and even those of us who are engaged in business have a very fair idea of politics. We alone regard a man who takes no interest in public affairs, not as a harmless, but as a useless character; and if few of us are originators, we are all sound judges of a policy. The great impediment to action is, in our opinion, not discussion, but the want of that knowledge which is gained by discussion preparatory to action. For we have a peculiar power of thinking before we act and of acting too, whereas other men are courageous from ignorance but hesitate upon reflection. And they are surely to be esteemed the bravest spirits who, having the clearest sense both of the pains and pleasures of life, do not on that account shrink from danger. In doing good, again, we are unlike others; we make our friends by conferring, not by receiving favors. Now he who confers a favor is the firmer friend, because he would fain by kindness keep alive the memory of an obligation; but the recipient is colder in his feelings, because he knows that in requiting another's generosity he will not be winning gratitude, but only paying a debt. We alone do good to our neighbors not upon a calculation of interest, but in the confidence of freedom and in a frank and fearless spirit. To sum up: I say that Athens is the school of Hellas, and that the individual Athenian in his own person seems to have the power of adapting himself to the most varied forms of action with the utmost versatility and grace. This is no passing and idle word, but truth and fact; and the assertion is verified by the position to which these qualities have raised the state. For in the hour of trial Athens alone among her contemporaries is superior to the report of her. No enemy who comes against her is indignant at the reverses which he sustains at the hands of such a city; no subject complains that his masters are unworthy of him. And we shall assuredly not be without witnesses; there are mighty monuments of our power which will make us the wonder of this and of succeeding ages; we shall not need the praises of Homer or of any other panegyrist whose poetry may please for the moment, although his representation of the facts will not bear the light of day. For we have compelled every land and every sea to open a path for our valor, and have everywhere planted eternal memorials of our friendship and of our enmity. Such is the city for whose sake these men nobly fought and died; they could not bear the thought that she might be taken from them; and every one of us who survive should gladly toil on her behalf.

"I have dwelt upon the greatness of Athens because I want to show you that we are contending for a higher prize then those who enjoy none of these privileges, and to establish by manifest proof the merit of these men whom I am now commemorating. Their loftiest praise has been already spoken. For in magnifying the city I have magnified them, and men like them whose virtues made her glorious. And of how few Hellenes can it be said as of them, that their deeds when weighed in the balance have been found equal to their fame! Methinks that a death such as theirs has been gives the true measure of a man's worth; it may be the first revelation of his virtues, but is at any rate their final seal. For even those who come short in other ways may justly plead the valor with which they have fought for their country; they have blotted out the evil with the good, and have benefited the state more by their public services than they have injured her by their private actions. None of these men were enervated by wealth or hesitated to resign the pleasures of life; none of them put off the evil day in the hope, natural to poverty, that a man, though poor, may one day become rich. But, deeming that the punishment of their enemies was sweeter than any of these things, and that they could fall in no nobler cause, they determined at the hazard of their lives to be honorably avenged, and to leave the rest. They resigned to hope their unknown chance of happiness; but in the face of death they resolved to rely upon themselves alone. And when the moment came they were minded to resist and suffer, rather than to fly and save their lives; they ran away from the word of dishonor, but on the battle-field their feet stood fast, and in an instant, at the height of their fortune, they passed away from the scene, not of their fear, but of their glory.

"Such was the end of these men; they were worthy of Athens, and the living need not desire to have a more heroic spirit although they may pray for a less fatal issue. The value of such a spirit is not to be expressed in words. Any one can discourse to you for ever about the advantages of a brave defence which you know already. But instead of listening to him I would have you day by day fix your eyes upon the greatness of Athens, until you become filled with the love of her; and when you are impressed by the spectacle of her glory, reflect that this empire has been acquired by men who knew their duty and had the courage to do it, who in the hour of conflict had the fear of dishonor always present to them, and who, if ever they failed in an enterprise, would not allow their virtues to be lost to their country, but freely gave their lives to her as the fairest offering which they could present at her feast. The sacrifice which they collectively made was individually repaid to them; for they received again each one for himself a praise which grows not old, and the noblest of all sepulchres—I speak not of that in which their remains are laid, but of that in which their glory survives, and is proclaimed always and on every fitting occasion both in word and deed. For the whole earth is the sepulchre of famous men; not only are they commemorated by columns and inscriptions in their own country, but in foreign lands there dwells also an unwritten memorial of them, graven not on stone but in the hearts of men. Make them your examples, and, esteeming courage to be freedom and freedom to be happiness, do not weigh too nicely the perils of war. The unfortunate who has no hope of a change for the better has less reason to throw away his life than the prosperous who, if he survive, is always liable to a change for the worse, and to whom any accidental fall makes the most serious difference. To a man of spirit, cowardice and disaster coming together are far more bitter than death, striking him unperceived at a time when he is full of courage and animated by the general hope.

"Wherefore I do not now commiserate the parents of the dead who stand here; I would rather comfort them. You know that your life has been passed amid manifold vicissitudes; and that they may be deemed fortunate who have gained most honor, whether an honorable death like theirs, or an honorable sorrow like yours, and whose days have been so ordered that the term of their happiness is likewise the term of their life. I know how hard it is to make you feel this, when the good fortune of others will too often remind you of the gladness which once lightened your hearts. And sorrow is felt at the want of those blessings, not which a man never knew, but which were a part of his life before they were taken from him. Some of you are of an age at which they may hope to have other children, and they ought to bear their sorrow better; not only will the children who may hereafter be born make them forget their own lost ones, but the city will be doubly a gainer. She will not be left desolate, and she will be safer. For a man's counsel cannot have equal weight or worth, when he alone has no children to risk in the general danger. To those of you who have passed their prime, I say; 'Congratulate yourselves that you have been happy during the greater part of your days; remember that your life of sorrow will not last long, and be comforted by the glory of those who are gone. For the love of honor alone is ever young, and not riches, as some say, but honor is the delight of men when they are old and useless.'

"To you who are the sons and brothers of the departed, I see that the struggle to emulate them will be an arduous one. For all men praise the dead, and, however pre-eminent your virtue may be, hardly will you be thought, I do not say to equal, but even to approach them. The living have their rivals and detractors, but when a man is out of the way, the honor and good-will which he receives is unalloyed. And, if I am to speak of womanly virtues to those of you who will henceforth be widows, let me sum them up in one short admonition: To a woman not to show more weakness than is natural to her sex is a great glory, and not to be talked about for good or for evil among men.

"I have paid the required tribute, in obedience to the law, making use of such fitting words as I had. The tribute of deeds has been paid in part; for the dead have been honorably interred, and it remains only that their children should be maintained at the public charge until they are grown up; this is the solid prize with which, as with a garland, Athens crowns her sons living and dead, after a struggle like theirs. For where the rewards of virtue are greatest, there the noblest citizens are enlisted in the service of the state. And now, when you have duly lamented, every one his own dead, you may depart."

Such was the order of the funeral celebrated in this winter, with the end of which ended the first year of the Peloponnesian War.

MELIAN DIALOGUE

The Melians[2] are colonists of the Lacedaemonians who would not submit to Athens like the other islanders. At first they were neutral and took no part. But when the Athenians tried to coerce them by ravaging their lands they were driven into open hostilities. The generals, Cleomedes the son of Lycomedes and Tisias the son of Tisimachus, encamped with the Athenian forces on the island. But before they did the country any harm they sent envoys to negotiate with the Melians. Instead of bringing these envoys before the people, the Melians desired them to explain their errand to the magistrates and to the chief men. They spoke as follows:—

"Since we are not allowed to speak to the people, lest, forsooth, they should be deceived by seductive and unanswerable arguments which they would hear set forth in a single uninterrupted oration (for we are perfectly aware that this is what you mean in bringing us before a select few), you who are sitting here may as well make assurance yet surer. Let us have no set speeches at all, but do you reply to each several statement of which you disapprove, and criticise it at once. Say first of all how you like this mode of proceeding."

The Melian representatives answered:—"The quiet interchange of explanations is a reasonable thing, and we do not object to that. But your warlike movements, which are present not only to our fears but to our eyes, seem to belie your words. We see that, although you may reason with us, you mean to be our judges; and that at the end of the discussion, if the justice of our cause prevail and we therefore refuse to yield, we may expect war; if we are convinced by you, slavery."

"ATHENIANS. 'Nay, but if you are only going to argue from fancies about the future, or if you meet us with any other purpose than that of looking your circumstances in the face and saving your city, we have done; but if this is your intention we will proceed.'

MELIANS. 'It is an excusable and natural thing that men in our position should have much to say and should indulge in many fancies. But we admit that this conference has met to consider the question of our preservation; and therefore let the argument proceed in the manner which you propose.'

ATHENIANS. 'Well, then, we Athenians will use no fine words; we

---

[2] The inhabitants of Melos, an island in the Aegean between Crete and Greece. The famed "Venus de Milo," now in the Louvre museum, was found here.

will not go out of our way to prove at length that we have a right to rule, because we overthrew the Persians; or that we attack you now because we are suffering any injury at your hands. We should not convince you if we did; nor must you expect to convince us by arguing that, although a colony of the Lacedaemonians, you have taken no part in their expeditions, or that you have never done us any wrong. But you and we should say what we really think, and aim only at what is possible, for we both alike know that into the discussion of human affairs the question of justice only enters where the pressure of necessity is equal, and that the powerful exact what they can, and the weak grant what they must.'

MELIANS.   'Well, then, since you set aside justice and invite us to speak of expediency, in our judgment it is certainly expedient that you should respect a principle which is for the common good; and that to every man when in peril a reasonable claim should be accounted a claim of right, and any plea which he is disposed to urge, even if failing of the point a little, should help his cause. Your interest in this principle is quite as great as ours, inasmuch as you, if you fall, will incur the heaviest vengeance, and will be the most terrible example to mankind.'

ATHENIANS.   'The fall of our empire, if it should fall, is not an event to which we look forward with dismay; for ruling states such as Lacedaemon are not cruel to their vanquished enemies. And we are fighting not as much against the Lacedaemonians as against our own subjects who may some day rise up and overcome their former masters. But this is a danger which you may leave to us. And we will now endeavor to show that we have come in the interests of our empire, and that in what we are about to say we are only seeking the preservation of your city. For we want to make you ours with the least trouble to ourselves, and it is for the interests of us both that you should not be destroyed.'

MELIANS.   'It may be your interest to be our masters, but how can it be ours to be your slaves?'

ATHENIANS.   'To you the gain will be that by submission you will avert the worst; and we shall be all the richer for your preservation.'

MELIANS.   'But must we be your enemies? Will you not receive us as friends if we are neutral and remain at peace with you?'

ATHENIANS.   'No, your enmity is not half so mischievous to us as your friendship; for the one is in the eyes of our subjects an argument of our power, the other of our weakness.'

MELIANS. 'But are your subjects really unable to distinguish between states in which you have no concern, and those which are chiefly your own colonies, and in some cases have revolted and been subdued by you?'

ATHENIANS. 'Why, they do not doubt that both of them have a good deal to say for themselves on the score of justice, but they think that states like yours are left free because they are able to defend themselves, and that we do not attack them because we dare not. So that your subjection will give us an increase of security, as well as an extension of empire. For we are masters of the sea, and you who are islanders, and insignificant islanders too, must not be allowed to escape us.'

MELIANS. 'But do you not recognize another danger? For once more, since you drive us from the plea of justice and press upon us your doctrine of expediency, we must show you what is for our interest, and, if it be for yours also, may hope to convince you:—Will you not be making enemies of all who are now neutrals? When they see how you are treating us they will expect you some day to turn against them; and if so, are you not strengthening the enemies whom you already have, and bringing upon you others who, if they could help, would never dream of being your enemies at all?'

ATHENIANS. 'We do not consider our really dangerous enemies to be any of the peoples inhabiting the mainland who, secure in their freedom, may defer indefinitely any measures of precaution which they take against us, but islanders who, like you, happen to be under no control, and all who may be already irritated by the necessity of submission of our empire—these are our real enemies, for they are the most reckless and most likely to bring themselves as well as us into a danger which they cannot but foresee.'

MELIANS. 'Surely then, if you and your subjects will brave all this risk, you to preserve your empire and they to be quit of it, how base and cowardly it would be in us, who retain our freedom, not to do and suffer anything rather than be your slaves.'

ATHENIANS. 'Not so, if you calmly reflect: for you are not fighting against equals to whom you cannot yield without disgrace, but you are taking counsel whether or no you shall resist an overwhelming force. The question is not one of honor but of prudence.'

MELIANS. 'But we know that the fortune of war is sometimes impartial, and not always on the side of numbers. If we yield now all is over; but if we fight there is yet a hope that we may stand upright.'

ATHENIANS.   'Hope is a good comforter in the hour of danger, and when men have something else to depend upon, although hurtful, she is not ruinous. But when her spendthrift nature has induced them to stake their all, they see her as she is in the moment of their fall, and not till then. While the knowledge of her might enable them to beware of her, she never fails. You are weak and a single turn of the scale might be your ruin. Do not you be thus deluded; avoid the error of which so many are guilty, who, although they might still be saved if they would take the natural means, when visible grounds of confidence forsake them, have recourse to the invisible, to prophecies and oracles and the like, which ruin men by the hopes which they inspire in them.'

MELIANS.   'We know only too well how hard the struggle must be against your power, and against fortune, if she does not mean to be impartial. Nevertheless we do not despair of fortune; for we hope to stand as high as you in the favor of heaven, because we are righteous, and you against whom we contend are unrighteous; and we are satisfied that our deficiency in power will be compensated by the aid of our allies the Lacedaemonians; they cannot refuse to help us, if only because we are their kinsmen, and for the sake of their own honor. And therefore our confidence is not so utterly blind as you suppose.'

ATHENIANS.   'As for the Gods, we expect to have quite as much of their favor as you: for we are not doing or claiming anything which goes beyond common opinion about divine or men's desires about human things. For of the Gods we believe, and of men we know, that by a law of their nature wherever they can rule they will. This law was not made by us, and we are not the first who have acted upon it; we did but inherit it, and shall bequeath it to all time, and we know that you and all mankind, if you were as strong as we are, would do as we do. So much for the Gods; we have told you why we expect to stand as high in their good opinion as you. And then as to the Lacedaemonians—when you imagine that out of very shame they will assist you, we admire the simplicity of your idea, but we do not envy you the folly of it. The Lacedamonians are exceedingly virtuous among themselves, and according to their national standard of morality. But in respect of their dealings with others, although many things might be said, a word is enough to describe them—of all men whom we know they are the most notorious for identifying what is pleasant with what is honorable, and what is expedient with what is just. But how inconsistent is such a character with your present blind hope of deliverance!'

MELIANS. 'That is the very reason why we trust them; they will look to their interest, and therefore will not be willing to betray the Melians, who are their own colonists, lest they should be distrusted by their friends in Hellas and play into the hands of their enemies.'

ATHENIANS. 'But do you not see that the path of expediency is safe, whereas justice and honor involve danger in practice, and such dangers the Lacedaemonians seldom care to face?'

MELIANS. 'On the other hand, we think that whatever perils there may be, they will be ready to face them for our sakes, and will consider danger less dangerous where we are concerned. For if they need our aid we are close at hand, and they can better trust our loyal feeling because we are their kinsmen.' . . .

ATHENIANS. 'If you are wise you will not run this risk; you ought to see that there can be no disgrace in yielding to a great city which invites you to become her ally on reasonable terms, keeping your own land, and merely paying tribute; and that you will certainly gain no honour if, having to choose between two alternatives, safety and war, you obstinately prefer the worse. To maintain our rights against equals, to be politic with superiors, and to be moderate towards inferiors is the path of safety. Reflect once more when we have withdrawn, and say to yourselves over and over again that you are deliberating about your one and only country, which may be saved or may be destroyed by a single decision.' "

The Athenian envoys returned to the army; and the generals, when they found that the Melians would not yield, immediately commenced hostilities. They surrounded the town of Melos with a wall, dividing the work among the several contingents. They then left troops of their own and of the allies to keep guard both by land and by sea, and retired with the greater part of their army; the remainder carried on the blockade.

About the same time the Argives[3] made an inroad into Phliasia, and lost nearly eighty men, who were caught in an ambuscade by the Phliasians and the Argive exiles. The Athenian garrison in Pylos took much spoil from the Lacedaemonians; nevertheless, the latter did not renounce the peace and go to war, but only notified by a

---

[3] Allies of Athens. The events mentioned in this paragraph refer chiefly to actions on the Greek mainland, affecting Melos only indirectly.

proclamation that if any one of their own people had a mind to make reprisals on the Athenians he might. The Corinthians next declared war upon the Athenians on some private grounds, but the rest of the Peloponnesians did not join them. The Melians took that part of the Athenian wall which looked towards the agora by a night assault, killed a few men, and brought in as much corn and other necessaries as they could; they then retreated and remained inactive. After this the Athenians set a better watch. So the summer ended.

In the following winter the Lacedaemonians had intended to make an expedition into the Argive territory, but finding that the sacrifices which they offered at the frontier were unfavorable they returned home. The Argives, suspecting that the threatened invasion was instigated by citizens of their own, apprehended some of them; others however escaped.

About the same time the Melians took another part of the Athenian wall; for the fortifications were insufficiently guarded. Whereupon the Athenians sent fresh troops, under the command of Philocrates the son of Demeas. The place was now closely invested, and there was treachery among the citizens themselves. So the Melians were induced to surrender at discretion. The Athenians thereupon put to death all who were of military age, and made slaves of the women and children. They then colonized the island, sending thither five hundred settlers of their own.

6

Xenophon

The Constitution of the Lacedaemonians

⊡

*Athens was not the only city-state extolled beyond its own borders. Lacedae-
mon (better known as Sparta), also had its admirers, particularly among
aristocrats and the wealthy. In the late fifth century* B.C. *pro-Spartan sentiment was conspicuous in the coterie about Socrates and among supporters of
the reactionary regime set up in Athens in 404* B.C. *by the victorious Spartans.*

One of the members of this circle was Xenophon (ca. 434–ca. 355 B.C.*),
a middle-class property-holding Athenian. After the downfall of the reactionary party he was among the Greeks who enlisted in the mercenary forces of a
prince who claimed the throne of Persia. The collapse of the expedition led to
a long, grim retreat northward to the Black Sea and safety. Later Xenophon
campaigned under the king of Sparta against the Persians, but when the latter became the allies of Athens, he was exiled and his property confiscated.
For the next twenty years Xenophon lived in retirement in Spartan-held territory as a country gentleman, hunting and writing vigorously.*

His best-known work is the Anabasis, *a spirited account of the great retreat, of which he had been the leader; but he also wrote three rather banal
books about Socrates, a long history continuing from where Thucydides left
off, and other works. His* Constitution of the Lacedaemonians, *reprinted
in part here, is perhaps the best general account of the Spartan way of life
available to us.*

*Not long after Xenophon's death, this regimented society—whose creation
is attributed to Lycurgus, an ancient and legendary lawgiver—broke down*

Xenophon, *The Constitution of the Lacedaemonians,* in *The Minor Works of Xenophon,*
trans. J. S. Watson (London: Bell [Bohn Classical Library], 1878), 204–209, 212–23.

forever. Of all the distinction won by Sparta at Thermopylae and in the Peloponnesian War, nothing remained but a high tradition. But it was a tradition destined for a long life. For through Xenophon and Plato, and later Plutarch, the aristocratic Spartan ideal of breeding and discipline was transmitted to the modern ruling classes of England and continental Europe, whose education, ever since the fifteenth century, has been based on the Greek and Roman classics.

THE REGULATIONS OF LYCURGUS RESPECTING MARRIAGE AND THE TREATMENT OF CHILDREN

But reflecting once how Sparta, one of the least populous of states, had proved the most powerful and celebrated city in Greece, I wondered by what means this result had been produced. When I proceeded, however, to contemplate the institutions of the Spartans, I wondered no longer.

Lycurgus, who made laws for them, by obedience to which they have flourished, I not only admire, but consider to have been in the fullest sense a wise man; for he rendered his country preëminent in prosperity, not by imitating other states, but by making ordinances contrary to those of most governments.

With regard, for example, to the procreation of children, that I may begin from the beginning, other people feed their young women, who are about to produce offspring, and who are of the class regarded as well brought up, on the most moderate quantity of vegetable food possible, and on the least possible quantity of meat, while they either keep them from wine altogether, or allow them to use it only when mixed with water; and as the greater number of the men engaged in trades are sedentary, so the rest of the Greeks think it proper that their young women should sit quiet and spin wool. But how can we expect that women thus treated should produce a vigorous progeny? Lycurgus, on the contrary, thought that female slaves were competent to furnish clothes; and, considering that the production of children was the noblest duty of the free, he enacted, in the first place, that the female should practise bodily exercises no less than the male sex; and he then appointed for the women contests with one another, just as for the men, expecting that when both parents were rendered strong, a stronger offspring would be born from them.

Observing, too, that the men of other nations, when women were united to husbands, associated with their wives during the early part of their intercourse without restraint, he made enactments quite at variance with this practice; for he ordained that a man should think it shame to be seen going in to his wife, or coming out from her. When married people meet in this way, they must feel stronger desire for the company of one another, and whatever offspring is produced must thus be rendered far more robust than if the parents were satiated with each other's society.

In addition to these regulations, he also took from the men the liberty of marrying when each of them pleased, and appointed that they should contract marriages only when they were in full bodily vigour, deeming this injunction also conducive to the production of an excellent offspring. Seeing also that if old men chanced to have young wives, they watched their wives with the utmost strictness, he made a law quite opposed to this feeling; for he appointed that an old man should introduce to his wife whatever man in the prime of life he admired for his corporeal and mental qualities, in order that she might have children by him. If, again, a man was unwilling to associate with his wife, and yet was desirous of having proper children, he made a provision also with respect to him, that whatever women he saw likely to have offspring, and of good disposition, he might, on obtaining the consent of her husband, have children by her. Many similar permissions he gave; for the women are willing to have two families, and the men to receive brothers to their children, who are equal to them in birth and standing, but have no claim to share in their property.

Let him who wishes, then, consider whether Lycurgus, in thus making enactments different from those of other legislators, in regard to the procreation of children, secured for Sparta a race of men eminent for size and strength.

ON THE TRAINING AND EDUCATION OF CHILDREN

Having given this account of the procreation of children, I wish also to detail the education of those of both sexes. Of the other Greeks, those who say that they bring up their sons best set slaves

over them to take charge of them, as soon as the children can understand what is said to them, and send them, at the same time, to
schoolmasters, to learn letters, and music, and the exercises of the
palaestra.[1] They also render their children's feet delicate by the use of
sandals, and weaken their bodies by changes of clothes; and as to
food, they regard their appetite as the measure of what they are to
take. But Lycurgus, instead of allowing each citizen to set slaves as
guardians over his children, appointed a man to have the care of
them all, one of those from whom the chief magistrates are chosen;
and he is called the paedonomus. He invested this man with full authority to assemble the boys, and, if he found that any one was
negligent of his duties, to punish him severely. He assigned him also
some of the grown-up boys as scourge-bearers, that they might
inflict whatever chastisement was necessary; so that great dread of
disgrace, and great willingness to obey, prevailed among them.

Instead, also, of making their feet soft with sandals, he enacted
that they should harden them by going without sandals; thinking
that, if they exercised themselves in this state, they would go up
steep places with far greater ease, and descend declivities with greater
safety; and that they would also leap, and skip, and run faster un-
shod, if they had their feet inured to doing so, than shod. Instead of
being rendered effeminate, too, by a variety of dresses, he made it a
practice that they should accustom themselves to one dress throughout the year; thinking that they would thus be better prepared to endure cold and heat.

As to food, he ordained that they should exhort the boys to take
only such a quantity as never to be oppressed with repletion, and not
to be strangers to living somewhat frugally; supposing that, being
thus brought up, they would be the better able, if they should be
required, to support toil under a scarcity of supplies, would be the
more likely to persevere in exertion, should it be imposed on them,
on the same quantity of provisions, and would be less desirous of
sauces, more easily satisfied with any kind of food, and pass their
lives in greater health. He also considered that the fare which rendered the body slender would be more conducive to increasing its
stature than that which expanded it with nutriment. Yet that the
boys might not suffer too much from hunger, Lycurgus, though he
did not allow them to take what they wanted without trouble, gave

[1] A public area used for athletic training.

them liberty to steal certain things to relieve the cravings of nature; and he made it honourable to steal as many cheeses as possible. That he did not give them leave to form schemes for getting food because he was at a loss what to allot them, I suppose no one is ignorant; as it is evident that he who designs to steal must be wakeful during the night, and use deceit, and lay plots; and, if he would gain anything of consequence, must employ spies. All these things, therefore, it is plain that he taught the children from a desire to render them more dexterous in securing provisions, and better qualified for warfare.

Some one may say, "Why, then, if he thought it honourable to steal, did he inflict a great number of stripes on him who was caught in the act?" I answer, that in other things which men teach, they punish him who does not follow his instructions properly; and that the Lacedaemonians accordingly punished those who were detected as having attempted to steal in an improper manner. These boys he gave in charge to others to scourge them at the altar of Diana Orthia; designing to show by this enactment that it is possible for a person, after enduring pain for a short time, to enjoy pleasure with credit for a long time. It is also shown by this punishment that, where there is need of activity, the inert person benefits himself the least, and occasions himself most trouble.

In order, too, that the boys, in case of the paedonomus being absent, may never be in want of a president, he appointed that whoever of the citizens may happen at any time to be present is to assume the direction of them, and to enjoin whatever he may think advantageous for them, and punish them if they do anything wrong. By doing this, Lycurgus has also succeeded in rendering the boys much more modest; for neither boys nor men respect any one so much as their rulers. And that if, on any occasion, no full-grown man happen to be present, the boys may not even in that case be without a leader, he ordained that the most active of the grown-up youths take the command of each band; so that the boys there are never without a superintendent.

It appears to me that I must say something also of the boys as objects of affection; for this has likewise some reference to education. Among the other Greeks, a man and boy either form a union, as among the Boeotians, and associate together, or, as among the Eleians, the men gain the favour of the youths by means of attentions bestowed upon them; but there are some of the Greeks who prohibit the suitors for the boys' favours from having the least conversation with them. But Lycurgus, acting contrary to all these people also, thought proper, if any man, being himself such as he ought to be, admired the disposition of a youth, and made it his object to render him a faultless friend, and to enjoy his society, to bestow praise upon him, and regarded this as the most excellent kind of education; but if any man showed that his affections were fixed only on the bodily attractions of a youth, Lycurgus, considering this as most unbecoming, appointed that at Lacedaemon suitors for the favours of boys should abstain from intimate connexion with them, not less strictly than parents abstain from such intercourse with their children, or children of the same family from that with one another. That such a state of things is disbelieved by some, I am not surprised; for in most states the laws are not at all adverse to the love of youths; but Lycurgus, for his part, took such precautions with reference to it.

• • •

MEALS TAKEN IN PUBLIC.   ON TEMPERANCE

The employments which Lycurgus appointed for each period of life have now been almost all specified. What mode of living he instituted for all the citizens, I will next endeavour to explain.

Lycurgus, then, having found the Spartans, like the other Greeks, taking their meals at home, and knowing that most were guilty of excess at them, caused their meals to be taken in public, thinking that his regulations would thus be less likely to be transgressed. He appointed them such a quantity of food, that they should neither be overfed nor feel stinted. Many extraordinary supplies are also furnished from what is caught in hunting, and for these the rich sometimes contribute bread; so that the table is never without provisions, as long as they design the meal to last, and yet is never expensive.

Having put a stop likewise to all unnecessary drinking, which weakens alike the body and the mind, he gave permission that every one should drink when he was thirsty, thinking that the drink would thus be most innoxious and most pleasant. When they take their meals together in this manner, how can any one ruin either himself or his family by gluttony or drunkenness? In other states, equals in age generally associate together, and with them modesty has but very little influence; but Lycurgus, at Sparta, mixed citizens of different ages, so that the younger are for the most part instructed by the experience of the older. It is a custom at these public meals, that whatever any one has done to his honour in the community is related; so that insolence, or disorder from intoxication, or any indecency in conduct or language, has there no opportunity of showing itself. The practice of taking meals away from home is also attended with these advantages, that the people are obliged to walk in taking their departure homewards, and to be careful that they may not stagger from the effects of wine, knowing that they will not remain where they dined, and that they must conduct themselves in the night just as in the day; for it is not allowable for any one who is still liable to military duty to walk with a torch.

As Lycurgus observed, too, that those who, after taking food, exercise themselves, become well-complexioned, plump, and robust, while those who are inactive are puffy, unhealthy-looking, and feeble, he did not neglect to give attention to that point; and as he perceived that when any one engages in labour from his own inclination, he proves himself to have his body in efficient condition, he ordered that the oldest in each place of exercise should take care that those belonging to it should never be overcome by taking too much food. With regard to this matter, he appears to me to have been by no means mistaken; for no one would easily find men more healthy, or more able-bodied, than the Spartans; for they exercise themselves alike in their legs, in their hands, and in their shoulders.

ORDINANCES REGARDING CHILDREN, SLAVES, AND PROPERTY

In the following particulars, also, he made enactments contrary to the usage of most states; for in other communities each individual has the control over his own children, and servants, and property; but Lycurgus, wishing to order things so that the citizens might enjoy some advantage from one another, unattended with any reciprocal injury, ordained that each should have authority not only over his own children, but over those of others. But when a person is conscious that his fellow-citizens are fathers of the children over whom he exercises authority, he must exercise it in such a way as he would wish it to be exercised over his own. If a boy, on any occasion, receive blows from another boy, and complain of that boy to his father, it is considered dishonourable in the father not to inflict additional blows on his son. Thus they trust to one another to impose nothing disgraceful on the children.

He enacted also that a person might use his neighbour's servants, if he had need of them. He introduced, too, a community of property in hunting-dogs; so that those who require them call on their owner to hunt, who, if he is not at leisure to hunt himself, cheerfully sends them out. They use horses also in like manner; for whoever is sick, or wants a vehicle, or desires to go to some place speedily, takes possession of a horse, if he sees one anywhere, and, after making proper use of it, restores it.

Nor, in regard to the following point, did he allow that which is customary among other people should be practised among his countrymen. For when men, from being overtaken by night in hunting, are in want of provisions, unless they have previously furnished themselves with them, he directed that, in such a case, those who have partaken of what they need, leave the rest ready for use, and that those who require a supply, having opened the seals, and taken as much as they want, seal the remainder up again and leave it. As they share thus, then, with one another, those who possess but little participate, whenever they are in need, in all the produce of the country.

RESTRICTIONS ON THE EMPLOYMENTS OF THE LACEDAEMONIANS

The following practices, too, Lycurgus established in Sparta, at variance with those of the rest of Greece. In other communities all gain as much by traffic as they can; one cultivates land, another trades by sea, another engages in general commerce, another maintains himself by art. But at Sparta, Lycurgus prohibited free men from having any connexion with traffic,[2] and enjoined them to consider as their only occupation whatever secures freedom to states. How, indeed, could wealth be eagerly sought in a community where he had appointed that the citizens should contribute equally to their necessary maintenance, and should take their meals in common, and had thus provided that they should not desire wealth with a view to

[2] That is, with commerce.

sensual gratifications? Nor had they, moreover, to get money for the sake of clothing; for they think themselves adorned, not by expensive raiment, but by a healthy personal appearance. Nor have they to gather money for the purpose of spending it on those who eat with them, since he has made it more honourable for a person to serve his neighbours by bodily exertion, than by putting himself to pecuniary expense; making it apparent that the one proceeds from the mind, and the other from fortune.

From acquiring money by unjust means, he prohibited them by such methods as the following. He instituted, in the first place, such a kind of money, that, even if but ten minae[3] came into a house, it could never escape the notice either of masters or of servants; for it would require much room, and a carriage to convey it. In the next place, gold and silver are searched after, and, if they are discovered anywhere, the possessor of them is punished. How, then, could gain by traffic be an object of pursuit, in a state where the possession of money occasions more pain than the use of it affords pleasure?

OBEDIENCE TO THE MAGISTRATES AND LAWS

That at Sparta the citizens pay the strictest obedience to the magistrates and laws, we all know. I suppose, however, that Lycurgus did not attempt to establish such an excellent order of things, until he had brought the most powerful men in the state to be of the same mind with regard to it. I form my opinion on this consideration, that, in other states, the more influential men are not willing even to appear to fear the magistrates, but think that such fear is unbecoming free men; but in Sparta, the most powerful men not only put themselves under the magistrates, but even count it an honour to humble themselves before them, and to obey, when they are called upon, not walking, but running; supposing that if they themselves are the first to pay exact obedience, others will follow their example; and such has been the case. It is probable, also, that the chief men established the magistracy of the Ephori,[4] in conjunction with Lycurgus, as they must have been certain that obedience is of the greatest benefit, alike

---

[3] Large iron coins of the Spartans.
[4] A five-man board, elected annually, that had unlimited powers, except command in war.

in a state, and in an army, and in a family; and they doubtless considered that the greater power magistrates have, the greater effect will they produce on the citizens in enforcing obedience. The Ephori, accordingly, have full power to impose a fine on whomsoever they please, and to exact the fine without delay; they have power also to degrade magistrates even while they are in office, and to put them in prison, and to bring them to trial for their life. Being possessed of such authority, they do not, like the magistrates in other states, always permit those who are elected to offices to rule during the whole year as they choose, but, like despots and presidents in gymnastic contests, punish on the instant whomsoever they find acting at all contrary to the laws.

Though there were many other excellent contrivances adopted by Lycurgus, to induce the citizens to obey the laws, the most excellent of all appears to me to be, that he did not deliver his laws to the people until he had gone, in company with the most eminent of his fellow-citizens, to Delphi, and consulted the god whether it would be more beneficial and advantageous for Sparta to obey the laws which he had made. As the god replied that it would be more beneficial in every way, he at once delivered them, deciding that it would be not only illegal, but impious, to disobey laws sanctioned by the oracle.

INFAMY AND PENALTIES OF COWARDICE

It is deserving of admiration, too, in Lycurgus, that he made it a settled principle in the community, that an honourable death is preferable to a dishonourable life; for whoever pays attention to the subject will find that fewer of those who hold this opinion die than of those who attempt to escape danger by flight. Hence we may say with truth, that safety attends for a much longer period on valour than on cowardice; for valour is not only attended with less anxiety and greater pleasure, but is also more capable of assisting and supporting us. It is evident, too, that good report accompanies valour; for almost everybody is willing to be in alliance with the brave.

How he contrived that such sentiments should be entertained, it is proper not to omit to mention. He evidently, then, intended a happy life for the brave, and a miserable one for the cowardly. In other communities, when a man acts as a coward, he merely brings on himself the name of coward, but the coward goes to the same market, and sits or takes exercise, if he pleases, in the same place with the brave men; at Lacedaemon, however, every one would be ashamed to admit a coward into the same tent with him, or to allow him to be his opponent in a match at wrestling. Frequently, too, a person of such a character, when they choose opposite parties to play at ball, is left without any place; and in forming a chorus he is thrust into the least honourable position. On the road he must yield the way to others, and at public meetings he must rise up, even before his juniors. His female relatives he must maintain at home, and they must pay the penalty of his want of spirit; he is also not allowed to have his hearth without a wife, and must at the same time pay a fine for being in that condition. He must not walk abroad anointed, or imitate the manners of persons of blameless character; else he will have to receive stripes from his betters. Since, then, such disgrace is inflicted on cowards, I do not at all wonder that death is preferred at Sparta to a life so dishonourable and infamous.

HONOURS PAID TO OLD AGE.
ENCOURAGEMENT OF VIRTUE

Lycurgus seems to me to have provided also, with great judgment, how virtue might be practised even to old age; for by adding to his other enactments the choice of senators at an advanced stage of life, he caused honour and virtue not to be disregarded even in old age.

It is worthy of admiration in him, too, that he attached consideration to the old age of the well-deserving; for by making the old men arbiters in the contest for superiority in mental qualifications, he rendered their old age more honourable than the vigour of those in the meridian of life. This contest is deservedly held in the greatest esteem among the people, for gymnastic contests are attended with honour, but they concern only bodily accomplishments; the contest for distinction in old age involves a decision respecting merits of the mind. In proportion, therefore, as the mind is superior to the body, so much are contests for mental eminence more worthy of regard than those concerning bodily superiority.

Is it not highly worthy of admiration, also, in Lycurgus, that when he saw that those who are disinclined to practice virtue are not qualified to increase the power of their country, he obliged all the citizens of Sparta to cultivate every kind of virtue publicly. As private individuals, accordingly, who practise virtue, are superior in it to those who neglect it, so Sparta is naturally superior in virtue to all other states, as it is the only one that engages in a public cultivation of honour and virtue. Is it not also deserving of commendation, that, when other states punish any person that injures another, Lycurgus inflicted no less punishment on any one that openly showed himself regardless of becoming as good a man as possible? He thought, as it appears, that by those who make others slaves, or rob them, or steal anything, the individual sufferers only are injured, but that by the unprincipled and cowardly whole communities are betrayed; so that he appears to me to have justly imposed the heaviest penalties on such characters.

He also imposed on his countrymen an obligation, from which there is no exception, of practising every kind of political virtue; for he made the privileges of citizenship equally available to all those who observed what was enjoined by the laws, without taking any account either of weakness of body or scantiness of means; but if any one was too indolent to perform what the laws prescribed, Lycurgus appointed that he should be no longer counted in the number of equally privileged citizens.

That these laws are extremely ancient is certain; for Lycurgus is said to have lived in the time of the Heracleidae;[5] but, ancient as they are, they are still very new to other communities; for, what is the most wonderful of all things, all men extol such institutions, but no state thinks proper to imitate them.

OF THE LACEDAEMONIAN ARMY

The regulations which I have mentioned are beneficial alike in peace and in war; but if any one wishes to learn what he contrived better than other legislators with reference to military proceedings, he may attend to the following particulars.

In the first place, then, the Ephori give the cavalry and infantry public notice of the years during which they must join the army, as well as the artisans; for the Lacedaemonians provide themselves in

[5] Children of the legendary hero Heracles.

the field with an abundance of all those things which people use in a city; and of whatever instruments an army may require in common, orders are given to bring some on waggons, and others on beasts of burden, as by this arrangement anything left behind is least likely to escape notice.

For engagements in the field he made the following arrangements. He ordered that each soldier should have a purple robe and a brazen shield; for he thought that such a dress had least resemblance to that of women, and was excellently adapted for the field of battle, as it is soonest made splendid, and is longest in growing soiled. He permitted also those above the age of puberty to let their hair grow, as he thought that they thus appeared taller, more manly, and more terrible in the eyes of the enemy.

When they were thus equipped, he divided them into six morae of cavalry and heavy-armed infantry. Each of these morae of the citizens has one polemarch, four centurions, eight captains of fifty, and sixteen enomotarchs. The men of these morae are sometimes, according to the command issued, formed in enomotiae,[6] sometimes by threes, sometimes by sixes. As to what most people imagine, that the arrangement of the Lacedaemonians under arms is extremely complex, they conceive the exact contrary to what is the fact; for in the Lacedaemonian order the officers are placed in the front ranks, and each rank is in a condition to perform everything which it is necessary for it to perform. So easy is it to understand this arrangement, that no one, who can distinguish one man from another, would fail of learning it; for it is assigned to some to lead, and enjoined on others to follow. Shiftings of place, by which the companies are extended or deepened, are ordered by the word of the enomotarch, as by a herald; and in these there is nothing in the least difficult to learn. But how it is possible for men in this arrangement, even if they are thrown into confusion, to fight with an enemy presenting themselves on any quarter alike, it is not so easy to understand, except for those who have been brought up under the institution of Lycurgus. The Lacedaemonians do with the greatest ease what appears extremely difficult to other men that are even accustomed to arms. For when they march in column, one enomotia follows in the rear of another; and if, when they are in this order, a body of the enemy shows itself in front, orders are given to each enomotarch to bring

---

[6] Platoons of thirty-two men.

up his enomotia to the front on the left; and this movement is made throughout the whole army, until it presents itself in full array against the enemy. But if again, while they are in this order, the enemy should show themselves in the rear, each rank performs an evolution, that the strongest may always be presented to the enemy.

But when the commander is on the left, they do not in that case consider themselves in a worse condition, but sometimes even in a better; for if an enemy should attempt to encompass them, he would come round, not on the defenceless, but on the armed side. If on any occasion, again, it should appear advantageous, for any particular object, that the commander should occupy the right wing, they wheel the troop towards the wing, and manoeuvre the main body, until the commander is on the right, and the rear becomes the left. But if, again, a body of the enemy appear on the right, marching in column, they do nothing else but turn each century round, like a ship, so as to front the enemy; and thus the century which was in the rear comes to the right. But if the enemy approach on the left, they do not allow them to come near, but repulse them, or turn their centuries round to face the enemy; and thus again the century that was in the rear takes its place on the left.

7

Aristophanes

Lysistrata

⊡

Aristophanes was born of upper-class parents, probably at Athens, around 445 B.C. and died there around 388 B.C. Regarding his life we have no sure details, saving those to be gleaned from his own plays. Of the forty-four he produced, only eleven have come down to us complete. The interests, attitudes, and spirit displayed in these works suggest that Aristophanes was an intellectual of a conservative turn of mind and lively wit. Unfortunately, many of his displays of wit involved contemporary and local allusions or plays upon words and thus are largely lost to the modern reader, especially when read in translation.

Although comedy was his medium, and he wrote plays often ribald in language and subject matter, Aristophanes sought to do more than entertain. In addition to being comedic, his plays were meant to be profoundly serious and critical appeals to the reason of the Athenian audience. Lysistrata, *the play presented here, is one of three Aristophanic comedies in which the imbecility of Greeks fighting Greeks is ridiculed. First staged about 412 B.C., only a few months after the total disaster experienced by Athenian forces at Syracuse, it has often been used to comment on modern wars and is today Aristophanes' most popular creation.*

Nothing testifies more forcibly to the values cherished in fifth-century Athens than the fact that the play was produced there under official auspices even while the state was at war. It is also significant that, after the fall of Athens from power, such productions ceased and what is known as the Old Comedy (of which Aristophanes' plays are the prime exemplars) became a thing of the past. The Golden Age of Greece was over.

Aristophanes, *Lysistrata*, trans. Charles T. Murphy, from *Greek Literature in Transition* edited by Whitney J. Oates and Charles T. Murphy. (New York: David McKay Co., 1944), 388–418. Copyright © 1944 by David McKay Co.; renewed in 1971 by Whitney J. Oates and Charles T. Murphy. Reprinted by permission of Longman, Inc.

Characters

LYSISTRATA ⎫
CALONICE ⎬   *Athenian women*
MYRRHINE ⎭
LAMPITO, *a Spartan woman*
CHORUS OF ATHENIAN MEN
CHORUS OF ATHENIAN WOMEN
ATHENIAN MAGISTRATE
CINESIAS, *an Athenian, husband of Myrrhine*
INFANT CHILD *of Cinesias and Myrrhine*
SPARTAN HERALD
SPARTAN AMBASSADORS
ATHENIAN AMBASSADORS
CHORUS OF SPARTANS
CHORUS OF ATHENIANS
SILENT CHARACTERS: A BOEOTIAN WOMAN; A CORINTHIAN WOMAN; A SCYTHIAN
    SLAVE-GIRL; FOUR SCYTHIAN POLICEMEN; CINESIAS' SLAVE.

TIME: early 411 B.C.

SCENE: *in Athens, beneath the Acropolis. In the center of the stage
is the Propylaea, or gateway to the Acropolis; to one side is a small
grotto, sacred to Pan. The Orchestra represents a slope leading up
to the gateway.*
    It is early in the morning. LYSISTRATA *is pacing impatiently up and
down.*

LYSISTRATA.   If they'd been summoned to worship the God of Wine,
    or Pan, or to visit the Queen of Love, why, you couldn't have
    pushed your way through the streets for all the timbrels. But
    now there's not a single woman here—except my neighbor; here
    she comes. [*Enter* CALONICE.] Good day to you, Calonice.
CALONICE.   And to you, Lysistrata. [*Noticing* LYSISTRATA'S *impatient
    air.*] But what ails you? Don't scowl, my dear; it's not becoming
    to you to knit your brows like that.
LYSISTRATA [*sadly*].   Ah, Calonice, my heart aches; I'm so annoyed
    at us women. For among men we have a reputation for sly
    trickery—

CALONICE. And rightly too, on my word!

LYSISTRATA. —but when they were told to meet here to consider a matter of no small importance, they lie abed and don't come.

CALONICE. Oh, they'll come all right, my dear. It's not easy for a woman to get out, you know. One is working on her husband, another is getting up the maid, another has to put the baby to bed, or wash and feed it.

LYSISTRATA. But after all, there are other matters more important than all that.

CALONICE. My dear Lysistrata, just what is this matter you've summoned us women to consider? What's up? Something big?

LYSISTRATA. Very big.

CALONICE [interested]. It is stout, too?

LYSISTRATA [smiling]. Yes indeed—both big and stout.

CALONICE. What? And the women still haven't come?

LYSISTRATA. It's not what you suppose; they'd have come soon enough for that. But I've worked up something, and for many a sleepless night I've turned it this way and that.

CALONICE [in mock disappointment]. Oh, I guess it's pretty fine and slender, if you've turned it this way and that.

LYSISTRATA. So fine that the safety of the whole of Greece lies in us women.

CALONICE. In us women? It depends on a very slender reed then.

LYSISTRATA. Our country's fortunes are in our hands; and whether the Spartans shall perish—

CALONICE. Good! Let them perish, by all means.

LYSISTRATA. —and the Boeotians shall be completely annihilated.

CALONICE. Not completely! Please spare the eels.

LYSISTRATA. As for Athens, I won't use any such unpleasant words. But you understand what I mean. But if the women will meet here—the Spartans, the Boeotians, and we Athenians—then all together we will save Greece.

CALONICE. But what could women do that's clever or distinguished? We just sit around all dolled up in silk robes, looking pretty in our sheer gowns and evening slippers.

LYSISTRATA. These are just the things I hope will save us: these silk robes, perfumes, evening slippers, rouge, and our chiffon blouses.

CALONICE. How so?

LYSISTRATA. So never a man alive will lift a spear against the foe—

CALONICE. I'll get a silk gown at once.

LYSISTRATA.   —or take up his shield—

CALONICE.   I'll put on my sheerest gown!

LYSISTRATA.   —or sword.

CALONICE.   I'll buy a pair of evening slippers.

LYSISTRATA.   Well then, shouldn't the women have come?

CALONICE.   Come? Why, they should have *flown* here.

LYSISTRATA.   Well, my dear, just watch: they'll act in true Athenian fashion—everything too late! And now there's not a woman here from the shore or from Salamis.

CALONICE.   They're coming, I'm sure; at daybreak they were laying—to their oars to cross the straits.

LYSISTRATA.   And those I expected would be the first to come—the women of Acharnae—they haven't arrived.

CALONICE.   Yet the wife of Theagenes means to come: she consulted Hecate about it. [*Seeing a group of women approaching.*] But look! Here come a few. And there are some more over here. Hurrah! Where do they come from?

LYSISTRATA.   From Anagyra.

CALONICE.   Yes indeed! We've raised up a quite a stink from Anagyra anyway.

[*Enter* MYRRHINE *in haste, followed by several other women.*]

MYRRHINE [*breathlessly*].   Have we come in time, Lysistrata? What do you say? Why so quiet?

LYSISTRATA.   I can't say much for you, Myrrhine, coming at this hour on such important business.

MYRRHINE.   Why, I had trouble finding my girdle in the dark. But if it's so important, we're here now; tell us.

LYSISTRATA.   No. Let's wait a little for the women from Boeotia and the Peloponnesus.

MYRRHINE.   That's a much better suggestion. Look! Here comes Lampito now.

[*Enter* LAMPITO *with two other women.*]

LYSISTRATA.   Greetings, my dear Spartan friend. How pretty you look, my dear. What a smooth complexion and well-developed figure! You could throttle an ox.

LAMPITO.   Faith, yes, I think I could. I take exercises and kick my heels against my bum. [*She demonstrates with a few steps of the Spartan "bottom-kicking" dance.*]

LYSISTRATA.   And what splendid breasts you have.

LAMPITO.   La! You handle me like a prize steer.

LYSISTRATA.   And who is this young lady with you?

LAMPITO.   Faith, she's an Ambassadress from Boeotia.

LYSISTRATA.   Oh yes, a Boeotian, and blooming like a garden too.

CALONICE [*lifting up her skirt*]. My word! How neatly her garden's weeded!

LYSISTRATA.   And who is the other girl?

LAMPITO.   Oh, she's a Corinthian swell.

MYRRHINE [*after a rapid examination*].   Yes indeed. She swells very nicely [*pointing*] here and here.

LAMPITO.   Who has gathered together this company of women?

LYSISTRATA.   I have.

LAMPITO.   Speak up, then. What do you want?

MYRRHINE.   Yes, my dear, do tell us what this important matter is.

LYSISTRATA.   Very well, I'll tell you. But before I speak, let me ask you a little question.

MYRRHINE.   Anything you like.

LYSISTRATA [*earnestly*].   Tell me: don't you yearn for the fathers of your children, who are away at the wars? I know you all have husbands abroad.

CALONICE.   Why, yes; mercy me! my husband's been away for five months in Thrace keeping guard on—Eucrates.

MYRRHINE.   And mine for seven whole months in Pylus.

LAMPITO.   And mine, as soon as ever he returns from the fray, read-justs his shield and flies out of the house again.

LYSISTRATA.   And as for lovers, there's not even a ghost of one left. Since the Milesians revolted from us,[1] I've not even seen an eight-inch dingus to be a leather consolation for us widows. Are you willing, if I can find a way, to help me end the war?

MYRRHINE.   Goodness, yes! I'd do it, even if I had to pawn my dress and—get drunk on the spot!

CALONICE.   And I, even if I had to let myself be split in two like a flounder.

LAMPITO.   I'd climb up Mt. Taygetus[2] if I could catch a glimpse of peace.

LYSISTRATA.   I'll tell you, then, in plain and simple words. My friends, if we are going to force our men to make peace, we must do without—

MYRRHINE.   Without what? Tell us.

---

[1] Miletus, formerly Athens' ally, the source of these devices, had gone over to Sparta the year before.

[2] A high mountain range dominating central Sparta.

LYSISTRATA.   Will you do it?

MYRRHINE.   We'll do it, if it kills us.

LYSISTRATA.   Well then, we must do without sex altogether. [*General consternation.*] Why do you turn away? Where go you? Why turn so pale? Why those tears? Will you do it or not? What means this hesitation?

MYRRHINE.   I won't do it! Let the war go on.

CALONICE.   Nor I! Let the war go on.

LYSISTRATA.   So, my little flounder? Didn't you say just now you'd split yourself in half?

CALONICE.   Anything else you like. I'm willing, even if I have to walk through fire. Anything rather than sex. There's nothing like it, my dear.

LYSISTRATA [*to* MYRRHINE].   What about you?

MYRRHINE [*sullenly*].   I'm willing to walk through fire, too.

LYSISTRATA.   Oh vile and cursed breed! No wonder they make tragedies about us: we're naught but "love affairs and bassinets." But you, my dear Spartan friend, if you alone are with me, our enterprise might yet succeed. Will you vote with me?

LAMPITO.   'Tis cruel hard, by my faith, for a woman to sleep alone without her nooky; but for all that, we certainly do need peace.

LYSISTRATA.   O my dearest friend! You're the only real woman here.

CALONICE [*wavering*].   Well, if we do refrain from— [*shuddering*] what you say (God forbid!), would that bring peace?

LYSISTRATA.   My goodness, yes! If we sit at home all rouged and powdered, dressed in our sheerest gowns, and neatly depilated, our men will get excited and want to take us; but if you don't come to them and keep away, they'll soon make a truce.

LAMPITO.   Aye; Menelaus caught sight of Helen's naked breast and dropped his sword, they say.

CALONICE.   What if the men give us up?

LYSISTRATA.   "Flay a skinned dog," as Pherecrates says.

CALONICE.   Rubbish! These make-shifts are no good. But suppose they grab us and drag us into the bedroom?

LYSISTRATA.   Hold on to the door.

CALONICE.   And if they beat us?

LYSISTRATA.   Give in with a bad grace. There's no pleasure in it for them when they have to use violence. And you must torment them in every possible way. They'll give up soon enough; a man gets no joy if he doesn't get along with his wife.

MYRRHINE.   If this is your opinion, we agree.

LAMPITO.   As for our own men, we can persuade them to make a just and fair peace; but what about the Athenian rabble? Who will persuade them not to start any more monkey-shines?

LYSISTRATA.   Don't worry. We guarantee to convince them.

LAMPITO.   Not while their ships are rigged so well and they have that mighty treasure in the temple of Athene.[3]

LYSISTRATA.   We've taken good care for that too: we shall seize the Acropolis today. The older women have orders to do this, and while we are making our arrangements, they are to pretend to make a sacrifice and occupy the Acropolis.

LAMPITO.   All will be well then. That's a very fine idea.

LYSISTRATA.   Let's ratify this, Lampito, with the most solemn oath.

LAMPITO.   Tell us what oath we shall swear.

LYSISTRATA.   Well said. Where's our Policewoman? [*To a Scythian slave.*] What are you gaping at? Set a shield upside-down here in front of me, and give me the sacred meats.

CALONICE.   Lysistrata, what sort of an oath are we to take?

LYSISTRATA.   What oath? I'm going to slaughter a sheep over the shield, as they do in Aeschylus.

CALONICE.   Don't, Lysistrata! No oaths about peace over a shield.

LYSISTRATA.   What shall the oath be, then?

CALONICE.   How about getting a white horse somewhere and cutting out its entrails for the sacrifice?

LYSISTRATA.   White horse indeed!

CALONICE.   Well then, how shall we swear?

MYRRHINE.   I'll tell you: let's place a large black bowl upside-down and then slaughter—a flask of Thasian wine. And then let's swear—not to pour in a single drop of water.

LAMPITO.   Lord! How I like that oath!

LYSISTRATA.   Someone bring out a bowl and a flask.

[*A slave brings the utensils for the sacrifice.*]

CALONICE.   Look, my friends! What a big jar! Here's a cup that 'twould give me joy to handle. [*She picks up the bowl.*]

LYSISTRATA.   Set it down and put your hands on our victim. [*As* CALONICE *places her hands on the flask.*] O Lady of Persuasion and dear Loving Cup, graciously vouchsafe to receive this sacrifice from us woman. [*She pours the wine into the bowl.*]

CALONICE.   The blood has a good color and spurts out nicely.

---

[3] The Parthenon, which housed the war-chest of Athens, accumulated by Pericles, the earlier Athenian leader.

LAMPITO.   Faith, it has a pleasant smell, too.

MYRRHINE.   Oh, let me be the first to swear, ladies!

CALONICE.   No, by our Lady! Not unless you're alloted the first turn.

LYSISTRATA.   Place all your hands on the cup, and one of you repeat on behalf of all what I say. Then all will swear and ratify the oath. *I will suffer no man, be he husband or lover,*

CALONICE.   *I will suffer no man, be he husband or lover,*

LYSISTRATA.   *To approach me all hot and horny.* [*As* CALONICE *hesitates.*] Say it!

CALONICE [*slowly and painfully*].   *To approach me all hot and horny.* O Lysistrata, I feel so weak in the knees!

LYSISTRATA.   *I will remain at home unmated,*

CALONICE.   *I will remain at home unmated,*

LYSISTRATA.   *Wearing my sheerest gown and carefully adorned,*

CALONICE.   *Wearing my sheerest gown and carefully adorned,*

LYSISTRATA.   *That my husband may burn with desire for me.*

CALONICE.   *That my husband may burn with desire for me.*

LYSISTRATA.   *And if he takes me by force against my will,*

CALONICE.   *And if he takes me by force against my will,*

LYSISTRATA.   *I shall do it badly and keep from moving.*

CALONICE.   *I shall do it badly and keep from moving.*

LYSISTRATA.   *I will not stretch my slippers toward the ceiling,*

CALONICE.   *I will not stretch my slippers toward the ceiling,*

LYSISTRATA.   *Nor will I take the posture of the lioness on the knifehandle.*

CALONICE.   *Nor will I take the posture of the lioness on the knifehandle.*

LYSISTRATA.   *If I keep this oath, may I be permitted to drink from this cup,*

CALONICE.   *If I keep this oath, may I be permitted to drink from this cup,*

LYSISTRATA.   *But if I break it, may the cup be filled with water.*

CALONICE.   *But if I break it, may the cup be filled with water.*

LYSISTRATA.   Do you all swear to this?

ALL.   I do, so help me!

LYSISTRATA.   Come then, I'll just consummate this offering. [*She takes a long drink from the cup.*]

CALONICE [*snatching the cup away*].   Shares, my dear! Let's drink to our continued friendship.

[*A shout is heard from off stage.*]

LAMPITO.   What's that shouting?

LYSISTRATA.   That's what I was telling you: the women have just seized the Acropolis. Now, Lampito, go home and arrange matters in Sparta; and leave these two ladies here as hostages. We'll enter the Acropolis to join our friends and help them lock the gates.

CALONICE.   Don't you suppose the men will come to attack us?

LYSISTRATA.   Don't worry about them. Neither threats nor fire will suffice to open the gates, except on the terms we've stated.

CALONICE.   I should say not! Else we'd belie our reputation as unmanageable pests.

[LAMPITO *leaves the stage. The other women retire and enter the Acropolis through the Propylaea. Enter the* CHORUS OF OLD MEN, *carrying fire-pots and a load of heavy sticks.*]

LEADER OF MEN.   Onward, Draces, step by step, though your shoulder's aching.

Cursèd logs of olive-wood, what a load you're making!

FIRST SEMICHORUS OF OLD MEN [*singing*].

Aye, many surprises await a man who lives to a ripe old age;

For who could suppose, Strymodorus my lad, that the women we've nourished (alas!),

> Who sat at home to vex our days,
> Would seize the holy image here,
> And occupy this sacred shrine,
> With bolts and bars, with fell design,
> To lock the Propylaea?

LEADER.   Come with speed, Philourgus, come! to the temple hast'ning.

There we'll heap these logs about in a circle round them,

And whoever has conspired, raising this rebellion,

Shall be roasted, scorched, and burnt, all without exception,

Doomed by one unanimous vote—but first the wife of Lycon.

SECOND SEMICHORUS [*singing*].

No, no! by Demeter, while I'm alive, no woman shall mock at me.

Not even the Spartan Cleomenes,[4] our citadel first to seize,

> Got off unscathed; for all his pride
> And haughty Spartan arrogance,
> He left his arms and sneaked away,
> Stripped to his shirt, unkempt, unshav'd,
> With six years' filth still on him.

---

[4] King Cleomenes I of Sparta had briefly occupied Athens, in 508 B.C., in order to assist the aristocratic party of that city.

LEADER.   I besieged that hero bold, sleeping at my station,
   Marshaled at these holy gates sixteen deep against him.
   Shall I not these cursèd pests punish for their daring,
   Burning these Euripides-and-God-detested women?
   Aye! or else may Marathon overturn my trophy.[5]

FIRST SEMICHORUS [*singing*].
      There remains of my road
      Just this brow of the hill;
      There I speed on my way.
   Drag the logs up the hill, though we've got no ass to help.
      (God! my shoulder's bruised and sore!)
      Onward still must we go.
      Blow the fire! Don't let it go out
      Now we're near the end of our road.

ALL [*blowing on the fire-pots*].
   Whew! Whew! Drat the smoke!

SECOND SEMICHORUS [*singing*].
      Lord, what smoke rushing forth
      From the pot, like a dog
      Running mad, bites my eyes!
   This must be Lemnos-fire. What a sharp and stinging smoke!
      Rushing onward to the shrine
      Aid the gods. Once for all
      Show your mettle, Laches my boy!
      To the rescue hastening all!

ALL [*blowing on the fire-pots*].
   Whew! Whew! Drat the smoke!
   [*The chorus has now reached the edge of the orchestra nearest the stage,
   in front of the Propylaea. They begin laying their logs and fire-pots on
   the ground.*]

LEADER. Thank heaven, this fire is still alive. Now let's first put
   down these logs here and place our torches in the pots to catch;
   then let's make a rush for the gates with a battering ram. If the
   women don't unbar the gate at our summons, we'll have to
   smoke them out.
       Let me put down my load. Ouch! That hurts! [*To the audi-
   ence.*] Would any of the generals in Samos like to lend a hand with
   this log! [*Throwing down a log.*] Well, *that* won't break my back
   any more, at any rate. [*Turning to his fire-pot.*] Your job, my little

---

[5] The speaker implies that he had won a trophy at the battle of Marathon.

pot, is to keep those coals alive and furnish me shortly with a red-hot torch.

O mistress Victory, be my ally and grant me to rout these audacious women in the Acropolis.

[*While the men are busy with their logs and fires, the* CHORUS OF OLD WOMEN *enters, carrying pitchers of water.*]

LEADER OF WOMEN.   What's this I see? Smoke and flames? Is that a fire ablazing?

Let's rush upon them. Hurry up! They'll find us women ready.

FIRST SEMICHORUS OF OLD WOMEN [*singing*].

   With wingèd foot onward I fly,
   Ere the flames consume Neodice;
   Lest Critylla be overwhelmed
  By a lawless, accurst herd of old men.
  I shudder with fear. Am I too late to aid them?
  At break of the day filled we our jars with water
Fresh from the spring, pushing our way straight through the crowds. Oh, what a din!

  Mid crockery crashing, jostled by slave-girls,
  Sped we to save them, aiding our neighbors,
  Bearing this water to put out the flames.

SECOND SEMICHORUS OF OLD WOMEN [*singing*].

   Such news I've heard: doddering fools
   Come with logs, like furnace-attendants,
   Loaded down with three hundred pounds,
  Breathing many a vain, blustering threat,
  That all these abhorred sluts will be burnt to charcoal.
  O goddess, I pray never may they be kindled;
Grant them to save Greece and our men; madness and war help them to end.

  With this as our purpose, golden-plumed Maiden,
  Guardian of Athens, seized we thy precinct.
  Be my ally, Warrior-maiden,
  'Gainst these old men, bearing water with me.

[*The women have now reached their position in the orchestra, and their* LEADER *advances toward the* LEADER OF THE MEN.]

LEADER OF WOMEN.   Hold on there! What's this, you utter scoundrels? No decent, God-fearing citizens would act like this.

LEADER OF MEN.   Oho! Here's something unexpected: a swarm of women have come out to attack us.

LEADER OF WOMEN.   What, do we frighten you? Surely you don't

think we're too many for you. And yet there are ten thousand
times more of us whom you haven't even seen.

LEADER OF MEN.   What say, Phaedria? Shall we let these women wag
their tongues? Shan't we take our sticks and break them over
their backs?

LEADER OF WOMEN.   Let's set our pitchers on the ground; then if
anyone lays a hand on us, they won't get in our way.

LEADER OF MEN.   By God! If someone gave them two or three
smacks on the jaw, like Bupalus, they wouldn't talk so much!

LEADER OF WOMEN.   Go on, hit me, somebody! Here's my jaw! But
no other bitch will bite a piece out of you before me.

LEADER OF MEN.   Silence! or I'll knock out your—senility!

LEADER OF WOMEN.   Just lay one finger on Stratyllis, I dare you!

LEADER OF MEN.   Suppose I dust you off with this fist? What will
you do?

LEADER OF WOMEN.   I'll tear the living guts out of you with my
teeth.

LEADER OF MEN.   No poet is more clever than Euripides: "There is
no beast so shameless as a woman."

LEADER OF WOMEN.   Let's pick up our jars of water, Rhodippe.

LEADER OF MEN.   Why have you come here with water, you detesta-
ble slut?

LEADER OF WOMEN.   And why have you come with fire, you funeral
vault? To cremate yourself?

LEADER OF MEN.   To light a fire and singe your friends.

LEADER OF WOMEN.   And I've brought water to put out your fire.

LEADER OF MEN.   What? You'll put out my fire?

LEADER OF WOMEN.   Just try and see!

LEADER OF MEN.   I wonder: shall I scorch you with this torch of
mine?

LEADER OF WOMEN.   If you've got any soap, I'll give you a bath.

LEADER OF MEN.   Give *me* a bath, you stinking hag?

LEADER OF WOMEN.   Yes—a bridal bath!

LEADER OF MEN.   Just listen to her! What crust!

LEADER OF WOMEN.   Well, I'm a free citizen.

LEADER OF MEN.   I'll put an end to your bawling. [*The men pick up
their torches.*]

LEADER OF WOMEN.   You'll never do jury duty[6] again. [*The women
pick up their pitchers.*]

[6] That is, his pay will stop. War refugees were often destitute except for the fees they
earned by serving as jurors.

LEADER OF MEN.   Singe her hair for her!

LEADER OF WOMEN.   Do your duty, water! [*The women empty their pitchers on the men.*]

LEADER OF MEN.   Ow! Ow! For heaven's sake!

LEADER OF WOMEN.   Is it too hot?

LEADER OF MEN.   What do you mean "hot"? Stop? What are you doing?

LEADER OF WOMEN.   I'm watering you, so you'll be fresh and green.

LEADER OF MEN.   But I'm all withered up with shaking.

LEADER OF WOMEN.   Well, you've got a fire; why don't you dry yourself?

[*Enter an Athenian* MAGISTRATE, *accompanied by four Scythian policemen.*][7]

MAGISTRATE.   Have these wanton women flared up again with their timbrels and their continual worship of Sabazius? Is this another Adonis dirge[8] upon the rooftops—which we heard not long ago in the Assembly? That confounded Demostratus was urging us to sail to Sicily, and the whirling women shouted, "Woe for Adonis!" And then Demostratus said we'd best enroll the infantry from Zacynthus, and a tipsy woman on the roof shrieked, "Beat your breasts for Adonis!" And that vile and filthy lunatic forced his measure through. Such license do our women take.

LEADER OF MEN.   What if you heard of the insolence of these women here? Besides their other violent acts, they threw water all over us, and we have to shake out our clothes just as if we'd leaked in them.

MAGISTRATE.   And rightly, too, by God! For we ourselves lead the women astray and teach them to play the wanton; from these roots such notions blossom forth. A man goes into the jeweler's shop and says, "About that necklace you made for my wife, goldsmith: last night, while she was dancing, the fastening-bolt slipped out of the hole. I have to sail over to Salamis today; if you're free, do come around tonight and fit in a new bolt for her." Another goes to the shoemaker, a strapping young fellow with manly parts, and says, "See here, cobbler, the sandal-strap chafes my wife's little—toe; it's so tender. Come around during

---

[7] The police of Athens, the "Archers," were drawn from the steppes of Scythia (the modern Ukraine).

[8] The dirge here was a lament for the loss of Adonis, a Nature demigod, who in winter descended to the abode of the dead.

the siesta and stretch it a little, so she'll be more comfortable." Now we see the results of such treatment: here I'm a special Councillor and need money to procure oars for the galleys; and I'm locked out of the Treasury by these women.

But this is no time to stand around. Bring up crow-bars there! I'll put an end to their insolence. [*To one of the policemen.*] What are you gaping at, you wretch? What are you staring at? Got an eye out for a tavern, eh? Set your crow-bars here to the gates and force them open. [*Retiring to a safe distance.*] I'll help from over here.

[*The gates are thrown open and* LYSISTRATA *comes out followed by several other women.*]

LYSISTRATA.   Don't force the gates; I'm coming out of my own accord. We don't need crow-bars here; what we need is good sound common-sense.

MAGISTRATE.   Is that so, you strumpet? Where's my policeman? Officer, arrest her and tie her arms behind her back.

LYSISTRATA.   By Artemis, if he lays a finger on me, he'll pay for it, even if he is a public servant.

[*The policeman retires in terror.*]

MAGISTRATE.   You there, are you afraid? Seize her round the waist—and you, too. Tie her up, both of you!

FIRST WOMAN [*as the second policeman approaches* LYSISTRATA].   By Pandrosus, if you but touch her with your hand, I'll kick the stuffings out of you.

[*The second policeman retires in terror.*]

MAGISTRATE.   Just listen to that: "kick the stuffings out." Where's another policeman? Tie *her* up first, for her chatter.

SECOND WOMAN.   By the Goddess of the Light, if you lay the tip of your finger on her, you'll soon need a doctor.

[*The third policeman retires in terror.*]

MAGISTRATE.   What's this? Where's my policeman? Seize *her* too. I'll soon stop your sallies.

THIRD WOMAN.   By the Goddess of Tauros, if you go near her, I'll tear out your hair until it shrieks with pain.

[*The fourth policeman retires in terror.*]

MAGISTRATE.   Oh, damn it all! I've run out of policemen. But women must never defeat us. Officers, let's charge them all together. Close up your ranks!

[*The policemen rally for a mass attack.*]

LYSISTRATA.   By heaven, you'll soon find out that we have four companies of warrior-women, all fully equipped within!

MAGISTRATE [*advancing*].   Twist their arms off, men!

LYSISTRATA [*shouting*].   To the rescue, my valiant women!

O sellers-of-barley-green-stuffs-and-eggs,

O sellers-of-garlic, ye keepers-of-taverns, and vendors-of-bread,
    Grapple! Smite! Smash!

Won't you heap filth on them? Give them a tongue-lashing!

[*The women beat off the policemen.*]

Halt! Withdraw! No looting on the field.

MAGISTRATE.   Damn it! My police force has put up a very poor show.

LYSISTRATA.   What did you expect? Did you think you were attacking slaves? Didn't you know that women are filled with passion?

MAGISTRATE.   Aye, passion enough—for a good strong drink!

LEADER OF MEN.   O chief and leader of this land, why spend your words in vain?

Don't argue with these shameless beasts. You know not how we've fared:

A soapless bath they've given us; our clothes are soundly soaked.

LEADER OF WOMEN.   Poor fool! You never should attack or strike a peaceful girl.

But if you do, your eyes must swell. For I am quite content

To sit unmoved, like modest maids, in peace and cause no pain;

But let a man stir up my hive, he'll find me like a wasp.

CHORUS OF MEN [*singing*].

O God, whatever shall we do with creatures like Womankind?

This can't be endured by any man alive. Question them!

    Let us try to find out what this means.

    To what end have they seized on this shrine,

        This steep and rugged, high and holy,

          Undefiled Acropolis?

LEADER OF MEN.   Come, put your questions; don't give in, and probe her every statement.

For base and shameful it would be to leave this plot untested.

MAGISTRATE.   Well then, first of all I wish to ask her this: for what purpose have you barred us from the Acropolis?

LYSISTRATA.   To keep the treasure safe, so you won't make war on account of it.

MAGISTRATE. What? Do we make war on account of the treasure?

LYSISTRATA. Yes, and you cause all our other troubles for it, too. Peisander and those greedy office-seekers keep things stirred up so they can find occasions to steal. Now let them do what they like: they'll never again make off with any of this money.

MAGISTRATE. What will you do?

LYSISTRATA. What a question! We'll administer it ourselves.

MAGISTRATE. *You* will administer the treasure?

LYSISTRATA. What's so strange in that? Don't we administer the household money for you?

MAGISTRATE. That's different.

LYSISTRATA. How is it different?

MAGISTRATE. We've got to make war with this money.

LYSISTRATA. But that's the very first thing: you mustn't make war.

MAGISTRATE. How else can we be saved?

LYSISTRATA. We'll save you.

MAGISTRATE. *You?*

LYSISTRATA. Yes, we!

MAGISTRATE. God forbid!

LYSISTRATA. We'll save you, whether you want it or not.

MAGISTRATE. Oh! This is terrible!

LYSISTRATA. You don't like it, but we're going to do it none the less.

MAGISTRATE. Good God! it's illegal!

LYSISTRATA. We *will* save you, my little man!

MAGISTRATE. Suppose I don't want you to?

LYSISTRATA. That's all the more reason.

MAGISTRATE. What business have you with war and peace?

LYSISTRATA. I'll explain.

MAGISTRATE [*shaking his fist*]. Speak up, or you'll smart for it.

LYSISTRATA. Just listen, and try to keep your hands still.

MAGISTRATE. I can't. I'm so mad I can't stop them.

FIRST WOMAN. Then you'll be the one to smart for it.

MAGISTRATE. Croak to yourself, old hag! [*To* LYSISTRATA.] Now then, speak up.

LYSISTRATA. Very well. Formerly we endured the war for a good long time with our usual restraint, no matter what you men did. You wouldn't let us say "boo," although nothing you did suited us. But we watched you well, and though we stayed at home we'd often hear of some terribly stupid measure you'd proposed. Then, though grieving at heart, we'd smile sweetly and say, "What was passed in the Assembly today about writing on the treaty-stone?"[9] "What's that to you?" my husband would say. "Hold your tongue!" And I held my tongue.

FIRST WOMAN.   But I wouldn't have—not I!

MAGISTRATE.   You'd have been soundly smacked, if you hadn't kept still.

LYSISTRATA.   So I kept still at home. Then we'd hear of some plan still worse than the first; we'd say, "Husband, how could you pass such a stupid proposal?" He'd scowl at me and say, "If you don't mind your spinning, your head will be sore for weeks. *War shall be the concern of Men.*"

MAGISTRATE.   And he was right, upon my word!

LYSISTRATA.   Why right, you confounded fool, when your proposals were so stupid and we weren't allowed to make suggestions?

"There's not a *man* left in the country," says one. "No, not one," says another. Therefore all we women have decided in council to make a common effort to save Greece. How long should we have waited? Now, if you're willing to listen to our excellent proposals and keep silence for us in your turn, we still may save you.

MAGISTRATE.   We men keep silence for you? That's terrible; I won't endure it!

LYSISTRATA.   Silence!

MAGISTRATE.   Silence for *you,* you wench, when you're wearing a snood? I'd rather die!

LYSISTRATA.   Well, if that's all that bothers you—here! Take my snood and tie it round your head. [*During the following words the women dress up the* MAGISTRATE *in women's garments.*] And *now* keep quiet! Here, take this spinning-basket, too, and card your wool with robes tucked up, munching on beans. *War shall be the concern of Women!*

LEADER OF WOMEN.   Arise and leave your pitchers, girls; no time is this to falter.

We too must aid our loyal friends; our turn has come for action.

---

[9] Treaties were engraved on stone tablets, which were placed where they might be seen by the people.

CHORUS OF WOMEN [*singing*].

I'll never tire of aiding them with song and dance; never may
Faintness keep my legs from moving to and fro endlessly.
For I yearn to do all for my friends;
They have charm, they have wit, they have grace,
With courage, brains and best of virtues—
Patriotic sapience.

LEADER OF WOMEN.   Come, child of manliest ancient dames, offspring of stinging nettles,
Advance with rage unsoftened; for fair breezes speed you onward.

LYSISTRATA.   If only sweet Eros and the Cyprian Queen of Love
shed charm over our breasts and limbs and inspire our men with
amorous longing and priapic spasms, I think we may soon be
called Peacemakers among the Greeks.

MAGISTRATE.   What will you do?

LYSISTRATA.   First of all, we'll stop those fellows who run madly
about the Marketplace in arms.

FIRST WOMAN.   Indeed we shall, by the Queen of Paphos.[10]

LYSISTRATA.   For now they roam about the market, amid the pots
and greenstuffs, armed to the teeth like Corybantes.

MAGISTRATE.   That's what manly fellows ought to do!

LYSISTRATA.   But it's so silly: a chap with a Gorgon-emblazoned
shield buying pickled herring.

FIRST WOMAN.   Why, just the other day I saw one of those long-
haired dandies who command our cavalry ride up on horseback
and pour into his bronze helmet the egg-broth he'd bought from
an old dame. And there was a Thracian slinger too, shaking his
lance like Tereus; he'd scared the life out of the poor fig-peddler
and was gulping down all her ripest fruit.

MAGISTRATE.   How can you stop all the confusion in the various
states and bring them together?

LYSISTRATA.   Very easily.

MAGISTRATE.   Tell me how.

LYSISTRATA.   Just like a ball of wool, when it's confused and snarled:
we take it thus, and draw out a thread here and a thread there
with our spindles; thus we'll unsnarl this war, if no one prevents

---

[10] Aphrodite, the goddess of love. The island of Cyprus and its city Paphos were
sacred to her.

us, and draw together the various states with embassies here and
embassies there.

MAGISTRATE. Do you suppose you can stop this dreadful business
with balls of wool and spindles, you nit-wits?

LYSISTRATA. Why, if *you* had any wits, you'd manage all affairs of
state like our wool-working.

MAGISTRATE. How so?

LYSISTRATA. First you ought to treat the city as we do when we
wash the dirt out of a fleece: stretch it out and pluck and thrash
out of the city all those prickly scoundrels; aye, and card out
those who conspire and stick together to gain office, pulling off
their heads. Then card the wool, all of it, into one fair basket of
goodwill, mingling in the aliens residing here, any loyal foreigners, and anyone who's in debt to the Treasury; and consider
that all our colonies lie scattered round about like remnants;
from all of these collect the wool and gather it together here,
wind up a great ball, and then weave a good stout cloak for the
democracy.

MAGISTRATE. Dreadful! Talking about thrashing and winding balls
of wool, when you haven't the slightest share in the war!

LYSISTRATA. Why, you dirty scoundrel, we bear more than twice as
much as you. First, we bear children and send off our sons as
soldiers.

MAGISTRATE. Hush! Let bygones be bygones!

LYSISTRATA. Then, when we ought to be happy and enjoy our
youth, we sleep alone because of your expeditions abroad. But
never mind us married women: I grieve most for the maids who
grow old at home unwed.

MAGISTRATE. Don't men grow old, too?

LYSISTRATA. For heaven's sake! That's not the same thing. When a
man comes home, no matter how gray he is, he soon finds a girl
to marry. But woman's bloom is short and fleeting; if she
doesn't grasp her chance, no man is willing to marry her and she
sits at home a prey to every fortune-teller.

MAGISTRATE [*coarsely*]. But if a man can still get it up—

LYSISTRATA. See here, you: what's the matter? Aren't you dead yet?
There's plenty of room for you. Buy yourself a shroud and I'll
bake you a honey-cake. [*Handing him a copper coin for his passage
across the Styx.*] Here's your fare! Now get yourself a wreath.
[*During the following dialogue the women dress up the* MAGISTRATE *as
a corpse.*]

FIRST WOMAN.   Here, take these fillets.

SECOND WOMAN.   Here, take this wreath.

LYSISTRATA.   What do you want? What's lacking? Get moving; off to the ferry! Charon is calling you; don't keep him from sailing.

MAGISTRATE.   Am I to endure these insults? By God! I'm going straight to the magistrates to show them how I've been treated.

LYSISTRATA.   Are you grumbling that you haven't been properly laid out? Well, the day after tomorrow we'll send around all the usual offerings early in the morning.

[*The* MAGISTRATE *goes out still wearing his funeral decorations.* LYSISTRATA *and the women retire into the Acropolis.*]

LEADER OF MEN.   Wake, ye sons of freedom, wake! 'Tis no time for sleeping.

Up and at them, like a man! Let us strip for action.

[*The* CHORUS OF MEN *remove their outer cloaks.*]

CHORUS OF MEN [*singing*].

Surely there is something here greater than meets the eye;
For without a doubt I smell Hippias'[11] tyranny.
Dreadful fear assails me lest certain bands of Spartan men,
Meeting here with Cleisthenes,[12] have inspired through treachery
All these god-detested women secretly to seize
Athens' treasure in the temple, and to stop that pay
  Whence I live at my ease.

LEADER OF MEN.   Now isn't it terrible for them to advise the state and chatter about shields, being mere women?

And they think to reconcile us with the Spartans—men who hold nothing sacred any more than hungry wolves. Surely this is a web of deceit, my friends, to conceal an attempt at tyranny. But they'll never lord it over me; I'll be on my guard and from now on,

  "The blade I bear   A myrtle spray shall wear."

I'll occupy the market under arms and stand next to Aristogeiton.[13]

  Thus I'll stand beside him. [*He strikes the pose of the famous*

---

[11] Hippias was a tyrant, or illegitimate ruler, of Athens in the sixth century B.C.

[12] A notorious homosexual who was believed, in consequence, to be pro-Sparta (homosexuality was reportedly condoned there).

[13] Harmodius and Aristogeiton attempted to end the tyranny of Hippias and his brother Hipparchus in 514 B.C.

statue of the tyrannicides, with one arm raised.] And here's my chance to take this accurst old hag and—[*striking the* LEADER OF WOMEN] smack her on the jaw!

LEADER OF WOMEN.   You'll go home in such a state your Ma won't recognize you!

Ladies all, upon the ground let us place these garments.

[*The* CHORUS OF WOMEN *remove their outer garments.*]

CHORUS OF WOMEN [*singing*].

Citizens of Athens, hear useful words for the state.
Rightly; for it nurtured me in my youth royally.
As a child of seven years carried I the sacred box;
Then I was a Miller-maid, grinding at Athene's shrine;
Next I wore the saffron robe and played Brauronia's Bear;
And I walked as Basket-bearer, wearing chains of figs,
     As a sweet maiden fair.

LEADER OF WOMEN.   Therefore, am I not bound to give good advice to the city?

Don't take it ill that I was born a woman, if I contribute something better than our present troubles. I pay my share; for I contribute MEN. But you miserable old fools contribute nothing, and after squandering our ancestral treasure, the fruit of the Persian Wars, you make no contribution in return. And now, all on account of you, we're facing ruin.

What, muttering, are you? If you annoy me, I'll take this hard, rough slipper and—[*striking the* LEADER OF MEN] smack you on the jaw!

CHORUS OF MEN [*singing*].

This is outright insolence! Things go from bad to worse.
If you're men with any guts, prepare to meet the foe.
Let us strip our tunics off! We need the smell of male
Vigor. And we cannot fight all swaddled up in clothes.
[*They strip off their tunics.*]
Come then, my comrades, on to the battle, ye who once to
     Leipsydrion came;
Then ye were MEN. Now call back your youthful vigor.
          With light, wingèd footstep advance,
     Shaking old age from your frame.

LEADER OF MEN. If any of us give these wenches the slightest hold, they'll stop at nothing: such is their cunning.

They will even build ships and sail against us, like Artemisia.[14] Or if they turn to mounting, I count our Knights as done for: a woman's such a tricky jockey when she gets astraddle, with a good firm seat for trotting. Just look at those Amazons[15] that Micon painted, fighting on horseback against men!

But we must throw them all in the pillory—[*seizing and choking the* LEADER OF WOMEN] grabbing hold of yonder neck!

CHORUS OF WOMEN [*singing*].
'Ware my anger! Like a boar 'twill rush upon you men.
Soon you'll bawl aloud for help, you'll be so soundly trimmed!
Come, my friends, let's strip with speed, and lay aside these
    robes;
Catch the scent of women's rage. Attack with tooth and nail!
[*They strip off their tunics.*]
Now then, come near me, you miserable man! You'll never eat
    garlic or black beans again.
And if you utter a single hard word, in rage I will "nurse" you
    as once
        The beetle requited her foe.
LEADER OF WOMEN.   For you don't worry me; no, not so long as my
    Lampito lives and our Theban friend, the noble Ismenia.
    You can't do anything, not even if you pass a dozen—decrees!
You miserable fool, all our neighbors hate you. Why, just the
    other day when I was holding a festival for Hecate, I invited as
    playmate from our neighbors the Boeotians a charming,
    well-bred Copaic—eel. But they refused to send me one on
    account of your decrees.
    And you'll never stop passing decrees until I grab your foot
    and—[*tripping up the* LEADER OF MEN] toss you down and break
    your neck!
    [*Here an interval of five days is supposed to elapse.*
    LYSISTRATA *comes out from the Acropolis.*]
LEADER OF WOMEN [*dramatically*].   Empress of this great emprise and
    undertaking,
        Why come you forth, I pray, with frowning brow?

---

[14] A queen of Halicarnassus, in Asia Minor; she joined the Persians against the Greeks
and fought beside them in the sea-battle of Salamis, near Athens, in 480 B.C.
[15] Female warriors said to have invaded Athens in the thirteenth century B.C.

LYSISTRATA.   Ah, these cursèd women! Their deeds and female notions make me pace up and down in utter despair.

LEADER OF WOMEN.   Ah, what sayest thou?

LYSISTRATA.   The truth, alas! the truth.

LEADER OF WOMEN.   What dreadful tale hast thou to tell thy friends?

LYSISTRATA.   'Tis shame to speak, and not to speak is hard.

LEADER OF WOMEN.   Hide not from me whatever woes we suffer.

LYSISTRATA.   Well then, to put it briefly, we want—laying!

LEADER OF WOMEN.   O Zeus, Zeus!

LYSISTRATA.   Why call on Zeus? That's the way things are. I can no longer keep them away from the men, and they're all deserting. I caught one wriggling through a hole near the grotto of Pan, another sliding down a rope, another deserting her post; and yesterday I found one getting on a sparrow's back to fly off to Orsilochus, and had to pull her back by the hair. They're digging up all sorts of excuses to get home. Look, here comes one of them now. [*A woman comes hastily out of the Acropolis.*] Here you! Where are you off to in such a hurry?

FIRST WOMAN.   I want to go home. My very best wool is being devoured by moths.

LYSISTRATA.   Moths? Nonsense! Go back inside.

FIRST WOMAN.   I'll come right back; I swear it. I just want to lay it out on the bed.

LYSISTRATA.   Well, you won't lay it out, and you won't go home, either.

FIRST WOMAN.   Shall I let my wool be ruined?

LYSISTRATA.   If necessary, yes.

[*Another woman comes out.*]

SECOND WOMAN.   Oh dear! Oh dear! My precious flax! I left it at home all unpeeled.

LYSISTRATA.   Here's another one, going home for her "flax." Come back here!

SECOND WOMAN.   But I just want to work it up a little and then I'll be right back.

LYSISTRATA.   No indeed! If you start this, all the other women will want to do the same.

[*A third woman comes out.*]

THIRD WOMAN.   O Eilithyia, goddess of travail, stop my labor till I come to a lawful spot![16]

---

[16] Childbirth was taboo on the Acropolis, it being holy ground.

LYSISTRATA.   What's this nonsense?

THIRD WOMAN.   I'm going to have a baby—right now!

LYSISTRATA.   But you weren't even pregnant yesterday.

THIRD WOMAN.   Well, I am today. O Lysistrata, do send me home to see a midwife, right away.

LYSISTRATA.   What are you talking about? [*Putting her hand on her stomach.*] What's this hard lump here?

THIRD WOMAN.   A little boy.

LYSISTRATA.   My goodness, what have you got there? It seems hollow; I'll just find out. [*Pulling aside her robe.*] Why, you silly goose, you've got Athene's sacred helmet there. And you said you were having a baby!

THIRD WOMAN.   Well, I *am* having one, I swear!

LYSISTRATA.   Then what's this helmet for?

THIRD WOMAN.   If the baby starts coming while I'm still in the Acropolis, I'll creep into this like a pigeon and give birth to it there.

LYSISTRATA.   Stuff and nonsense! It's plain enough what you're up to. You just wait here for the christening of this—helmet.

THIRD WOMAN.   But I can't sleep in the Acropolis since I saw the sacred snake.[17]

FIRST WOMAN.   And I'm dying for lack of sleep: the hooting of the owls keeps me awake.

LYSISTRATA.   Enough of these shams, you wretched creatures. You want your husbands, I suppose. Well, don't you think they want us? I'm sure they're spending miserable nights. Hold out, my friends, and endure for just a little while. There's an oracle that we shall conquer, if we don't split up. [*Producing a roll of paper.*] Here it is.

FIRST WOMAN.   Tell us what it says.

LYSISTRATA.   Listen.

"When in the length of time the Swallows shall gather together,

Fleeing the Hoopoe's amorous flight and the Cockatoo shunning,

Then shall your woes be ended and Zeus who thunders in heaven

Set what's below on top—"

FIRST WOMAN.   What? Are we going to be on top?

---

[17] The serpent was associated with the cult of Athene as guardian of the Acropolis.

LYSISTRATA. "But if the Swallows rebel and flutter away from the
　temple,
　Never a bird in the world shall seem more wanton and worth-
　less."

FIRST WOMAN. That's clear enough, upon my word!

LYSISTRATA. By all that's holy, let's not give up the struggle now.
　Let's go back inside. It would be a shame, my dear friends, to
　disobey the oracle.

　[*The women all retire to the Acropolis again.*]

CHORUS OF MEN [*singing*].

　　　　　I have a tale to tell,
　　　　　Which I know full well.
　　　　　　It was told me
　　　　　　In the nursery.

　　　　　Once there was a likely lad,
　　　　　　Melanion they name him;
　　　　　The thought of marriage made him mad,
　　　　　　For which I cannot blame him.

　　　　　So off he went to mountains fair;
　　　　　　(No women to upbraid him!)
　　　　　A mighty hunter of the hare,
　　　　　　He had a dog to aid him.

　　　　　He never came back home to see
　　　　　　Detested women's faces.
　　　　　He showed a shrewd mentality.
　　　　　　With him I'd fain change places!

ONE OF THE MEN [*to one of the women*].
　　　　　Come here, old dame; give me a kiss.

WOMAN. You'll ne'er eat garlic, if you dare!

MAN. I want to kick you—just like this!

WOMAN. Oh, there's a leg with bushy hair!

MAN. Myronides and Phormio
　　　　　Were hairy—and they thrashed the foe.

CHORUS OF WOMEN [*singing*].
　　　　　I have another tale,
　　　　　With which to assail

Your contention
'Bout Melanion.

Once upon a time a man
   Named Timon left our city,
To live in some deserted land.
   (We thought him rather witty.)

He dwelt alone amidst the thorn;
   In solitude he brooded.
From some grim Fury he was born:
   Such hatred he exuded.

He cursed you men, as scoundrels through
   And through, till life he ended.
He couldn't stand the sight of YOU
   But women he befriended.

WOMAN [*to one of the men*].   I'll smash your face in, if you like.
MAN.   Oh no, please don't! You frighten me.
WOMAN.   I'll lift my foot—and thus I'll strike.
MAN.   Aha! Look there! What's that I see?
WOMAN.   Whate'er you see, you cannot say
   That I'm not neatly trimmed today.

[LYSISTRATA *appears on the wall of the Acropolis.*]
LYSISTRATA.   Hello! Hello! Girls, come here quick!
   [*Several women appear beside her.*]
WOMAN.   What is it? Why are you calling?
LYSISTRATA.   I see a man coming: he's in a dreadful state. He's mad
   with passion. O Queen of Cyprus, Cythera, and Paphos, just
   keep on this way!
WOMAN.   Where is the fellow?
LYSISTRATA.   There, beside the shrine of Demeter.
WOMAN.   Oh yes, so he is. Who is he?
LYSISTRATA.   Let's see. Do any of you know him?
MYRRHINE.   Yes indeed. That's my husband, Cinesias.
LYSISTRATA.   It's up to you, now: roast him, rack him, fool him,
   love him—and leave him! Do everything, except what our oath
   forbids.
MYRRHINE.   Don't worry; I'll do it.

LYSISTRATA.   I'll stay here to tease him and warm him up a bit. Off with you.

[*The other women retire from the wall. Enter* CINESIAS *followed by a slave carrying a baby.* CINESIAS *is obviously in great pain and distress.*]

CINESIAS [*groaning*].   Oh-h! Oh-h-h! This is killing me! O God, what tortures I'm suffering!

LYSISTRATA [*from the wall*].   Who's that within our lines?

CINESIAS.   Me.

LYSISTRATA.   *A man?*

CINESIAS [*pointing*].   A *man,* indeed!

LYSISTRATA.   Well, go away!

CINESIAS.   Who are you to send me away?

LYSISTRATA.   The captain of the guard.

CINESIAS.   Oh, for heaven's sake, call out Myrrhine for me.

LYSISTRATA.   Call Myrrhine? Nonsense! Who are you?

CINESIAS.   Her husband, Cinesias of Paionidai.

LYSISTRATA [*appearing much impressed*].   Oh, greetings, friend. Your name is not without honor here among us. Your wife is always talking about you, and whenever she takes an egg or an apple, she says, "Here's to my dear Cinesias!"

CINESIAS [*quivering with excitement*].   Oh, ye gods in heaven!

LYSISTRATA.   Indeed she does! And whenever our conversations turn to men, your wife immediately says, "All others are mere rubbish compared with Cinesias."

CINESIAS [*groaning*].   Oh! Do call her for me.

LYSISTRATA.   Why should I? What will you give me?

CINESIAS.   Whatever you want. All I have is yours—and you see what I've got!

LYSISTRATA.   Well then, I'll go down and call her. [*She descends.*]

CINESIAS.   And hurry up! I've had no joy of life ever since she left home. When I go in the house, I feel awful: everything seems so empty and I can't enjoy my dinner. I'm in such a state all the time!

MYRRHINE [*from behind the wall*].   I *do* love him so. But he won't let me love him. No, no! Don't ask me to see him!

CINESIAS.   O my darling, O Myrrhine honey, why do you do this to me? [MYRRHINE *appears on the wall.*] Come down here!

MYRRHINE.   No, I won't come down.

CINESIAS.   Won't you come, Myrrhine, when *I* call you?

MYRRHINE.   No; you don't want me.

CINESIAS.   *Don't want you?* I'm in agony!

MYRRHINE.   I'm going now.

CINESIAS.   Please don't! At least, listen to your baby. [*To the baby.*] Here you, call your mamma! [*Pinching the baby.*]

BABY.   Ma-ma! Ma-ma! Ma-ma!

CINESIAS [*to* MYRRHINE].   What's the matter with you? Have you no pity for your child, who hasn't been washed or fed for five whole days?

MYRRHINE.   Oh, poor child; your father pays no attention to you.

CINESIAS.   Come down then, you heartless wretch, for the baby's sake.

MYRRHINE.   Oh, what it is to be a mother! I've got to come down, I suppose. [*She leaves the wall and shortly reappears at the gate.*]

CINESIAS [*to himself*].   She seems much younger, and she has such a sweet look about her. Oh, the way she teases me! And her pretty, provoking ways make me burn with longing.

MYRRHINE [*coming out of the gate and taking the baby*].   O my sweet little angel. Naughty papa! Here, let Mummy kiss you, Mamma's little sweetheart! [*She fondles the baby lovingly.*]

CINESIAS [*in despair*].   You heartless creature, why do you do this? Why follow these other women and make both of us suffer so? [*He tries to embrace her.*]

MYRRHINE.   Don't touch me!

CINESIAS.   You're letting all our things at home go to wrack and ruin.

MYRRHINE.   I don't care.

CINESIAS.   You don't care that your wool is being plucked to pieces by the chickens?

MYRRHINE.   Not in the least.

CINESIAS.   And you haven't celebrated the rites of Aphrodite for ever so long. Won't you come home?

MYRRHINE.   Not on your life, unless you men make a truce and stop the war.

CINESIAS.   Well then, if that pleases you, we'll do it.

MYRRHINE.   Well then, if that pleases *you,* I'll come home—afterwards! Right now I'm on oath not to.

CINESIAS.   Then just lie down here with me for a moment.

MYRRHINE.   No—[*in a teasing voice*] and yet, I won't say I don't love you.

CINESIAS.   You love me? Oh, do lie down here, Myrrhine dear!

MYRRHINE.   What, you silly fool in front of the baby?

CINESIAS [*hastily thrusting the baby at the slave*].   Of course not. Here—home! Take him, Manes! [*The slave goes off with the baby.*] See, the baby's out of the way. Now won't you lie down?

MYRRHINE.   But where, my dear?

CINESIAS.   Where? The grotto of Pan's a lovely spot.

MYRRHINE.   How could I purify myself before returning to the shrine?

CINESIAS.   Easily: just wash here in the Clepsydra.

MYRRHINE.   And then, shall I go back on my oath?

CINESIAS.   On my head be it! Don't worry about the oath.

MYRRHINE.   All right, then. Just let me bring out a bed.

CINESIAS.   No, don't. The ground's all right.

MYRRHINE.   Heavens, no! Bad as you are, I won't let you lie on the bare ground. [*She goes into the Acropolis.*]

CINESIAS.   Why, she really loves me; it's plain to see.

MYRRHINE [*returning with a bed*]   There! Now hurry up and lie down. I'll just slip off this dress. But—let's see; oh yes, I must fetch a mattress.

CINESIAS.   Nonsense! No mattress for me.

MYRRHINE.   Yes indeed! It's not nice on the bare springs.

CINESIAS.   Give me a kiss.

MYRRHINE [*giving him a hasty kiss*].   There! [*She goes.*]

CINESIAS [*in mingled distress and delight*].   Oh-h! Hurry back!

MYRRHINE [*returning with a mattress*].   Here's the mattress; lie down on it. I'm taking my things off now—but—let's see: you have no pillow.

CINESIAS.   I don't *want* a pillow!

MYRRHINE.   But I do. [*She goes.*]

CINESIAS.   Cheated again, just like Heracles and his dinner![18]

MYRRHINE [*returning with a pillow*].   Here, lift your head. [*To herself, wondering how else to tease him.*] Is that all?

CINESIAS.   Surely that's all! Do come here, precious!

MYRRHINE.   I'm taking off my girdle. But remember: don't go back on your promise about the truce.

CINESIAS.   Hope to die, if I do.

---

[18] Cinesias' appetite, like that of the hungry demigod Heracles, had not been appeased.

MYRRHINE.   You don't have a blanket.

CINESIAS [*shouting in exasperation*].   *I don't want one!* I WANT TO—

MYRRHINE.   Sh-h! There, there, I'll be back in a minute. [*She goes.*]

CINESIAS.   She'll be the death of me with these bedclothes.

MYRRHINE [*returning with a blanket*].   Here, get up.

CINESIAS.   I've got *this* up!

MYRRHINE.   Would you like some perfume?

CINESIAS.   Good heavens, no! I won't have it!

MYRRHINE.   Yes, you shall, whether you want it or not. [*She goes.*]

CINESIAS.   O lord! Confound all perfumes anyway!

MYRRHINE [*returning with a flask*].   Stretch out your hand and put some on.

CINESIAS [*suspiciously*].   By God, I don't much like this perfume. It smacks of shilly-shallying, and has no scent of the marriage-bed.

MYRRHINE.   Oh dear! This is Rhodian perfume I've brought.

CINESIAS.   It's quite all right, dear. Never mind.

MYRRHINE.   Don't be silly! [*She goes out with the flask.*]

CINESIAS.   Damn the man who first concocted perfumes!

MYRRHINE [*returning with another flask*].   Here, try this flask.

CINESIAS.   I've got another one all ready for you. Come, you wretch, lie down and stop bringing me things.

MYRRHINE.   All right; I'm taking off my shoes. But, my dear, see that you vote for peace.

CINESIAS [*absently*].   I'll consider it. [MYRRHINE *runs away to the Acropolis.*] I'm ruined! The wench has skinned me and run away! [*Chanting, in tragic style.*] Alas! Alas! Deceived, deserted by this fairest of women, whom shall I—lay? Ah, my poor little child, how shall I nurture thee? Where's Cynalopex?[19] I needs must hire a nurse!

LEADER OF MEN [*chanting*].   Ah, wretched man, in dreadful wise beguiled, betrayed, thy soul is sore distressed. I pity thee, alas! alas! What soul, what loins, what liver could stand this strain? How firm and unyielding he stands, with naught to aid him of a morning.

CINESIAS.   O lord! O Zeus! What tortures I endure!

LEADER OF MEN.   This is the way she's treated you, that vile and cursèd wanton.

LEADER OF WOMEN.   Nay, not vile and cursèd, but sweet and dear.

[19] A well-known pimp.

LEADER OF MEN.   Sweet, you say? Nay, hateful, hateful!

CINESIAS.   Hateful indeed! O Zeus, Zeus!

> Seize her and snatch her away,
> Like a handful of dust, in a mighty,
> Fiery tempest! Whirl her aloft, then let her drop
> Down to the earth, with a crash, as she falls—
> On the point of this waiting
>   Thingummybob!   [*He goes out.*]

[*Enter a Spartan* HERALD, *in an obvious state of excitement, which he is doing his best to conceal.*]

HERALD.   Where can I find the Senate or the Pyrtanes? I've got an important message. [*The Athenian* MAGISTRATE *enters.*]

MAGISTRATE.   Say there, are you a man or Priapus?[20]

HERALD [*in annoyance*].   I'm a herald, you lout! I've come from Sparta about the truce.

MAGISTRATE.   Is that a spear you've got under your cloak?

HERALD.   No, of course not!

MAGISTRATE.   Why do you twist and turn so? Why hold your cloak in front of you? Did you rupture yourself on the trip?

HERALD.   By gum, the fellow's an old fool.

MAGISTRATE [*pointing*].   Why, you dirty rascal, you're all excited.

HERALD.   Not at all. Stop this tom-foolery.

MAGISTRATE.   Well, what's that I see?

HERALD.   A Spartan message-staff.

MAGISTRATE.   Oh, certainly! That's just the kind of message-staff I've got. But tell me the honest truth: how are things going in Sparta?

HERALD.   All the land of Sparta is up in arms—and our allies are up, too. We need Pellene.

MAGISTRATE.   What brought this trouble on you? A sudden Panic?

HERALD.   No, Lampito started it and then all the other women in Sparta with one accord chased their husbands out of their beds.

MAGISTRATE.   How do you feel?

HERALD.   Terrible. We walk around the city bent over like men lighting matches in a wind. For our women won't let us touch them until we all agree and make peace throughout Greece.

MAGISTRATE.   This is a general conspiracy of the women; I see it now. Well, hurry back and tell the Spartans to send ambassadors

---

[20] An Asiatic fertility god represented by a large phallic symbol.

here with full powers to arrange a truce. And I'll go tell the Council to choose ambassadors from here; I've got a little something here that will soon persuade them!

HERALD.   I'll fly there; for you've made an excellent suggestion.

[*The* HERALD *and the* MAGISTRATE *depart on opposite sides of the stage.*]

LEADER OF MEN.   No beast or fire is harder than womankind to tame,

Nor is the spotted leopard so devoid of shame.

LEADER OF WOMEN.   Knowing this, you dare provoke us to attack?

I'd be your steady friend, if you'd but take us back.

LEADER OF MEN.   I'll never cease my hatred keen of womankind.

LEADER OF WOMEN.   Just as you will. But now just let me help you find

That cloak you threw aside. You look so silly there

Without your clothes. Here, put it on and don't go bare.

LEADER OF MEN.   That's very kind, and shows you're not entirely bad.

But I threw off my things when I was good and mad.

LEADER OF WOMEN.   At last you seem a man, and won't be mocked, my lad.

If you'd been nice to me, I'd take this little gnat

That's in your eye and pluck it out for you, like that.

LEADER OF MEN.   So that's what's bothered me and bit my eye so long!

Please dig it out for me. I own that I've been wrong.

LEADER OF WOMEN.   I'll do so, though you've been a most ill-natured brat.

Ye gods! See here! A huge and monstrous little gnat!

LEADER OF MEN.   Oh, how that helps! For it was digging wells in me.

And now it's out, my tears can roll down hard and free.

LEADER OF WOMEN.   Here, let me wipe them off, although you're such a knave,

And kiss me.

LEADER OF MEN.   No!

LEADER OF WOMEN.   Whate'er you say, a kiss I'll have.

[*She kisses him.*]

LEADER OF MEN.   Oh, confound these women! They've a coaxing way about them.

He was wise and never spoke a truer word, who said,
"We can't live with women, but we cannot live without them."
Now I'll make a truce with you. We'll fight no more; instead,
    I will not injure you if you do me no wrong.
    And now let's join our ranks and then begin a song.

COMBINED CHORUS [*singing*].
    Athenians, we're not prepared,
        To say a single ugly word
        About our fellow citizens.
Quite the contrary: we desire but to say and to do
Naught but good. Quite enough are the ills now on hand.

    Men and women, be advised:
        If anyone requires
    Money—minae two or three—
        We've got what he desires.

    My purse is yours, on easy terms:
        When Peace shall reappear,
    Whate'er you've borrowed will be due.
        So speak up without fear.

    You needn't pay me back, you see,
        If you can get a cent from me!

    We're about to entertain
        Some foreign gentlemen;
    We've soup and tender, fresh-killed pork.
        Come round to dine at ten.

    Come early; wash and dress with care,
        And bring the children, too.
    Then step right in, no "by your leave."
        We'll be expecting you.

    Walk in as if you owned the place.
    You'll find the door—shut in your face!

[*Enter a group of Spartan* AMBASSADORS; *they are in the same desperate condition as the* HERALD *in the previous scene.*]

LEADER OF CHORUS.   Here come the envoys from Sparta, sprouting
long beards and looking for all the world as if they were carrying pigpens in front of them.

Greetings, gentlemen of Sparta. Tell me, in what state have you come?

SPARTAN.   Why waste words? You can plainly see what state we've come in!

LEADER OF CHORUS.   Wow! You're in a pretty high-strung condition, and it seems to be getting worse.

SPARTAN.   It's indescribable. Won't someone please arrange a peace for us—in any way you like.

LEADER OF CHORUS.   Here come our own, native ambassadors, crouching like wrestlers and holding their clothes in front of them; this seems an athletic kind of malady.

[*Enter several Athenian* AMBASSADORS.]

ATHENIAN.   Can anyone tell us where Lysistrata is? You see our condition.

LEADER OF CHORUS.   Here's another case of the same complaint. Tell me, are the attacks worse in the morning?

ATHENIAN.   No, we're always afflicted this way. If someone doesn't soon arrange this truce, you'd better not let me get my hands on—Cleisthenes!

LEADER OF CHORUS.   If you're smart, you'll arrange your cloaks so none of the fellows who smashed the Hermae[21] can see you.

ATHENIAN.   Right you are; a very good suggestion.

SPARTAN.   Aye, by all means. Here, let's hitch up our clothes.

ATHENIAN.   Greetings, Spartan. We've suffered dreadful things.

SPARTAN.   My dear fellow, we'd have suffered still worse if one of those fellows had seen us in this condition.

ATHENIAN.   Well, gentlemen, we must get down to business. What's your errand here?

SPARTAN.   We're ambassadors about peace.

ATHENIAN.   Excellent; so are we. Only Lysistrata can arrange things for us; shall we summon her?

SPARTAN.   Aye, and Lysistratus too, if you like.

LEADER OF CHORUS.   No need to summon her, it seems. She's coming out of her own accord.

[*Enter* LYSISTRATA *accompanied by a statue of a nude female figure, which represents Reconciliation.*]

---

[21] Squared stone posts, with phallus, set up at Athenian doorways, each bearing the head of the god Hermes. Their mutilation one night in 415 B.C. caused dismay and has remained a mystery.

Hail, noblest of women; now must thou be
A judge shrewd and subtle, mild and severe,
Be sweet yet majestic: all manners employ.
The leaders of Hellas, caught by thy love-charms,
Have come to thy judgment, their charges submitting.

LYSISTRATA. This is no difficult task, if one catch them still in amorous passion, before they've resorted to each other. But I'll soon find out. Where's Reconciliation? Go, first bring the Spartans here, and don't seize them rudely and violently, as our tactless husbands used to do, but as befits a woman, like an old, familiar friend; if they won't give you their hands, take them however you can. Then go fetch these Athenians here, taking hold of whatever they offer you. Now then, men of Sparta, stand here beside me, and you Athenians on the other side, and listen to my words.

I am a woman, it is true, but I have a mind; I'm not badly off in native wit, and by listening to my father and my elders, I've had a decent schooling.

Now I intend to give you a scolding which you both deserve. With one common font you worship at the same altars, just like brothers, at Olympia, at Thermopylae, at Delphi—how many more might I name, if time permitted;—and the Barbarians stand by waiting with their armies; yet you are destroying the men and towns of Greece.

ATHENIAN. Oh, this tension is killing me!

LYSISTRATA. And now, men of Sparta—to turn to you—don't you remember how the Spartan Pericleidas came here once as a suppliant, and sitting at our altar, all pale with fear in his crimson cloak, begged us for an army? For all Messene[22] had attacked you and the god sent an earthquake too? Then Cimon went forth with four thousand hoplites and saved all Lacedaemon.[23] Such was the aid you received from Athens, and now you lay waste the country which once treated you so well.

ATHENIAN [hotly]. They're in the wrong, Lysistrata, upon my word, they are!

---

[22] The Messenians, once conquered and reduced to serfdom by the Spartans, rose in a rebellion.
[23] Another name for Sparta.

SPARTAN [*absently, looking at the statue of Reconciliation*].   We're in the wrong. What hips! How lovely they are!

LYSISTRATA.   Don't think I'm going to let you Athenians off. Don't you remember how the Spartans came in arms when you were wearing the rough, sheepskin cloak of slaves and slew the host of Thessalians, the comrades and allies of Hippias? Fighting with you on that day, alone of all the Greeks, they set you free and instead of a sheepskin gave your folk a handsome robe to wear.

SPARTAN [*looking at* LYSISTRATA].   I've never seen a more distinguished woman.

ATHENIAN [*looking at Reconciliation*].   I've never seen a more voluptuous body!

LYSISTRATA.   Why then, with these many noble deeds to think of, do you fight each other? Why don't you stop this villainy? Why not make peace? Tell me, what prevents it?

SPARTAN [*waving vaguely at Reconciliation*].   We're willing, if you're willing to give up your position on yonder flank.

LYSISTRATA.   What position, my good man?

SPARTAN.   Pylus; we've been panting for it for ever so long.

ATHENIAN.   No, by God! You shan't have it!

LYSISTRATA.   Let them have it, my friend.

ATHENIAN.   Then what shall we have to rouse things up?

LYSISTRATA.   Ask for another place in exchange.

ATHENIAN.   Well, let's see: first of all [*pointing to various parts of Reconciliation's anatomy*] give us Echinus here, this Maliac Inlet in back there, and these two Megarian legs.[24]

SPARTAN.   No, by heavens! You can't have *everything,* you crazy fool!

LYSISTRATA.   Let it go. Don't fight over a pair of legs.

ATHENIAN [*taking off his cloak*].   I think I'll strip and do a little planting now.

SPARTAN [*following suit*].   And I'll just do a little fertilizing, by gosh!

LYSISTRATA.   Wait until the truce is concluded. Now if you've decided on this course, hold a conference and discuss the matter with your allies.

ATHENIAN.   Allies? Don't be ridiculous! They're in the same state we

---

[24] In Greek the words in this phrase make obscene puns upon geographical names— puns that elude the comparable English terms.

are. Won't all our allies want the same thing we do—to jump in bed with their women?

SPARTAN.   Ours will, I know.

ATHENIAN.   Especially the Carystians, by God!

LYSISTRATA.   Very well. Now purify yourselves, that your wives may feast and entertain you in the Acropolis; we've provisions by the basketfull. Exchange your oaths and pledges there, and then each of you may take his wife and go home.

ATHENIAN.   Let's go at once.

SPARTAN.   Come on, where you will.

ATHENIAN.   For God's sake, let's hurry!

[*They all go into the Acropolis.*]

CHORUS [*singing*].
>   Whate'er I have of coverlets
>   And robes of varied hue
>   And golden trinklets—without stint
>   I offer them to you.
>
>   Take what you will and bear it home,
>   Your children to delight,
>   Or if your girl's a Basket-maid;
>   Just choose whate'er's in sight.
>
>   There's naught within so well secured
>   You cannot break the seal
>   And bear it off; just help yourselves;
>   No hesitation feel.
>
>   But you'll see nothing, though you try,
>   Unless you've sharper eyes than I!
>
>   If anyone needs bread to feed
>   A growing family,
>   I've lots of wheat and full-grown loaves;
>   So just apply to me.
>
>   Let every poor man who desires
>   Come round and bring a sack
>   To fetch the grain; my slave is there
>   To load it on his back.

But don't come near my door, I say:
Beware the dog, and stay away!

[*An* ATHENIAN *enters carrying a torch; he knocks at the gate.*]

ATHENIAN.   Open the door! [*To the* CHORUS, *which is clustered around the gate.*] Make way, won't you! What are you hanging around for? Want me to singe you with this torch? [*To himself.*] No; it's a stale trick, I won't do it! [*To the audience.*] Still, if I've got to do it to please *you,* I suppose I'll have to take the trouble.

[*A second* ATHENIAN *comes out of the gate.*]

SECOND ATHENIAN.   And I'll help you.

FIRST ATHENIAN [*waving his torch at the* CHORUS].   Get out! Go bawl your heads off! Move on there, so the Spartans can leave in peace when the banquet's over.

[*They brandish their torches until the* CHORUS *leaves the Orchestra.*]

SECOND ATHENIAN.   I've never seen such a pleasant banquet: the Spartans are charming fellows, indeed they are! And we Athenians are very witty in our cups.

FIRST ATHENIAN.   Naturally: for when we're sober we're never at our best. If the Athenians would listen to me, we'd always get a little tipsy on our embassies. As things are now, we go to Sparta when we're sober and look around to stir up trouble. And then we don't hear what they say—and as for what they *don't* say, we have all sort of suspicions. And then we bring back varying reports about the mission. But this time everything is pleasant; even if a man should sing the Telamon-song when he ought to sing "Cleitagoras," we'd praise him and swear it was excellent.

[*The two* CHORUSES *return, as a* CHORUS OF ATHENIANS *and a* CHORUS OF SPARTANS.]

Here they come back again. Go to the devil, you scoundrels!

SECOND ATHENIAN.   Get out, I say! They're coming out from the feast.

[*Enter the Spartan and Athenian envoys, followed by* LYSISTRATA *and all the women.*]

SPARTAN [*to one of his fellow envoys*].   My good fellow, take up your pipes; I want to do a fancy two-step and sing a jolly song for the Athenians.

ATHENIAN.   Yes, do take your pipes, by all means. I'd love to see you dance.

SPARTAN [*singing and dancing with the* CHORUS OF SPARTANS].
       These youths inspire

To song and dance, O Memory;
Stir up my Muse, to tell how we
And Athens' men, in your galleys clashing
At Artemisium,[25] 'gainst foemen dashing
          In godlike ire,
Conquered the Persian and set Greece free.

          Leonidas[26]
Led on his valiant warriors
Whetting their teeth like angry boars.
Abundant foam on their lips was flow'ring,
A stream of sweat from their limbs was show'ring.
          The Persian was
Numberless as the sand on the shores.

O Huntress[27] who slayest the beasts in the glade,
O Virgin divine, hither come to our truce,
Unite us in bonds which all time will not loose.
Grant us to find in this treaty, we pray,
An unfailing source of true friendship today,
And all of our days, helping us to refrain
From weaseling tricks which bring war in their train.
          Then hither, come hither! O huntress maid.

LYSISTRATA.   Come then, since all is fairly done, men of Sparta, lead
away your wives, and you, Athenians, take yours. Let every
man stand beside his wife, and every wife beside her man, and
then, to celebrate our fortune, let's dance. And in the future,
let's take care to avoid these misunderstandings.

CHORUS OF ATHENIANS [*singing and dancing*].
     Lead on the dances, your graces revealing.
     Call Artemis hither, call Artemis' twin,
     Leader of dances, Apollo the Healing,
     Kindly God—hither! let's summon him in!

          Nysian Bacchus call,
     Who with his Maenads, his eyes flashing fire,
          Dances, and last of all

----

[25] The northern cape of the large island of Euboea, scene of a sea battle between
Greeks and Persians in 480 B.C.
[26] A king of Sparta; he died in 480 B.C. in the battle to hold the pass at Thermopylae.
[27] Artemis, goddess of hunting and protector of women (twin sister of Apollo).

Zeus of the thunderbolt flaming, the Sire,
And Hera in majesty,
Queen of prosperity.

Come, ye Powers who dwell above
Unforgetting, our witnesses be
Or Peace with bonds of harmonious love—
The Peace which Cypris[28] has wrought for me.
Alleluia! Io Paean!
Leap in joy—hurrah! hurrah!
'Tis victory—hurrah! hurrah!
Euoi! Euoi! Euai! Euai!

LYSISTRATA [*to the Spartans*]. Come now, sing a new song to cap ours.

CHORUS OF SPARTANS [*singing and dancing*].
Leaving Taygetus fair and renown'd,
Muse of Laconia,[29] hither come:
Amyclae's god in hymns resound,
Athene of the Brazen Home,
And Castor and Pollux, Tyndareus' sons,
Who sport where Eurotas murmuring runs.
On with the dance! Heia! Ho!
All leaping along,
Mantles a-swinging as we go!
Of Sparta our song.
There the holy chorus ever gladdens,
There the beat of stamping feet,
As our winsome fillies, lovely maidens,
Dance, beside Eurotas' banks a-skipping,—
Nimbly go to and and fro
Hast'ning, leaping feet in measures tripping,
Like the Bacchae's revels, hair a-streaming.
Leda's child, divine and mild,
Leads the holy dance, her fair face beaming.
On with the dance! As your hand
Presses the hair

---

[28] Aphrodite.
[29] Area surrounding Sparta. All of the references following are to personages and places sacred to the Spartans.

Streaming away unconfined.
    Leap in the air
Light as the deer; footsteps resound
Aiding our dance, beating the ground.
Praise Athene, Maid divine, unrivaled in her might,
Dweller in the Brazen Home, unconquered in the fight.

[All go out singing and dancing.]

8

Plato

Phaedo

Ꝺ

Neither Socrates nor Jesus, the most famous and most beloved teachers of the ancient world, are known through their own writings. For our knowledge of both we must depend mainly upon the works of disciples, who saw them as beings without human parallel. In the case of Socrates, our primary source is Plato, in whose dialogues the Athenian sage is the foremost figure.

Socrates (ca. 470–399 B.C.) lived in an age that was, like our own, one of intellectual and moral unrest. In Athens the most venerable orthodoxies were being exposed to radical criticism and revaluation, especially by a group of teachers known as the Sophists. Socrates himself contributed to the shaking of popular beliefs by constantly questioning them with everyone he met; this challenging of tradition was largely responsible for his being brought to trial and put to death.

But his place in history does not derive from this negative influence. Socrates had no doubt at all that truth exists. Truth, he maintained, is in the possession of everyone, hidden under smug self-satisfaction and narrow dogmatism, and needs only to be liberated by the judicious examination and testing of opinion. This "Socratic method" was aimed at revealing the eternal principles of human conduct, upon which personal happiness and social stability depend. Socrates' mode of truth-seeking (dialectic) is illustrated in the following selection from Plato's Phaedo, *a dialogue that ranks among the masterworks of Western literature.*

In Phaedo, *Socrates spends the last hours before his execution in comforting his friends. Persisting in his outlook and method, he tells them that behind the immediate world of appearances lies the unseen eternal order. It is*

Plato, *Phaedo,* in *The Dialogues of Plato,* trans. Benjamin Jowett (Oxford: Clarendon Press, 1953), Steph. 1–5, 8–13, 25–28, 30–34, 65–66.

for this, the eternal world, that people should live; when freed through death, the souls of those who have lived wisely will at last rejoin the eternal world.

Centuries later this philosophy was to contribute mightily to the intellectual capital of Christianity. In addition, since he subjected everything to the test of reason and based morality upon human values, Socrates is regarded as a leading spirit in the rationalist and humanist tradition.

Persons of the Dialogue

PHAEDO, who is the narrator of the Dialogue to
ECHECRATES of Phlius
SOCRATES
ATTENDANT OF THE PRISON
APOLLODORUS
SIMMIAS
CEBES
CRITO

SCENE. *The Prison of Socrates*
PLACE OF THE NARRATION. *Phlius*

ECHECRATES. Were you yourself, Phaedo, in the prison with Socrates on the day when he drank the poison?

PHAEDO. Yes, Echecrates, I was.

ECHECRATES. I should so like to hear about his death. What did he say in his last hours? We were informed that he died by taking poison, but no one knew anything more; for no Phliasian ever goes to Athens now, and it is a long time since any stranger from Athens has found his way hither; so that we had no clear account.

PHAEDO. Did you not hear of the proceedings at the trial?

ECHECRATES. Yes; some one told us about the trial, and we could not understand why, having been condemned, he should have been put to death, not at the time, but long afterwards. What was the reason of this?

PHAEDO.   An accident, Echecrates: the stern of the ship which the Athenians send to Delos happened to have been crowned on the day before he was tried.

ECHECRATES.   What is this ship?

PHAEDO.   It is the ship in which, according to Athenian tradition, Theseus went to Crete when he took with him the fourteen youths, and was the saviour of them and of himself. And they are said to have vowed to Apollo at the time, that if they were saved they would send a yearly mission to Delos.[1] Now this custom still continues, and the whole period of the voyage to and from Delos, beginning when the priest of Apollo crowns the stern of the ship, is a holy season, during which the city is not allowed to be polluted by public executions; and when the vessel is detained by contrary winds, the time spent in going and returning is very considerable. As I was saying, the ship was crowned on the day before the trial, and this was the reason why Socrates lay in prison and was not put to death until long after he was condemned.

ECHECRATES.   What was the manner of his death, Phaedo? What was said or done? And which of his friends were with him? Or did the authorities forbid them to be present—so that he had no friends near him when he died?

PHAEDO.   No; there were several of them with him.

ECHECRATES.   If you have nothing to do, I wish that you would tell me what passed, as exactly as you can.

PHAEDO.   I have nothing at all to do, and will try to gratify your wish. To be reminded of Socrates is always the greatest delight to me, whether I speak myself or hear another speak of him.

ECHECRATES.   You will have listeners who are of the same mind with you, and I hope that you will be as exact as you can.

PHAEDO.   I had a singular feeling at being in his company. For I could hardly believe that I was present at the death of a friend, and therefore I did not pity him, Echecrates; he died so fearlessly, and his words and bearing were so noble and gracious, that to me he appeared blessed. I thought that in going to the other world he could not be without a divine call, and that he would be happy, if any man ever was, when he arrived there; and

---

[1] An island in the Aegean famous as the birthplace of Apollo (and Artemis). A shrine sacred to him had been erected there.

therefore I did not pity him as might have seemed natural at such an hour. But I had not the pleasure which I usually feel in philosophical discourse (for philosophy was the theme of which we spoke). I was pleased, but in the pleasure there was also a strange admixture of pain; for I reflected that he was soon to die, and this double feeling was shared by us all; we were laughing and weeping by turns, especially the excitable Apollodorus— you know the sort of man?

ECHECRATES. Yes.

PHAEDO. He was quite beside himself, and I and all of us were greatly moved.

ECHECRATES. Who were present?

PHAEDO. Of native Athenians there were, besides Apollodorus, Critobulus and his father Crito, Hermogenes, Epigenes, Aeschines, Antisthenes; likewise Ctesippus of the deme of Paeania, Menexenus, and some others; Plato, if I am not mistaken, was ill.

ECHECRATES. Were there any strangers?

PHAEDO. Yes, there were; Simmias the Theban, and Cebes, and Phaedondes; Euclid and Terpsion, who came from Megara.

ECHECRATES. And was Aristippus there, and Cleombrotus?

PHAEDO. No, they were said to be in Aegina.

ECHECRATES. Any one else?

PHAEDO. I think that these were nearly all.

ECHECRATES. Well, and what did you talk about?

PHAEDO. I will begin at the beginning, and endeavour to repeat the entire conversation. On the previous days we had been in the habit of assembling early in the morning at the court in which the trial took place, and which is not far from the prison. There we used to wait talking with one another until the opening of the doors (for they were not opened very early); then we went in and generally passed the day with Socrates. On the last morning we assembled sooner than usual, having heard on the day before when we quitted the prison in the evening that the sacred ship had come from Delos; and so we arranged to meet very early at the accustomed place. On our arrival the jailer who answered the door, instead of admitting us, came out and told us to stay until he called us. 'For the Eleven,' he said, 'are now with Socrates; they are taking off his chains, and giving orders that he is to die to-day.' He soon returned and said that we might come in. On entering we found Socrates just released from chains, and Xanthippè,[2] whom you know, sitting by him, and holding his child in her arms. When she saw us she uttered a cry and said, as women will: 'O Socrates, this is the last time that either you will converse with your friends, or they with you.' Socrates turned to Crito and said: 'Crito, let some one take her home.' Some of Crito's people accordingly led her away, crying out and beating herself. And when she was gone, Socrates, sitting up on the couch, bent and rubbed his leg, saying, as he was rubbing: How singular is the thing called pleasure, and how curiously related to pain, which might be thought to be the opposite of it; for they are never present to a man at the same instant, and yet he who pursues either is generally compelled to take the other; their bodies are two, but they are joined by a single head. And I cannot help thinking that if Aesop had remembered them, he would have made a fable about God trying to reconcile their strife, and how, when he could not, he fastened their heads together; and this is the reason why when one comes the other follows: as I know by my own experience now, when after the pain in my leg which was caused by the chain pleasure appears to succeed.

Upon this Cebes said: I am glad, Socrates, that you have mentioned the name of Aesop. For it reminds me of a question which has been asked by many, and was asked of me only the day before yesterday by Evenus the poet—he will be sure to ask it again, and therefore if you would like me to have an answer ready for him, you may as well tell me what I should say to him:—he wanted to know why you, who never before wrote a line of poetry, now that you are in prison are turning Aesop's fables into verse, and also composing that hymn in honour of Apollo.

Tell him, Cebes, he replied, what is the truth—that I had no idea of rivalling him or his poems; to do so as I knew, would be no easy task. But I wanted to see whether I could purge away a scruple which I felt about the meaning of certain dreams. In the course of my life I have often had intimations in dreams 'that I should compose music.' The same dream came to me sometimes in one form, and sometimes in another, but always saying the same or nearly the same words: 'Cultivate and make music,'

---

[2] The wife of Socrates; her name has become synonymous with "shrew."

said the dream. And hitherto I had imagined that this was only intended to exhort and encourage me in the study of philosophy, which has been the pursuit of my life, and is the noblest and best of music. The dream was bidding me do what I was already doing, in the same way that the competitor in a race is bidden by the spectators to run when he is already running. But I was not certain of this; for the dream might have meant music in the popular sense of the word, and being under sentence of death, and the festival giving me a respite, I thought that it would be safer for me to satisfy the scruple, and, in obedience to the dream, to compose a few verses before I departed. And first I made a hymn in honour of the god of the festival, and then considering that a poet, if he is really to be a poet, should not only put together words, but should invent stories, and that I have no invention, I took some fables of Aesop, which I had ready at hand and which I knew—they were the first I came upon—and turned them into verse. Tell this to Evenus, Cebes, and bid him be of good cheer; say that I would have him come after me if he be a wise man, and not tarry; and that to-day I am likely to be going, for the Athenians say that I must.

Simmias said: What a message for such a man! having been a frequent companion of his I should say that, as far as I know him, he will never take your advice unless he is obliged.

Why, said Socrates,—is not Evenus a philosopher?

I think that he is, said Simmias.

Then he, or any man who has the spirit of philosophy, will be willing to die; but he will not take his own life, for that is held to be unlawful.

Here he changed his position, and put his legs off the couch on to the ground, and during the rest of the conversation he remained sitting.

Why do you say, enquired Cebes, that a man ought not to take his own life, but that the philosopher will be ready to follow the dying?

Socrates replied: And have you, Cebes and Simmias, who are the disciples of Philolaus, never heard him speak of this?

Yes, but his language was obscure, Socrates.

My words, too, are only an echo; but there is no reason why I should not repeat what I have heard: and indeed, as I am going

to another place, it is very meet for me to be thinking and talking of the nature of the pilgrimage which I am about to make.
What can I do better in the interval between this and the setting
of the sun?

•   •   •

And now, O my judges, I desire to prove to you that the real
philosopher has reason to be of good cheer when he is about to
die, and that after death he may hope to obtain the greatest good
in the other world. And how this may be, Simmias and Cebes, I
will endeavour to explain. For I deem that the true votary of
philosophy is likely to be misunderstood by other men; they do
not perceive that he is always pursuing death and dying; and if
this be so, and he has had the desire of death all his life long,
why when his time comes should he repine at that which he has
been always pursuing and desiring?

Simmias said laughingly: Though not in a laughing humour,
you have made me laugh, Socrates; for I cannot help thinking
that the many when they hear your words will say how truly
you have described philosophers, and our people at home will
likewise say that the life which philosophers desire is in reality
death, and that they have found them out to be deserving of the
death which they desire.

And they are right, Simmias, in thinking so, with the exception of the words 'they have found them out'; for they have not
found out either what is the nature of that death which the true
philosopher deserves, or how he deserves or desires death. But
enough of them:—let us discuss the matter among ourselves. Do
we believe that there is such a thing as death?

To be sure, replied Simmias.

Is it not the separation of soul and body? And to be dead is the
completion of this; when the soul exists in herself, and is released from the body and the body is released from the soul,
what is this but death?

Just so, he replied.

There is another question, which will probably throw light on
our present enquiry if you and I can agree about it:—Ought the
philosopher to care about the pleasures—if they are to be called
pleasures—of eating and drinking?

Certainly not, answered Simmias.

And what about the pleasures of love—should he care for them?

By no means.

And will he think much of the other ways of indulging the body, for example, the acquisition of costly raiment, or sandals, or other adornments of the body? Instead of caring about them, does he not rather despise anything more than nature needs? What do you say?

I should say that the true philosopher would despise them.

Would you not say that he is entirely concerned with the soul and not with the body? He would like, as far as he can, to get away from the body and to turn to the soul.

Quite true.

In matters of this sort philosophers, above all other men, may be observed in every sort of way to dissever the soul from the communion of the body.

Very true.

Whereas, Simmias, the rest of the world are of opinion that to him who has no sense of pleasure and no part in bodily pleasure, life is not worth having; and that he who is indifferent about them is as good as dead.

That is also true.

What again shall we say of the actual acquirement of knowledge?—is the body, if invited to share in the enquiry, a hinderer or a helper? I mean to say, have sight and hearing any truth in them? Are they not, as the poets are always telling us, inaccurate witnesses? and yet, if even they are inaccurate and indistinct, what is to be said of the other senses—for you will allow that they are the best of them?

Certainly, he replied.

Then when does the soul attain truth?—for in attempting to consider anything in company with the body she is obviously deceived.

True.

Then must not true existence be revealed to her in thought, if at all?

Yes.

And thought is best when the mind is gathered into herself and none of these things trouble her—neither sounds nor sights nor pain nor any pleasure,—when she takes leave of the body, and has as little as possible to do with it, when she has no bodily sense or desire, but is aspiring after true being?

Certainly.

And in this the philosopher dishonours the body; his soul runs away from his body and desires to be alone and by herself?

That is true.

Well, but there is another thing, Simmias: Is there or is there not an absolute justice?

Assuredly there is.

And an absolute beauty and absolute good?

Of course.

But did you ever behold any of them with your eyes?

Certainly not.

Or did you ever reach them with any other bodily sense?—and I speak not of these alone, but of absolute greatness, and health, and strength, and of the essence or true nature of everything. Has the reality of them ever been perceived by you through the bodily organs? or rather, is not the nearest approach to the knowledge of their several natures made by him who so orders his intellectual vision as to have the most exact conception of the essence of each thing which he considers?

Certainly.

And he attains to the purest knowledge of them who goes to each with the mind alone, not introducing or intruding in the act of thought, sight, or any other sense together with reason, but with the very light of the mind in her own clearness searches into the very truth of each; he who has got rid, as far as he can, of eyes and ears and, so to speak, of the whole body, these being in his opinion distracting elements which when they infect the soul hinder her from acquiring truth and knowledge—who, if not he, is likely to attain to the knowledge of true being?

What you say has a wonderful truth in it, Socrates, replied Simmias.

And when real philosophers consider all these things, will they not be led to make a reflection which they will express in words something like the following? 'Have we not found,' they will say, 'a path of thought which seems to bring us and our argument to the conclusion, that while we are in the body, and while the soul is infected with the evils of the body, our desire will not be satisfied? and our desire is of the truth. For the body is a source of endless trouble to us by reason of the mere requirement of food; and is liable also to diseases which overtake and impede us in the search after true being: it fills us full of loves, and lusts, and fears, and fancies of all kinds, and endless foolery, and in fact, as men say, takes away from us the power of thinking at all. Whence come wars, and fightings, and factions? whence but from the body and the lusts of the body? Wars are occasioned by the love of money, and money has to be acquired for the sake and in the service of the body; and by reason of all these impediments we have no time to give to philosophy; and, last and worst of all, even if we are at leisure and betake ourselves to some speculation, the body is always breaking in upon us, causing turmoil and confusion in our enquiries, and so amazing us that we are prevented from seeing the truth. It has been proved to us by experience that if we would have pure knowledge of anything we must be quit of the body—the soul in herself must behold things in themselves; and then we shall attain the wisdom which we desire, and of which we say that we are lovers; not while we live, but after death; for if while in company with the body, the soul cannot have pure knowledge, one of two things follows—either knowledge is not to be attained at all, or, if at all, after death. For then, and not till then, the soul will be parted from the body and exist in herself alone. In this present life, I reckon that we make the nearest approach to knowledge when we have the least possible intercourse or communion with the body, and are not surfeited with the bodily nature, but keep ourselves pure until the hour when God himself is pleased to release us. And thus having got rid of the foolishness of the body we shall be pure and hold converse with the pure, and know of ourselves the clear light everywhere, which is no other than the light of truth.' For the impure are not permitted to approach the pure. These are the sort of words, Simmias, which the true lovers of knowledge cannot help saying to one another and thinking. You would agree; would you not?

Undoubtedly, Socrates.

But, O my friend, if this be true, there is great reason to hope that, going whither I go, when I have come to the end of my journey, I shall attain that which has been the pursuit of my life. And therefore I go on my way rejoicing, and not I only, but every other man who believes that his mind has been made ready and that he is in a manner purified.

Certainly, replied Simmias.

And what is purification but the separation of the soul from the body, as I was saying before; the habit of the soul gathering and collecting herself into herself from all sides out of the body; the dwelling in her own place alone, as in another life, so also in this, as far as she can;—the release of the soul from the chains of the body?

Very true, he said.

And this separation and release of the soul from the body is termed death?

To be sure, he said.

And the true philosophers, and they only, are ever seeking to release the soul. Is not the separation and release of the soul from the body their especial study?

That is true.

And, as I was saying at first, there would be a ridiculous contradiction in men studying to live as nearly as they can in a state of death, and yet repining when it comes upon them.

Clearly.

And the true philosophers, Simmias, are always occupied in the practice of dying, wherefore also to them least of all men is death terrible. Look at the matter thus:—if they have been in every way the enemies of the body, and are wanting to be alone with the soul, when this desire of theirs is granted, how inconsistent would they be if they trembled and repined, instead of rejoicing at their departure to that place where, when they arrive, they hope to gain that which in life they desired—and this was wisdom—and at the same time to be rid of the company of their enemy. Many a man has been willing to go to the world below animated by the hope of seeing there an earthly love, or wife, or son, and conversing with them. And will he who is a true lover of wisdom, and is strongly persuaded in like manner that only in the world below he can worthily enjoy her, still repine at death? Will he not depart with joy? Surely he will, O my friend, if he be a true philosopher. For he will have a firm conviction that there, and there only, he can find wisdom in her purity. And if this be true, he would be very absurd, as I was saying, if he were afraid of death.

He would indeed, replied Simmias.

And when you see a man who is repining at the approach of death, is not his reluctance a sufficient proof that he is not a lover of wisdom, but a lover of the body, and probably at the same time a lover of either money or power, or both?

Quite so, he replied.

And is not courage, Simmias, a quality which is specially characteristic of the philosopher?

Certainly.

There is temperance again, which even by the vulgar [3] is supposed to consist in the control and regulation of the passions, and in the sense of superiority to them—is not temperance a virtue belonging to those only who despise the body, and who pass their lives in philosophy?

Most assuredly.

For the courage and temperance of other men, if you will consider them, are really a contradiction.

How so?

Well, he said, you are aware that death is regarded by men in general as a great evil.

Very true, he said.

And do not courageous men face death because they are afraid of yet greater evils?

That is quite true.

Then all but the philosophers are courageous only from fear, and because they are afraid; and yet that a man should be courageous from fear, and because he is a coward, is surely a strange thing.

Very true.

And are not the temperate exactly in the same case? They are temperate because they are intemperate—which might seem to be a contradiction, but is nevertheless the sort of thing which happens with this foolish temperance. For there are pleasures which they are afraid of losing; and in their desire to keep them, they abstain from some pleasures, because they are overcome by others; and although to be conquered by pleasure is called by men intemperance, to them the conquest of pleasure consists in being conquered by pleasure. And that is what I mean by saying

---

[3] That is, even in popular usage.

that, in a sense, they are made temperate through intemperance.

Such appears to be the case.

Yet the exchange of one fear or pleasure or pain for another fear or pleasure or pain, and of the greater for the less, as if they were coins, is not the exchange of virtue. O my blessed Simmias, is there not one true coin for which all things ought to be exchanged?—and that is wisdom; and only in exchange for this, and in company with this, is anything truly bought or sold, whether courage or temperance or justice. And is not all true virtue the companion of wisdom, no matter what fears or pleasures or other similar goods or evils may or may not attend her? But the virtue which is made up of these goods, when they are severed from wisdom and exchanged with one another, is a shadow of virtue only, nor is there any freedom or health or truth in her; but in the true exchange there is a purging away of all these things, and temperance, and justice, and courage, and wisdom herself are the purgation of them. The founders of the mysteries would appear to have had a real meaning, and were not talking nonsense when they intimated in a figure long ago that he who passes unsanctified and uninitiated into the world below will lie in a slough, but that he who arrives there after initiation and purification will dwell with the gods. For 'many,' as they say in the mysteries, 'are the thyrsus-bearers, but few are the mystics,'—meaning, as I interpret the words, 'the true philosophers.' In the number of whom, during my whole life, I have been seeking, according to my ability, to find a place;—whether I have sought in a right way or not, and whether I have succeeded or not, I shall truly know in a little while, if God will, when I myself arrive in the other world—such is my belief. And therefore I maintain that I am right, Simmias and Cebes, in not grieving or repining at parting from you and my masters in this world, for I believe that I shall equally find good masters and friends in another world. But most men do not believe this saying; if then I succeed in convincing you by my defence better than I did the Athenian judges, it will be well.

• • •

And were we not saying long ago that the soul when using the body as an instrument of perception, that is to say, when using the sense of sight or hearing or some other sense (for the meaning of perceiving through the body is perceiving through the senses)—were we not saying that the soul too is then dragged by the body into the region of the changeable, and wanders and is confused; the world spins round her, and she is like a drunkard, when she touches change?

Very true.

But when returning into herself she reflects, then she passes into the other world, the region of purity, and eternity, and immortality, and unchangeableness, which are her kindred, and with them she ever lives, when she is by herself and is not let or hindered; then she ceases from her erring ways, and being in communion with the unchanging is unchanging. And this state of the soul is called wisdom?

That is well and truly said, Socrates, Cebes replied.

And to which class is the soul more nearly alike and akin, as far as may be inferred from this argument, as well as from the preceding one?

I think, Socrates, that, in the opinion of every one who follows the argument, the soul will be infinitely more like the unchangeable—even the most stupid person will not deny that.

And the body is more like the changing?

Yes.

Yet once more consider the matter in another light: When the soul and the body are united, then nature orders the soul to rule and govern, and the body to obey and serve. Now which of these two functions is akin to the divine? and which to the mortal? Does not the divine appear to you to be that which naturally orders and rules, and the mortal to be that which is subject and servant?

True.

And which does the soul resemble?

The soul resembles the divine, and the body the mortal—there can be no doubt of that, Socrates.

Then reflect, Cebes: of all which has been said is not this the conclusion?—that the soul is in the very likeness of the divine, and immortal, and intellectual, and uniform, and indissoluble, and unchangeable; and that the body is in the very likeness of the human, and mortal, and unintellectual, and multiform, and dissoluble, and changeable. Can this, my dear Cebes, be denied?

It cannot.

But if it be true, then is not the body liable to speedy dissolution? and is not the soul almost or altogether indissoluble?

Certainly.

And do you further observe, that after a man is dead, the body, or visible part of him, which is lying in the visible world, and is called a corpse, and would naturally be dissolved and decomposed and dissipated, is not dissolved or decomposed at once, but may remain for some time, nay even for a long time, if the constitution be sound at the time of death, and the season of the year favourable? For the body when shrunk and embalmed, as the manner is in Egypt, may remain almost entire through infinite ages; and even in decay, there are still some portions, such as the bones and ligaments, which are practically indestructible:—Do you agree?

Yes.

And is it likely that the soul, which is invisible, in passing to the place of the true Hades,[4] which like her is invisible, and pure, and noble, and on her way to the good and wise God, whither, if God will, my soul is also soon to go,—that the soul, I repeat, if this be her nature and origin, will be blown away and destroyed immediately on quitting the body, as the many say? That can never be, my dear Simmias and Cebes. The truth rather is, that the soul which is pure at departing and draws after her no bodily taint, having never voluntarily during life had connection with the body, which she is ever avoiding, herself gathered into herself;—and making such abstraction her perpetual study—which means that she has been a true disciple of philosophy; and therefore has in fact been always engaged in the practice of dying? For is not philosophy the study of death?—

Certainly—

That soul, I say, herself invisible, departs to the invisible world—to the divine and immortal and rational: thither arriving, she is secure of bliss and is released from the error and folly of men, their fears and wild passions and all other human ills, and for ever dwells, as they say of the initiated, in company with the gods. Is not this true, Cebes?

Yes, said Cebes, beyond a doubt.

---

[4] The king of the underworld or the underworld itself. The literal meaning of the word is "unseen" or "hidden."

But the soul which has been polluted, and is impure at the time of her departure, and is the companion and servant of the body always, and is in love with and fascinated by the body and by the desires and pleasures of the body, until she is led to believe that the truth only exists in a bodily form, which a man may touch and see and taste, and use for the purposes of his lusts,—the soul, I mean, accustomed to hate and fear and avoid the intellectual principle, which to the bodily eye is dark and invisible, and can be attained only by philosophy;—do you suppose that such a soul will depart pure and unalloyed?

Impossible, he replied.

She is held fast by the corporeal, which the continual association and constant care of the body have wrought into her nature.

Very true.

And this corporeal element, my friend, is heavy and weighty and earthy, and is that element of sight by which a soul is depressed and dragged down again into the visible world, because she is afraid of the invisible and of the world below—prowling about tombs and sepulchres, near which, as they tell us, are seen certain ghostly apparitions of souls which have not departed pure, but are cloyed with sight and therefore visible.

That is very likely, Socrates.

Yes, that is very likely, Cebes; and these must be the souls, not of the good, but of the evil, which are compelled to wander about such places in payment of the penalty of their former evil way of life; and they continue to wander until through the craving after the corporeal which never leaves them, they are imprisoned finally in another body. And they may be supposed to find their prisons in the same natures which they have had in their former lives.

What natures do you mean, Socrates?

What I mean is that men who have followed after gluttony, and wantonness, and drunkenness, and have had no thought of avoiding them, would pass into asses and animals of that sort. What do you think?

I think such an opinion to be exceedingly probable.

And those who have chosen the portion of injustice, and tyranny, and violence, will pass into wolves, or into hawks and kites;—whither else can we suppose them to go?

Yes, said Cebes; with such natures, beyond question.

And there is no difficulty, he said, in assigning to all of them places answering to their several natures and propensities?

There is not, he said.

Some are happier than others; and the happiest both in themselves and in the place to which they go are those who have practised the civil and social virtues which are called temperance and justice, and are acquired by habit and attention without philosophy and mind.

Why are they the happiest?

Because they may be expected to pass into some gentle and social kind which is like their own, such as bees or wasps or ants, or back again into the form of man, and just and moderate men may be supposed to spring from them.

Very likely.

No one who has not studied philosophy and who is not entirely pure at the time of his departure is allowed to enter the company of the Gods, but the lover of knowledge only. And this is the reason, Simmias and Cebes, why the true votaries of philosophy abstain from all fleshly lusts, and hold out against them and refuse to give themselves up to them,—not because they fear poverty or the ruin of their families, like the lovers of money, and the world in general; nor like the lovers of power and honour, because they dread the dishonour or disgrace of evil deeds.

No, Socrates, that would not become them, said Cebes.

No indeed, he replied; and therefore they who have any care of their own souls, and do not merely live moulding and fashioning the body, say farewell to all this; they will not walk in the ways of the blind: and when philosophy offers them purification and release from evil, they feel that they ought not to resist her influence, and whither she leads they turn and follow.

What do you mean, Socrates?

I will tell you, he said. The lovers of knowledge are conscious that the soul was simply fastened and glued to the body—until philosophy received her, she could only view real existence through the bars of a prison, not in and through herself; she was wallowing in the mire of every sort of ignorance, and by reason of lust had become the principal accomplice in her own captivity. This was her original state; and then, as I was saying, and as the lovers of knowledge are well aware, philosophy, seeing how terrible was her confinement, of which she was to herself the cause, received and gently comforted her and sought to release her, pointing out that the eye and the ear and the other senses are full of deception, and persuading her to retire from them, and abstain from all but the necessary use of them, and be gathered up and collected into herself, bidding her trust in herself and her own pure apprehension of pure existence, and to mistrust whatever comes to her through other channels and is subject to variation; for such things are visible and tangible, but what she sees in her own nature is intelligible and invisible. And the soul of the true philosopher thinks that she ought not to resist this deliverance, and therefore abstains from pleasures and desires and pains and fears, as far as she is able; reflecting that when a man has great joys or sorrows or fears or desires, he suffers from them, not merely the sort of evil which might be anticipated—as for example, the loss of his health or property which he has sacrificed to his lusts—but an evil greater far, which is the greatest and worst of all evils, and one of which he never thinks.

What is it, Socrates? said Cebes.

The evil is that when the feeling of pleasure or pain is most intense, every soul of man imagines the objects of this intense feeling to be then plainest and truest: but this is not so, they are really the things of sight.

Very true.

And is not this the state in which the soul is most enthralled by the body?

How so?

Why, because each pleasure and pain is a sort of nail which nails and rivets the soul to the body, until she becomes like the body, and believes that to be true which the body affirms to be true; and from agreeing with the body and having the same delights she is obliged to have the same habits and haunts, and is not likely ever to be pure at her departure to the world below, but is always infected by the body; and so she sinks into another body and there germinates and grows, and has therefore no part in the communion of the divine and pure and simple.

Most true, Socrates, answered Cebes.

And this, Cebes, is the reason why the true lovers of knowledge are temperate and brave; and not for the reason which the world gives.

Certainly not.

Certainly not! The soul of a philosopher will reason in quite another way; she will not ask philosophy to release her in order that when released she may deliver herself up again to the thraldom of pleasures and pains, doing a work only to be undone again, weaving instead of unweaving her Penelope's web. But she will calm passion, and follow reason, and dwell in the contemplation of her, beholding the true and divine (which is not matter of opinion), and thence deriving nourishment. Thus she seeks to live while she lives, and after death she hopes to go to her own kindred and to that which is like her, and to be freed from human ills. Never fear, Simmias and Cebes, that a soul which has been thus nurtured and has had these pursuits, will at her departure from the body be scattered and blown away by the winds and be nowhere and nothing.

• • •

When he had spoken these words, he arose and went into a chamber to bathe; Crito followed him, and told us to wait. So we remained behind, talking and thinking of the subject of discourse, and also of the greatness of our sorrow; he was like a father of whom we were being bereaved, and we were about to pass the rest of our lives as orphans. When he had taken the bath his children were brought to him—(he had two young sons and an elder one); and the women of the family also came, and he talked to them and gave them a few directions in the presence of Crito; then he dismissed them and returned to us.

Now the bow of sunset was near, for a good deal of time had passed while he was within. When he came out, he sat down with us again after his bath, but not much was said. Soon the jailer, who was the servant of the Eleven, entered and stood by him, saying:—To you, Socrates, whom I know to be the noblest and gentlest and best of all who ever came to this place, I will not impute the angry feelings of other men, who rage and swear at me, when, in obedience to the authorities, I bid them drink the poison—indeed, I am sure that you will not be angry with me; for others, as you are aware, and not I, are to blame. And so fare you well, and try to bear lightly what must needs be—you know my errand. Then bursting into tears he turned away and went out.

Socrates looked at him, and said: I return your good wishes, and will do as you bid. Then turning to us, he said, How charming the man is: since I have been in prison he has always been coming to see me, and at times he would talk to me, and was as good to me as could be, and now see how generously he sorrows on my account. We must do as he says, Crito; and therefore let the cup be brought, if the poison is prepared: if not, let the attendant prepare some.

Yet, said Crito, the sun is still upon the hill-tops, and I know that many a one has taken the draught late, and after the announcement has been made to him, he has eaten and drunk, and enjoyed the society of his beloved; do not hurry—there is time enough.

Socrates said: Yes, Crito, and they of whom you speak are right in so acting, for they think that they will be gainers by the delay; but I am right in not following their example, for I do not think that I should gain anything by drinking the poison a little later; I should only be ridiculous in my own eyes for sparing and saving a life which is already forfeit. Please then to do as I say, and not to refuse me.

Crito made a sign to the servant, who was standing by; and he went out, and having been absent for some time, returned with the jailer carrying the cup of poison. Socrates said: You, my good friend, who are experienced in these matters, shall give me directions how I am to proceed. The man answered: You have only to walk about until your legs are heavy, and then to lie down, and the poison will act. At the same time he handed the cup to Socrates, who in the easiest and gentlest manner, without the least fear or change of colour or feature, looking at the man with all his eyes, Echecrates, as his manner was, took the cup and said: What do you say about making a libation out of this cup to any god? May I, or not? The man answered: We only prepare, Socrates, just so much as we deem enough. I understand, he said: but I may and must ask the gods to prosper my journey from this to the other world—even so—and so be it according to my prayer. Then raising the cup to his lips, quite readily and cheerfully he drank off the poison. And hitherto most of us had been able to control our sorrow; but now when we saw him drinking, and saw too that he had finished the draught, we could no longer forbear, and in spite of myself my own tears were flowing fast; so that I covered my face and wept, not for him, but at the thought of my own calamity in having to part from such a friend. Nor was I the first; for Crito, when he found himself unable to restrain his tears, had got up, and I followed; and at that moment, Apollodorus, who had been weeping all the time, broke out in a loud and passionate cry which made cowards of us all. Socrates alone retained his calmness: What is this strange outcry? he said. I sent away the women mainly in order that they might not misbehave in this way, for I have been told that a man should die in peace. Be quiet then, and have patience. When we heard his words we were ashamed, and refrained our tears; and he walked about until, as he said, his legs began to fail, and then he lay on his back, according to the directions, and the man who gave him the poison now and then looked at his feet and legs; and after a while he pressed his foot hard, and asked him if he could feel; and he said, No; and then his leg, and so upwards and upwards, and showed us that he was cold and stiff. And he felt them himself, and said: When the poison reaches the heart, that will be the end. He was beginning to grow cold about the groin, when he uncovered his face, for he had covered himself up, and said—they were his last words—he said: Crito, I owe a cock to Asclepius;[5] will you remember to pay the debt? The debt shall be paid, said Crito; is there anything else? There was no answer to this question; but in a minute or two a movement was heard, and the attendants uncovered him; his eyes were set, and Crito closed his eyes and mouth.

Such was the end, Echecrates, of our friend; concerning whom I may truly say, that of all the men of his time whom I have known, he was the wisest and justest and best.

---

[5] The god of healing. Socrates is referring to the sacrifice of a bird that he had promised the deity.

9

Plato

The Republic

To Plato (ca. 427–ca. 347 B.C.), Socrates' most brilliant disciple, the trial and death of the master came as a profound shock. Born a member of the Athenian ruling class, Plato had grown up in an atmosphere of war and revolution. He had seen the discredited Athenian democracy go down in ruin and had looked to a government by gentlemen to restore order and justice— only to be disillusioned by the incompetence of those installed by Sparta—the "Thirty Tyrants." The death of his revered master turned Plato from a life of prospective public service, normal for an aristocrat, to the propagation and application of the Socratic ideals. In 387 B.C., after a prolonged absence following the events described in the Phaedo, *he returned to Athens and proceeded to gather about himself a community of young disciples, teaching them the principles of his beloved teacher.*

The basic human problem, it seemed to Plato, was this: How can society be reconstituted so that all individuals may know happiness and justice? To facilitate a formal inquiry into this problem, Plato instituted a school in a private garden on the outskirts of Athens, called the Academy. The Academy was to be used to train philosopher-statesmen, who, he hoped, would one day govern Athens. Soon, however, it became not only a pan-Hellenic center for study and research, but a magnet for philosophers throughout the world, and it was to remain such for almost a thousand years.

Here, until his death, Plato taught and developed the thought of Socrates and continued to write the dialogues; among them were the Phaedo *(preceding selection) and* The Republic, *from which the following passages are*

Plato, *The Republic,* trans. F. M. Cornford (New York and London: Oxford University Press, Inc., 1945), 103–11, 148–50, 152–58, 163–64, 176–79, 227–31, 234. Reprinted by permission of the publishers.

taken. Although the Spartan polity is taken as an imperfect working model, the central thesis of The Republic *is that government is a task only for those qualified; that the disinterested lover of truth, the philosopher, alone is qualified to govern; and that until philosophy and political power meet in one authority there will be no end to human misery.*

The Republic *is a discussion of great intellectual richness and breadth, and, as Plato's most widely read work, it has exercised a profound influence upon Western thought. To many it is known only as a utopian program, the first of its kind in the literature of the West; but to others, perhaps reflecting upon the social horrors and stupidities of the twentieth century, it is regarded as the greatest work of political philosophy ever written.*

The dialogue as a whole is concerned with the nature of justice and how a just social order may be realized. Socrates (the "I" of the dialogue) develops the true meaning of justice and draws an unforgettable picture of an ideal society in which justice has been made real. The excerpt reprinted here deals with the proposed ruling élite (called Guardians); with the roles and relationships of men, women, and children; with the central place of philosophy in human affairs; and, in the famous "Allegory of the Cave," with the crucial function of philosophers as educators and governors. The persons who participate in the imaginary dialogue are, besides Socrates himself, Glaucon and Adeimantus, the brothers of Plato. The setting is the house of a mutual friend in the Piraeus, a port about five miles south of Athens.

[Earlier in the dialogue, the discussion has turned about the preliminary education of the Guardians,[1] ending at the age of twenty, intended to develop a harmony of mental, physical, and "philosophic" elements in their character. As we begin the selected passage, Socrates moves on to a higher level of training: to the "kingly science" that fits the best for rule. *Ed.*]

Good, said Socrates; and what is the next point to be settled? Is it not the question, which of these Guardians are to be rulers and which are to obey?

No doubt, said Glaucon.

Well, it is obvious that the elder must have authority over the young, and that the rulers must be the best.

---

[1] The Guardians were authoritarian, but their function was custodianship, not leadership. Unlike some twentieth-century dictators, they would work to preserve values, not to bring about change.

Yes.

And as among farmers the best are those with a natural turn for farming, so, if we want the best among our Guardians, we must take those naturally fitted to watch over a commonwealth. They must have the right sort of intelligence and ability; and also they must look upon the commonwealth as their special concern—the sort of concern that is felt for something so closely bound up with oneself that its interests and fortunes, for good or ill, are held to be identical with one's own.

Exactly.

So the kind of men we must choose from among the Guardians will be those who, when we look at the whole course of their lives, are found to be full of zeal to do whatever they believe is for the good of the commonwealth and never willing to act against its interest.

Yes, they will be the men we want.

We must watch them, I think, at every age and see whether they are capable of preserving this conviction that they must do what is best for the community, never forgetting it or allowing themselves to be either forced or bewitched into throwing it over.

How does this throwing over come about?

I will explain. When a belief passes out of the mind, a man may be willing to part with it, if it is false and he has learnt better, or unwilling, if it is true.

I see how he might be willing to let it go; but you must explain how he can be unwilling.

Where is your difficulty? Don't you agree that men are unwilling to be deprived of good, though ready enough to part with evil? Or that to be deceived about the truth is evil, to possess it good? Or don't you think that possessing truth means thinking of things as they really are?

You are right. I do agree that men are unwilling to be robbed of a true belief.

When that happens to them, then, it must be by theft, or violence, or bewitchment.

Again I do not understand.

Perhaps my metaphors are too high-flown. I call it theft when one is persuaded out of one's belief or forgets it. Argument in the one case, and time in the other, steal it away without one's knowing what is happening. You understand now?

Yes.

And by violence I mean being driven to change one's mind by pain or suffering.

That too I understand, and you are right.

And bewitchment, as I think you would agree, occurs when a man is beguiled out of his opinion by the allurements of pleasure or scared out of it under the spell of panic.

Yes, all delusions are like a sort of bewitchment.

As I said just now, then, we must find out who are the best guardians of this inward conviction that they must always do what they believe to be best for the commonwealth. We shall have to watch them from earliest childhood and set them tasks in which they would be most likely to forget or to be beguiled out of this duty. We shall then choose only those whose memory holds firm and who are proof against delusion.

Yes.

We must also subject them to ordeals of toil and pain and watch for the same qualities there. And we must observe them when exposed to the test of yet a third kind of bewitchment. As people lead colts up to alarming noises to see whether they are timid, so these young men must be brought into terrifying situations and then into scenes of pleasure, which will put them to severer proof than gold tried in the furnace. If we find one bearing himself well in all these trials and resisting every enchantment, a true guardian of himself, preserving always that perfect rhythm and harmony of being which he has acquired from his training in music and poetry, such a one will be of the greatest service to the commonwealth as well as to himself. Whenever we find one who has come unscathed through every test in childhood, youth, and manhood, we shall set him as a Ruler to watch over the commonwealth; he will be honoured in life, and after death receive the highest tribute of funeral rites and other memorials. All who do not reach this standard we must reject. And that, I think, my dear Glaucon, may be taken as an outline of the way in which we shall select Guardians to be set in authority as Rulers.

I am very much of your mind.

These, then, may properly be called Guardians in the fullest sense, who will ensure that neither foes without shall have the power, nor friends within the wish, to do harm. Those young men whom up to now we have been speaking of as Guardians, will be better described as Auxiliaries, who will enforce the decisions of the Rulers.

I agree.

Now, said I, can we devise something in the way of those convenient fictions we spoke of earlier, a single bold flight of invention,[2]
which we may induce the community in general, and if possible the
Rulers themselves, to accept?

What kind of fiction?

Nothing new; something like an Eastern tale of what, according to
the poets, has happened before now in more than one part of the
world. The poets have been believed; but the thing has not happened
in our day, and it would be hard to persuade anyone that it could
ever happen again.

You seem rather shy of telling this story of yours.

With good reason, as you will see when I have told it.

Out with it; don't be afraid.

Well, here it is; though I hardly know how to find the courage or
the words to express it. I shall try to convince, first the Rulers and
the soldiers, and then the whole community, that all that nurture and
education which we gave them was only something they seemed to
experience as it were in a dream. In reality they were the whole time
down inside the earth, being moulded and fostered while their arms
and all their equipment were being fashioned also; and at last, when
they were complete, the earth sent them up from her womb into the
light of day. So now they must think of the land they dwell in as a
mother and nurse, whom they must take thought for and defend
against any attack, and of their fellow citizens as brothers born of the
same soil.

You might well be bashful about coming out with your fiction.

No doubt; but still you must hear the rest of the story. It is true,
we shall tell our people in this fable, that all of you in this land are
brothers; but the god who fashioned you mixed gold in the composition of those among you who are fit to rule, so that they are of the
most precious quality; and he put silver in the Auxiliaries, and iron
and brass in the farmers and craftsmen. Now, since you are all of one
stock, although your children will generally be like their parents,
sometimes a golden parent may have a silver child or a silver parent a
golden one, and so on with all the other combinations. So the first
and chief injunction laid by heaven upon the Rulers is that, among all

[2] Sometimes translated as "the noble lie"; but, although a fiction, it was "true in
spirit" and intended for the good of all. The Guardians themselves were to accept it.

the things of which they must show themselves good guardians, there is none that needs to be so carefully watched as the mixture of metals in the souls of the children. If a child of their own is born with an alloy of iron or brass, they must, without the smallest pity, assign him the station proper to his nature and thrust him out among the craftsmen or the farmers. If, on the contrary, these classes produce a child with gold or silver in his composition, they will promote him, according to his value, to be a Guardian or an Auxiliary. They will appeal to a prophecy that ruin will come upon the state when it passes into the keeping of a man of iron or brass. Such is the story; can you think of any device to make them believe it?

Not in the first generation; but their sons and descendants might believe it, and finally the rest of mankind.

Well, said I, even so it might have a good effect in making them care more for the commonwealth and for one another; for I think I see what you mean.

So, I continued, we will leave the success of our story to the care of popular tradition; and now let us arm these sons of Earth and lead them, under the command of their Rulers, to the site of our city. There let them look round for the best place to fix their camp, from which they will be able to control any rebellion against the laws from within and to beat off enemies who may come from without like wolves to attack the fold. When they have pitched their camp and offered sacrifice to the proper divinities, they must arrange their sleeping quarters; and these must be sufficient to shelter them from winter cold and summer heat.

Naturally. You mean they are going to live there?

Yes, said I; but live like soldiers, not like men of business.

What is the difference?

I will try to explain. It would be very strange if a shepherd were to disgrace himself by keeping, for the protection of his flock, dogs who were so ill-bred and badly trained that hunger or unruliness or some bad habit or other would set them worrying the sheep and behaving no better than wolves. We must take every precaution against our Auxiliaries treating the citizens in any such way and, because they are stronger, turning into savage tyrants instead of friendly allies; and they will have been furnished with the best of safeguards, if they have really been educated in the right way.

But surely there is nothing wrong with their education.

We must not be too positive about that, my dear Glaucon; but we can be sure of what we said not long ago, that if they are to have the best chance of being gentle and humane to one another and to their charges, they must have the right education, whatever that may be.

We were certainly right there.

Then besides that education, it is only common sense to say that the dwellings and other belongings provided for them must be such as will neither make them less perfect Guardians nor encourage them to maltreat their fellow citizens.

True.

With that end in view, let us consider how they should live and be housed. First, none of them must possess any private property beyond the barest necessaries. Next, no one is to have any dwelling or store-house that is not open for all to enter at will. Their food, in the quantities required by men of temperance and courage who are in training for war, they will receive from the other citizens as the wages of their guardianship, fixed so that there shall be just enough for the year with nothing over; and they will have meals in common and all live together like soldiers in a camp. Gold and silver, we shall tell them, they will not need, having the divine counterparts of those metals always in their souls as a god-given possession, whose purity it is not lawful to sully by the acquisition of that mortal dross, current among mankind, which has been the occasion of so many unholy deeds. They alone of all the citizens are forbidden to touch and handle silver or gold, or to come under the same roof with them, or wear them as ornaments, or drink from vessels made of them. This manner of life will be their salvation and make them the saviours of the commonwealth. If ever they should come to possess land of their own and houses and money, they will give up their guardianship for the management of their farms and households and become tyrants at enmity with their fellow citizens instead of allies. And so they will pass all their lives in hating and being hated, plotting and being plotted against, in much greater fear of their enemies at home than of any foreign foe, and fast heading for the destruction that will soon overwhelm their country with themselves. For all these reasons let us say that this is how our Guardians are to be housed and otherwise provided for, and let us make laws accordingly.

By all means, said Glaucon.

Here Adeimantus interposed. Socrates, he said, how would you meet the objection that you are not making these people particularly happy? It is their own fault too, if they are not; for they are really masters of the state, and yet they get no good out of it as other rulers do, who own lands, build themselves fine houses with handsome furniture, offer private sacrifices to the gods, and entertain visitors from abroad; who possess, in fact, that gold and silver you spoke of, with everything else that is usually thought necessary for happiness. These people seem like nothing so much as a garrison of mercenaries posted in the city and perpetually mounting guard.

Yes, I said, and what is more they will serve for their food only without getting a mercenary's pay, so that they will not be able to travel on their own account or to make presents to a mistress or to spend as they please in other ways, like the people who are commonly thought happy. You have forgotten to include these counts in your indictment, and many more to the same effect.

Well, take them as included now.

And you want to hear the answer?

Yes.

We shall find one, I think, by keeping to the line we have followed so far. We shall say that, though it would not be surprising if even these people were perfectly happy under such conditions, our aim in founding the commonwealth was not to make any one class specially happy, but to secure the greatest possible happiness for the community as a whole. We thought we should have the best chance of finding justice in a state so constituted, just as we should find injustice where the constitution was of the worst possible type; we could then decide the question which has been before us all this time. For the moment, we are constructing, as we believe, the state which will be happy as a whole, not trying to secure the well-being of a select few; we shall study a state of the opposite kind presently. It is as if we were colouring a statue[3] and someone came up and blamed us for not putting the most beautiful colours on the noblest parts of the figure; the eyes, for instance, should be painted crimson, but we had made them black. We should think it a fair answer to say: Really, you must not expect us to paint eyes so handsome as not to look like eyes at all. This applies to all the parts: the question is whether, by giving each its proper colour, we make the whole beautiful. So too, in the present case, you must not press us to endow our Guardians with a happiness that will make them anything rather than guardians. We could quite easily clothe our farmers in gorgeous robes,

---

[3] Greek sculpture was usually painted.

crown them with gold, and invite them to till the soil at their pleasure; or we might set our potters to lie on couches by their fire, passing round the wine and making merry, with their wheel at hand to work at whenever they felt so inclined. We could make all the rest happy in the same sort of way, and so spread this well-being through the whole community. But you must not put that idea into our heads; if we take your advice, the farmer will be no farmer, the potter no longer a potter; none of the elements that make up the community will keep its character. In many cases this does not matter so much: if a cobbler goes to the bad and pretends to be what he is not, he is not a danger to the state; but, as you must surely see, men who make only a vain show of being guardians of the laws and of the commonwealth bring the whole state to utter ruin, just as, on the other hand, its good government and well-being depend entirely on them. We, in fact, are making genuine Guardians who will be the last to bring harm upon the commonwealth; if our critic aims rather at producing a happiness like that of a party of peasants feasting at a fair, what he has in mind is something other than a civic community. So we must consider whether our aim in establishing Guardians is to secure the greatest possible happiness for them, or happiness is something of which we should watch the development in the whole commonwealth. If so, we must compel these Guardians and Auxiliaries of ours to second our efforts; and they, and all the rest with them, must be induced to make themselves perfect masters each of his own craft. In that way, as the community grows into a well-ordered whole, the several classes may be allowed such measure of happiness as their nature will compass.

I think that is an admirable reply.

• • •

We must go back, then, said Socrates, to a subject which ought, perhaps, to have been treated earlier in its proper place; though, after all, it may be suitable that the women should have their turn on the stage when the men have quite finished their performance, especially since you are so insistent. In my judgement, then, the question under what conditions people born and educated as we have described should possess wives and children, and how they should treat them, can be rightly settled only by keeping to the course on which we started them at the outset. We undertook to put these men in the position of watch-dogs guarding a flock. Suppose we follow up the analogy and imagine them bred and reared in the same sort of way. We can then see if that plan will suit our purpose.

How will that be?

In this way. Which do we think right for watch-dogs: should the females guard the flock and hunt with the males and take a share in all they do, or should they be kept within doors as fit for no more than bearing and feeding their puppies, while all the hard work of looking after the flock is left to the males?

They are expected to take their full share, except that we treat them as not quite so strong.

Can you employ any creature for the same work as another, if you do not give them both the same upbringing and education?

No.

Then, if we are to set women to the same tasks as men, we must teach them the same things. They must have the same two branches of training for mind and body and also be taught the art of war, and they must receive the same treatment.

That seems to follow.

Possibly, if these proposals were carried out, they might be ridiculed as involving a good many breaches of custom.

They might indeed.

The most ridiculous—don't you think?—being the notion of women exercising naked along with the men in the wrestling-schools; some of them elderly women too, like the old men who still have a passion for exercise when they are wrinkled and not very agreeable to look at.

Yes, that would be thought laughable, according to our present notions.

Now we have started on this subject, we must not be frightened of the many witticisms that might be aimed at such a revolution, not only in the matter of bodily exercise but in the training of women's minds, and not least when it comes to their bearing arms and riding on horseback. Having begun upon these rules, we must not draw back from the harsher provisions. The wits may be asked to stop being witty and try to be serious; and we may remind them that it is not so long since the Greeks, like most foreign nations of the present day, thought it ridiculous and shameful for men to be seen naked. When gymnastic exercises were first introduced in Crete and later at Sparta, the humorists had their chance to make fun of them; but when experience had shown that nakedness is better uncovered than muffled up, the laughter died down and a practice which the reason approved ceased to look ridiculous to the eye. This shows how idle it is to think anything ludicrous but what is base. One who tries to raise a laugh at any spectacle save that of baseness and folly will also, in his serious moments, set before himself some other standard than goodness of what deserves to be held in honour.

Most assuredly.

The first thing to be settled, then, is whether these proposals are feasible; and it must be open to anyone, whether a humorist or serious-minded, to raise the question whether, in the case of mankind, the feminine nature is capable of taking part with the other sex in all occupations, or in none at all, or in some only; and in particular under which of these heads this business of military service falls. Well begun is half done, and would not this be the best way to begin?

Yes.

Shall we take the other side in this debate and argue against ourselves? We do not want the adversary's position to be taken by storm for lack of defenders.

I have no objection.

Let us state his case for him. "Socrates and Glaucon," he will say, "there is no need for others to dispute your position; you yourselves, at the very outset of founding your commonwealth, agreed that everyone should do the one work for which nature fits him." Yes, of course; I suppose we did. "And isn't there a very great difference in nature between man and woman?" Yes, surely. "Does not that natural difference imply a corresponding difference in the work to be given to each?" Yes. . . .

If, then, we find that either the male sex or the female is specially qualified for any particular form of occupation, then that occupation, we shall say, ought to be assigned to one sex or the other. But if the only difference appears to be that the male begets and the female brings forth, we shall conclude that no difference between man and woman has yet been produced that is relevant to our purpose. We shall continue to think it proper for our Guardians and their wives to share in the same pursuits.

And quite rightly.

The next thing will be to ask our opponent to name any profession or occupation in civic life for the purposes of which woman's nature is different from man's.

That is a fair question.

He might reply, as you did just now, that it is not easy to find a satisfactory answer on the spur of the moment, but that there would be no difficulty after a little reflection.

Perhaps.

Suppose, then, we invite him to follow us and see if we can convince him that there is no occupation concerned with the management of social affairs that is peculiar to women. We will confront him with a question: When you speak of a man having a natural talent for something, do you mean that he finds it easy to learn, and after a little instruction can find out much more for himself; whereas a man who is not so gifted learns with difficulty and no amount of instruction and practice will make him even remember what he has been taught? Is the talented man one whose bodily powers are readily at the service of his mind, instead of being a hindrance? Are not these the marks by which you distinguish the presence of a natural gift for any pursuit?

Yes, precisely.

Now do you know of any human occupation in which the male sex is not superior to the female in all these respects? Need I waste time over exceptions like weaving and watching over saucepans and batches of cakes, though women are supposed to be good at such things and get laughed at when a man does them better?

It is true, he replied, in almost everything one sex is easily beaten by the other. No doubt many women are better at many things than many men; but taking the sexes as a whole, it is as you say.

To conclude, then, there is no occupation concerned with the management of social affairs which belongs either to woman or to man, as such. Natural gifts are to be found here and there in both creatures alike; and every occupation is open to both, so far as their natures are concerned, though woman is for all purposes the weaker.

Certainly.

• • •

It follows that one woman will be fitted by nature to be a Guardian, another will not; because these were the qualities for which we selected our men Guardians. So for the purpose of keeping watch over the commonwealth, woman has the same nature as man, save in so far as she is weaker.

So it appears.

It follows that women of this type must be selected to share the life and duties of Guardians with men of the same type, since they are competent and of a like nature, and the same natures must be allowed the same pursuits.

Yes.

We come round, then, to our former position, that there is nothing contrary to nature in giving our Guardians' wives the same training for mind and body. The practice we proposed to establish was not impossible or visionary, since it was in accordance with nature. Rather, the contrary practice which now prevails turns out to be unnatural.

So it appears.

Well, we set out to inquire whether the plan we proposed was feasible and also the best. That it is feasible is now agreed; we must next settle whether it is the best.

Obviously.

Now, for the purpose of producing a woman fit to be a Guardian, we shall not have one education for men and another for women, precisely because the nature to be taken in hand is the same.

True.

What is your opinion on the question of one man being better than another? Do you think there is no such difference?

Certainly I do not.

And in this commonwealth of ours which will prove the better men—the Guardians who have received the education we described, or the shoemakers who have been trained to make shoes?

It is absurd to ask such a question.

Very well. So these Guardians will be the best of all the citizens?

By far.

And these women the best of all the women?

Yes.

Can anything be better for a commonwealth than to produce in it men and women of the best possible type?

No.

And that result will be brought about by such a system of mental and bodily training as we have described?

Surely.

We may conclude that the institution we proposed was not only practicable, but also the best for the commonwealth.

Yes.

The wives of our Guardians, then, must strip for exercise, since they will be clothed with virtue, and they must take their share in war and in the other social duties of guardianship. They are to have no other occupation; and in these duties the lighter part must fall to the women, because of the weakness of their sex. The man who laughs at naked women, exercising their bodies for the best of reasons, is like one that "gathers fruit unripe," for he does not know what it is that he is laughing at or what he is doing. There will never be a finer saying than the one which declares that whatever does good should be held in honour, and the only shame is in doing harm.

That is perfectly true. . . . So far, then, in regulating the position of women, we may claim to have come safely through with one hazardous proposal, that male and female Guardians shall have all occupations in common. The consistency of the argument is an assurance that the plan is a good one and also feasible. We are like swimmers who have breasted the first wave without being swallowed up.

Not such a small wave either.

You will not call it large when you see the next.

Let me have a look at the next one, then.

Here it is: a law which follows from that principle and all that has gone before, namely that, of these Guardians, no one man and one woman are to set up house together privately: wives are to be held in common by all; so too are the children, and no parent is to know his own child, nor any child his parent.

It will be much harder to convince people that that is either a feasible plan or a good one.

As to its being a good plan, I imagine no one would deny the immense advantage of wives and children being held in common, provided it can be done. I should expect dispute to arise chiefly over the question whether it is possible.

There may well be a good deal of dispute over both points.

You mean, I must meet attacks on two fronts. I was hoping to escape one by running away: if you agreed it was a good plan, then I should only have had to inquire whether it was feasible.

No, we have seen through that maneuvre. You will have to defend both positions.

Well, I must pay the penalty for my cowardice. But grant me one favour. Let me indulge my fancy, like one who entertains himself with idle day-dreams on a solitary walk. Before he has any notion how his desires can be realized, he will set aside that question, to save himself the trouble of reckoning what may or may not be possible. He will assume that his wish has come true, and amuse himself with settling all the details of what he means to do then. So a lazy mind encourages itself to be lazier than ever; and I am giving way to the same weakness myself. I want to put off till later that question, how the thing can be done. For the moment, with your leave, I shall assume it to be possible, and ask how the Rulers will work out the details in practice; and I shall argue that the plan, once carried into effect, would be the best thing in the world for our commonwealth and for its Guardians. That is what I shall now try to make out with your help, if you will allow me to postpone the other question.

Very good; I have no objection.

Well, if our Rulers are worthy of the name, and their Auxiliaries likewise, these latter will be ready to do what they are told, and the Rulers, in giving their commands, will themselves obey our laws and will be faithful to their spirit in any details we leave to their discretion.

No doubt.

It is for you, then, as their lawgiver, who have already selected the men, to select for association with them women who are so far as possible of the same natural capacity. Now since none of them will have any private home of his own, but they will share the same dwelling and eat at common tables, the two sexes will be together; and meeting without restriction for exercise and all through their upbringing, they will surely be drawn towards union with one another by a necessity of their nature—necessity is not too strong a word, I think?

Not too strong for the constraint of love, which for the mass of mankind is more persuasive and compelling than even the necessity of mathematical proof.

Exactly. But in the next place, Glaucon, anything like unregulated unions would be a profanation in a state whose citizens lead the good life. The Rulers will not allow such a thing.

No, it would not be right.

Clearly, then, we must have marriages, as sacred as we can make them; and this sanctity will attach to those which yield the best results.

Certainly. . . .

This, then, Glaucon, is the manner in which the Guardians of your commonwealth are to hold their wives and children in common. Must we not next find arguments to establish that it is consistent with our other institutions and also by far the best plan?

Yes, surely.

We had better begin by asking what is the greatest good at which the lawgiver should aim in laying down the constitution of a state, and what is the worst evil. We can then consider whether our proposals are in keeping with that good and irreconcilable with the evil.

By all means.

Does not the worst evil for a state arise from anything that tends to rend it asunder and destroy its unity, while nothing does it more good than whatever tends to bind it together and make it one?

That is true.

And are not citizens bound together by sharing in the same pleasures and pains, all feeling glad or grieved on the same occasions of gain or loss; whereas the bond is broken when such feelings are no longer universal, but any event of public or personal concern fills some with joy and others with distress?

Certainly.

And this disunion comes about when the words "mine" and "not mine," "another's" and "not another's" are not applied to the same things throughout the community. The best ordered state will be the one in which the largest number of persons use these terms in the same sense, and which accordingly most nearly resembles a single person. When one of us hurts his finger, the whole extent of those bodily connexions which are gathered up in the soul and unified by its ruling element is made aware and it all shares as a whole in the pain of the suffering part; hence we say that the man has a pain in his finger. The same thing is true of the pain or pleasure felt when any other part of the person suffers or is relieved.

Yes; I agree that the best organized community comes nearest to that condition.

And so it will recognize as a part of itself the individual citizen to whom good or evil happens, and will share as a whole in his joy or sorrow.

• • •

But really, Socrates, Glaucon continued, if you are allowed to go on like this, I am afraid you will forget all about the question you thrust aside some time ago: whether a society so constituted can ever come into existence, and if so, how. No doubt, if it did exist, all manner of good things would come about. I can even add some that you have passed over. Men who acknowledged one another as fathers, sons, or brothers and always used those names among themselves would never desert one another; so they would fight with unequalled bravery. And if their womenfolk went out with them to war, either in the ranks or drawn up in the rear to intimidate the enemy and act as a reserve in case of need, I am sure all this would make them invincible. At home, too, I can see many advantages you have not mentioned. But, since I admit that our commonwealth would have all these merits and any number more, if once it came into existence, you need not describe it in further detail. All we have now to do is to convince ourselves that it can be brought into being and how.

This is a very sudden onslaught, said I; you have no mercy on my shilly-shallying. Perhaps you do not realize that, after I have barely escaped the first two waves,[4] the third, which you are now bringing down upon me, is the most formidable of all. When you have seen what it is like and heard my reply, you will be ready to excuse the very natural fears which made me shrink from putting forward such a paradox for discussion.

The more you talk like that, he said, the less we shall be willing to let you off from telling us how this constitution can come into existence; so you had better waste no more time.

Well, said I, let me begin by reminding you that what brought us to this point was our inquiry into the nature of justice and injustice.

True; but what of that?

Merely this: suppose we do find out what justice is, are we going to demand that a man who is just shall have a character which exactly corresponds in every respect to the ideal of justice? Or shall we be satisfied if he comes as near to the ideal as possible and has in him a larger measure of that quality than the rest of the world?

That will satisfy me.

If so, when we set out to discover the essential nature of justice and injustice and what a perfectly just and a perfectly unjust man would be like, supposing them to exist, our purpose was to use them

---

[4] Socrates is referring to the difficulties (waves) he has overcome in proposing equality for women and an end to the traditional family unit.

as ideal patterns: we were to observe the degree of happiness or unhappiness that each exhibited, and to draw the necessary inference that our own destiny would be like that of the one we most resembled. We did not set out to show that these ideals could exist in fact.

That is true.

Then suppose a painter had drawn an ideally beautiful figure complete to the last touch, would you think any the worse of him, if he could not show that a person as beautiful as that could exist?

No, I should not.

Well, we have been constructing in discourse the pattern of an ideal state. Is our theory any the worse, if we cannot prove it possible that a state so organized could be actually founded?

Surely not.

That, then, is the truth of the matter. But if, for your satisfaction, I am to do my best to show under what conditions our ideal would have the best chance of being realized, I must ask you once more to admit that the same principle applies here. Can theory ever be fully realized in practice? Is it not in the nature of things that action should come less close to truth than thought? People may not think so; but do you agree or not?

I do.

Then you must not insist upon my showing that this construction we have traced in thought could be reproduced in fact down to the last detail. You must admit that we shall have found a way to meet your demand for realization, if we can discover how a state might be constituted in the closest accordance with our description. Will not that content you? It would be enough for me.

And for me too.

Then our next attempt, it seems, must be to point out what defect in the working of existing states prevents them from being so organized, and what is the least change that would effect a transformation into this type of government—a single change if possible, or perhaps two; at any rate let us make the changes as few and insignificant as may be.

By all means.

Well, there is one change which, as I believe we can show, would bring about this revolution—not a small change, certainly, nor an easy one, but possible.

What is it?

I have now to confront what we called the third and greatest wave. But I must state my paradox, even though the wave should break in laughter over my head and drown me in ignominy. Now mark what I am going to say.

Go on.

Unless either philosophers become kings in their countries or those who are now called kings and rulers come to be sufficiently inspired with a genuine desire for wisdom; unless, that it to say, political power and philosophy meet together, while the many natures who now go their several ways in the one or the other direction are forcibly debarred from doing so, there can be no rest from troubles, my dear Glaucon, for states, nor yet, as I believe, for all mankind; nor can this commonwealth which we have imagined ever till then see the light of day and grow to its full stature. This it was that I have so long hung back from saying; I knew what a paradox it would be, because it is hard to see that there is no other way of happiness either for the state or for the individual.

• • •

Next, said I, here is a parable[5] to illustrate the degrees in which our nature may be enlightened or unenlightened. Imagine the condition of men living in a sort of cavernous chamber underground, with an entrance open to the light and a long passage all down the cave. Here they have been from childhood, chained by the leg and also by the neck, so that they cannot move and can see only what is in front of them, because the chains will not let them turn their heads. At some distance higher up is the light of a fire burning behind them; and between the prisoners and the fire is a track with a parapet built along it, like the screen at a puppetshow, which hides the performers while they show their puppets over the top.

I see, said he.

Now behind this parapet imagine persons carrying along various artificial objects, including figures of men and animals in wood or stone or other materials, which project above the parapet. Naturally, some of these persons will be talking, others silent.

It is a strange picture, he said, and a strange sort of prisoners.

Like ourselves, I replied; for in the first place prisoners so confined would have seen nothing of themselves or of one another, except the

---

[5] What follows is Plato's view of human alienation—not from a personal God or from society, but from Plato's concept of Reality. This parable has often been referred to as the "Allegory of the Cave."

shadows thrown by the fire-light on the wall of the Cave facing them, would they?

Not if all their lives they had been prevented from moving their heads.

And they would have seen as little of the objects carried past.

Of course.

Now, if they could talk to one another, would they not suppose that their words referred only to those passing shadows which they saw?

Necessarily.

And suppose their prison had an echo from the wall facing them? When one of the people crossing behind them spoke, they could only suppose that the sound came from the shadow passing before their eyes.

No doubt.

In every way, then, such prisoners would recognize as reality nothing but the shadows of those artificial objects.

Inevitably.

Now consider what would happen if their release from the chains and the healing of their unwisdom should come about in this way. Suppose one of them set free and forced suddenly to stand up, turn his head, and walk with eyes lifted to the light; all these movements would be painful, and he would be too dazzled to make out the objects whose shadows he had been used to see. What do you think he would say, if someone told him that what he had formerly seen was meaningless illusion, but now, being somewhat nearer to reality and turned towards more real objects, he was getting a truer view? Suppose further that he were shown the various objects being carried by and were made to say, in reply to questions, what each of them was. Would he not be perplexed and believe the objects now shown him to be not so real as what he formerly saw?

Yes, not nearly so real.

And if he were forced to look at the fire-light itself, would not his eyes ache, so that he would try to escape and turn back to the things which he could see distinctly, convinced that they really were clearer than these other objects now being shown to him?

Yes.

And suppose someone were to drag him away forcibly up the steep and rugged ascent and not let him go until he had hauled him out into the sunlight, would he not suffer pain and vexation at such treatment, and, when he had come out into the light, find his eyes so full of its radiance that he could not see a single one of the things that he was now told were real?

Certainly he would not see them all at once.

He would need, then, to grow accustomed before he could see things in that upper world. At first it would be easiest to make out shadows, and then the images of men and things reflected in water, and later on the things themselves. After that, it would be easier to watch the heavenly bodies and the sky itself by night, looking at the light of the moon and stars rather than the Sun and the Sun's light in the day-time.

Yes, surely.

Last of all, he would be able to look at the Sun and contemplate its nature, not as it appears when reflected in water or any alien medium, but as it is in itself in its own domain.

No doubt.

And now he would begin to draw the conclusion that it is the Sun that produces the seasons and the course of the year and controls everything in the visible world, and moreover is in a way the cause of all that he and his companions used to see.

Clearly he would come at last to that conclusion.

Then if he called to mind his fellow prisoners and what passed for wisdom in his former dwelling-place, he would surely think himself happy in the change and be sorry for them. They may have had a practice of honouring and commending one another, with prizes for the man who had the keenest eye for the passing shadows and the best memory for the order in which they followed or accompanied one another, so that he could make a good guess as to which was going to come next. Would our released prisoner be likely to covet those prizes or to envy the men exalted to honour and power in the Cave? Would he not feel like Homer's Achilles, that he would far sooner "be on earth as a hired servant in the house of a landless man" or endure anything rather than go back to his old beliefs and live in the old way?

Yes, he would prefer any fate to such a life.

Now imagine what would happen if he went down again to take his former seat in the Cave. Coming suddenly out of the sunlight, his eyes would be filled with darkness. He might be required once more to deliver his opinion on those shadows, in competition with the prisoners who had never been released, while his eyesight was still dim and unsteady; and it might take some time to become used to the darkness. They would laugh at him and say that he had gone up only to come back with his sight ruined; it was worth no one's while even to attempt the ascent. If they could lay hands on the man who was trying to set them free and lead them up, they would kill him.[6]

Yes, they would.

Every feature in this parable, my dear Glaucon, is meant to fit our earlier analysis. The prison dwelling corresponds to the region revealed to us through the sense of sight, and the fire-light within it to the power of the Sun. The ascent to see the things in the upper world you may take as standing for the upward journey of the soul into the region of the intelligible; then you will be in possession of what I surmise, since that is what you wish to be told. Heaven knows whether it is true; but this, at any rate, is how it appears to me. In the world of knowledge, the last thing to be perceived and only with great difficulty is the essential Form of Goodness. Once it is perceived, the conclusion must follow that, for all things, this is the cause of whatever is right and good; in the visible world it gives birth to light and to the lord of light, while it is itself sovereign in the intelligible world and the parent of intelligence and truth. Without having had a vision of this Form no one can act with wisdom, either in his own life or in matters of state.

So far as I can understand, I share your belief. . . .

You will see, then, Glaucon, that there will be no real injustice in compelling our philosophers to watch over and care for the other citizens. We can fairly tell them that their compeers in other states may quite reasonably refuse to collaborate: there they have sprung up, like a self-sown plant, in despite of their country's institutions; no one has fostered their growth, and they cannot be expected to show gratitude for a care they have never received. "But," we shall say, "it is not so with you. We have brought you into existence for your country's sake as well as for your own, to be like leaders and king-bees in a hive; you have been better and more thoroughly educated than those others and hence you are more capable of playing your part both as men of thought and as men of action. You must go down, then, each in his turn, to live with the rest and let your eyes grow accustomed to the darkness. You will then see a thousand

---

[6] As was the case with Socrates.

times better than those who live there always; you will recognize every image for what it is and know what it represents, because you have seen justice, beauty, and goodness in their reality; and so you and we shall find life in our commonwealth no mere dream, as it is in most existing states, where men live fighting one another about shadows and quarrelling for power, as if that were a great prize; whereas in truth government can be at its best and free from dissension only where the destined rulers are least desirous of holding office."

10

Aristotle

Nicomachean Ethics

🔲

Today many people accept the idea that morals are relative—relative, that is, to the cultural environment; but most influential thinkers among the ancient Greeks rejected this view. They believed it possible to arrive, rationally, at values true for all times and places. That their pursuit of such values was carried on so brilliantly is one of the marvels of Western culture.

In this achievement no one took a greater part than Aristotle (384–322 B.C.). He was born at Stagira in Chalcidice, and his father was physician to the king of Macedon. From the age of seventeen to the death of Plato, twenty years later, Aristotle studied under the master at the Academy; he then spent three years as tutor to the young Alexander of Macedon. In 335 Aristotle set up his famous Lyceum at Athens, a rival school to the Academy. During the next dozen years he taught and lectured, while producing a wealth of writings. Upon Alexander's death in 323 he was forced by the anti-Macedonian party to flee Athens, and he died in exile a year later.

Throughout his works, which cover a wide range of subjects, Aristotle was concerned (as was Plato) with the search for reality, for objective truth; but, more down-to-earth than Plato, he sought to show that sense objects are no less real than the world of Forms or Ideas. Thus in the Nicomachean Ethics,★ *which deals with the problem of the good life, values are tested by Aristotle's observation of things as they are, rather than by a vision of the ideal as in Plato.*

Although Aristotle constantly strove for permanent and universal values,

Aristotle, *The Nicomachean Ethics,* trans. F. H. Peters (London: Kegan Paul, Trench, Truebner, 1886), 1–4, 12–17, 23–27, 36–38, 41–55, 113–19.

★ The book's title reflects the fact that the author reportedly wrote it for his son, Nicomachus.

the Ethics *reflects conditions peculiar to Hellenic life. Its ideals are always aristocratic—concerned with the good life for the perceptive few, not for the indifferent masses. Thus, after many centuries of Christian and democratic influences, it is not always easy for the modern Western reader to understand the Aristotelian "high-minded man" or the virtues he represents. Nevertheless, the book has made a lasting impression on Western thought and conduct; to this day, wherever the all-round amateur is prized, wherever manners are appreciated, and wherever narrow professionalism is deplored, the spirit of the* Ethics *still lives.*

Every art and every kind of inquiry, and likewise every act and purpose, seems to aim at some good: and so it has been well said that the good is that at which everything aims.

But a difference is observable among these aims or ends. What is aimed at is sometimes the exercise of a faculty, sometimes a certain result beyond that exercise. And where there is an end beyond the act, there the result is better than the exercise of the faculty.

Now since there are many kinds of actions and many arts and sciences, it follows that there are many ends also; *e.g.* health is the end of medicine, ships of shipbuilding, victory of the art of war, and wealth of economy.

But when several of these are subordinated to some one art or science,—as the making of bridles and other trappings to the art of horsemanship, and this in turn, along with all else that the soldier does, to the art of war, and so on,—then the end of the master-art is always more desired than the ends of the subordinate arts, since these are pursued for its sake. And this is equally true whether the end in view be the mere exercise of a faculty or something beyond that, as in the above instances.

If then in what we do there be some end which we wish for on its own account, choosing all the others as means to this, but not every end without exception as a means to something else (for so we should go on *ad infinitum,* and desire would be left void and objectless),—this evidently will be the good or the best of all things.

And surely from a practical point of view it much concerns us to know this good; for then, like archers shooting at a definite mark, we shall be more likely to attain what we want.

If this be so, we must try to indicate roughly what it is, and first of all to which of the arts or sciences it belongs.

It would seem to belong to the supreme art or science, that one which most of all deserves the name of master-art or master-science.

Now Politics seems to answer to this description. For it prescribes which of the sciences a state needs, and which each man shall study, and up to what point; and to it we see subordinated even the highest arts, such as economy, rhetoric, and the art of war.

Since then it makes use of the other practical sciences, and since it further ordains what men are to do and from what to refrain, its end must include the ends of the others, and must be the proper good of man.

For though this good is the same for the individual and the state, yet the good of the state seems a grander and more perfect thing both to attain and to secure; and glad as one would be to do this service for a single individual, to do it for a people and for a number of states is nobler and more divine.

This then is the aim of the present inquiry, which is a sort of political inquiry.

We must be content if we can attain to so much precision in our statement as the subject before us admits of; for the same degree of accuracy is no more to be expected in all kinds of reasoning than in all kinds of manufacture.

Now what is noble and just (with which Politics deals) is so various and so uncertain, that some think these are merely conventional and not natural distinctions.

There is a similar uncertainty also about what is good, because good things often do people harm: men have before now been ruined by wealth, and have lost their lives through courage.

Our subject, then, and our data being of this nature, we must be content if we can indicate the truth roughly and in outline, and if, in dealing with matters that are not amenable to immutable laws, and reasoning from premises that are but probable, we can arrive at probable conclusions.

• • •

Leaving these matters, then, let us return once more to the question, what this good can be of which we are in search.

It seems to be different in different kinds of action and in different arts,—one thing in medicine and another in war, and so on. What then is the good in each of these cases? Surely that for the sake of which all else is done. And that in medicine is health, in war is victory, in building is a house,—a different thing in each different case, but always, in whatever we do and in whatever we choose, the end. For it is always for the sake of the end that all else is done.

If then there be one end of all that man does, this end will be the realizable good,—or these ends, if there be more than one.

Our argument has thus come round by a different path to the same point as before. This point we must try to explain more clearly.

We see that there are many ends. But some of these are chosen only as means, as wealth, flutes, and the whole class of instruments. And so it is plain that not all ends are final.

But the best of all things must, we conceive, be something final.

If then there be only one final end, this will be what we are seeking,—or if there be more than one, then the most final of them.

Now that which is pursued as an end in itself is more final than that which is pursued as means to something else, and that which is never chosen as means than that which is chosen both as an end in itself and as means, and that is strictly final which is always chosen as an end in itself and never as means.

Happiness seems more than anything else to answer to this description: for we always choose it for itself, and never for the sake of something else; while honour and pleasure and reason, and all virtue or excellence, we choose partly indeed for themselves (for, apart from any result, we should choose each of them), but partly also for the sake of happiness, supposing that they will help to make us happy. But no one chooses happiness for the sake of these things, or as a means to anything else at all.

We seem to be led to the same conclusion when we start from the notion of self-sufficiency.

The final good is thought to be self-sufficing [or all-sufficing]. In applying this term we do not regard a man as an individual leading a solitary life, but we also take account of parents, children, wife, and, in short, friends and fellow-citizens generally, since man is naturally a social being. Some limit must indeed be set to this; for if you go on to parents and descendants and friends of friends, you will never come to a stop. But this we will consider further on: for the present we will take self-sufficing to mean what by itself makes life desirable and in want of nothing. And happiness is believed to answer to this description.

And further, happiness is believed to be the most desirable thing in the world, and that not merely as one among other good things: if it were merely one among other good things [so that other things could be added to it], it is plain that the addition of the least of other goods must make it more desirable; for the addition becomes a surplus of good, and of two goods the greater is always more desirable.

Thus it seems that happiness is something final and self-sufficing, and is the end of all that man does.

But perhaps the reader thinks that though no one will dispute the statement that happiness is the best thing in the world, yet a still more precise definition of it is needed.

This will best be gained, I think, by asking, What is the function of man? For as the goodness and the excellence of a piper or a sculptor, or the practiser of any art, and generally of those who have any function or business to do, lies in that function, so man's good would seem to lie in his function, if he has one.

But can we suppose that, while a carpenter and a cobbler has a function and a business of his own, man has no business and no function assigned him by nature? Nay, surely as his several members, eye and hand and foot, plainly have each his own function, so we must suppose that man also has some function over and above all these.

What then is it?

Life evidently he has in common even with the plants, but we want that which is peculiar to him. We must exclude, therefore, the life of mere nutrition and growth.

Next to this comes the life of sense; but this too he plainly shares with horses and cattle and all kinds of animals.

There remains then the life whereby he acts—the life of his rational nature, with its two sides or divisions, one rational as obeying reason, the other rational as having and exercising reason.

But as this expression is ambiguous, we must be understood to mean thereby the life that consists in the exercise of the faculties; for this seems to be more properly entitled to the name.

The function of man, then, is exercise of his vital faculties [or soul] on one side in obedience to reason, and on the other side with reason.

But what is called the function of a man of any profession and the function of a man who is good in that profession are generically the same, *e.g.* of a harper and of a good harper; and this holds in all cases without exception, only that in the case of the latter his superior excellence at his work is added; for we say a harper's function is to harp, and a good harper's to harp well.

Man's function then being, as we say, a kind of life—that is to say, exercise of his faculties and action of various kinds with reason—the good man's function is to do this well and beautifully [or nobly].

But the function of anything is done well when it is done in accordance with the proper excellence of that thing.

Putting all this together, then, we find that the good of man is exercise of his faculties in accordance with excellence or virtue, or, if there be more than one, in accordance with the best and most complete virtue.

But there must also be a full term of years for this exercise; for one swallow or one fine day does not make a spring, nor does one day or any small space of time make a blessed or happy man.

This, then, may be taken as a rough outline of the good; for this, I think, is the proper method.

• • •

Are we, then, to call no man happy as long as he lives, but to wait for the end, as Solon[1] said?

And, supposing we have to allow this, do we mean that he actually is happy after he is dead? Surely that is absurd, especially for us who say that happiness is a kind of activity or life.

But if we do not call the dead man happy, and if Solon meant not this, but that only then could we safely apply the term to a man, as being now beyond the reach of evil and calamity, then here too we find some ground for objection. For it is thought that both good and evil may in some sort befall a dead man (just as they may befall a living man, although he is unconscious of them), *e.g.* honours rendered to him, or the reverse of these, and again the prosperity or the misfortune of his children and all his descendants.

But this, too, has its difficulties; for after a man has lived happily to a good old age, and ended as he lived, it is possible that many changes may befall him in the persons of his descendants, and that some of them may turn out good and meet with the good fortune they deserve, and others the reverse. It is evident too that the degree in which the descendants are related to their ancestors may vary to

[1] A sixth-century Athenian sage and lawgiver. (See the selection from Herodotus, pp. 76–79).

any extent. And it would be a strange thing if the dead man were to change with these changes and become happy and miserable by turns. But it would also be strange to suppose that the dead are not affected at all, even for a limited time, by the fortunes of their posterity.

But let us return to our former question; for its solution will, perhaps, clear up this other difficulty.

The saying of Solon may mean that we ought to look for the end and then call a man happy, not because he now is, but because he once was happy.

But surely it is strange that when he is happy we should refuse to say what is true of him, because we do not like to apply the term to living men in view of the changes to which they are liable, and because we hold happiness to be something that endures and is little liable to change, while the fortunes of one and the same man often undergo many revolutions: for, it is argued, it is plain that, if we follow the changes of fortune, we shall call the same man happy and miserable many times over, making the happy man "a sort of chameleon and one who rests on no sound foundation."

We reply that it cannot be right thus to follow fortune. For it is not in this that our weal or woe lies; but, as we said, though the life of man needs these gifts of fortune, yet it is the excellent employment of his powers that constitutes his happiness, as the reverse of this constitutes his misery.

But the discussion of this difficulty leads to a further confirmation of our account. For nothing human is so constant as the excellent exercise of our faculties. The sciences themselves seem to be less abiding. And the highest of these exercises are the most abiding, because the happy are occupied with them most of all and most continuously (for this seems to be the reason why we do not forget how to do them).

The happy man, then, as we define him, will have this required property of permanence, and all through life will preserve his character; for he will be occupied continually, or with the least possible interruption, in excellent deeds and excellent speculations; and, whatever his fortune be, he will take it in the noblest fashion, and bear himself always and in all things suitably, since he is truly good and "foursquare without a flaw."

But the dispensations of fortune are many, some great, some small. The small ones, whether good or evil, plainly are of no weight in the scale; but the great ones, when numerous, will make life happier if they be good; for they help to give a grace to life themselves, and their use is noble and good; but, if they be evil, will enfeeble and spoil happiness; for they bring pain, and often impede the exercise of our faculties.

But nevertheless true worth shines out even here, in the calm endurance of many great misfortunes, not through insensibility, but through nobility and greatness of soul. And if it is what man does that determines the character of his life, as we said, then no happy man will become miserable, for he will never do what is hateful and base. For we hold that the man who is truly good and wise will bear with dignity whatever fortune sends, and will always make the best of his circumstances, as a good general will turn the forces at his command to the best account, and a good shoemaker will make the best shoe that can be made out of a given piece of leather, and so on with all other crafts.

If this be so, the happy man will never become miserable, though he will not be truly happy if he meets with the fate of Priam.[2]

But yet he is not unstable and lightly changed: he will not be moved from his happiness easily, nor by any ordinary misfortunes, but only by many heavy ones; and after such, he will not recover his happiness again in short time, but if at all, only in a considerable period, which has a certain completeness, and in which he attains to great and noble things.

We shall meet all objections, then, if we say that a happy man is "one who exercises his faculties in accordance with perfect excellence, being duly furnished with external goods, not for any chance time, but for a full term of years": to which perhaps we should add, "and who shall continue to live so, and shall die as he lived," since the future is veiled to us, but happiness we take to be the end and in all ways perfectly final or complete.

If this be so, we may say that those living men are blessed or perfectly happy who both have and shall continue to have these characteristics, but happy as men only.

• • •

But our present inquiry has not, like the rest, a merely speculative aim; we are not inquiring merely in order to know what excellence

---

[2] King of Troy. Slain by Achilles' son upon the fall of the city.

or virtue is, but in order to become good; for otherwise it would profit us nothing. We must ask therefore about these acts, and see of what kind they are to be; for, as we said, it is they that determine our habits or character.

• • •

First of all, then, we must observe that, in matters of this sort, to fall short and to exceed are alike fatal. This is plain (to illustrate what we cannot see by what we can see) in the case of strength and health. Too much and too little exercise alike destroy strength, and to take too much meat and drink, or to take too little, is equally ruinous to health, but the fitting amount produces and increases and preserves them. Just so, then, is it with temperance also, and courage, and the other virtues. The man who shuns and fears everything and never makes a stand, becomes a coward; while the man who fears nothing at all, but will face anything, becomes foolhardy. So, too, the man who takes his fill of any kind of pleasure, and abstains from none, is a profligate, but the man who shuns all (like him whom we call a "boor") is devoid of sensibility. For temperance and courage are destroyed both by excess and defect, but preserved by moderation.

• • •

But here we may be asked what we mean by saying that men can become just and temperate only by doing what is just and temperate: surely, it may be said, if their acts are just and temperate, they themselves are already just and temperate, as they are grammarians and musicians if they do what is grammatical and musical.

We may answer, I think, firstly, that this is not quite the case even with the arts. A man may do something grammatical [or write something correctly] by chance, or at the prompting of another person: he will not be grammatical till he not only does something grammatical, but also does it grammatically [or like a grammatical person], *i.e.* in virtue of his own knowledge of grammar.

But, secondly, the virtues are not in this point analogous to the arts. The products of art have their excellence in themselves, and so it is enough if when produced they are of a certain quality; but in the case of the virtues, a man is not said to act justly or temperately [or like a just or temperate man] if what he does merely be of a certain sort—he must also be in a certain state of mind when he does it; *i.e.,* first of all, he must know what he is doing; secondly, he must choose it, and choose it for itself; and, thirdly, his act must be the expression of a formed and stable character. Now, of these conditions, only one, the knowledge, is necessary for the possession of any art; but for the possession of the virtues knowledge is of little or no avail, while the other conditions that result from repeatedly doing what is just and temperate are not a little important, but all-important.

The thing that is done, therefore, is called just or temperate when it is such as the just or temperate man would do; but the man who does it is not just or temperate, unless he also does it in the spirit of the just or the temperate man.

It is right, then, to say that by doing what is just a man becomes just, and temperate by doing what is temperate, while without doing thus he has no chance of ever becoming good.

But most men, instead of doing thus, fly to theories, and fancy that they are philosophizing and that this will make them good, like a sick man who listens attentively to what the doctor says and then disobeys all his orders. This sort of philosophizing will no more produce a healthy habit of mind than this sort of treatment will produce a healthy habit of body.

• • •

We have thus found the genus to which virtue belongs; but we want to know, not only that it is a trained faculty, but also what species of trained faculty it is.

We may safely assert that the virtue or excellence of a thing causes that thing both to be itself in good condition and to perform its function well. The excellence of the eye, for instance, makes both the eye and its work good; for it is by the excellence of the eye that we see well. So the proper excellence of the horse makes a horse what he should be, and makes him good at running, and carrying his rider, and standing a charge.

If, then, this holds good in all cases, the proper excellence or virtue of man will be a habit or trained faculty that makes a man good and makes him perform his function well.

How this is to be done we have already said, but we may exhibit the same conclusion in another way, by inquiring what the nature of this virtue is.

Now, if we have any quantity, whether continuous or discrete, it is possible to take either a larger [or too large], or a smaller [or too small], or an equal [or fair] amount, and that either absolutely or relatively to our own needs.

By an equal or fair amount I understand a mean amount, or one that lies between excess and deficiency.

By the absolute mean, or mean relatively to the thing itself, I understand that which is equidistant from both extremes, and this is one and the same for all.

By the mean relatively to us I understand that which is neither too much nor too little for us; and this is not one and the same for all.

For instance, if ten be larger [or too large] and two be smaller [or too small], if we take six we take the mean relatively to the thing itself [or the arithmetical mean]; for it exceeds one extreme by the same amount by which it is exceeded by the other extreme: and this is the mean in arithmetical proportion.

But the mean relatively to us cannot be found in this way. If ten pounds of food is too much for a given man to eat, and two pounds too little, it does not follow that the trainer will order him six pounds: for that also may perhaps be too much for the man in question, or too little; too little for Milo, too much for the beginner. The same holds true in running and wrestling.

And so we may say generally that a master in any art avoids what is too much and what is too little, and seeks for the mean and chooses it—not the absolute but the relative mean.

Every art or science, then, perfects its work in this way, looking to the mean and bringing its work up to this standard; so that people are wont to say of a good work that nothing could be taken from it or added to it, implying that excellence is destroyed by excess or deficiency, but secured by observing the mean. And good artists, as we say, do in fact keep their eyes fixed on this in all that they do.

Virtue therefore, since like nature it is more exact and better than any art, must also aim at the mean—virtue of course meaning moral virtue or excellence; for it has to do with passions and actions, and it is these that admit of excess and deficiency and the mean. For instance, it is possible to feel fear, confidence, desire, anger, pity, and generally to be affected pleasantly and painfully, either too much or too little, in either case wrongly; but to be thus affected at the right times, and on the right occasions, and towards the right persons, and with the right object, and in the right fashion, is the mean course and the best course, and these are characteristics of virtue. And in the same way our outward acts also admit of excess and deficiency, and the mean or due amount.

Virtue, then, has to deal with feelings or passions and with outward acts, in which excess is wrong and deficiency also is blamed, but the mean amount is praised and is right—both of which are characteristics of virtue.

Virtue, then, is a kind of moderation inasmuch as it aims at the mean or moderate amount.

Again, there are many ways of going wrong (for evil is infinite in nature, to use a Pythagorean figure, while good is finite), but only one way of going right; so that the one is easy and the other hard— easy to miss the mark and hard to hit. On this account also, then, excess and deficiency are characteristic of vice, hitting the mean is characteristic of virtue:

> "Goodness is simple, ill takes any shape."

Virtue, then, is a habit or trained faculty of choice, the characteristic of which lies in observing the mean relatively to the persons concerned, and which is guided by reason, *i.e.* by the judgment of the prudent man.

And it is a moderation, firstly, inasmuch as it comes in the middle or mean between two vices, one on the side of excess, the other on the side of defect; and, secondly, inasmuch as, while these vices fall short of or exceed the due measure in feeling and in action, it finds and chooses the mean, middling, or moderate amount.

Regarded in its essence, therefore, or according to the definition of its nature, virtue is a moderation or middle state, but viewed in its relation to what is best and right it is the extreme of perfection.

But it is not all actions nor all passions that admit of moderation; there are some whose very names imply badness, as malevolence, shamelessness, envy, and, among acts, adultery, theft, murder. These and all other like things are blamed as being bad in themselves, and not merely in their excess or deficiency. It is impossible therefore to go right in them; they are always wrong: rightness and wrongness in such things (*e.g.* in adultery) does not depend upon whether it is the right person and occasion and manner, but the mere doing of any one of them is wrong.

It would be equally absurd to look for moderation or excess or deficiency in unjust cowardly or profligate conduct; for then there would be moderation in excess or deficiency, and excess in excess, and deficiency in deficiency.

The fact is that just as there can be no excess or deficiency in temperance or courage because the mean or moderate amount is, in a sense, an extreme, so in these kinds of conduct also there can be no moderation or excess or deficiency, but the acts are wrong however they be done. For, to put it generally, there cannot be moderation in excess or deficiency, nor excess or deficiency in moderation.

But it is not enough to make these general statements [about virtue and vice]: we must go on and apply them to particulars [i.e. to the several virtues and vices]. For in reasoning about matters of conduct general statements are too vague, and do not convey so much truth as particular propositions. It is with particulars that conduct is concerned: our statements, therefore, when applied to these particulars, should be found to hold good.

These particulars then [i.e. the several virtues and vices and the several acts and affections with which they deal], we will take from the following table.

Moderation in the feelings of fear and confidence is courage: of those that exceed, he that exceeds in fearlessness has no name (as often happens), but he that exceeds in confidence is foolhardy, while he that exceeds in fear, but is deficient in confidence, is cowardly.

Moderation in respect of certain pleasures and also (though to a less extent) certain pains is temperance, while excess is profligacy. But defectiveness in the matter of these pleasures is hardly ever found, and so this sort of people also have as yet received no name: let us put them down as "void of sensibility."

In the matter of giving and taking money, moderation is liberality, excess and deficiency are prodigality and illiberality. But these two vices exceed and fall short in contrary ways: the prodigal exceeds in spending, but falls short in taking; while the illiberal man exceeds in taking, but falls short in spending.

(For the present we are but giving an outline or summary, and aim at nothing more; we shall afterwards treat these points in greater detail.)

But, besides these, there are other dispositions in the matter of money: there is a moderation which is called magnificence (for the magnificent is not the same as the liberal man: the former deals with large sums, the latter with small), and an excess which is called bad taste or vulgarity, and a deficiency which is called meanness; and these vices differ from those which are opposed to liberality: how they differ will be explained later.

With respect to honour and disgrace, there is a moderation which is high-mindedness, an excess which may be called vanity, and a deficiency which is little-mindedness.

But just as we said that liberality is related to magnificence, differing only in that it deals with small sums, so here there is a virtue related to high-mindedness, and differing only in that it is concerned with small instead of great honours. A man may have a due desire for honour, and also more or less than a due desire: he that carries this desire to excess is called ambitious, he that has not enough of it is called unambitious, but he that has the due amount has no name. There are also no abstract names for the characters, except "ambition," corresponding to ambitious. And on this account those who occupy the extremes lay claim to the middle place. And in common parlance, too, the moderate man is sometimes called ambitious and sometimes unambitious, and sometimes the ambitious man is praised and sometimes the unambitious. Why this is we will explain afterwards; for the present we will follow out our plan and enumerate the other types of character.

In the matter of anger also we find excess and deficiency and moderation. The characters themselves hardly have recognized names, but as the moderate man is here called gentle, we will call his character gentleness; of those who go into extremes, we may take the term wrathful for him who exceeds, with wrathfulness for the vice, and wrathless for him who is deficient, with wrathfulness for his character.

Besides these, there are three kinds of moderation, bearing some resemblance to one another, and yet different. They all have to do with intercourse in speech and action, but they differ in that one has to do with the truthfulness of this intercourse, while the other two have to do with its pleasantness—one of the two with pleasantness in matters of amusement, the other with pleasantness in all the relations of life. We must therefore speak of these qualities also in order that we may the more plainly see how, in all cases, moderation is praiseworthy, while the extreme courses are neither right nor praiseworthy, but blamable.

In these cases also names are for the most part wanting, but we must try, here as elsewhere, to coin names ourselves, in order to make our argument clear and easy to follow.

In the matter of truth, then, let us call him who observes the mean a true (or truthful) person, and observance of the mean truth (or truthfulness): pretence, when it exaggerates, may be called boasting, and the person a boaster; when it understates, let the names be irony and ironical.

With regard to pleasantness in amusement, he who observes the mean may be called witty, and his character wittiness; excess may be called buffoonery, and the man a buffoon; while boorish may stand for the person who is deficient, and boorishness for his character.

With regard to pleasantness in the other affairs of life, he who makes himself properly pleasant may be called friendly, and his moderation friendliness; he that exceeds may be called obsequious if he have no ulterior motive but a flatterer if he has an eye to his own advantage; he that is deficient in this respect, and always makes himself disagreeable, may be called a quarrelsome or peevish fellow.

Moreover, in mere emotions and in our conduct with regard to them, there are ways of observing the mean; for instance, shame is not a virtue, but yet the modest man is praised. For in these matters also we speak of this man as observing the mean, of that man as going beyond it (as the shame-faced man whom the least thing makes shy), while he who is deficient in the feeling, or lacks it altogether, is called shameless; but the term modest is applied to him who observes the mean.

Righteous indignation, again, hits the mean between envy and malevolence. These have to do with feelings of pleasure and pain at what happens to our neighbors. A man is called righteously indignant when he feels pain at the sight of undeserved prosperity, but your envious man goes beyond him and is pained by the sight of any one in prosperity, while the malevolent man is so far from being pained that he actually exults in the sight of prosperous iniquity.

But we shall have another opportunity of discussing these matters.

As for justice, the term is used in more senses than one; we will, therefore, after disposing of the above questions, distinguish these various senses, and show how each of these kinds of justice is a kind of moderation.

And then we will treat of the intellectual virtues in the same way.

There are, as we said, three classes of disposition, viz. two kinds of vice, one marked by excess, the other by deficiency, and one kind of virtue, the observance of the mean.

Now, the extreme dispositions are opposed both to the mean or moderate disposition and to one another, while the moderate disposition is opposed to both the extremes. Just as a quantity which is equal to a given quantity is also greater when compared with a less, and less when compared with a greater quantity, so the mean or moderate dispositions exceed as compared with the defective dispositions, and fall short as compared with the excessive dispositions, both in feeling and in action; *e.g.* the courageous man seems fool-hardy as compared with the coward, and cowardly as compared with the foolhardy; and similarly the temperate man appears profligate in comparison with the insensible, and insensible in comparison with the profligate man; and the liberal man appears prodigal by the side of the illiberal man, and illiberal by the side of the prodigal man.

And so the extreme characters try to displace the mean or moderate character, and each represents him as falling into the opposite extreme, the coward calling the courageous man foolhardy, the foolhardy calling him coward, and so on in other cases.

But while the mean and the extremes are thus opposed to one another, the extremes are still more contrary to each other than to the mean; for they are further removed from one another than from the mean, as that which is greater than a given magnitude is further from that which is less, and that which is less is further from that which is greater, than either the greater or the less is from that which is equal to the given magnitude.

Sometimes, again, an extreme, when compared with the mean, has a sort of resemblance to it, as foolhardiness to courage, or prodigality to liberality; but there is the greatest possible dissimilarity between the extremes.

Again, "things that are as far as possible removed from each other" is the accepted definition of contraries, so that the further things are removed from each other the more contrary they are.

In comparison with the mean, however, it is sometimes the deficiency that is the more opposed, and sometimes the excess; *e.g.* foolhardiness, which is excess, is not so much opposed to courage as cowardice, which is deficiency; but insensibility, which is lack of feeling, is not so much opposed to temperance as profligacy, which is excess.

The reasons for this are two. One is the reason derived from the nature of the matter itself: since one extreme is, in fact, nearer and more similar to the mean, we naturally do not oppose it to the mean so strongly as the other; *e.g.* as foolhardiness seems more similar to courage and nearer to it, and cowardice more dissimilar, we speak of cowardice as the opposite rather than the other: for that which is further removed from the mean seems to be more opposed to it.

This, then, is one reason, derived from the nature of the thing itself. Another reason lies in ourselves: and it is this—those things to which we happen to be more prone by nature appear to be more opposed to the mean: *e.g.* our natural inclination is rather towards in-dulgence in pleasure, and so we more easily fall into profligate than into regular habits: those courses, then, in which we are more apt to run to great lengths are spoken of as more opposed to the mean; and thus profligacy, which is an excess, is more opposed to temperance than the deficiency is.

We have sufficiently explained, then, that moral virtue is modera-tion or observance of the mean, and in what sense, viz. (1) as holding a middle position between two vices, one on the side of excess, and the other on the side of deficiency, and (2) as aiming at the mean or moderate amount both in feeling and in action.

And on this account it is a hard thing to be good; for finding the middle or the mean in each case is a hard thing, just as finding the middle or centre of a circle is a thing that is not within the power of everybody, but only of him who has the requisite knowledge.

• • •

High-mindedness would seem from its very name to have to do with great things; let us first ascertain what these are.

It will make no difference whether we consider the quality itself, or the man who exhibits the quality.

By a high-minded man we seem to mean one who claims much and deserves much: for he who claims much without deserving it is a fool; but the possessor of a virtue is never foolish or silly. The man we have described, then, is high-minded.

He who deserves little and claims little is temperate [or modest], but not high-minded: for high-mindedness [or greatness of soul] implies greatness, just as beauty implies stature; small men may be neat and well proportioned, but cannot be called beautiful.

He who claims much without deserving it is vain (though not every one who claims more than he deserves is vain).

He who claims less than he deserves is little-minded, whether his deserts be great or moderate, or whether they be small and he claims still less: but this little-mindedness is most conspicuous in him whose deserts are great; for what would he do if his deserts were less than they are?

The high-minded man, then, in respect of the greatness of his deserts occupies an extreme position, but in that he behaves as he ought, observes the mean; for he claims that which he deserves, while all the others claim too much or too little.

But now if he deserves much and claims much, and most of all deserves and claims the greatest things, there will be one thing with which he will be especially concerned. For desert has reference to external good things. Now, the greatest of external good things we may assume to be that which we render to the Gods as their due, and that which people in high stations most desire, and which is the prize appointed for the noblest deeds. But the thing that answers to this description is honour, which, we may safely say, is the greatest of all external goods. Honours and dishonours, therefore, are the field in which the high-minded man behaves as he ought.

And indeed we may see, without going about to prove it, that honour is what high-minded men are concerned with; for it is honour that great men claim and deserve.

The little-minded man falls short, whether we compare his claims with his own deserts or with what the high-minded man claims for himself.

The vain or conceited man exceeds what is due to himself, though he does not exceed the high-minded man in his claims.

But the high-minded man, as he deserves the greatest things, must be a perfectly good or excellent man; for the better man always deserves the greater things, and the best possible man the greatest possible things. The really high-minded man, therefore, must be a good or excellent man. And indeed greatness in every virtue or excellence would seem to be necessarily implied in being a high-minded or great-souled man.

It would be equally inconsistent with the high-minded man's character to run along swinging his arms, and to commit an act of injustice; for what thing is there for love of which he would do anything unseemly, seeing that all things are of little account to him?

Survey him point by point and you will find that the notion of a high-minded man that is not a good or excellent man is utterly absurd. Indeed, if we were not good, he could not be worthy of honour; for honour is the prize of virtue, and is rendered to the good as their due.

High-mindedness, then, seems to be the crowning grace, as it were, of the virtues; it makes them greater, and cannot exist without them. And on this account it is a hard thing to be truly high-minded; for it is impossible without the union of all the virtues.

The high-minded man, then, exhibits his character especially in the matter of honours and dishonours and at great honour from good men he will be moderately pleased, as getting nothing more than his due, or even less; for no honour can be adequate to complete virtue; but nevertheless he will accept it, as they have nothing greater to offer him. But honour from ordinary men and on trivial grounds he will utterly despise; for that is not what he deserves. And dishonour likewise he will make light of; for he will never merit it.

But though it is especially in the matter of honours, as we have said, that the high-minded man displays his character, yet he will also observe the mean in his feelings with regard to wealth and power and all kinds of good and evil fortune, whatever may befall him, and will neither be very much exalted by prosperity, nor very much cast down by adversity; seeing that not even honour affects him as if it were a very important thing. For power and wealth are desirable for honour's sake (at least, those who have them wish to gain honour by them). He then who thinks lightly of honour must think lightly of them also.

And so high-minded men seem to look down upon everything.

But the gifts of fortune also are commonly thought to contribute to high-mindedness. For those who are well born are thought worthy of honour, and those who are powerful or wealthy; for they are in a position of superiority, and that which is superior in any good thing is always held in greater honour. And so these things do make people more high-minded in a sense; for such people find honour from some. But in strictness it is only the good man that is worthy of honour, though he that has both goodness and good fortune is commonly thought to be more worthy of honour. Those, however, who have these good things without virtue, neither have any just claim to great things, nor are properly to be called high-minded; for neither is possible without complete virtue.

But those who have these good things readily come to be supercilious and insolent. For without virtue it is not easy to bear the gifts of fortune becomingly; and so, being unable to bear them, and thinking themselves superior to everybody else, such people look down upon others, and yet themselves do whatever happens to please them. They imitate the high-minded man without being really like him, and they imitate him where they can; that is to say, they do not exhibit virtue in their acts, but they look down upon others. Only the high-minded man never looks down upon others without justice (for he estimates them correctly), while most men do so for quite irrelevant reasons.

The high-minded man is not quick to run into petty dangers, and indeed does not love danger, since there are few things that he much values; but he is ready to incur a great danger, and whenever he does so is unsparing of his life, as a thing that is not worth keeping at all costs.

It is his nature to confer benefits, but he is ashamed to receive them; for the former is the part of a superior, the latter of an inferior. And when he has received a benefit, he is apt to confer a greater in return; for thus his creditor will become his debtor and be in the position of a recipient of his favour.

It is thought, moreover, that such men remember those on whom they have conferred favours better than those from whom they have received them; for the recipient of a benefit is inferior to the benefactor, but such a man wishes to be in the position of a superior. So he likes to be reminded of the one, but dislikes to be reminded of the other; and this is the reason why we read that Thetis[3] would not mention to Zeus[4] the services she had done him, and why the Lacedaemonians,[5] in treating with the Athenians, reminded them of the benefits received by Sparta rather than of those conferred by her.

It is characteristic of the high-minded man, again, never or reluctantly to ask favours, but to be ready to confer them, and to be lofty in his behaviour to those who are high in station and favoured by fortune, but affable to those of the middle ranks; for it is a difficult thing and a dignified thing to assert superiority over the former, but easy to assert it over the latter. A haughty demeanour in dealing with the great is quite consistent with good breeding, but in dealing with those of low estate is brutal, like showing off one's strength upon a cripple.

Another of his characteristics is not to rush in wherever honour is to be won, nor to go where others take the lead, but to hold aloof and to shun an enterprise, except when great honour is to be gained, or a great work to be done—not to do many things, but great things and notable.

Again, he must be open in his hate and in his love; for concealment shows fear.

He must care for truth more than for what men will think of him,

---

[3] A minor deity and sea nymph who pleaded on behalf of her son Achilles.
[4] The principal Greek god.
[5] Spartans.

and speak and act openly; he will not hesitate to say all that he thinks, as he looks down upon mankind. So he will speak the truth, except when he speaks ironically; and irony he will employ in speaking to the generality of men.

Another of his characteristics is that he cannot fashion his life to suit another, except he be a friend; for that is servile; and so all flatterers or hangers on of great men are of a slavish nature, and men of low natures become flatterers.

Nor is he easily moved to admiration; for nothing is great to him.

He readily forgets injuries; for it is not consistent with his character to brood on the past, especially on past injuries, but rather to overlook them.

He is no gossip; he will neither talk about himself nor about others; for he cares not that men should praise him, nor that others should be blamed (though, on the other hand, he is not very ready to bestow praise); and so he is not apt to speak evil of others, not even of his enemies, except with the express purpose of giving offence.

When an event happens that cannot be helped or is of slight importance, he is the last man in the world to cry out or to beg for help; for that is the conduct of a man who thinks these events very important.

He loves to possess beautiful things that bring no profit, rather than useful things that pay; for this is characteristic of the man whose resources are in himself.

Further, the character of the high-minded man seems to require that his gait should be slow, his voice deep, his speech measured; for a man is not likely to be in a hurry when there are few things in which he is deeply interested, nor excited when he holds nothing to be of very great importance; and these are the causes of a high voice and rapid movements.

This, then, is the character of the high-minded man.

But he that is deficient in this quality is called little-minded; he that exceeds, vain or conceited.

11

Aristotle

Politics

The Greek polis (city-state) and its culture were the affair of a small minority of privileged citizens who, ideally, placed honor and the esteem of their peers above power and profit. This fact is abundantly reflected in the writings of Plato, Thucydides, and Xenophon. All these writers held antidemocratic views. Aristotle, growing up as he did in Macedonian court circles, also had no democratic sympathies, as evidenced in the Ethics; to him a rekindling of the Athenian politics of the Periclean Age would be contrary to all reason.

Aristotle held that ethics and politics were complementary ways of going about the same thing: attainment of the good life for man, or rather for men capable of attaining it. This aspiration is the subject of his Politics, which, for most readers, stands second in interest to the Ethics.

Aristotle believed that man is a "political animal" and that his moral character could be perfected only in the community life of the polis. But what kind of polis? The selection that follows gives Aristotle's concept of the "perfect" state. Its purpose would not be rule by the many, equality for all, or a high material standard of life, but rather promotion of the good life for "highminded" citizens—just as a modern community might aim to produce industrial wares.

Nowhere are the limitations of Greek political speculation better demonstrated than in Aristotle's inability to divorce his reasoning from the actualities of his time. Despite his learning, he did not realize that the day of the small city-state was past, and he lacked the wide-ranging imagination of his pupil, Alexander, whose career and policy pointed dramatically to the emergence of the great leader and the great state.

Aristotle, *Politics*, trans. Benjamin Jowett, in *The Works of Aristotle*, ed. W. D. Ross (Oxford: Clarendon Press, 1921), Book VII, 278–97.

227

He who would duly inquire about the best form of a state ought first to determine which is the most eligible life; while this remains uncertain the best form of the state must also be uncertain; for, in the natural order of things, those may be expected to lead the best life who are governed in the best manner of which their circumstances admit. We ought therefore to ascertain, first of all, which is the most generally eligible life, and then whether the same life is or is not best for the state and for individuals.

Assuming that enough has been already said in discussions outside the school concerning the best life, we will now only repeat what is contained in them. Certainly no one will dispute the propriety of that partition of goods which separates them into three classes, viz. external goods, goods of the body, and goods of the soul, or deny that the happy man must have all three. For no one would maintain that he is happy who has not in him a particle of courage or temperance or justice or prudence, who is afraid of every insect which flutters past him, and will commit any crime, however great, in order to gratify his lust of meat or drink, who will sacrifice his dearest friend for the sake of half-a-farthing, and is as feeble and false in mind as a child or a madman. These propositions are almost universally acknowledged as soon as they are uttered, but men differ about the degree or relative superiority of this or that good. Some think that a very moderate amount of virtue is enough, but set no limit to their desires of wealth, property, power, reputation, and the like. To whom we reply by an appeal to facts, which easily prove that mankind do not acquire or preserve virtue by the help of external goods, but external goods by the help of virtue, and that happiness, whether consisting in pleasure or virtue, or both, is more often found with those who are most highly cultivated in their mind and in their character, and have only a moderate share of external goods, than among those who possess external goods to a useless extent but are deficient in higher qualities; and this is not only matter of experience, but, if reflected upon, will easily appear to be in accordance with reason. For, whereas external goods have a limit, like any other instrument, and all things useful are of such a nature that where there is too much of them they must either do harm, or at any rate be of no use, to their possessors, every good of the soul, the greater it is, is also of greater use, if the epithet useful as well as noble is appropriate to such subjects. No proof is required to show that the best state of one thing in relation to another corresponds in degree of excellence to the interval between the natures of which we say that these very states are states: so that, if the soul is more noble than our possessions or our bodies, both absolutely and in relation to us, it must be admitted that the best state of either has a similar ratio to the other. Again, it is for the sake of the soul that goods external and goods of the body are eligible at all, and all wise men ought to choose them for the sake of the soul, and not the soul for the sake of them.

Let us acknowledge then that each one has just so much of happiness as he has of virtue and wisdom, and of virtuous and wise action. God is a witness to us of this truth, for he is happy and blessed, not by reason of any external good, but in himself and by reason of his own nature. And herein of necessity lies the difference between good fortune and happiness; for external goods come of themselves, and chance is the author of them, but no one is just or temperate by or through chance. In like manner, and by a similar train of argument, the happy state may be shown to be that which is best and which acts rightly; and rightly it cannot act without doing right actions, and neither individual nor state can do right actions without virtue and wisdom. Thus the courage, justice, and wisdom of a state have the same form and nature as the qualities which give the individual who possesses them the name of just, wise, or temperate.

Thus much may suffice by way of preface: for I could not avoid touching upon these questions, neither could I go through all the arguments affecting them; these are the business of another science.

Let us assume then that the best life, both for individuals and states, is the life of virtue, when virtue has external goods enough for the performance of good actions. If there are any who controvert our assertion, we will in this treatise pass them over, and consider their objections hereafter.

There remains to be discussed the question, Whether the happiness of the individual is the same as that of the state, or different? Here again there can be no doubt—no one denies that they are the same. For those who hold that the well-being of the individual consists in his wealth, also think that riches make the happiness of the whole state, and those who value most highly the life of a tyrant deem that city the happiest which rules over the greatest number; while they who approve an individual for his virtue say that the more virtuous a city is, the happier it is. Two points here present themselves for consideration: first (1), which is the more eligible life, that of a citizen who is a member of a state, or that of an alien who has no political ties; and again (2), which is the best form of constitution or the best condition of a state, either on the supposition that political privileges are desirable for all, or for a majority only? Since the good of the state and not of the individual is the proper subject of political thought and speculation, and we are engaged in a political discussion, while the first of these two points has a secondary interest for us, the latter will be the main subject of our inquiry.

Now it is evident that the form of government is best in which every man, whoever he is, can act best and live happily. But even those who agree in thinking that the life of virtue is the most eligible raise a question, whether the life of business and politics is or is not more eligible than one which is wholly independent of external goods, I mean than a contemplative life, which by some is maintained to be the only one worthy of a philosopher. For these two lives—the life of the philosopher and the life of the statesman—appear to have been preferred by those who have been most keen in the pursuit of virtue, both in our own and in other ages. Which is the better is a question of no small moment; for the wise man, like the wise state, will necessarily regulate his life according to the best end. There are some who think that while a despotic rule over others is the greatest injustice, to exercise a constitutional rule over them, even though not unjust, is a great impediment to a man's individual well-being. Others take an opposite view; they maintain that the true life of man is the practical and political, and that every virtue admits of being practised, quite as much by statesmen and rulers as by private individuals. Others, again, are of opinion that arbitrary and tyrannical rule alone consists with happiness; indeed, in some states the entire aim both of the laws and of the constitution is to give men despotic power over their neighbours. And, therefore, although in most cities the laws may be said generally to be in a chaotic state, still, if they aim at anything, they aim at the maintenance of power: thus in Lacedaemon and Crete the system of education and the greater part of the laws are framed with a view to war. And in all nations which are able to gratify their ambition military power is held in esteem, for example among the Scythians and Persians and Thracians and Celts. In some nations there are even laws tending to stimulate the warlike virtues, as at Carthage, where we are told that men obtain the honour of wearing as many armlets as they have served campaigns. There was once a law in Macedonia that he who had not killed an enemy should wear a halter, and among the Scythians no one who had not slain his man was allowed to drink out of the cup which was handed round at a certain feast. Among the Iberians, a warlike nation, the number of enemies whom a man has slain is indicated by the number of obelisks which are fixed in the earth round his tomb; and there are numerous practices among other nations of a like kind, some of them established by law and others by custom. Yet to a reflecting mind it must appear very strange that the statesman should be always considering how he can dominate and tyrannize over others, whether they will or not. How can that which is not even lawful be the business of the statesman or the legislator? Unlawful it certainly is to rule without regard to justice, for there may be might where there is no right. The other arts and sciences offer no parallel; a physician is not expected to persuade or coerce his patients, nor a pilot the passengers in his ship. Yet most men appear to think that the art of despotic government is statesmanship, and what men affirm to be unjust and inexpedient in their own case they are not ashamed of practising towards others; they demand just rule for themselves, but where other men are concerned they care nothing about it. Such behaviour is irrational; unless the one party is, and the other is not, born to serve, in which case men have a right to command, not indeed all their fellows, but only those who are intended to be subjects; just as we ought not to hunt mankind, whether for food or sacrifice, but only the animals which may be hunted for food or sacrifice, this is to say, such wild animals as are eatable. And surely there may be a city happy in isolation, which we will assume to be well-governed (for it is quite possible that a city thus isolated might be well-administered and have good laws); but such a city would not be constituted with any view to war or the conquest of enemies—all that sort of thing must be excluded. Hence we see very plainly that warlike pursuits, although generally to be deemed honourable, are not the supreme end of all things, but only means. And the good lawgiver should inquire how states and races of men and communities may participate in a good life, and in the happiness which is attainable by them. His enactments will not be always the same; and where there are neighbours he will have to see what sort of studies should be practised in relation to their several characters, or how the measures appropriate in relation to each are to be adopted. The end at which the best form of government should aim may be properly made a matter of future consideration.

Let us now address those who, while they agree that the life of virtue is the most eligible, differ about the manner of practising it. For some renounce political power, and think that the life of the freeman is different from the life of the statesman and the best of all; but others think the life of the statesman best. The argument of the latter is that he who does nothing cannot do well, and that virtuous activity is identical with happiness. To both we say: 'you are partly right and partly wrong.' The first class are right in affirming that the life of the freeman is better than the life of the despot; for there is nothing grand or noble in having the use of a slave, in so far as he is a slave; or in issuing commands about necessary things. But it is an error to suppose that every sort of rule is despotic like that of a master over slaves, for there is as great a difference between the rule over freemen and the rule over slaves as there is between slavery by nature and freedom by nature, about which I have said enough at the commencement of this treatise. And it is equally a mistake to place inactivity above action, for happiness is activity, and the actions of the just and wise are the realization of much that is noble.

But perhaps some one, accepting these premises, may still maintain that supreme power is the best of all things, because the possessors of it are able to perform the greatest number of noble actions. If so, the man who is able to rule, instead of giving up anything to his neighbour, ought rather to take away his power; and the father should make no account of his son, nor the son of his father, nor friend of friend; they should not bestow a thought on one another in comparison with this higher object, for the best is the most eligible and 'doing well' is the best. There might be some truth in such a view if we assume that robbers and plunderers attain the chief good. But this can never be; their hypothesis is false. For the actions of a ruler cannot really be honourable, unless he is as much superior to other men as a husband is to a wife, or a father to his children, or a master to his slaves. And therefore he who violates the law can never recover by any success, however great, what he has already lost in departing from virtue. For equals the honourable and the just consist in sharing alike, as is just and equal. But that the unequal should be given to equals, and the unlike to those who are like, is contrary to nature, and nothing which is contrary to nature is good. If therefore, there is any one superior in virtue and in the power of performing the best actions, him we ought to follow and obey, but he must have the capacity for action as well as virtue.

If we are right in our view, and happiness is assumed to be virtuous activity, the active life will be the best, both for every city collectively, and for individuals. Not that a life of action must necessarily have relation to others, as some persons think, nor are those ideas only to be regarded as practical which are pursued for the sake of practical results, but much more the thoughts and contemplations which are independent and complete in themselves; since virtuous activity, and therefore a certain kind of action, is an end, and even in the case of external actions the directing mind is most truly said to act. Neither, again, is it necessary that states which are cut off from others and choose to live alone should be inactive; for activity, as well as other things, may take place by sections; there are many ways in which the sections of a state act upon one another. The same thing is equally true of every individual. If this were otherwise, God and the universe, who have no external actions over and above their own energies, would be far enough from perfection. Hence it is evident that the same life is best for each individual, and for states and for mankind collectively.

Thus far by way of introduction. In what has preceded I have discussed other forms of government; in what remains the first point to be considered is what should be the conditions of the ideal or perfect state; for the perfect state cannot exist without a due supply of the means of life. And therefore we must pre-suppose many purely imaginary conditions, but nothing impossible. There will be a certain number of citizens, a country in which to place them, and the like. As the weaver or shipbuilder or any other artisan must have the material proper for his work (and in proportion as this is better prepared, so will the result of his art be nobler), so the statesman or legislator must also have the materials suited to him.

First among the materials required by the statesman is population: he will consider what should be the number and character of the citizens, and then what should be the size and character of the country. Most persons think that a state in order to be happy ought to be large; but even if they are right, they have no idea what is a large and what a small state. For they judge of the size of the city by the number of the inhabitants; whereas they ought to regard, not their number, but their power. A city too, like an individual, has a work to do; and that city which is best adapted to the fulfillment of its work is to be deemed greatest, in the same sense of the word great in which Hippocrates[1] might be called greater, not as a man, but as a physician, than some one else who was taller. And even if we reckon greatness by numbers, we ought not to include everybody, for there must always be in cities a multitude of slaves and sojourners and foreigners; but we should include those only who are members of the state, and who form an essential part of it. The number of the latter is a proof of the greatness of a city; but a city which produces numerous artisans and comparatively few soldiers cannot be great, for a great city is not to be confounded with a populous one. Moreover, experience shows that a very populous city can rarely, if ever, be well governed; since all cities which have a reputation for good government have a limit of population. We may argue on grounds of reason, and the same result will follow. For law is order, and good law is good order; but a very great multitude cannot be orderly: to introduce order into the unlimited is the work of a divine power—of such a power as holds together the universe. Beauty is realized in number and magnitude, and the state which combines magnitude with good order must necessarily be the most beautiful. To the size of states there is a limit, as there is to other things, plants, animals, implements; for none of these retain their natural power when they are too large or too small, but they either wholly lose their nature, or are spoiled. For example, a ship which is only a span long will not be a ship at all, nor a ship a quarter of a mile long; yet there may be a ship of a certain size, either too large or too small, which will still be a ship, but bad for sailing. In like manner a state when composed of too few is not, as a state ought to be, self-sufficing; when of too many, though self-sufficing in all mere necessaries, as a nation may be, it is not a state, being almost incapable of constitutional government. For who can be the general of such a vast multitude, or who the herald, unless he have the voice of a Stentor?[2]

A state, then, only begins to exist when it has attained a population sufficient for a good life in the political community: it may indeed, if it somewhat exceed this number, be a greater state. But, as I was saying, there must be a limit. What should be the limit will be

---

[1] A noted Greek physician of the fifth century B.C.
[2] A herald in Homer's *Iliad,* known for his powerful voice.

easily ascertained by experience. For both governors and governed have duties to perform; the special functions of a governor are to command and to judge. But if the citizens of a state are to judge and to distribute offices according to merit, then they must know each other's characters; where they do not possess this knowledge, both the election to offices and the decision of lawsuits will go wrong. When the population is very large they are manifestly settled at haphazard, which clearly ought not to be. Besides, in an over-populous state foreigners and metics will readily acquire the rights of citizens, for who will find them out? Clearly then the best limit of the population of a state is the largest number which suffices for the purposes of life, and can be taken in at a single view. Enough concerning the size of a state.

Much the same principle will apply to the territory of the state: every one would agree in praising the territory which is most entirely self-sufficing; and that must be the territory which is all-producing, for to have all things and to want nothing is sufficiency. In size and extent it should be such as may enable the inhabitants to live at once temperately and liberally in the enjoyment of leisure. Whether we are right or wrong in laying down this limit we will inquire more precisely hereafter, when we have occasion to consider what is the right use of property and wealth: a matter which is much disputed, because men are inclined to rush into one of two extremes, some into meanness, others into luxury.

It is not difficult to determine the general character of the territory which is required (there are, however, some points on which military authorities should be heard); it should be difficult of access to the enemy, and easy of egress to the inhabitants. Further, we require that the land as well as the inhabitants of whom we were just now speaking should be taken in at a single view, for a country which is easily seen can be easily protected. As to the position of the city, if we could have what we wish, it should be well situated in regard both to sea and land. This then is one principle, that it should be a convenient centre for the protection of the whole country: the other is, that it should be suitable for receiving the fruits of the soil, and also for the bringing in of timber and any other products that are easily transported.

Whether a communication with the sea is beneficial to a well-ordered state or not is a question which has often been asked. It is argued that the introduction of strangers brought up under other laws, and the increase of population, will be adverse to good order; the increase arises from their using the sea and having a crowd of merchants coming and going, and is inimical to good government. Apart from these considerations, it would be undoubtedly better, both with a view to safety and to the provision of necessaries, that the city and territory should be connected with the sea; the defenders of a country, if they are to maintain themselves against an enemy, should be easily relieved both by land and by sea; and even if they are not able to attack by sea and land at once, they will have less difficulty in doing mischief to their assailants on one element, if they themselves can use both. Moreover, it is necessary that they should import from abroad what is not found in their own country, and that they should export what they have in excess; for a city ought to be a market, not indeed for others, but for herself.

Those who make themselves a market for the world only do so for the sake of revenue, and if a state ought not to desire profit of this kind it ought not to have such an emporium. Nowadays we often see in countries and cities dockyards and harbours very conveniently placed outside the city, but not too far off; and they are kept in dependence by walls and similar fortifications. Cities thus situated manifestly reap the benefit of intercourse with their ports; and any harm which is likely to accrue may be easily guarded against by the laws, which will pronounce and determine who may hold communication with one another, and who may not.

There can be no doubt that the possession of a moderate naval force is advantageous to a city; the city should be formidable not only to its own citizens but to some of its neighbours, or, if necessary, able to assist them by sea as well as by land. The proper number or magnitude of this naval force is relative to the character of the state; for if her function is to take a leading part in politics, her naval power should be commensurate with the scale of her enterprises. The population of the state need not be much increased, since there is no necessity that the sailors should be citizens: the marines who have the control and command will be freemen, and belong also to the infantry; and wherever there is a dense population of Perioeci[3] and husbandmen, there will always be sailors more than enough. Of this we see instances at the present day. The city of

---

[3] Free aliens, usually in commercial or farming occupations. Husbandmen are farmers.

Heraclea, for example, although small in comparison with many others, can man a considerable fleet. Such are our conclusions respecting the territory of the state, its harbours, its towns, its relations to the sea, and its maritime power.

Having spoken of the number of the citizens, we will proceed to speak of what should be their character. This is a subject which can be easily understood by any one who casts his eye on the more celebrated states of Hellas,[4] and generally on the distribution of races in the habitable world. Those who live in a cold climate and in Europe are full of spirit, but wanting in intelligence and skill; and therefore they retain comparative freedom, but have no political organization, and are incapable of ruling over others. Whereas the natives of Asia are intelligent and inventive, but they are wanting in spirit, and therefore they are always in a state of subjection and slavery. But the Hellenic race, which is situated between them, is likewise intermediate in character, being high-spirited and also intelligent. Hence it continues free, and is the best-governed of any nation, and, if it could be formed into one state, would be able to rule the world. There are also similar differences in the different tribes of Hellas; for some of them are of a one-sided nature, and are intelligent or courageous only, while in others there is a happy combination of both qualities. And clearly those whom the legislator will most easily lead to virtue may be expected to be both intelligent and courageous. Some say that the guardians should be friendly towards those whom they know, fierce towards those whom they do not know. Now, passion is the quality of the soul which begets friendship and enables us to love; notably the spirit within us is more stirred against our friends and acquaintances than against those who are unknown to us, when we think that we are despised by them; for which reason Archilochus, complaining of his friends, very naturally addresses his soul in these words,

> 'For surely thou art plagued on account of friends.'

The power of command and the love of freedom are in all men based upon this quality, for passion is commanding and invincible. Nor is it right to say that the guardians should be fierce towards those whom they do not know, for we ought not to be out of

---

[4] The Greek world.

temper with any one; and a lofty spirit is not fierce by nature, but only when excited against evil-doers. And this, as I was saying before, is a feeling which men show most strongly towards their friends if they think they have received a wrong at their hands: as indeed is reasonable; for, besides the actual injury, they seem to be deprived of a benefit by those who owe them one. Hence the saying,

'Cruel is the strife of brethren,'

and again,

'They who love in excess also hate in excess.'

Thus we have nearly determined the number and character of the citizens of our state, and also the size and nature of their territory. I say 'nearly,' for we ought not to require the same minuteness in theory as in the facts given by perception.

As in other natural compounds the conditions of a composite whole are not necessarily organic parts of it, so in a state or in any other combination forming a unity not everything is a part, which is a necessary condition. The members of an association have necessarily some one thing the same and common to all, in which they share equally or unequally; for example, food or land or any other thing. But where there are two things of which one is a means and the other an end, they have nothing in common except that the one receives what the other produces. Such, for example, is the relation in which workmen and tools stand to their work; the house and the builder have nothing in common, but the art of the builder is for the sake of the house. And so states require property, but property, even though living beings are included in it, is no part of a state; for a state is not a community of living beings only, but a community of equals, aiming at the best life possible. Now, whereas happiness is the highest good, being a realization and perfect practice of virtue, which some can attain, while others have little or none of it, the various qualities of men are clearly the reason why there are various kinds of states and many forms of government; for different men seek after happiness in different ways and by different means, and so make for themselves different modes of life and forms of government. We must see also how many things are indispensable to the existence of a state, for what we call the parts of a state will be found among the indispensables. Let us then enumerate the functions of a state, and we shall easily elicit what we want:

First, there must be food; secondly, arts, for life requires many instruments; thirdly, there must be arms, for the members of a community have need of them, and in their own hands, too, in order to maintain authority both against disobedient subjects and against external assailants; fourthly, there must be a certain amount of revenue, both for internal needs, and for the purposes of war; fifthly, or rather first, there must be a care of religion, which is commonly called worship; sixthly, and most necessary of all, there must be a power of deciding what is for the public interest, and what is just in men's dealings with one another.

These are the services which every state may be said to need. For a state is not a mere aggregate of persons, but a union of them sufficing for the purposes of life; and if any of these things be wanting, it is as we maintain impossible that the community can be absolutely self-sufficing. A state then should be framed with a view to the fulfillment of these functions. There must be husbandmen to procure food, and artisans, and a warlike and a wealthy class, and priests, and judges to decide what is necessary and expedient.

Having determined these points, we have in the next place to consider whether all ought to share in every sort of occupation. Shall every man be at once husbandman, artisan, councillor, judge, or shall we suppose the several occupations just mentioned assigned to different persons? or, thirdly, shall some employments be assigned to individuals and others common to all? The same arrangement, however, does not occur in every constitution; as we were saying, all may be shared by all, or not all by all, but only by some; and hence arise the differences of constitutions, for in democracies all share in all, in oligarchies the opposite practice prevails. Now, since we are here speaking of the best form of government, i.e. that under which the state will be most happy (and happiness, as has been already said, cannot exist without virtue), it clearly follows that in the state which is best governed and possesses men who are just absolutely, and not merely relatively to the principle of the constitution, the citizens[5] must not lead the life of mechanics or tradesmen, for such a life is ignoble, and inimical to virtue. Neither must they be husbandmen since leisure is necessary both for the development of virtue and the performance of political duties.

[5] Male citizens alone exercise political power; citizenship in Greece was normally limited to those individuals born of citizens.

Again, there is in a state a class of warriors, and another of councillors, who advise about the expedient and determine matters of law, and these seem in an especial manner parts of a state. Now, should these two classes be distinguished, or are both functions to be assigned to the same persons? Here again there is no difficulty in seeing that both functions will in one way belong to the same, in another, to different persons. To different persons in so far as these employments are suited to different primes of life, for the one requires wisdom and the other strength. But on the other hand, since it is an impossible thing that those who are able to use or to resist force should be willing to remain always in subjection, from this point of view the persons are the same; for those who carry arms can always determine the fate of the constitution. It remains therefore that both functions should be entrusted by the ideal constitution to the same persons, not, however, at the same time, but in the order prescribed by nature, who has given to young men strength and to older men wisdom. Such a distribution of duties will be expedient and also just, and is founded upon a principle of conformity to merit. Besides, the ruling class should be the owners of property, for they are citizens, and the citizens of a state should be in good circumstances; whereas mechanics or any other class which is not a producer of virtue have no share in the state. This follows from our first principle, for happiness cannot exist without virtue, and a city is not to be termed happy in regard to a portion of the citizens, but in regard to them all. And clearly property should be in their hands, since the husbandmen will of necessity be slaves or barbarian[6] Perioeci.

Of the classes enumerated there remain only the priests, and the manner in which their office is to be regulated is obvious. No husbandman or mechanic should be appointed to it; for the Gods should receive honour from the citizens only. Now since the body of the citizens is divided into two classes, the warriors and the councillors, and it is beseeming that the worship of the Gods should be duly performed, and also a rest provided in their service for those who from age have given up active life, to the old men of these two classes should be assigned the duties of the priesthood.

We have shown what are the necessary conditions, and what the parts of a state: husbandmen, craftsmen, and labourers of all kinds

---

[6] The Greeks used the term *barbarian* to mean, simply, non-Greek.

are necessary to the existence of states, but the parts [7] of the state are the warriors and councillors. And these are distinguished severally from one another, the distinction being in some cases permanent, in others not.

[7] The active *citizen* elements that, strictly speaking, constitute the state.

12

Livy

The History of Rome

🔲

*Neither Herodotus nor Thucydides wrote merely to encourage patriotism and
ancestral ways. The greatness of the Hellenic founders of history lay in their
emphasis upon the spirit of impartial inquiry.*

*Quite the opposite was true, however, of the great Roman historian,
Titus Livius (59 B.C.–A.D. 17). Livy was born at Patavium (the modern
Padua) in northern Italy. Apparently of aristocratic stock, he seems to have
had the means to devote his long life to the writing of* The History of
Rome, *or, as he called it,* From the Founding of the City. *This prose
epic traces the story of Rome from the mythical Father Aeneas to Livy's
time.*

*His upbringing in an old-fashioned country town seems to have instilled in
Livy an enduring love of the simple life and traditional moral discipline—a
rare virtue in Rome during the ugly last years of the Republic. Thus
equipped, Livy was thoroughly in harmony with the official moral and
religious revival promoted by the Emperor Augustus, and the two men came
to be and remained on terms of friendly intimacy.*

Livy's History, *then, is a long glorification of the Roman Republic; of its
heroes, such as King Romulus, Lucius Junius Brutus, and Titus Manlius
Torquatus; and of its heroines, such as Lucretia, whose characters and deeds
are celebrated in the following selection. Livy's picture of Rome's hazy past
is often mythical and always idealized, and his use of source material is
uncritical. He lacked the practical knowledge of war and politics necessary to
describe the rise of a community of soldier-farmers to world domination. But
a scholarly treatise was not what he intended; rather, he created a morally
edifying work of literature. Livy hoped that its style and content would*

Livy, *The History of Rome*, trans. D. Spillan (London: Bell & Daldy, 1850–1872), I,
2–4, 8–11, 14–16, 65, 71–78, 510–13.

inspire his countrymen to imitate the old Roman virtues, renew their sense of common destiny, and seal their determination to rule the world.

Whether in tracing the history of the Roman people, from the foundation of the city, I shall employ myself to a useful purpose, I am neither very certain, nor, if I were, dare I say: inasmuch as I observe, that it is both an old and hackneyed practice, later authors always supposing that they will either adduce something more authentic in the facts, or, that they will excel the less polished ancients in their style of writing.

Be that as it may, it will, all events, be a satisfaction to me, that I too have contributed my share to perpetuate the achievements of a people, the lords of the world; and if, amidst so great a number of historians, my reputation should remain in obscurity, I may console myself with the celebrity and lustre of those who shall stand in the way of my fame. Moreover, the subject is both of immense labour, as being one which must be traced back for more than seven hundred years, and which, having set out from small beginnings, has increased to such a degree that it is now distressed by its own magnitude.

And, to most readers, I doubt not but that the first origin and the events immediately succeeding, will afford but little pleasure, while they will be hastening to these later times, in which the strength of this overgrown people has for a long period been working its own destruction. I, on the contrary, shall seek this, as a reward of my labour, viz. to withdraw myself from the view of the calamities, which our age has witnessed for so many years, so long as I am reviewing with my whole attention these ancient times, being free from every care that may distract a writer's mind, though it cannot warp it from the truth.

The traditions which have come down to us of what happened before the building of the city, or before its building was contemplated, as being suitable rather to the fictions of poetry than to the genuine records of history, I have no intention either to affirm or refute. This indulgence is conceded to antiquity, that by blending things human with divine, it may make the origin of cities appear more venerable; and if any people might be allowed to consecrate their origin, and to ascribe it to the gods as its authors, such is the renown of the Roman people in war, that when they represent Mars,[1] in particular, as their own parent and that of their founder, the nations of the world may submit to this as patiently as they submit to their sovereignty.

But in whatever way these and such like matters shall be attended to, or judged of, I shall not deem of great importance. I would have every man apply his mind seriously to consider these points, viz. what their life and what their manners were; through what men and by what measures, both in peace and in war, their empire was acquired and extended; then, as discipline gradually declined, let him follow in his thoughts their morals, at first as slightly giving way, anon how they sunk more and more, then began to fall headlong, until he reaches the present times, when we can neither endure our vices, nor their remedies. This it is which is particularly salutary and profitable in the study of history, that you behold instances of every variety of conduct displayed on a conspicuous monument; that from thence you may select for yourself and for your country that which you may imitate; thence *note* what is shameful in the undertaking, and shameful in the result, which you may avoid. But either a fond partiality for the task I have undertaken deceives me, or there never was any state either greater, or more moral, or richer in good examples, nor one into which luxury and avarice made their entrance so late, and where poverty and frugality were so much and so long honoured; so that the less wealth there was, the less desire was there. Of late, riches have introduced avarice, and excessive pleasures a longing for them, amidst luxury and a passion for ruining ourselves and destroying everything else. But let complaints, which will not be agreeable even then, when perhaps they will be also necessary, be kept aloof at least from the first stage of commencing so great a work. We should rather, if it was usual with us (historians) as it is with poets, begin with good omens, vows and prayers to the gods and goddesses to vouchsafe good success to our efforts in so arduous an undertaking.

● ● ●

In my opinion, the origin of so great a city, and the establishment of an empire next in power to that of the gods, was due to the Fates.

---

[1] The god of war (Ares to the Greeks).

The vestal Rhea,[2] being deflowered by force, when she had brought forth twins, declares Mars to be the father of her illegitimate off-spring, either because she believed it to be so, or because a god was a more creditable author of her offence. But neither gods nor men pro-tect her or her children from the king's cruelty: the priestess is bound and thrown into prison; the children he commands to be thrown into the current of the river. By some interposition of providence, the Tiber having overflowed its banks in stagnant pools, did not admit of any access to the regular bed of the river; and the bearers supposed that the infants could be drowned in water however still; thus, as if they had effectually executed the king's orders, they expose the boys in the nearest land-flood, where now stands the ficus Ruminalis[3] (they say that it was called Romularis).

The country thereabout was then a vast wilderness. The tradition is, that when the water, subsiding, had left the floating trough, in which the children had been exposed, on dry ground, a thirsty she-wolf, coming from the neighbouring mountains, directed her course to the cries of the infants, and that she held down her dugs to them with so much gentleness, that the keeper of the king's flock found her licking the boys with her tongue. It is said his name was Faustu-lus; and that they were carried by him to his homestead to be nursed by his wife Laurentia. Some are of opinion that she was called Lupa among the shepherds, from her being a common prostitute, and that this gave rise to the surprising story. The children thus born and thus brought up, when arrived at the years of manhood, did not loiter away their time in tending the folds or following the flocks, but roamed and hunted in the forests. Having by this exercise improved their strength and courage, they not only encountered wild beasts, but even attacked robbers laden with plunder, and afterwards di-vided the spoil among the shepherds. And in company with these, the number of their young associates daily increasing, they carried on their business and their sports.

They say, that the festival of the lupercal, as now celebrated, was even at that time solemnized on the Palatine hill[4] . . . in such man-ner, that young men ran about naked in sport and wantonness, doing honour to Pan Lycaeus, whom the Romans afterwards called Inuus.

[2] The vestals were selected virgin priestesses whose lives were devoted to tending the sacred fire in the temple of Vesta (Roman goddess of the family hearth).
[3] A fig-tree under which the twin boys were said to have been found.
[4] One of the famed Seven Hills of Rome.

That the robbers, through rage at the loss of their booty, having lain in wait for them whilst intent on this sport, as the festival was now well known, whilst Romulus vigorously defended himself, took Remus prisoner; that they delivered him up, when taken, to King Amulius, accusing him with the utmost effrontery. They principally alleged it as a charge against them, that they had made incursions upon Numitor's[5] lands, and plundered them in a hostile manner, having assembled a band of young men for the purpose. Upon this Remus was delivered to Numitor to be punished.

Now, from the very first, Faustulus had entertained hopes that the boys whom he was bringing up were of the blood royal; for he both knew that the children had been exposed by the king's orders, and that the time at which he had taken them up agreed exactly with that period; but he had been unwilling that the matter, as not being yet ripe for discovery, should be disclosed, till either a fit opportunity or necessity should arise. Necessity came first; accordingly, compelled by fear, he reveals the whole affair to Romulus. By accident also, whilst he had Remus in custody, and had heard that the brothers were twins, on comparing their age, and observing their turn of mind entirely free from servility, the recollection of his grand-children struck Numitor; and on making inquiries he arrived at the same conclusion, so that he was well-nigh recognising Remus. Thus a plot is formed against the king on all sides. Romulus, not accompanied by a body of young men (for he was unequal to open force) but having commanded the shepherds to come to the palace by different roads at a fixed time, forces his way to the king; and Remus, with another party from Numitor's house, assists his brother, and so they kill the king.[6]

Numitor . . . when he saw the young men, after they had killed the king, advancing to congratulate him, immediately called an assembly of the people, and represented to them the unnatural behavior of his brother towards him, the ancestry of his grandchildren, the manner of their birth and education, and how they came to be discovered; then he informed them of the king's death, and that he was killed by his orders. When the young princes, coming up with their band through the middle of the assembly, saluted their grandfather king, an approving shout, following from

[5] Numitor was the father of the vestal Rhea, hence, grandfather of the twins Romulus and Remus.
[6] The king, Amulius, had usurped the throne of his brother, Numitor.

all the people present, ratified to him both that title and the sovereignty.

Thus the government of Alba[7] being committed to Numitor, a desire seized Romulus and Remus to build a city on the spot where they had been exposed and brought up. And there was an overflowing population of Albans and of Latins. The shepherds too had come into that design, and all these readily inspired hopes, that Alba and Lavinium would be but petty places in comparison with the city which they intended to build. But ambition of the sovereignty, the bane of their grandfather, interrupted these designs, and thence arose a shameful quarrel from a beginning sufficiently amicable. For as they were twins, and the respect due to seniority could not determine the point, they agreed to leave to the tutelary gods of the place to choose, by augury, which should give a name to the new city, which govern it when built.

Romulus chose the Palatine and Remus the Aventine hill as their stands to make their observations. It is said, that to Remus an omen came first, six vultures; and now, the omen having been declared, when double the number presented itself to Romulus, his own party saluted each king; the former claimed the kingdom on the ground of priority of time, the latter on account of the number of birds. Upon this, having met in an altercation, from the contest of angry feelings they turn to bloodshed; there Remus fell from a blow received in the crowd. A more common account is, that Remus, in derision of his brother, leaped over his new-built wall, and was, for that reason, slain by Romulus in a passion; who, after sharply chiding him, added words to this effect: "So shall every one fare, who shall dare to leap over my fortifications." Thus Romulus got the sovereignty to himself; the city, when built, was called after the name of its founder.

• • •

And now the Roman state had become so powerful, that it was a match for any of the neighbouring nations in war, but, from the paucity of women, its greatness could only last for one age of man; for they had no hope of issue at home, nor had they any intermarriages with their neighbours. Therefore, by the advice of the Fathers,[8] Romulus sent ambassadors to the neighbouring states to

---

[7] An ancient Italian town, founded (according to legend) by the Trojan hero, Aeneas. It was the core-site for the building of Rome.
[8] The elders (senators).

solicit an alliance and the privilege of intermarriage for his new subjects. . . .

Nowhere did the embassy obtain a favourable hearing: so much did they at the same time despise, and dread for themselves and their posterity, so great a power growing up in the midst of them. They were dismissed by the great part with the repeated question, "Whether they had opened any asylum for women also, for that such a plan only could obtain them suitable matches?"

The Roman youth resented this conduct bitterly, and the matter unquestionably began to point towards violence. Romulus, in order that he might afford a favourable time and place for this, dissembling his resentment, purposely prepares games in honour of Neptunus Equestris; he calls them Consualia. He then orders the spectacle to be proclaimed among their neighbours; and they prepare for the celebration with all the magnificence they were then acquainted with, or were capable of doing, that they might render the matter famous, and an object of expectation. Great numbers assembled, from a desire also of seeing the new city; especially their nearest neighbours, the Caeninenses, Crustumini, and Antemnates. Moreover the whole multitude of the Sabines came, with their wives and children. Having been hospitably invited to the different houses, when they had seen the situation, and fortifications, and the city crowded with houses, they became astonished that the Roman power had increased so rapidly.

When the time of the spectacle came on, and while their minds and eyes were intent upon it, according to plan a tumult began, and upon a signal given the Roman youth ran different ways to carry off the virgins by force. A great number were carried off haphazardly, according as they fell into their hands. Persons from the common people, who had been charged with the task, conveyed to their houses some women of surpassing beauty, destined for the leading senators. . . .

The festival being disturbed by this alarm, the parents of the young women retire in grief, appealing to the compact of violated hospitality, and invoking the god, to whose festival and games they had come, deceived by the pretence of religion and good faith. Neither had the ravished virgins better hopes of their condition, or less indignation. But Romulus in person went about and declared, "That what was done was owing to the pride of their fathers, who had refused to grant the privilege of marriage to their neighbours; but notwithstanding, they should be joined in lawful wedlock, participate in all their possessions and civil privileges, and, than which nothing can be dearer to the human heart, in their common children. He begged them only to assuage the fierceness of their anger, and cheerfully surrender their affections to those to whom fortune had consigned their persons." [He added,] "That from injuries love and friendship often arise; and that they should find them kinder husbands on this account, because each of them, besides the performance of his conjugal duty, would endeavour to the utmost of his power to make up for the want of their parents and native country." To this the caresses of the husbands were added, excusing what they had done on the plea of passion and love, arguments that work most successfully on women's hearts.

. . .

After this period Tarquin[9] began his reign, whose actions procured him the surname of the Proud. . . . He surrounded his person with armed men, for he had no claim to the kingdom except force, inasmuch as he reigned without either the order of the people or the sanction of the senate. To this was added (the fact) that, as he reposed no hope in the affection of his subjects, he found it necessary to secure his kingdom by terror; and in order to strike this into the greater number, he took cognizance of capital cases solely by himself without assessors; and under that pretext he had it in his power to put to death, banish, or fine, not only those who were suspected or hated, but those also from whom he could obtain nothing else but plunder. The number of the fathers more especially being thus diminished, he determined to elect none into the senate, in order that the order might become contemptible by their very paucity, and that they might feel the less resentment at no business being transacted by them. For he was the first king who violated the custom derived from his predecessors of consulting the senate on all subjects; he administered the public business by family councils. War, peace, treaties, alliances, he contracted and dissolved with whomsoever he pleased, without the sanction of the people and senate. The nation of the Latins in particular he wished to attach to him, so that by foreign influence also he might be more secure among his own subjects; and

[9] An Etruscan king of Rome—expelled by the citizens in 510 B.C.

he contracted not only ties of hospitality but affinities also with their leading men.

. . .

Then he turned his thoughts to the business of the city. The chief whereof was that of leaving behind him the temple of Jupiter [10] on the Tarpeian mount, as a monument of his name and reign. . . . It is reported that the head of a man, with the face entire, appeared to the workmen when digging the foundation of the temple. The sight of this phenomenon unequivocally presaged that this temple should be the metropolis of the empire, and the head of the world; and so declared the soothsayers, both those who were in the city, and those whom they had sent for from Etruria, to consult on this subject. . . .

Tarquin, intent upon finishing this temple, having sent for workmen from all parts of Etruria, employed on it not only the public money, but the manual labour of the people; and when this labour, by no means inconsiderable in itself, was added to their military service, still the people murmured less at their building the temples of the gods with their own hands; they were afterwards transferred to other works, which, whilst less in show, required still greater toil: such as erecting benches in the circus, and conducting under ground the principal sewer, the receptacle of all the filth of the city; to which two works even modern splendour can scarcely produce any thing equal. . . .

While he was thus employed a frightful prodigy appeared to him. A serpent sliding out of a wooden pillar, after causing dismay and a run into the palace, not so much struck the king's heart with sudden terror, as filled him with anxious solicitude. Accordingly . . . he determined on sending persons to Delphi to the most celebrated oracle in the world; and not venturing to intrust the responses of the oracle to any other person, he despatched his two sons to Greece through lands unknown at that time, and seas still more so. Titus and Aruns were the two who went. To them were added, as a companion, L. Junius Brutus, the son of Tarquinia, sister to the king, a youth of an entirely different quality of mind from that of the disguise which he had assumed.

[10] The principal Roman deity, later identified with the Greek Zeus.

Brutus, on hearing that the chief men of the city, and among others his own brother, had been put to death by his uncle, resolved to leave nothing in his intellects that might be dreaded by the king, nor any thing in his fortune to be coveted, and thus to be secure in contempt, where there was but little protection in justice. Therefore designedly fashioning himself to the semblance of foolishness, after he suffered himself and his whole estate to become a prey to the king, he did not refuse to take even the surname of Brutus, that, concealed under the cover of such a cognomen, that genius that was to liberate the Roman people might await its proper time. He, being brought to Delphi by the Tarquinii [11] rather as a subject of sport than as a companion, is said to have brought with him as an offering to Apollo a golden rod, enclosed in a staff of cornel-wood hollowed out for the purpose, a mystical emblem of his own mind.

When they arrived there, their father's commission being executed, a desire seized the young men of inquiring on which of them the sovereignty of Rome should devolve. They say that a voice was returned from the bottom of the cave, "Young men, whichever of you shall first kiss his mother shall enjoy the sovereign power at Rome." The Tarquinii order the matter to be kept secret with the utmost care, that Sextus, who had been left behind at Rome, might be ignorant of the response, and have no share in the kingdom; they cast lots among themselves, as to which of them should first kiss his mother, after they had returned to Rome. Brutus, thinking that the Delphic response had another meaning, as if he had stumbled and fallen, touched the ground with his lips; she being, forsooth, the common mother of all mankind. After this they all returned to Rome, where preparations were being made with the greatest vigour for a war against the Rutulians. [12]

The Rutulians, a nation very wealthy, considering the country and age they lived in, were at that time in possession of Ardea. Their riches gave occasion to the war; for the king of the Romans, being exhausted of money by the magnificence of his public works, was desirous both to enrich himself, and by a large booty to soothe the minds of his subjects, who, besides other instances of his tyranny, were incensed against his government, because they were indignant that they had been kept so long a time by the king in the employments of mechanics, and in labour fit for slaves.

[11] The two sons of King Tarquin.
[12] Neighbors of the Romans.

An attempt was made to take Ardea by storm; when that did not succeed, the enemy began to be distressed by a blockade, and by works raised around them. As it commonly happens in standing camps, the war being rather tedious than violent, furloughs were easily obtained, more so by the officers, however, than the common soldiers. The young princes sometimes spent their leisure hours in feasting and entertainments. One day as they were drinking in the tent of Sextus Tarquin, where Collatinus Tarquinius, the son of Egerius, was also at supper, mention was made of wives. Every one commended his own in an extravagant manner, till a dispute arising about it, Collatinus said, "There is no occasion for words; it might be known in a few hours how far Lucretia excels all the rest. If then we have any share of the vigour of youth, let us mount our horses and examine the behaviour of our wives; that must be most satisfactory to every one, what shall meet his eyes on the unexpected arrival of the husband." They were heated with wine; "Come on, then," say all. They immediately galloped to Rome, where they arrived in the dusk of the evening. From thence they went to Collatia,[13] where they find Lucretia, not like the king's daughters-in-law, whom they had seen spending their time in luxurious entertainments with their equals, but though at an advanced time of night, employed at her wool, sitting in the middle of the house amid her maids working around her. The merit of the contest regarding the ladies was assigned to Lucretia. Her husband on his arrival, and the Tarquinii, were kindly received; the husband, proud of his victory, gives the young princes a polite invitation. There the villanous passion for violating Lucretia by force seizes Sextus Tarquin; both her beauty, and her approved purity, act as incentives. And then, after this youthful frolic of the night, they return to the camp.

A few days after, without the knowledge of Collatinus, Sextus came to Collatia with one attendant only; where, being kindly received by them, as not being aware of his intention, after he had been conducted after supper into the guests' chamber, burning with passion, when every thing around seem sufficiently secure, and all fast asleep, he comes to Lucretia, as she lay asleep, with a naked sword, and with his left hand pressing down the woman's breast, he says, "Be silent, Lucretia; I am Sextus Tarquin; I have a sword in my hand; you shall die, if you utter a word." When awaking terrified from sleep, the woman beheld no aid, impending death nigh at hand; then Tarquin acknowledged his passion, entreated, mixed threats with entreaties, tried the female's mind in every possible way. When he saw her inflexible, and that she was not moved even by the terror of death, he added to terror the threat of dishonour; he says that he will lay a murdered slave naked by her side when dead, so that she may be said to have been slain in infamous adultery.

When by the terror of this disgrace his lust, as it were victorious, had overcome her inflexible chastity, and Tarquin had departed, exulting in having triumphed over a lady's honour, Lucretia, in melancholy distress at so dreadful a misfortune, despatches the same messenger to Rome to her father, and to Ardea to her husband, that they would come each with one trusted friend; that it was necessary to do so, and that quickly. Sp. Lucretius comes with P. Valerius, the son of Volesus, Collatinus with L. Junius Brutus, with whom, as he was returning to Rome, he happened to be met by his wife's messenger. They find Lucretia sitting in her chamber in sorrowful dejection. On the arrival of her friends the tears burst from her eyes; and to her husband, on his inquiry "whether all was right," she says, "By no means, for what can be right with a woman who has lost her honour? The traces of another man are on your bed, Collatinus. But the body only has been violated, the mind is guiltless; death shall be my witness. But give me your right hands, and your honour, that the adulterer shall not come off unpunished. It is Sextus Tarquin, who, an enemy in the guise of a guest, has borne away hence a triumph fatal to me, and to himself, if you are men."

They all pledge their honour; they attempt to console her, distracted as she was in mind, by turning away the guilt from her, constrained by force, on the perpetrator of the crime; that it is the mind sins, not the body; and that where intention was wanting guilt could not be. "It is for you to see," says she, "what is due to him. As for me, though I acquit myself of guilt, from punishment I do not discharge myself; nor shall any woman survive her dishonour pleading the example of Lucretia." The knife, which she kept concealed beneath her garment, she plunges into her heart, and falling forward on the wound, she dropped down expiring. The husband and father shriek aloud.

Brutus, while they were overpowered with grief, having drawn the knife out of the wound, and holding it up before him reeking with blood, said, "By this blood, most pure before the pollution of royal villany, I swear, and I call you, O gods, to witness my oath, that I shall pursue Lucius Tarquin the Proud, his wicked wife, and all their race, with fire, sword, and all other means in my power; nor shall I ever suffer them or any other to reign at Rome." Then he gave the knife to Collatinus, and after him to Lucretius and Valerius, who were surprised at such extraordinary mind in the breast of Brutus. However, they all take the oath as they were directed, and converting their sorrow into rage, follow Brutus as their leader, who from that time ceased not to solicit them to abolish the regal power. . . .

Nor does the heinousness of the circumstance excite less violent emotions at Rome than it had done at Collatia; accordingly they run from all parts of the city into the forum, whither, when they came, the public crier summoned them to attend the tribune of the celeres, with which office Brutus happened to be at that time vested. There an harangue was delivered by him, by no means of that feeling and capacity which had been counterfeited up to that day, concerning the violence and lust of Sextus Tarquin, the horrid violation of Lucretia and her lamentable death, the bereavement of Tricipitinus, to whom the cause of his daughter's death was more exasperating and deplorable than the death itself. To this was added the haughty insolence of the king himself, and the sufferings and toils of the people, buried in the earth in cleansing sinks and sewers; that the Romans, the conquerors of all the surrounding states, instead of warriors had become labourers and stone-cutters. . . .

By stating these and other, I suppose, more exasperating circumstances, which though by no means easily detailed by writers, the heinousness of the case suggested at the time, he persuaded the multitude, already incensed, to deprive the king of his authority, and to order the banishment of L. Tarquin with his wife and children. He himself having selected and armed some of the young men, who readily gave in their names, set out for Ardea to the camp to excite the army against the king. . . .

News of these transactions reached the camp when the king, alarmed at this sudden revolution, was going to Rome to quell the commotions. Brutus, for he had notice of his approach, turned out of the way, that he might not meet him; and much about the same time Brutus and Tarquin arrived by different routes, the one at Ardea, the other at Rome. The gates were shut against Tarquin, and an act of banishment passed against him; the deliverer of the state the camp received with great joy, and the king's sons were expelled. Two of them followed their father, and went into banishment to Caere, a city of Etruria. Sextus Tarquin, having gone to Gabii, as to his own kingdom, was slain by the avengers of the old feuds, which he had raised against himself by his rapines and murders.

Lucius Tarquin the Proud reigned twenty-five years; the regal form of government had lasted from the building of the city to this period of its deliverance, two hundred and forty-four years. Two consuls, viz. Lucius Junius Brutus and Lucius Tarquinius Collatinus, were elected by the prefect of the city at the comitia by centuries,[14] according to the commentaries of Servius Tullius.

* * *

The consuls, after raising two armies, marched into the territories of the Marsians and Pelignians, the army of the Samnites having joined them, and pitched their camp near Capua, where the Latins and their allies had now assembled. . . .

What excited their attention particularly was, that they had to contend against Latins, who coincided with themselves in language, manners, in the same kind of arms, and more especially in military institutions; soldiers had been mixed with soldiers, centurions with centurions, tribunes with tribunes, as comrades and colleagues, in the same armies, and often in the same companies. Lest in consequence of this the soldiers should be involved in any mistake, the consuls issue orders that no one should fight against an enemy out of his post.[15]

It happened that among the other prefects[16] of the troops, who had been sent out in all directions to reconnoitre, Titus Manlius, the consul's son, came with his troop to the back of the enemy's camp, so near that he was scarcely distant a dart's throw from the next post. In that place were some Tusculan cavalry; they were commanded by Geminus Metius, a man distinguished among his countrymen both by birth and exploits. When he recognised the Roman cavalry, and conspicuous among them the consul's son marching at their head, (for they were all known to each other, especially the

---

[14] The comitia was one of several citizen assemblies in ancient Rome.
[15] That is, away from the Roman camp.
[16] Commanders.

men of note,) "Romans, are ye going to wage war with the Latins and allies with a single troop? What in the interim will the consuls, what will the two consular armies be doing?" "They will be here in good time," says Manlius, "and with them will be Jupiter himself, as a witness of the treaties violated by you, who is stronger and more powerful. If we fought at the lake Regillus until you had quite enough, here also we shall so act, that a line of battle and an encounter with us may afford you no very great gratification." In reply to this, Geminus, advancing some distance from his own party, says, "Do you choose then, until that day arrives on which you are to put your armies in motion with such mighty labour, to enter the lists with me, that from the result of a contest between us both, it may be seen how much a Latin excels a Roman horseman?"

Either resentment, or shame at declining the contest, or the invincible power of fate, arouses the determined spirit of the youth. Forgetful therefore of his father's command, and the consul's edict, he is driven headlong to that contest, in which it made not much difference whether he conquered or was conquered. The other horsemen being removed to a distance as if to witness the sight, in the space of clear ground which lay between them they spurred on their horses against each other; and when they were together in fierce encounter, the spear of Manlius passed over the helmet of his antagonist, that of Metius across the neck of the other's horse. Then wheeling round their horses, when Manlius arose to repeat the blow, he fixed his javelin between the ears of his opponent's horse. When, by the pain of this wound, the horse, having raised his fore-feet on high, tossed his head with great violence, he shook off his rider, whom, when he was raising himself from the severe fall, by leaning on his spear and buckler, Manlius pierced through the throat, so that the steel passed out through the ribs, and pinned him to the earth; and having collected the spoils, he returned to his own party, and with his troop, who were exulting with joy. He proceeds to the camp, and thence to the general's tent to his father, ignorant of what awaited him, whether praise or punishment had been merited. "Father," says he, "that all may truly represent me as sprung from your blood; when challenged, I slew my adversary, and have taken from him these equestrian spoils."

When the consul heard this, immediately turning away from his son, he ordered an assembly to be summoned by sound of trumpet. When these assembled in great numbers, "Since you, Titus Manlius," says he, "revering neither the consular power nor a father's majesty, have fought against the enemy out of your post contrary to our orders, and, as far as in you lay, have subverted military discipline, by which the Roman power has stood to this day, and have brought me to this necessity, that I must either forget the republic, or myself and mine; we shall expiate our own transgressions rather than the republic should sustain so serious a loss for our misdeeds. We shall be a melancholy example, but a profitable one, to the youth of future ages. As for me, both the natural affection for my children, as well as that instance of bravery which has led you astray by the false notion of honour, affects me for you. But since either the authority of consuls is to be established by your death, or by your forgiveness to be for ever annulled; I do not think that even you, if you have any of our blood in you, will refuse to restore, by your punishment, the military discipline which has been subverted by your misconduct. Go, lictor,[17] bind him to the stake." All became motionless, more through fear than discipline, astounded by so cruel an order, each looking on the axe as if drawn against himself. Therefore when they stood in profound silence, suddenly, when the blood spouted from his severed neck, their minds recovering, as it were, from a state of stupefaction, then their voices arose together in free expressions of complaint, so that they spared neither lamentations nor execrations; and the body of the youth, being covered with the spoils, was burned on a pile erected outside the rampart, with all the military zeal with which any funeral could be celebrated; and Manlian orders were considered with horror, not only for the present, but of the most austere severity for future times.

The severity of the punishment, however, rendered the soldiers more obedient to the general; the guards and watches and the regulation of the posts were everywhere more strictly attended to, and such severity was also profitable in the final struggle when they came into the field of battle.

---

[17] An official who carried rods and an axe, for the imposition of disciplinary punishments.

13

Plutarch

Lives: Marcus Cato

Greek literature did not end with the decline of the Greek polis, but it re-mained predominantly the interest of the privileged and bookish few. Litera-ture continued to grow, and from the fourth century B.C. *a new form made its appearance: the short biography, presenting not a "type," as previously, but a specific person with unique traits. As Greek letters took a new lease on life in the early Roman Empire, this "modern" biographical writing came into vogue and may even have provided a pattern for the Christian gospels. Certainly the form reached its peak in Plutarch (ca.* A.D. *46–ca. 120).*

Little is known of Plutarch's own life. After student days in Athens, he spent some years lecturing in Rome. An amiable man of wide interests, broad learning, and cultivated taste, he was on close terms with the "mighty"; the Emperor Trajan made him a consul and provincial governor. Plutarch, how-ever, preferred the life of a country gentleman; he returned to his native Chaeronea, in Greece, where he happily filled its petty offices and priest-hoods. It was then that he composed his major work, the Parallel Lives, *a biographical study of famous Greek soldiers and statesmen, paired with their Roman counterparts, in which, above all, he sought to inculcate the ethical ideals of Hellenic culture.*

The following selection from the Lives *is taken from Plutarch's ac-count of Marcus Porcius Cato (234–149* B.C.*), usually known as Cato the Elder, or the Censor. It is a memorable picture of one of the Roman Repub-lic's great personalities and patriotic heroes who, throughout his private and public life, sought to stem the alien cultural tide that was eroding the ances-tral ways of the Roman people—once the most puritanical of antiquity.*

Plutarch, *Lives,* trans. called Dryden's, corr. and rev. A. H. Clough (Boston: Little, Brown, 1875), II, 316–18, 321–34, 341–47, 350–51.

If only because they are based on sources now lost to us, the Lives *are invaluable. Their wide popularity among readers over the centuries gives Plutarch first place among the Greek authors who shaped an image of the ancient world for later ages. Among great men of letters, Shakespeare, Montaigne, Corneille, and Racine are all indebted to him.*

Marcus Cato, we are told, was born at Tusculum, though (till he betook himself to civil and military affairs) he lived and was bred up in the country of the Sabines, where his father's estate lay. His ancestors seeming almost entirely unknown, he himself praises his father Marcus, as a worthy man and a brave soldier, and Cato, his great grandfather too, as one who had often obtained military prizes, and who, having lost five horses under him, received, on the account of his valor, the worth of them out of the public exchequer. Now it being the custom among the Romans to call those who, having no repute by birth, made themselves eminent by their own exertions, new men or upstarts, they called even Cato himself so, and so he confessed himself to be as to any public distinction or employment, but yet asserted that in the exploits and virtues of his ancestors he was very ancient. His third name originally was not Cato, but Priscus, though afterwards he had the surname of Cato, by reason of his abilities; for the Romans call a skilful or experienced man, *Catus.* He was of a ruddy complexion, and grey-eyed; as the writer, who, with no good-will, made the following epigram upon him, lets us see:—

> Porcius, who snarls at all in every place,
> With his grey eyes, and with his fiery face,
> Even after death will scarce admitted be
> Into the infernal realms by Hecate.[1]

He gained, in early life, a good habit of body by working with his own hands, and living temperately, and serving in war; and seemed to have an equal proportion both of health and strength. And he exerted and practised his eloquence through all the neighborhood and

---

[1] A goddess usually associated with sorcery and death. Reputedly ugly, she guarded the gates of Hades (the underworld).

little villages; thinking it as requisite as a second body, and an all but
necessary organ to one who looks forward to something above a
mere humble and inactive life. He would never refuse to be counsel
for those who needed him, and was, indeed, early reckoned a good
lawyer, and, ere long, a capable orator.

Hence his solidity and depth of character showed itself gradually,
more and more to those with whom he was concerned, and claimed,
as it were, employment in great affairs, and places of public command. Nor did he merely abstain from taking fees for his counsel
and pleading, but did not even seem to put any high price on the
honor which proceeded from such kind of combats, seeming much
more desirous to signalize himself in the camp and in real fights; and
while yet but a youth, had his breast covered with scars he had
received from the enemy; being (as he himself says) but seventeen
years old, when he made his first campaign; in the time when Hannibal, in the height of his success, was burning and pillaging all Italy.
In engagements he would strike boldly, without flinching, stand firm
to his ground, fix a bold countenance upon his enemies, and with a
harsh threatening voice accost them, justly thinking himself and telling others, that such a rugged kind of behavior sometimes terrifies
the enemy more than the sword itself. In his marches, he bore his
own arms on foot, whilst one servant only followed, to carry the
provisions for his table, with whom he is said never to have been
angry or hasty, whilst he made ready his dinner or supper, but
would, for the most part, when he was free from military duty, assist and help him himself to dress it. When he was with the army, he
used to drink only water; unless, perhaps, when extremely thirsty,
he might mingle it with a little vinegar; or if he found his strength
fail him, take a little wine.

The little country house of Manius Curius, who had been thrice
carried in triumph,[2] happened to be near his farm; so that often
going thither, and contemplating the small compass of the place, and
plainness of the dwelling, he formed an idea of the mind of the person, who, being one of the greatest of the Romans, and having
subdued the most warlike nations, nay, had driven Pyrrhus[3] out of
Italy, now, after three triumphs, was contented to dig in so small a
piece of ground, and live in such a cottage. Here it was that the am-

[2] A ceremonious procession held in Rome for a victorious general.
[3] A king of Epirus; he invaded Italy in 280 B.C.

bassadors of the Samnites, finding him boiling turnips in the chimney corner, offered him a present of gold; but he sent them away with this saying; that he, who was content with such a supper, had no need of gold; and that he thought it more honorable to conquer those who possessed the gold, than to possess the gold itself. Cato, after reflecting upon these things, used to return, and reviewing his own farm, his servants, and housekeeping, increase his labor, and retrench all superfluous expenses.

* * *

He himself says, that he never wore a suit of clothes which cost more than a hundred drachmas; and that, when he was general and consul, he drank the same wine which his workmen did; and that the meat or fish which was bought in the market for his dinner, did not cost above thirty *asses*.[4] All which was for the sake of the commonwealth, that so his body might be the hardier for the war. Having a piece of embroidered Babylonian tapestry left him, he sold it; because none of his farm-houses were so much as plastered. Nor did he ever buy a slave for above fifteen hundred drachmas, as he did not seek for effeminate and handsome ones, but able, sturdy workmen, horse-keepers and cow-herds; and these he thought ought to be sold again, when they grew old, and no useless servants fed in his house. In short, he reckoned nothing a good bargain, which was superfluous; but whatever it was, though sold for a farthing, he would think it a great price, if you had no need of it; and was for the purchase of lands for sowing and feeding, rather than grounds for sweeping and watering.

Some imputed these things to petty avarice, but others approved of him, as if he had only the more strictly denied himself for the rectifying and amending of others. Yet certainly, in my judgment, it marks an over-rigid temper, for a man to take the work out of his servants as out of brute beasts, turning them off and selling them in their old age, and thinking there ought to be no further commerce between man and man, than whilst there arises some profit by it. . . . As to myself, I would not so much as sell my draught ox on the account of his age, much less for a small piece of money sell a poor old man, and so chase him, as it were, from his own country, by

---

[4] Romans of Cato's day regarded the bronze *as* much as we do our copper coins. The drachma was made of silver and valued at from ten to twenty-nine *asses*.

turning him not only out of the place where he has lived a long while, but also out of the manner of living he has been accustomed to, and that more especially when he would be as useless to the buyer as to the seller. Yet Cato for all this glories that he left that very horse in Spain, which he used in the wars when he was consul, only because he would not put the public to the charge of his freight. Whether these acts are to be ascribed to the greatness or pettiness of his spirit, let everyone argue as they please.

For his general temperance, however, and self-control, he really deserves the highest admiration. For when he commanded the army, he never took for himself, and those that belonged to him, above three bushels of wheat for a month, and somewhat less than a bushel and a half a day of barley for his baggage-cattle. And when he entered upon the government of Sardinia, where his predecessors had been used to require tents, bedding, and clothes upon the public account, and to charge the state heavily with the cost of provisions and entertainments for a great train of servants and friends, the difference he showed in his economy was something incredible. There was nothing of any sort for which he put the public to expense; he would walk without a carriage to visit the cities, with one only of the common town officers, who carried his dress, and a cup to offer libation with. Yet, though he seemed thus easy and sparing to all who were under his power, he, on the other hand, showed most inflexible severity and strictness, in what related to public justice, and was rigorous and precise in what concerned the ordinances of the commonwealth; so that the Roman government, never seemed more terrible, nor yet more mild, than under his administration.

• • •

He was also a good father, an excellent husband to his wife, and an extraordinary economist; and as he did not manage his affairs of this kind carelessly, and as things of little moment, I think I ought to record a little further whatever was commendable in him in these points. He married a wife more noble than rich; being of opinion, that the rich and the high-born are equally haughty and proud; but that those of noble blood, would be more ashamed of base things, and consequently more obedient to their husbands in all that was fit and right. A man who beat his wife or child, laid violent hands, he said, on what was most sacred; and a good husband he reckoned worthy of more praise than a great senator; and he admired the ancient Socrates for nothing so much, as for having lived a temperate and contented life with a wife who was a scold, and children who were half-witted.

As soon as he had a son born, though he had never such urgent business upon his hands, unless it were some public matter, he would be by when his wife washed it, and dressed it in its swaddling clothes. For she herself suckled it, nay, she often too gave her breast to her servants' children, to produce, by sucking the same milk, a kind of natural love in them to her son. When he began to come to years of discretion, Cato himself would teach him to read, although he had a servant, a very good grammarian, called Chilo, who taught many others; but he thought not fit, as he himself said, to have his son reprimanded by a slave, or pulled, it may be, by the ears when found tardy in his lesson; nor would he have him owe to a servant the obligation of so great a thing as his learning; he himself, therefore, (as we were saying,) taught him his grammar, law, and his gymnastic exercises. Nor did he only show him, too, how to throw a dart,[5] to fight in armor, and to ride, but to box also and to endure both heat and cold, and to swim over the most rapid and rough rivers. He says, likewise, that he wrote histories, in large characters, with his own hand, that so his son, without stirring out of the house, might learn to know about his countrymen and forefathers; nor did he less abstain from speaking any thing obscene before his son, than if it had been in the presence of the sacred virgins, called vestals. Nor would he ever go into the bath with him, which seems indeed to have been the common custom of the Romans. Sons-in-law used to avoid bathing with fathers-in-law, disliking to see one another naked; but having, in time, learned of the Greeks to strip before men, they have since taught the Greeks to do it even with the women themselves.

Thus, like an excellent work, Cato formed and fashioned his son to virtue; nor had he any occasion to find fault with his readiness and docility; but as he proved to be of too weak a constitution for hardships, he did not insist on requiring of him any very austere way of living. However, though delicate in health, he proved a stout man in the field, and behaved himself valiantly when Aemilius Paulus fought against Perseus.[6] . . . Afterwards he married Tertia, Aemi-

---

[5] A javelin.
[6] The last king of Macedonia, which was conquered and annexed by Rome in 171 B.C.

lius Paulus's daughter, and sister to Scipio;[7] nor was he admitted into this family less for his own worth than his father's. So that Cato's care in his son's education came to a very fitting result.

He purchased a great many slaves out of the captives taken in war, but chiefly bought up the young ones, who were capable to be, as it were, broken and taught like whelps and colts. None of these ever entered another man's house, except sent either by Cato himself or his wife. If any one of them were asked what Cato did, they answered merely, that they did not know. When a servant was at home, he was obliged either to do some work or sleep; for indeed Cato loved those most who used to lie down often to sleep, accounting them more docile than those who were wakeful, and more fit for any thing when they were refreshed with a little slumber. Being also of opinion, that the great cause of the laziness and misbehavior of slaves was their running after their pleasures, he fixed a certain price for them to pay for permission amongst themselves, but would suffer no connections out of the house. At first, when he was but a poor soldier, he would not be difficult in anything which related to his eating, but looked upon it as a pitiful thing to quarrel with a servant for the belly's sake; but afterwards, when he grew richer, and made any feasts for his friends and colleagues in office, as soon as supper was over he used to go with a leathern thong and scourge those who had waited or dressed the meat carelessly. He always contrived, too, that his servants should have some difference one among another, always suspecting and fearing a good understanding between them. Those who had committed any thing worthy of death, he punished, if they were found guilty by the verdict of their fellow-servants. But being after all much given to the desire of gain, he looked upon agriculture rather as a pleasure than profit; resolving, therefore, to lay out his money in safe and solid things, he purchased ponds, hot baths, grounds full of fuller's earth, remunerative lands, pastures, and woods, from which he drew large returns; so that Jupiter himself, he used to say, could do him little damage. He was also given to the form of usury, which is considered most odious, in traffic by sea; and that thus:—he desired that those whom he put out his money to, should have many partners; and when the number of them and their ships came to be fifty, he himself took one share through Quintio his freedman, who therefore was to sail with the adventurers, and take a

---

[7] A distinguished Roman consul and general.

part in all their proceedings; so that thus there was no danger of losing his whole stock, but only a little part, and that with a prospect of great profit. He likewise lent money to those of his slaves who wished to borrow, with which they bought also other young ones, whom, when they had taught and bred up at his charges, they would sell again at the year's end; but some of them Cato would keep for himself, giving just as much for them as another had offered. To incline his son to be of this kind of temper, he used to tell him, that it was not like a man, but rather like a widow woman, to lessen an estate. But the strongest indication of Cato's avaricious nature was when he took the boldness to affirm, that he was a most wonderful, nay, a godlike man, who left more behind him than he had received.

He was now grown old, when Carneades the Academic,[8] and Diogenes the Stoic, came as deputies from Athens to Rome, praying for release from a penalty of five hundred talents laid on the Athenians, in a suit, to which they did not appear, in which the Oropians were plaintiffs, and Sicyonians judges. All the most studious youth immediately waited on these philosophers, and frequently, with admiration, heard them speak. But the gracefulness of Carneades's oratory, whose ability was really greatest, and his reputation equal to it, gathered large and favorable audiences, and erelong filled, like a wind, all the city with the sound of it. So that it soon began to be told, that a Greek, famous even to admiration, winning and carrying all before him, had impressed so strange a love upon the young men, that quitting all their pleasures and pastimes, they ran mad, as it were, after philosophy; which indeed much pleased the Romans in general; nor could they but with much pleasure see the youth receive so welcomely the Greek literature, and frequent the company of learned men. But Cato, on the other side, seeing this passion for words flowing into the city, from the beginning, took it ill, fearing lest the youth should be diverted that way, and so should prefer the glory of speaking well before that of arms, and doing well. And when the fame of the philosophers increased in the city, and Caius Acilius, a person of distinction, at his own request, became their interpreter to the senate at their first audience, Cato resolved, under some specious pretence, to have all philosophers cleared out of the

---

[8] An appellation given to each of the philosophers who succeeded Plato at the famous Academy, which he had founded. Carneades (214–129 B.C.) was famed for his skepticism.

city; and, coming into the senate, blamed the magistrates for letting these deputies stay so long a time without being despatched, though they were persons that could easily persuade the people to what they pleased; that therefore in all haste something should be determined about their petition, that so they might go home again to their own schools, and declaim to the Greek children, and leave the Roman youth, to be obedient, as hitherto, to their own laws and governors.

Yet he did this not out of any anger, as some think, to Carneades; but because he wholly despised philosophy, and out of a kind of pride, scoffed at the Greek studies and literature; as, for example, he would say, that Socrates was a prating seditious fellow, who did his best to tyrannize over his country, to undermine the ancient customs, and to entice and withdraw the citizens to opinions contrary to the laws. Ridiculing the school of Isocrates, he would add, that his scholars grew old men before they had done learning with him, as if they were to use their art and plead causes in the court of Minos[9] in the next world. And to frighten his son from any thing that was Greek, in a more vehement tone than became one of his age, he pronounced, as it were, with the voice of an oracle, that the Romans would certainly be destroyed when they began once to be infected with Greek literature; though time indeed has shown the vanity of this his prophecy; as, in truth, the city of Rome has risen to its highest fortune, while entertaining Grecian learning.

Nor had he an aversion only against the Greek philosophers, but the physicians also; for having, it seems, heard how Hippocrates,[10] when the king of Persia sent for him, with offers of a fee of several talents, said, that he would never assist barbarians who were enemies to the Greeks; he affirmed, that this was now become a common oath taken by all physicians, and enjoined his son to have a care and avoid them; for that he himself had written a little book of prescriptions for curing those who were sick in his family; he never enjoined fasting to any one, but ordered them either vegetables, or the meat of a duck, pigeon, or leveret;[11] such kind of diet being of light digestion, and fit for sick folks, only it made those who ate it, dream a little too much; and by the use of this kind of physic, he said, he not only made himself and those about him well, but kept them so.

• • •

[9] In Greco-Roman mythology, a judge of dead souls in the underworld.
[10] A famous Greek physician of the fifth century B.C.
[11] A young hare.

Some will have the overthrow of Carthage[12] to have been one of his last acts of state, when, indeed, Scipio the Younger, did by his valor give it the last blow; but the war, chiefly by the counsel and advice of Cato, was undertaken on the following occasion. Cato was sent to the Carthaginians and Masinissa, king of Numidia, who were at war with one another, to know the cause of their difference. He, it seems, had been a friend of the Romans from the beginning; and they, too, since they were conquered by Scipio, were of the Roman confederacy, having been shorn of their power by loss of territory, and a heavy tax. Finding Carthage, not (as the Romans thought) low and in an ill condition, but well manned, full of riches and all sorts of arms and ammunition, and perceiving the Carthaginians carry it high, he conceived that it was not a time for the Romans to adjust affairs between them and Masinissa; but rather that they themselves would fall into danger, unless they should find means to check this rapid new growth of Rome's ancient irreconcilable enemy. Therefore, returning quickly to Rome, he acquainted the senate, that the former defeats and blows given to the Carthaginians, had not so much diminished their strength, as it had abated their imprudence and folly; that they were not become weaker, but more experienced in war, and did only skirmish with the Numidians, to exercise themselves the better to cope with the Romans; that the peace and league they had made was but a kind of suspension of war which awaited a fairer opportunity to break out again.

Moreover, they say that, shaking his gown, he took occasion to let drop some African figs before the senate. And on their admiring the size and beauty of them, he presently added, that the place that bore them was but three days' sail from Rome. Nay, he never after this gave his opinion, but at the end he would be sure to come out with this sentence, "Also, Carthage, methinks, ought utterly to be destroyed." . . . For seeing his countrymen to be grown wanton and insolent, and the people made, by their prosperity, obstinate and disobedient to the senate, and drawing the whole city, whither they would, after them, he would have had the fear of Carthage to serve as a bit to hold in the rebelliousness of the multitude; and he looked upon the Carthaginians as too weak to overcome the Romans, and too great to be despised by them. On the other side, it seemed a perilous thing to Cato, that a city which had been always great, and was

---

[12] The great rival city against which the Roman Republic waged the Punic Wars, three wars fought during the third and second centuries B.C.

now grown sober and wise, by reason of its former calamities, should still lie, as it were, in wait for the follies and dangerous excesses of the overpowerful Roman people; so that he thought it the wisest course to have all outward dangers removed, when they had so many inward ones among themselves.

14

Cicero

De Legibus

With Cicero we come not only to the imperial world of Rome but to
Rome in the golden age of its literature (70 B.C.–A.D. 14). Cicero
gave perfect expression to the dominant tradition of classical man, for all his
works—oratorical, philosophical, epistolary, and poetic—are pervaded by
the highest sense of public interest and duty. We find in them also a supreme
regard for humanitas, *a word coined by Cicero, meaning the mental and
moral qualities that make for civilized living.*

Marcus Tullius Cicero (106–43 B.C.*) was born in Arpinum, south of
Rome, to a family of only local note; as a "new man" (the Roman term for
a parvenu), he had to make his way against aristocratic prejudice. After
schooling in Rome, Athens, and Rhodes, he quickly rose to leadership in jurisprudence; he became a consul in 63* B.C. *and, later, a provincial governor.
After the murder of Caesar in 44* B.C.*, Cicero backed the senatorial party; as
a consequence, in the following year he was put to death by order of Marcus
Antonius, whom he had offended.*

*The writings of Cicero are more voluminous than those of any other au-
thor of ancient times, and his role as selector and transmitter of Greco-Roman
thought and values is of enormous importance. He was a master of Latin
prose and rhetorical form, and his stylistic influence (Ciceronianism), especially strong during the Renaissance, has been transmitted to modern times.*

Cicero's De Legibus (On the Laws), *which was begun ca. 52* B.C. *but
never finished, is an exposition of the ideal state and takes the form of a dialogue between Cicero, his brother Quintus, and his friend Pomponius At-*

Cicero, *De Legibus,* trans. Clinton W. Keyes (Loeb Classical Library—London: Heinemann and New York: Putnam, 1928), 311, 313, 315, 317, 319, 321, 323, 325, 327,
329, 331, 333, 335, 341, 343, 345, 347, 351, 353. Reprinted by permission of the publishers and the Loeb Classical Library.

ticus. Book I, from which the following selection is drawn, sets forth the thesis (previously advanced by the Stoic philosophers) that divine justice is the source of all law, everywhere. Existing codes and statutes, constituting "positive" law, therefore derive their validity and justification from this "higher" or "natural" law, which is also identical with right reason. This doctrine of natural law, with its ideals of freedom and equality, was to have a long and influential life, becoming the jus naturale *of Roman jurisprudence, finding embodiment in the laws of the medieval Church, and reaching its acme of influence in the eighteenth century—as the foundation for the American and French revolutions.*

ATTICUS. Why do you not, then, in the present "odds and ends of time," as you call them, expound this very subject to us, and compose a treatise on the civil law, going into it more deeply than your predecessors? For I remember that you were interested in law even in your early youth, when I too was studying with Scaevola,[1] and it has never seemed to me that you have become so absorbed in oratory as to turn your back completely upon the civil law.

MARCUS [Cicero].   You are urging me to a long discussion, Atticus, but nevertheless I will undertake it, unless Quintus prefers some other occupation; and, as we are at leisure, I will state my views on this topic.

QUINTUS.   I should be very glad to listen to you; for what occupation could I prefer, or how could I spend the day more profitably?

MARCUS.   Then let us go to those promenades and seats of ours, so that when we have enough of walking, we may rest. Surely we shall not lack entertainment as we take up one question after another.

ATTICUS.   We agree; and indeed, if you approve, we might walk here by the Liris, in the shade along its bank. But kindly begin without delay the statement of your opinions on the civil law.

MARCUS.   My opinions? Well then, I believe that there have been most eminent men in our State whose customary function it was to interpret the law to the people and answer questions in regard to it, but that these men, though they have made great claims, have spent their time on unimportant details. What subject indeed is so vast as the law of the State? But what is so trivial as the task of those who give

---

[1] A prominent Roman teacher of law in first century B.C.

legal advice? It is, however, necessary for the people. But, while I do not consider that those who have applied themselves to this profession have lacked a conception of universal law, yet they have carried their studies of this civil law, as it is called, only far enough to accomplish their purpose of being useful to the people. Now all this amounts to little so far as learning is concerned, though for practical purposes it is indispensable. What subject is it, then, that you are asking me to expound? To what task are you urging me? Do you want me to write a treatise on the law of eaves and house-walls? Or to compose formulas for contracts and court procedure? These subjects have been carefully treated by many writers, and are of a humbler character, I believe, than what is expected of me.

ATTICUS.   Yet if you ask what I expect of you, I consider it a logical thing that, since you have already written a treatise on the constitution of the ideal State, you should also write one on its laws. For I note that this was done by your beloved Plato, whom you admire, revere above all others, and love above all others.

MARCUS.   Is it your wish, then, that, as he discussed the institutions of States and the ideal laws with Clinias and the Spartan Megillus in Crete on a summer day amid the cypress groves and forest paths of Cnossus, sometimes walking about, sometimes resting—you recall his description—we, in like manner, strolling or taking our ease among these stately poplars on the green and shady river bank, shall discuss the same subjects along somewhat broader lines than the practice of the courts calls for?

ATTICUS.   I should certainly like to hear such a conversation.

MARCUS.   What does Quintus say?

QUINTUS.   No other subject would suit me better.

MARCUS.   And you are wise, for you must understand that in no other kind of discussion can one bring out so clearly what Nature's gifts to man are, what a wealth of most excellent possessions the human mind enjoys, what the purpose is, to strive after and accomplish which we have been born and placed in this world, what it is that unites men, and what natural fellowship there is among them. For it is only after all these things have been made clear that the origin of Law and Justice can be discovered.

ATTICUS.   Then you do not think that the science of law is to be derived from the praetor's edit,[2] as the majority do now, or from the

_____

[2] The praetor was a magistrate elected annually and given wide powers. Upon taking office his edict declared the rules of law that would guide him. Such edicts became a source of Roman Law.

Twelve Tables,[3] as people used to think, but from the deepest mysteries of philosophy?

MARCUS.   Quite right; for in our present conversation, Pomponius, we are not trying to learn how to protect ourselves legally, or how to answer clients' questions. Such problems may be important, and in fact they are; for in former times many eminent men made a specialty of their solution, and at present one person performs this duty with the greatest authority and skill. But in our present investigation we intend to cover the whole range of universal Justice and Law in such a way that our own civil law, as it is called, will be confined to a small and narrow corner. For we must explain the nature of Justice, and this must be sought for in the nature of man; we must also consider the laws by which States ought to be governed; then we must deal with the enactments and decrees of nations which are already formulated and put in writing; and among these the civil law, as it is called, of the Roman people will not fail to find a place.

QUINTUS.   You probe deep, and seek, as you should, the very fountain-head, to find what we are after, brother. And those who teach the civil law in any other way are teaching not so much the path of justice as of litigation.

MARCUS.   There you are mistaken, Quintus, for it is rather ignorance of the law than knowledge of it that leads to litigation. But that will come later; now let us investigate the origins of Justice.

Well then, the most learned men have determined to begin with Law, and it would seem that they are right, if, according to their definition, Law is the highest reason, implanted in Nature, which commands what ought to be done and forbids the opposite. This reason, when firmly fixed and fully developed in the human mind, is Law. And so they believe that Law is intelligence, whose natural function it is to command right conduct and forbid wrongdoing. . . .

Now if this is correct, as I think it to be in general, then the origin of Justice is to be found in Law, for Law is a natural force; it is the mind and reason of the intelligent man, the standard by which Justice and Injustice are measured. But since our whole discussion has to do with the reasoning of the populace, it will sometimes be necessary to speak in the popular manner, and give the name of law to that which in written form decrees whatever it wishes either by command or

---

[3] The basic laws of Rome, previously unwritten, were inscribed on these tablets in the fifth century B.C.

prohibition. For such is the crowd's definition of law. But in determining what Justice is, let us begin with that supreme Law which had its origin ages before any written law existed or any State had been established.

QUINTUS.   Indeed that will be preferable and more suitable to the character of the conversation we have begun.

MARCUS.   Well, then, shall we seek the origin of Justice itself at its fountain-head? For when that is discovered we shall undoubtedly have a standard by which the things we are seeking may be tested.

QUINTUS.   I think that is certainly what we must do.

• • •

MARCUS.   I will not make the argument long. Your admission leads us to this: that animal which we call man, endowed with foresight and quick intelligence, complex, keen, possessing memory, full of reason and prudence, has been given a certain distinguished status by the supreme God who created him; for he is the only one among so many different kinds and varieties of living beings who has a share in reason and thought, while all the rest are deprived of it. But what is more divine, I will not say in man only, but in all heaven and earth, than reason? And reason, when it is full grown and perfected, is rightly called wisdom. Therefore, since there is nothing better than reason, and since it exists both in man and God, the first common possession of man and God is reason. But those who have reason in common must also have right reason in common. And since right reason is Law, we must believe that men have Law also in common with the gods. Further, those who share Law must also share Justice; and those who share these are to be regarded as members of the same commonwealth. If indeed they obey the same authorities and powers, this is true in a far greater degree; but as a matter of fact they do obey this celestial system, the divine mind, and the God of transcendent power. Hence we must now conceive of this whole universe as one commonwealth of which both gods and men are members.

And just as in States distinctions in legal status are made on account of the blood relationships of families, according to a system which I shall take up in its proper place, so in the universe the same thing holds true, but on a scale much vaster and more splendid, so that men are grouped with gods on the basis of blood relationship and descent.

For when the nature of man is examined, the theory is usually advanced (and in all probability it is correct) that through constant changes and revolutions in the heavens, a time came which was suitable for sowing the seed of the human race. And when this seed was scattered and sown over the earth, it was granted the divine gift of the soul. For while the other elements of which man consists were derived from what is mortal, and are therefore fragile and perishable, the soul was generated in us by God. Hence we are justified in saying that there is a blood relationship between ourselves and the celestial beings; or we may call it a common ancestry or origin. Therefore among all the varieties of living beings, there is no creature except man which has any knowledge of God, and among men themselves there is no race either so highly civilized or so savage as not to know that it must believe in a god, even if it does not know in what sort of god it ought to believe. Thus it is clear that man recognizes God because, in a way, he remembers and recognizes the source from which he sprang.

Moreover, virtue exists in man and God alike, but in no other creature besides; virtue, however, is nothing else than Nature perfected and developed to its highest point; therefore there is a likeness between man and God. As this is true, what relationship could be closer or clearer than this one? For this reason, Nature has lavishly yielded such a wealth of things adapted to man's convenience and use that what she produces seems intended as a gift to us, and not brought forth by chance; and this is true, not only of what the fertile earth bountifully bestows in the form of grain and fruit, but also of the animals; for it is clear that some of them have been created to be man's slaves, some to supply him with their products, and others to serve as his food. Moreover, innumerable arts have been discovered through the teachings of Nature; for it is by a skilful imitation of her that reason has acquired the necessities of life. Nature has likewise not only equipped man himself with nimbleness of thought, but has also given him the senses, to be, as it were, his attendants and messengers; she has laid bare the obscure and none too obvious meanings of a great many things, to serve as the foundations of knowledge, as we may call them; and she has granted us a bodily form which is convenient and well suited to the human mind. For while she has bent the other creatures down toward their food, she has made man alone erect, and has challenged him to look up toward heaven, as being, so to speak, akin to him, and his first home. In addition, she has so formed his features as to portray therein the character that lies hidden deep within him; for not only do the eyes declare with exceeding clearness the innermost feelings of our hearts, but also the countenance, as we Romans call it, which can be found in no living thing save man, reveals the character. (The Greeks are familiar with the meaning which this word "countenance" conveys, though they have no name for it.) I will pass over the special faculties and aptitudes of the other parts of the body, such as the varying tones of the voice and the power of speech, which is the most effective promoter of human intercourse; for all these things are not in keeping with our present discussion or the time at our disposal; and besides, this topic has been adequately treated, as it seems to me, by Scipio in the books which you have read. But, whereas God has begotten and equipped man, desiring him to be the chief of all created things, it should now be evident, without going into all the details, that Nature, alone and unaided, goes a step farther; for, with no guide to point the way, she starts with those things whose character she has learned through the rudimentary beginnings of intelligence, and, alone and unaided, strengthens and perfects the faculty of reason.

ATTICUS.   Ye immortal gods, how far back you go to find the origins of Justice! And you discourse so eloquently that I not only have no desire to hasten on to the consideration of the civil law, concerning which I was expecting you to speak, but I should have no objection to your spending even the entire day on your present topic; for the matters which you have taken up, no doubt, merely as preparatory to another subject, are of greater import than the subject itself to which they form an introduction.

MARCUS.   The points which are now being briefly touched upon are certainly important; but out of all the material of the philosophers' discussions, surely there comes nothing more valuable than the full realization that we are born for Justice, and that right is based, not upon men's opinions, but upon Nature. This fact will immediately be plain if you once get a clear conception of man's fellowship and union with his fellow-men. For no single thing is so like another, so exactly its counterpart, as all of us are to one another. Nay, if bad habits and false beliefs did not twist the weaker minds and turn them in whatever direction they are inclined, no one would be so like his own self as all men would be like all others. And so, however we may define man, a single definition will apply to all. This is a sufficient proof that there is no difference in kind between man and man; for if there were, one definition could not be applicable to all men; and indeed reason, which alone raises us above the level of the beasts and enables us to draw inferences, to prove and disprove, to discuss and solve problems, and to come to conclusions, is certainly common to us all, and, though varying in what it learns, at least in the capacity to learn it is invariable. For the same things are invariably perceived by the senses, and those things which stimulate the senses, stimulate them in the same way in all men; and those rudimentary beginnings of intelligence to which I have referred, which are imprinted on our minds, are imprinted on all minds alike; and speech, the mind's interpreter, though differing in the choice of words, agrees in the sentiments expressed. In fact, there is no human being of any race who, if he finds a guide, cannot attain to virtue.

The similarity of the human race is clearly marked in its evil tendencies as well as in its goodness. For pleasure also attracts all men; and even though it is an enticement to vice, yet it has some likeness to what is naturally good. For it delights us by its lightness and agreeableness; and for this reason, by an error of thought, it is embraced as something wholesome. It is through a similar misconception that we shun death as though it were a dissolution of nature, and cling to life because it keeps us in the sphere in which we were born; and that we look upon pain as one of the greatest of evils, not only because of its cruelty, but also because it seems to lead to the destruction of nature. In the same way, on account of the similarity between moral worth and renown, those who are publicly honoured are considered happy, while those who do not attain fame are thought miserable. Troubles, joys, desires, and fears haunt the minds of all men without distinction, and even if different men have different beliefs, that does not prove, for example, that it is not the same quality of superstition that besets those races which worship dogs and cats as gods, as that which torments other races. But what nation does not love courtesy, kindliness, gratitude, and remembrance of favours bestowed? What people does not hate and despise the haughty, the wicked, the cruel, and the ungrateful? Inasmuch as these considerations prove to us that the whole human race is bound together in unity, it follows, finally, that knowledge of the principles of right living is what makes men better.

If you approve of what has been said, I will go on to what follows. But if there is anything that you care to have explained, we will take that up first.

ATTICUS.   We have no questions, if I may speak for both of us.

MARCUS.   The next point, then, is that we are so constituted by Nature as to share the sense of Justice with one another and to pass it on to all men. And in this whole discussion I want it understood that what I shall call Nature is that which is implanted in us by Nature; that, however, the corruption caused by bad habits is so great that the sparks of fire, so to speak, which Nature has kindled in us are extinguished by this corruption, and the vices which are their opposites spring up and are established. But if the judgments of men were in agreement with Nature, so that, as the poet[4] says, they considered "nothing alien to them which concerns mankind," then Justice would be equally observed by all. For those creatures who have received the gift of reason from Nature have also received right reason, and therefore they have also received the gift of Law, which is right reason applied to command and prohibition. And if they have received Law, they have received Justice also. Now all men have received reason; therefore all men have received Justice. Consequently Socrates was right when he cursed, as he often did, the man who first separated utility from Justice; for this separation, he complained, is the source of all mischief. For what gave rise to Pythagoras'[5] famous words about friendship? . . . From this it is clear that, when a wise man shows toward another endowed with equal virtue the kind of benevolence which is so widely diffused among men, that will then have come to pass which, unbelievable as it seems to some, is after all the inevitable result—namely, that he loves himself no whit more than he loves another. For what difference can there be among things which are all equal? But if the least distinction should be made in friendship, then the very name of friendship would perish forthwith; for its essence is such that, as soon as either friend prefers anything for himself, friendship ceases to exist.

Now all this is really a preface to what remains to be said in our discussion, and its purpose is to make it more easily understood that Justice is inherent in Nature. After I have said a few words more on this topic, I shall go on to the civil law, the subject which gives rise to all this discourse.

• • •

But if it were a penalty and not Nature that ought to keep men from injustice, what anxiety would there be to trouble the wicked

---

[4] Terence, Roman writer of the second century B.C.
[5] Greek mathematician and philosopher of the sixth century B.C.

when the danger of punishment was removed? But in fact there has never been a villain so brazen as not to deny that he had committed a crime, or else invent some story of just anger to excuse its commission, and seek justification for his crime in some natural principle of right. Now if even the wicked dare to appeal to such principles, how jealously should they be guarded by the good! But if it is a penalty, the fear of punishment, and not the wickedness itself, that is to keep men from a life of wrongdoing and crime, then no one can be called unjust, and wicked men ought rather to be regarded as imprudent; furthermore, those of us who are not influenced by virtue itself to be good men, but by some consideration of utility and profit, are merely shrewd, not good. For to what lengths will that man go in the dark who fears nothing but a witness and a judge? What will he do if, in some desolate spot, he meets a helpless man, unattended, whom he can rob of a fortune? Our virtuous man, who is just and good by nature, will talk with such a person, help him, and guide him on his way; but the other, who does nothing for another's sake, and measures every act by the standard of his own advantage—it is clear enough, I think, what he will do! If, however, the latter does deny that he would kill the man and rob him of his money, he will not deny it because he regards it as a naturally wicked thing to do, but because he is afraid that his crime may become known—that is, that he may get into trouble. Oh, what a motive, that might well bring a blush of shame to the cheek, not merely of the philosopher, but even of the simple rustic!

But the most foolish notion of all is the belief that everything is just which is found in the customs or laws of nations. Would that be true, even if these laws had been enacted by tyrants? If the well-known Thirty[6] had desired to enact a set of laws at Athens, or if the Athenians without exception were delighted by the tyrants' laws, that would not entitle such laws to be regarded as just, would it? No more, in my opinion, should that law be considered just which a Roman interrex proposed, to the effect that a dictator might put to death with impunity any citizen he wished, even without a trial. For Justice is one; it binds all human society, and is based on one Law, which is right reason applied to command and prohibition. Whoever knows not this Law, whether it has been recorded in writing anywhere or not, is without Justice.

---

[6] Thirty men placed in power at Athens by the victorious Spartans after the Peloponnesian War (fifth century B.C.).

But if Justice is conformity to written laws and national customs, and if, as the same persons claim, everything is to be tested by the standard of utility, then anyone who thinks it will be profitable to him will, if he is able, disregard and violate the laws. It follows that Justice does not exist at all, if it does not exist in Nature, and if that form of it which is based on utility can be overthrown by that very utility itself. And if Nature is not to be considered the foundation of Justice, that will mean the destruction of the virtues on which human society depends. For where then will there be a place for generosity, or love of country, or loyalty, or the inclination to be of service to others or to show gratitude for favours received? For these virtues originate in our natural inclination to love our fellow-men, and this is the foundation of Justice. Otherwise not merely consideration for men but also rites and pious observances in honour of the gods are done away with; for I think that these ought to be maintained, not through fear, but on account of the close relationship which exists between man and God. But if the principles of Justice were founded on the decrees of peoples, the edicts of princes, or the decisions of judges, then Justice would sanction robbery and adultery and forgery of wills, in case these acts were approved by the votes or decrees of the populace. But if so great a power belongs to the decisions and decrees of fools that the laws of Nature can be changed by their votes, then why do they not ordain that what is bad and baneful shall be considered good and salutary? Or, if a law can make Justice out of Injustice, can it not also make good out of bad? But in fact we can perceive the difference between good laws and bad by referring them to no other standard than Nature; indeed, it is not merely Justice and Injustice which are distinguished by Nature, but also and without exception things which are honourable and dishonourable. For since an intelligence common to us all makes things known to us and formulates them in our minds, honourable actions are ascribed by us to virtue, and dishonourable actions to vice; and only a madman would conclude that these judgments are matters of opinion, and not fixed by Nature.

• • •

To close now our discussion of this whole subject, the conclusion, which stands clearly before our eyes from what has already been said, is this: Justice and all things honourable are to be sought for their own sake. And indeed all good men love fairness in itself and Justice in itself, and it is unnatural for a good man to make such a mistake as to love what does not deserve love for itself alone. Therefore Justice must be sought and cultivated for her own sake; and if this is true of Justice, it is also true of equity; and if this is the case with equity, then all the other virtues are also to be cherished for their own sake. What of generosity? Is it disinterested or does it look to a recompense? If a man is kind without any reward, then it is disinterested; but if he receives payment then it is hired. It cannot be doubted that he who is called generous or kind answers the call of duty, not of gain. Therefore equity also demands no reward or price; consequently it is sought for its own sake. And the same motive and purpose characterize all the virtues.

In addition, if it be true that virtue is sought for the sake of other benefits and not for its own sake, there will be only one virtue, which will most properly be called a vice. For in proportion as anyone makes his own advantage absolutely the sole standard of all his actions, to that extent he is absolutely not a good man; therefore those who measure virtue by the reward it brings believe in the existence of no virtue except vice. For where shall we find a kindly man, if no one does a kindness for the sake of anyone else than himself? Who can be considered grateful, if even those who repay favours have no real consideration for those to whom they repay them? What becomes of that sacred thing, friendship, if even the friend himself is not loved for his own sake, "with the whole heart," as people say? Why, according to this theory, a friend should even be deserted and cast aside as soon as there is no longer hope of benefit and profit from his friendship! But what could be more inhuman than that? If, on the other hand, friendship is to be sought for its own sake, then the society of our fellow-men, fairness, and Justice, are also to be sought for their own sake. If this is not the case then there is no such thing as Justice at all, for the very height of injustice is to seek pay for Justice. But what shall we say of sobriety, moderation, and self-restraint; of modesty, self-respect, and chastity? Is it for fear of disgrace that we should not be wanton, or for fear of the laws and the courts? In that case men are innocent and modest in order to be well spoken of, and they blush in order to gain a good reputation! I am ashamed even to mention chastity! Or rather I am ashamed of those philosophers who believe it honourable to avoid condemnation for a crime without having avoided the crime itself.

15

Suetonius

The Lives of the Twelve Caesars: Augustus

🔲

The Romans had always been absorbed in the lives of their great leaders, as shown by the preservation of commemorative death masks and the development of portrait sculpture. When autocrats came to dominate all others under the Empire, it was natural that their biographies should be written, and for a long time biography eclipsed narrative history.

This trend began with Gaius Suetonius Tranquillus (ca. A.D. 69–ca. 140), the son of a well-to-do family. Even more than Plutarch, he is known almost entirely through his writings; for, apart from the fact that he was secretary to the Emperor Hadrian for a time, we know little of him. Most of his writings are lost to us as well. His only surviving work is The Lives of the Twelve Caesars, *published in A.D. 120.*

Suetonius was an industrious scholar and through his official post had access to archival materials now lost forever; but as a biographer he makes no attempt to present well-rounded portraits of his subjects, to set them in the background of their times, or even to comment upon them. If we knew nothing more of the Emperor Augustus than what Suetonius tells us, we would be left wondering how this man could have been master of the world— the man referred to in a provincial inscription as "the savior of the whole human race . . . god of god . . . Zeus of father Zeus."

In this respect Suetonius differs from Plutarch, his Greek contemporary, who offers lessons in conduct rather than informatory sketches. But, although lacking in style and insight, the studies by Suetonius abound in lively

Suetonius, *The Lives of the Twelve Caesars,* trans. Alexander Thompson, rev. and corr. T. Forester (London: Bell, 1893), 75–76, 80–82, 84–85, 87, 91–100, 109–10, 112, 114–16, 128–30.

anecdotes and gossipy details, often sensational in nature. And, of course, they deal with twelve extraordinary men. These features account in large measure for the enduring popularity of Suetonius.

He lost his father when he was only four years of age; and, in his twelfth year, pronounced a funeral oration in praise of his grandmother Julia. Four years afterwards, having assumed the robe of manhood, he was honoured with several military rewards by Caesar in his African triumph, although he took no part in the war on account of his youth. Upon his uncle's[1] expedition to Spain against the sons of Pompey, he was followed by his nephew, although he was scarcely recovered from a dangerous sickness; and after being shipwrecked at sea, and travelling with very few attendants through roads that were infested with the enemy, he at last came up with him. This activity gave great satisfaction to his uncle, who soon conceived an increasing affection for him, on account of such indications of character. After the subjugation of Spain, while Caesar was meditating an expedition against the Dacians and Parthians, he was sent before him to Apollonia, where he applied himself to his studies; until receiving intelligence that his uncle was murdered, and that he was appointed his heir, he hesitated for some time whether he should call to his aid the legions stationed in the neighbourhood; but he abandoned the design as rash and premature. However, returning to Rome, he took possession of his inheritance, although his mother was apprehensive that such a measure might be attended with danger, and his step-father, Marcius Philippus, a man of consular rank, very earnestly dissuaded him from it. From this time, collecting together a strong military force, he first held the government in conjunction with Mark Antony and Marcus Lepidus, then with Antony only for nearly twelve years, and at last in his own hands during a period of four and forty.

Having thus given a very short summary of his life, I shall prosecute the several parts of it, not in order of time, but arranging his acts into distinct classes, for the sake of perspicuity. He was engaged in five civil wars, namely those of Modena, Philippi,

---

[1] His "uncle" was Julius Caesar (actually, his great-uncle).

Perugia, Sicily, and Actium; the first and last of which were against Antony, and the second against Brutus and Cassius; the third against Lucius Antonius, the triumvir's brother, and the fourth against Sextus Pompeius, the son of Cneius Pompeius.

The motive which gave rise to all these wars was the opinion he entertained that both his honour and interest were concerned in revenging the murder of his uncle, and maintaining the state of affairs he had established.

• • •

The alliance between him and Antony, which had always been precarious, often interrupted, and ill cemented by repeated reconciliations, he at last entirely dissolved. And to make it known to the world how far Antony had degenerated from patriotic feelings, he caused a will of his, which had been left at Rome, and in which he had nominated Cleopatra's children, amongst others, as his heirs, to be opened and read in an assembly of the people. . . . And not long afterwards he defeated him in a naval engagement near Actium, which was prolonged to so late an hour, that, after the victory, he was obliged to sleep on board his ship.

From Actium he went to the isle of Samos to winter; but being alarmed with the accounts of a mutiny amongst the soldiers he had selected from the main body of his army sent to Brundisium after the victory, who insisted on their being rewarded for their service and discharged, he returned to Italy. . . .

He remained only twenty-seven days at Brundisium, until the demands of the soldiers were settled, and then went, by way of Asia [2] and Syria, to Egypt, where laying siege to Alexandria, whither Antony had fled with Cleopatra, he made himself master of it in a short time. He drove Antony to kill himself, after he had used every effort to obtain conditions of peace, and he saw his corpse. Cleopatra he anxiously wished to save for his triumph; and when she was supposed to have been bit to death by an asp, he sent for the Psylli to endeavor to suck out the poison. He allowed them to be buried together in the same grave, and ordered a mausoleum, begun by themselves, to be completed. The eldest of Antony's two sons by Fulvia he commanded to be taken by force from the statue of Julius Caesar, to which he had fled, after many fruitless supplications for

[2] The Roman province located in the western portion of Asia Minor.

his life, and put him to death. The same fate attended Caesarion, Cleopatra's son by Caesar, as he pretended, who had fled for his life, but was retaken. The children which Antony had by Cleopatra he saved, and brought up and cherished in a manner suitable to their rank, just as if they had been his own relations.

· · ·

He conducted in person only two foreign wars; the Dalmatian, whilst he was yet but a youth; and, after Antony's final defeat, the Cantabrian. He was wounded in the former of these wars; in one battle he received a contusion in the right knee from a stone—and in another, he was much hurt in one leg and both arms, by the fall of a bridge. His other wars he carried on by his lieutenants; but occasionally visited the army, in some of the wars of Pannonia and Germany, or remained at no great distance, proceeding from Rome as far as Ravenna, Milan, or Aquileia.

He conquered, however, partly in person, and partly by his lieutenants, Cantabria, Aquitania and Pannonia, Dalmatia, with all Illyricum and Rhaetia, besides the two Alpine nations, the Vindelici and the Salassii. He also checked the incursions of the Dacians, by cutting off three of their generals with vast armies, and drove the Germans beyond the river Elbe; removing two other tribes who submitted, the Ubii and Sicambri, into Gaul, and settling them in the country bordering on the Rhine. Other nations also, which broke into revolt, he reduced to submission. But he never made war upon any nation without just and necessary cause; and was so far from being ambitious either to extend the empire, or advance his own military glory, that he obliged the chiefs of some barbarous tribes to swear in the temple of Mars the Avenger, that they would faithfully observe their engagements, and not violate the peace which they had implored. Of some he demanded a new description of hostages, their women, having found from experience that they cared little for their men when given as hostages; but he always afforded them the means of getting back their hostages whenever they wished it.

Even those who engaged most frequently and with the greatest perfidy in their rebellion, he never punished more severely than by selling their captives, on the terms of their not serving in any neighbouring country, nor being released from their slavery before the expiration of thirty years. By the character which he thus acquired, for virtue and moderation, he induced even the Indians and Scythians,[3] nations before known to the Romans by report only, to solicit his friendship, and that of the Roman people, by ambassadors. The Parthians[4] readily allowed his claim to Armenia; restoring at his demand, the standards which they had taken from Marcus Crassus and Mark Antony, and offering him hostages besides. Afterwards, when a contest arose between several pretenders to the crown of that kingdom, they refused to acknowledge any one who was not chosen by him.

· · ·

In military affairs he made many alterations, introducing some practices entirely new, and reviving others, which had become obsolete. He maintained the strictest discipline among the troops; and would not allow even his lieutenants the liberty to visit their wives, except reluctantly, and in the winter season only. A Roman knight having cut off the thumbs of his two young sons, to render them incapable of serving in the wars, he exposed both him and his estate to public sale. But upon observing the farmers of the revenue very greedy for the purchase, he assigned him to a freedman of his own, that he might send him into the country, and suffer him to retain his freedom. The tenth legion becoming mutinous, he disbanded it with ignominy; and did the same by some others which petulantly demanded their discharge; withholding from them the rewards usually bestowed on those who had served their stated time in the wars. The cohorts which yielded their ground in time of action, he decimated, and fed with barley. Centurions, as well as common sentinels, who deserted their posts when on guard, he punished with death. For other misdemeanors he inflicted upon them various kinds of disgrace; such as obliging them to stand all day before the praetorium, sometimes in their tunics only, and without their belts, sometimes to carry poles ten feet long, or sods of turf.

· · ·

He twice entertained thoughts of restoring the republic; first, immediately after he had crushed Antony, remembering that he had often charged him with being the obstacle to its restoration. The sec-

---

[3] Inhabitants of an area now called the Ukraine.
[4] Successors to the ancient Persians.

ond was in consequence of a long illness, when he sent for the magistrates and the senate to his own house, and delivered them a particular account of the state of the empire. But reflecting at the same time that it would be both hazardous to himself to return to the condition of a private person, and might be dangerous to the public to have the government placed again under the control of the people, he resolved to keep it in his own hands, whether with the better event or intention, is hard to say. His good intentions he often affirmed in private discourse, and also published an edict, in which it was declared in the following terms: "May it be permitted me to have the happiness of establishing the commonwealth on a safe and sound basis, and thus enjoy the reward of which I am ambitious, that of being celebrated for moulding it into the form best adapted to present circumstances; so that, on my leaving the world, I may carry with me the hope that the foundations which I have laid for its future government, will stand firm and stable."

The city, which was not built in a manner suitable to the grandeur of the empire, and was liable to inundations of the Tiber, as well as to fires, was so much improved under his administration, that he boasted, not without reason, that he "found it of brick, but left it of marble." He also rendered it secure for the time to come against such disasters, as far as could be effected by human foresight.

A great number of public buildings were erected by him, the most considerable of which were a forum, containing the temple of Mars the Avenger, the temple of Apollo on the Palatine hill, and the temple of Jupiter Tonans in the capitol. The reason of his building a new forum was the vast increase in the population, and the number of causes to be tried in the courts, for which, the two already existing not affording sufficient space, it was thought necessary to have a third. It was therefore opened for public use before the temple of Mars was completely finished; and a law was passed, that causes should be tried, and judges chosen by lot, in that place. The temple of Mars was built in fulfilment of a vow made during the war of Philippi, undertaken by him to avenge his father's murder. He ordained that the senate should always assemble there when they met to deliberate respecting wars and triumphs; that thence should be despatched all those who were sent into the provinces in the command of armies; and that in it those who returned victorious from the wars, should lodge the trophies of their triumphs. He erected the temple of Apollo in that part of his house on the Palatine hill which had been struck with lightning, and which, on that account, the soothsayers declared the God to have chosen. He added porticos to it, with a library of Latin and Greek authors; and when advanced in years, used frequently there to hold the senate, and examine the rolls of the judges.

He dedicated the temple to Apollo Tonans, in acknowledgment of his escape from a great danger in his Cantabrian expedition; when, as he was travelling in the night, his litter was struck by lightning, which killed the slave who carried a torch before him. He likewise constructed some public buildings in the name of others; for instance, his grandsons, his wife, and sister. Thus he built the portico and basilica of Lucius and Caius, and the porticos of Livia and Octavia, and the theatre of Marcellus. He also often exhorted other persons of rank to embellish the city by new buildings, or repairing and improving the old, according to their means. In consequence of this recommendation, many were raised; such as the temple of Hercules and the Muses, by Marcius Philippus; a temple of Diana by Lucius Cornificius; the Court of Freedom by Asinius Pollio; a temple of Saturn by Munatius Plancus; a theatre by Cornelius Balbus; an amphitheatre by Statilius Taurus; and several other noble edifices by Marcus Agrippa.

He divided the city into regions and districts, ordaining that the annual magistrates should take by lot the charge of the former; and that the latter should be superintended by wardens chosen out of the people of each neighbourhood. He appointed a nightly watch to be on their guard against accidents from fire; and, to prevent the frequent inundations, he widened and cleansed the bed of the Tiber, which had in the course of years been almost dammed up with rubbish, and the channel narrowed by the ruins of houses. To render the approaches to the city more commodious, he took upon himself the charge of repairing the Flaminian way as far as Ariminum, and distributed the repairs of the other roads amongst several persons who had obtained the honour of a triumph; to be defrayed out of the money arising from the spoils of war. Temples decayed by time, or destroyed by fire, he either repaired or rebuilt; and enriched them, as well as many others, with splendid offerings. On a single occasion, he deposited in the cell of the temple of Jupiter Capitolinus, sixteen thousand pounds of gold, with jewels and pearls to the amount of fifty millions of sesterces.

• • •

He restored the calendar, which had been corrected by Julius Caesar, but through negligence had again fallen into confusion, to its former regularity; and upon that occasion called the month Sextilis by his own name, August, rather than September, in which he was born; because in it he had obtained his first consulship, and all his most considerable victories. He increased the number, dignity, and revenues of the priests, and especially those of the Vestal Virgins.[5] And when, upon the death of one of them, a new one was to be taken, and many persons made interest that their daughters' names might be omitted in the lists for election, he replied with an oath, "If either of my own grand-daughters were old enough, I would have proposed her."

He likewise revived some old religious customs, which had become obsolete; as the augury of public health, the office of high priest of Jupiter, the religious solemnity of the Lupercalia, with the Secular, and Compitalian games. He prohibited young boys from running in the Lupercalia; and in respect of the Secular games, issued an order, that no young persons of either sex should appear at any public diversions in the night-time, unless in the company of some elderly relation. He ordered the household gods to be decked twice a year with spring and summer flowers, in the Compitalian festival.

Next to the immortal gods, he paid the highest honours to the memory of those generals who had raised the Roman state from its low origin to the highest pitch of grandeur. He accordingly repaired or rebuilt the public edifices erected by them; preserving the former inscriptions, and placing statues of them all, with triumphal emblems, in both the porticos of his forum, issuing an edict on the occasion, in which he made the following declaration: "My design in so doing is, that the Roman people may require from me, and all succeeding princes, a conformity to those illustrious examples." He likewise removed the statue of Pompey from the senate-house, in which Caius Caesar had been killed, and placed it under a marble arch, fronting the palace attached to Pompey's theatre.

He corrected many ill practices, which, to the detriment of the public, had either survived the licentious habits of the late civil wars, or else originated in the long peace. Bands of robbers showed themselves openly, completely armed, under colour of self-defence; and in

---

[5] Selected young women who devoted their lives to attending the flame in the temple of Vesta (goddess of the family hearth).

different parts of the country, travellers, freemen and slaves without distinction, were forcibly carried off, and kept to work in the houses of correction. Several associations were formed under the specious name of a new college, which banded together for the perpetration of all kinds of villany. The bandits he quelled by establishing posts of soldiers in suitable stations for the purpose; the houses of correction were subjected to a strict superintendance; all associations, those only excepted which were of ancient standing, and recognised by the laws, were dissolved.

He burnt all the notes of those who had been a long time in arrear with the treasury, as being the principal source of vexatious suits and prosecutions. Places in the city claimed by the public, where the right was doubtful, he adjudged to the actual possessors. He struck out of the list of criminals the names of those over whom prosecutions had been long impending, where nothing further was intended by the informers than to gratify their own malice, by seeing their enemies humiliated; laying it down as a rule, that if any one chose to renew a prosecution, he should incur the risk of the punishment which he sought to inflict. And that crimes might not escape punishment, nor business be neglected by delay, he ordered the courts to sit during the thirty days which were spent in celebrating honorary games. . . .

He was himself assiduous in his functions as a judge, and would sometimes prolong his sittings even into the night: if he were indisposed, his litter[6] was placed before the tribunal, or he administered justice reclining on his couch at home; displaying always not only the greatest attention, but extreme leniency. To save a culprit, who evidently appeared guilty of parricide, from the extreme penalty of being sewn up in a sack, because none were punished in that manner but such as confessed the fact, he is said to have interrogated him thus: "Surely you did not kill your father, did you?" And when, in a trial of a cause about a forged will, all those who had signed it were liable to the penalty of the Cornelian law, he ordered that his colleagues on the tribunal should not only be furnished with the two tablets by which they decided, "guilty or not guilty," but with a third likewise, ignoring the offence of those who should appear to have given their signatures through any deception or mistake. All appeals in causes between inhabitants of Rome, he assigned every

[6] A portable couch.

year to the praetor of the city; and where provincials were concerned, to men of consular rank, to one of whom the business of
each province was referred.

Some laws he abrogated, and he made some new ones; such as the
sumptuary law, that relating to adultery and the violation of chastity,
the law against bribery in elections, and likewise that for the encour-
agement of marriage. Having been more severe in his reform of this
law than the rest, he found the people utterly averse to submit to it,
unless the penalties were abolished or mitigated, besides allowing an
interval of three years after a wife's death, and increasing the pre-
miums on marriage. . . . But finding that the force of the law was
eluded by marrying girls under the age of puberty and by frequent
change of wives, he limited the time for consummation after es-
pousals, and imposed restrictions on divorce.

By two separate scrutinies[7] he reduced to their former number and
splendour the senate, which had been swamped by a disorderly
crowd; for they were now more than a thousand and some of them
very mean persons, who, after Caesar's death, had been chosen by
dint of interest and bribery, so that they had the nickname of Orcini
among the people. The first of these scrutinies was left to themselves, each senator naming another; but the last was conducted by
himself and Agrippa. On this occasion he is believed to have taken
his seat as he presided, with a coat of mail under his tunic, and a
sword by his side, and with ten of the stoutest men of senatorial
rank, who were his friends, standing round his chair. Cordus Cre-
mutius relates that no senator was suffered to approach him, except
singly, and after having his bosom searched [for secreted daggers].
Some he obliged to have the grace of declining the office; these he
allowed to retain the privileges of wearing the distinguishing dress,
occupying the seats at the solemn spectacles, and of feasting publicly,
reserved to the senatorial order.

That those who were chosen and approved of, might perform
their functions under more solemn obligations, and with less inconvenience, he ordered that every senator, before he took his seat in the
house, should pay his devotions, with an offering of frankincense
and wine, at the altar of that God in whose temple the senate then assembled, and that their stated meetings, should be only twice in the
month, namely, on the calends and ides;[8] and that in the months of

---

[7] Reviews of the senate membership.
[8] The first and the middle days of the month.

September and October, a certain number only, chosen by lot, such as the law required to give validity to a decree, should be required to attend. For himself, he resolved to choose every six months a new council, with whom he might consult previously upon such affairs as he judged proper at any time to lay before the full senate. He also took the votes of the senators upon any subject of importance, not according to custom, nor in regular order, but as he pleased; that every one might hold himself ready to give his opinion, rather than a mere vote of assent.

• • •

Having thus regulated the city and its concerns, he augmented the population of Italy by planting in it no less than twenty-eight colonies, and greatly improved it by public works, and a beneficial application of the revenues. In rights and privileges, he rendered it in a measure equal to the city itself, by inventing a new kind of suffrage, which the principal officers and magistrates of the colonies might take at home, and forward under seal to the city, against the time of the elections. To increase the number of persons of condition, and of children among the lower ranks, he granted the petitions of all those who requested the honour of doing military service on horseback as knights, provided their demands were seconded by the recommendation of the town in which they lived; and when he visited the several districts of Italy, he distributed a thousand sesterces a head to such of the lower class as presented him with sons or daughters.

The more important provinces, which could not with ease or safety be entrusted to the government of annual magistrates, he reserved for his own administration: the rest he distributed by lot amongst the proconsuls: but sometimes he made exchanges, and frequently visited most of both kinds in person. Some cities in alliance with Rome, but which by their great licentiousness were hastening to ruin, he deprived of their independence. Others, which were much in debt, he relieved, and rebuilt such as had been destroyed by earthquakes. To those that could produce any instance of their having deserved well of the Roman people, he presented the freedom of Latium, or even that of the City. There is not, I believe, a province, except Africa and Sardinia, which he did not visit. . . .

Kingdoms, of which he had made himself master by the right of conquest, a few only excepted, he either restored to their former possessors, or conferred upon aliens. Between kings in alliance with Rome, he encouraged most intimate union; being always ready to promote or favour any proposal of marriage or friendship amongst them; and, indeed, treated them all with the same consideration, as if they were members and parts of the empire. To such of them as were minors or lunatics he appointed guardians, until they arrived at age, or recovered their senses; and the sons of many of them he brought up and educated with his own.

With respect to the army, he distributed the legions and auxiliary troops throughout the several provinces. He stationed a fleet at Misenum, and another at Ravenna, for the protection of the Upper and Lower Seas. A certain number of the forces were selected, to occupy the posts in the city, and partly for his own body-guard; but he dismissed the Spanish guard, which he retained about him till the fall of Antony; and also the Germans, whom he had amongst his guards, until the defeat of Varus. Yet he never permitted a greater force than three cohorts [9] in the city, and had no (praetorian) camps. [10] The rest he quartered in the neighbourhood of the nearest towns, in winter and summer camps.

All the troops throughout the empire he reduced to one fixed model with regard to their pay and their pensions; determining these according to their rank in the army, the time they had served, and their private means; so that after their discharge, they might not be tempted by age or necessities to join the agitators for a revolution. For the purpose of providing a fund always ready to meet their pay and pensions, he instituted a military exchequer, and appropriated new taxes to that object. In order to obtain the earliest intelligence of what was passing in the provinces, he established posts, consisting at first of young men stationed at moderate distances along the military roads, and afterwards of regular couriers with fast vehicles; which appeared to him the most commodious, because the persons who were the bearers of dispatches, written on the spot, might then be questioned about the business, as occasion occurred.

• • •

He always abhorred the title of *Lord,* as ill-omened and offensive. And when, in a play, performed at the theatre, at which he was present, these words were introduced, "O just and gracious lord," and the whole company, with joyful acclamations, testified their

[9] Each cohort, a subdivision of a Roman "legion," included about 500 men.
[10] Praetorian troops were special guards for the chief magistrate of the city.

approbation of them, as applied to him, he instantly put a stop to their indecent flattery, by waving his hand, and frowning sternly, and the next day publicly declared his displeasure, in a proclamation. He never afterwards would suffer himself to be addressed in that manner, even by his own children or grand-children, either in jest or earnest and forbad them the use of all such complimentary expressions to one another.

He rarely entered any city or town, or departed from it, except in the evening or the night, to avoid giving any person the trouble of complimenting him. During his consulships, he commonly walked the streets on foot; but at other times, rode in a closed carriage. He admitted to court even plebeians, in common with people of the higher ranks; receiving the petitions of those who approached him with so much affability, that he once jocosely rebuked a man, by telling him, "You present your memorial with as much hesitation as if you were offering money to an elephant." On senate days, he used to pay his respects to the Conscript Fathers[11] only in the house, addressing them each by name as they sat, without any prompter; and on his departure, he bade each of them farewell, while they retained their seats. In the same manner, he maintained with many of them a constant intercourse of mutual civilities, giving them his company upon occasions of any particular festivity in their families; until he became advanced in years, and was incommoded by the crowd at a wedding.

• • •

How much he was beloved for his worthy conduct in all these respects, it is easy to imagine. I say nothing of the decrees of the senate in his honour, which may seem to have resulted from compulsion or deference. The Roman knights[12] voluntarily, and with one accord, always celebrated his birth for two days together; and all ranks of the people, yearly, in performance of a vow they had made, threw a piece of money into the Curtian lake, as an offering for his welfare. They likewise, on the calends [first] of January, presented for his acceptance new-year's gifts in the capitol, though he was not present: with which donations he purchased some costly images of the Gods,

[11] The senate.
[12] A class of wealthy citizens, next below the senatorial class in political influence. Originally a cavalry corps.

which he erected in several streets of the city; as that of Apollo Sandaliarius, Jupiter Tragoedus, and others.

When his house on the Palatine hill was accidentally destroyed by fire, the veteran soldiers, the judges, the tribes, and even the people, individually, contributed, according to the ability of each, for rebuilding it; but he would accept only of some small portion out of the several sums collected, and refused to take from any one person more than a single denarius. Upon his return home from any of the provinces, they attended him not only with joyful acclamations, but with songs. It is also remarked, that as often as he entered the city, the infliction of punishment was suspended for the time.

The whole body of the people, upon a sudden impulse, and with unanimous consent, offered him the title of Father of His Country. It was announced to him first at Antium, by a deputation from the people, and upon his declining the honour, they repeated their offer on his return to Rome, in a full theatre, when they were crowned with laurel. The senate soon afterwards adopted the proposal.

• • •

Having thus given an account of the manner in which he filled his public offices both civil and military, and his conduct in the government of the empire, both in peace and war; I shall now describe his private and domestic life.

• • •

He ate sparingly (for I must not omit even this), and commonly used a plain diet. He was particularly fond of coarse bread, small fishes, new cheese made of cow's milk, and green figs of the sort which bear fruit twice a year. He did not wait for supper, but took food at any time, and in any place, when he had an appetite. The following passages relative to this subject, I have transcribed from his letters. "I ate a little bread and some small dates, in my carriage." Again. "In returning home from the palace in my litter, I ate an ounce of bread, and a few raisins." Again. "No Jew, my dear Tiberius, ever keeps such strict fast upon the Sabbath, as I have to-day; for while in the bath, and after the first hour of the night, I only ate two biscuits, before I began to be rubbed with oil." From this great indifference about his diet, he sometimes supped by himself, before his company began, or after they had finished, and would not touch a morsel at table with his guests.

He was by nature extremely sparing in the use of wine. Cornelius Nepos says that he used to drink only three times at supper in the camp at Modena; and when he indulged himself the most, he never exceeded a pint; or if he did, his stomach rejected it. Of all wines, he gave the preference to the Rhaetian,[13] but scarcely ever drank any in the day-time. Instead of drinking, he used to take a piece of bread dipped in cold water, or a slice of cucumber, or some leaves of lettuce, or a green, sharp, juicy apple.

After a slight repast at noon, he used to seek repose, dressed as he was, and with his shoes on, his feet covered, and his hand held before his eyes. After supper he commonly withdrew to his study, a small closet, where he sat late, until he had put down in his diary all or most of the remaining transactions of the day, which he had not before registered. He would then go to bed, but never slept above seven hours at most, and that not without interruption; for he would wake three or four times during that time. If he could not again fall asleep, as sometimes happened, he called for some one to read or tell stories to him, until he became drowsy, and then his sleep was usually protracted till after day-break. He never liked to lie awake in the dark, without somebody to sit by him. Very early rising was apt to disagree with him. On which account, if he was sometimes obliged to rise, for any civil or religious functions, in order to guard as much as possible against the inconvenience resulting from it, he used to lodge in some apartment near the spot, belonging to any of his attendants. It at any time a fit of drowsiness seized him in passing along the streets, his litter was set down while he snatched a few moments' sleep.

In person he was handsome and graceful, through every period of his life. But he was negligent in his dress; and so careless about dressing his hair, that he usually had it done in great haste by several barbers at a time. His beard he sometimes clipped, and sometimes shaved; and either read or wrote during the operation. His countenance, either when discoursing or silent, was so calm and serene that a Gaul of the first rank declared amongst his friends that he was so softened by it, as to be restrained from throwing him down a precipice, in his passage over the Alps, when he had been admitted to approach him, under pretence of conferring with him. His eyes were

[13] Rhaetia was a Roman province that included areas now part of Switzerland and Austria.

bright and piercing; and he was willing it should be thought that there was something of a divine vigour in them. He was likewise not a little pleased to see people, upon his looking stedfastly at them, lower their countenances, as if the sun shone in their eyes. But in his old age, he saw very imperfectly with his left eye. His teeth were thin set, small and scaly, his hair a little curled, and inclining to a yellow colour. His eye-brows met; his ears were small, and he had an aquiline nose. His complexion was betwixt brown and fair; his stature but low; though Julius Marathus, his freedman, says he was five feet and nine inches in height. This, however, was so much concealed by the just proportion of his limbs, that it was only perceivable upon comparison with some taller person standing by him.

He is said to have been born with many spots upon his breast and belly, answering to the figure, order, and number of the stars in the constellation of the Bear. He had besides several callosities resembling scars, occasioned by an itching in his body, and the constant and violent use of the strigil in being rubbed. He had a weakness in his left hip, thigh, and leg, insomuch that he often halted on that side; but he received much benefit from the use of sand and reeds. He likewise sometimes found the fore-finger of his right hand so weak that, when it was benumbed and contracted with cold, to use it in writing he was obliged to have recourse to a circular piece of horn. He had occasionally a complaint in the bladder; but upon voiding some stones in his urine, he was relieved from that pain.

16

Horace

Odes

Propaganda contributed as much to the triumph of the Emperor Augustus as force, and once he was master of the world he centralized and systematized the influencing of opinion. Augustus spared no effort in reconciling all to his new order and in proclaiming the mission of a regenerated Rome. Fortunately for him and for the world, among those who lent themselves to his purposes were several writers of genius.

One of these was Quintus Horatius Flaccus (65–8 B.C.), born at Venusia in southern Italy, the son of a freedman who gave him the education of a gentleman. While at school in Athens, Horace joined the losing cause of Brutus in the civil war and returned home to poverty. His bitter early verses brought him to the attention of the great epic poet Vergil, who helped him to meet some influential people; in 33 B.C. the gift of a farm from a rich patron, Maecenas, made him financially independent and showed that he had accepted the Augustan regime.

The 103 lyrics called the Odes, his finest work, must not, however, be regarded as a mere product of patronage. They are the voice of true Roman feeling, devoted to the ideals of the Augustan age: love of the soil, martial virtues, and traditional religious and moral values. But not all the Odes are grave in tone; some are graceful, witty, or trivial expressions of Horace's personality, giving first place to the pleasures of friendship, vintage wine, and a life of leisure on his beloved farm. Thus, though showing the same derivative relationship to Greek prototypes that characterizes Latin literature in general, the Odes strike a distinctive Roman note of their own.

In 23 B.C., when most of the Odes were first published, Horace boasted that he had "erected a monument more enduring than bronze." Certainly, since Petrarch "rediscovered" him in the fourteenth century, he has been the most popular of Latin poets, mainly, perhaps, because of his quotability and Roman common sense.

I: 5

What slim and sweetly scented boy
presses you to the roses, Pyrrha,
   in your favorite grotto?
     For whom is your blond hair styled,

deceptively simple? Ah, how often he'll sob
over your faithless conversions, staring
   stupidly at the black
     winds and wild seas. He has you

now, for him you have a golden glow,
ever contented, ever loving
   he hopes, unaware of the
     tricky breeze. Poor things, for whom

you glitter before you're tried. The temple
wall with its plaque serves notice: I
   have hung my wet clothes up
     and bowed to the sea god's power.[1]

I: 20

Cheap Sabine wine will be your drink, in plain
tankards; from a Greek jar, though, where I stored
and sealed it myself, that day they filled the theater
   with applause for you,

dear lord Maecenas,[2] and the banks of Tiber,
the river of your homeland, and the playful

I: 5 and I: 20. Reprinted from *The Odes and Epodes of Horace, A Modern English Verse Translation,* by Joseph P. Clancy, by permission of The University of Chicago Press. © 1960 by The University of Chicago. [Pp. 30, 51.]

[1] It was customary for sailors who had survived a shipwreck to dedicate a plaque to the sea god.

[2] Horace's wealthy patron. The poet refers to the day Maecenas reappeared in public after an illness.

echo from Mount Vatican answered
the sounds of your praise.

The best vintages, Caecuban, Calenian,
you may drink when you wish; my goblets hold
no flavor of wine from the vines of Falernus
or Formia's hills.

II: 15

Idle the plough, since the rich men's lordly piles
Usurped the fruitful acres; pond and stew,
Broad as the Lucrine water,[3] miles on miles,
Make sights for tourists gaping at the view.

The spinster plane drives out the wedded elm;[4]
Myrtle and violet, every odious weed,
Dispense their perfumes in the olive's realm,
Whose erstwhile masters fed the public need,

And close-bough'd laurels weave luxurious shade—
Not thus our bearded fathers built the State,
When Romulus or Cato were obeyed,
And in her rugged plainness Rome was great.

Wealth for the City, not the citizen,
Was massed; no upstart burgess felled his trees
And with nice compass plotted on the plain
Verandahs cool to take the northern breeze.

Men roofed their homes with turves from every field,
While at the general charge their towns grew fine
With stately buildings, and the quarry's field
With new-cut stone adorned each holy shrine.

II: 15. Horace, *The Odes of Horace,* trans. Edward Marsh (London: Macmillan & Company Ltd. and St. Martin's Press, Inc., 1941), 80. Reprinted by permission of the publishers.

[3] A reference to a small coastal lake located in a fashionable area near Naples.
[4] Elms were generally used to support grapevines; plane trees were used for decorative purposes only.

II: 16

Peace, he begs of the gods, caught on the open
Aegean, with black clouds holding the moon in
hiding, and the stars no longer steadily
    shining for sailors;

peace is the prayer of battle-maddened Thrace;
peace, beg Parthians with their painted quivers:
it is not bought, Grosphus, with purple cloths, with
    jewels or with gold.

No, neither royal treasures nor a consul's
lictor[5] can clear the crowd of worries away
from the mind, and the troubles that flutter near
    the paneled ceilings.

He lives well with little, the man whose fathers'
salt dish shines on his impoverished table,
and whose easy sleep is not stolen by fear
    or by filthy greed.

Why do we try for so much so hard with such
little time? Why do we turn to countries warmed
by a different sun? What exile from home
    escapes himself too?

The disease of worry boards the bronze-prowed ship,
and troops of horsemen cannot leave it behind,
swifter than stags and swifter than the Eastwind
    driving the stormclouds.

Joyful here and now, may the spirit despise
concern for what lies beyond and dilute the
bitter with a calm smile. Nothing is wholly
    filled with happiness.

II: 16. Reprinted from *The Odes and Epodes of Horace, A Modern English Verse Translation,* by Joseph P. Clancy, by permission of The University of Chicago Press. © 1960 by The University of Chicago. [Pp. 95–96.]

[5] An official who bore symbols of authority (fasces) before the consuls, and cleared a
  way before them.

Sudden death took Achilles in his glory,
his long old age wasted Tithonus[6] away,
and to me perhaps this hour will offer
    what you are denied.

You are surrounded by a hundred mooing
herds of Sicilian cattle, you can hear
your racehorse whinny, you are dressed in wool
    double-dyed with Af–

rican purple; I was not cheated by Fate,
who gave me a little farm and a spirit
sensitive to Grecian poetry, above
    the crowd and its spite.

III: 6

You, the guiltless, will pay for your fathers' sins,
Roman, until you repair the decaying
    temples and shrines of the gods and their
        images, filthy with blackening smoke.

When you act as servant of the gods, you rule:
from them all beginning, leave them the ending;
    neglected, the gods have brought many
        sorrows to suffering Italy.

Twice now Monaeses and Pacorus' army,[7]
when omens were evil, have smashed our attack
    to bits, and they grin as they fasten
        our trophies to their skimpy necklaces.

In the grip of civil conflicts the city
was nearly wiped out by Egypt and Dacia,

III: 6. Reprinted from *The Odes and Epodes of Horace, A Modern English Verse Translation,* by Joseph P. Clancy, by permission of The University of Chicago Press. © 1960
by The University of Chicago. [Pp. 117–18.]

[6] A goddess (Aurora) had given him immortality but not eternal youth; thus, although
he remained alive like his divine love, he aged, growing ever more wrinkled and
emaciated.

[7] The army of two Parthian commanders that invaded Roman Syria.

the one with a frightening fleet, and
the other with superior archers.[8]

Breeder of vices, our age has polluted
first marriage vows and the children and the home;
from this spring, a river of ruin
has flooded our country and our people.

The blossoming virgin enjoys her course in
Ionic dancing, and even now practices
all the tricks, and thoughts of sinful loves
fill her to the tender tips of her toes.

Soon she is after, at her husband's parties,
younger lovers, and is not particular
about the one she hastily gives
the forbidden thrills when the lights go out;

then called for, her husband there and knowing it,
she responds, whether a salesman summons her
or the master of a Spanish ship,
a wealthy trader in adulteries.

Not from parents like these were the young men born
who stained the sea with Carthaginian blood
and struck down Pyrrhus and the mighty
Antiochus and dreadful Hannibal;[9]

no, they were men, the descendants of farm-bred
soldiers, who were raised to turn over the clods
with their Sabine hoes, and to chop wood
and carry it in at their stern mother's

orders, as the Sungod shifted the shadows
of the mountains, and gave the weary oxen
relief from the yoke, bringing an hour
of rest as his chariot departed.

---

[8] Civil war brought an end to the Roman Republic, signaled by the triumph of Augustus. Cleopatra of Egypt had opposed him with her navy, and soldiers from Dacia had simultaneously attacked his troops on land.
[9] Three powerful enemy generals of the second century B.C. All were eventually defeated by the Romans.

What does time's decaying leave undiminished?
Our parent's age, worse than their parents', brought forth
    us, who are still worse, who soon will breed
        descendants even more degenerate.

IV: 15

Of stricken fields and conquered towns I planned
High singing; but Apollo on his lyre
    Twanged a warning, not to aspire
So high, nor risk my skiff too far from land.

Thine age, great Caesar [10] to our fields restores
Their fatness; now in Jove's avengèd shrine
    Once more the captured eagles shine
That blazed our shame on Parthia's temple doors. [11]

And Janus' [12] Gates of War stand shut. Thy rein
Hath curbed the stubborn passions that had brought
    Our honour and our pride to nought,
And to the ancient arts we turn again

Which nursed the strength of Italy, and spread
Far forth her empire's majesty and fame,
    Emblazoning the Latin name
From the sun's rising to his Western bed.

Under thy guardian hand, no storm of hate
Shall banish peace, no kindred blood outpoured,
    Nor wrath, fell anvil of the sword,
Mover of woeful strife in city and state,

No tribe that drinks of Danube or of Don,
Nor Tartar fire nor Persian treachery,

IV: 15.   Horace, *The Odes of Horace,* trans. Edward Marsh (London: Macmillan & Company Ltd. and St. Martin's Press, Inc., 1941), 181–82. Reprinted by permission of the publishers.

[10] Augustus, the emperor.

[11] A reference to the great defeat of the Romans in Mesopotamia in 53 B.C., a defeat in which the standards were captured by the army of Parthia (formerly, Persia).

[12] The god Janus was invoked at the start of any important enterprise. The doors of his temple in Rome stood open when war was in progress and closed during peace.

The Julian edict [13] shall defy;
No Thracian highland but thy sway shall own.

And we, on work-a-day and holy days,
Blessing good Bacchus for his gifts of mirth,
    With wives and children round our hearth,
Paying the Gods their due of prayer and praise,

Will sing our storied names with rites of yore
And jocund harmony of voice and lyre,
    Telling of Troy and our great sire [14]
Whom bounteous Venus to Anchises bore.

[13] The law of Augustus.
[14] Aeneas—according to legend, a forefather of Rome and the Roman people. He was believed to be the son of the goddess Venus and the Trojan hero Anchises.

17

Ovid

The Art of Love

꒡

Publius Ovidius Naso was born in central Italy in 43 B.C. Although he was from a family of local prominence and was trained for an official career, he chose the free and frivolous life of the capital, where he won a reputation for both his poetic talent and his rakish ways.

Unluckily for Ovid, Rome would soon change its official demeanor. The Augustan revolution (like many great social upheavals) brought with it a movement that looked backward to the austere traditional manners and morals of simpler Republican days; and it was a trend dear to Augustus himself.

But all this Ovid deliberately flouted, not only in his loose way of life but in his writings, particularly his Art of Love, *an impudent manual of sexual hide-and-seek published in A.D. 1. If, as some speculate, there was a more intimate reason for what happened to Ovid soon after, it is not known to us. Whatever its stimulus, the imperial wrath fell harshly on the poet, who was exiled from the Empire—to the uncivilized west coast of the Black Sea. There, despite his appeals, he remained until his death in A.D. 17.*

Ovid's Art of Love *is a long poem that celebrates yet another ancient-world concept of the good life—one less common in classical literature than in ancient practice: the full liberation of the senses. Despite its erotic worldliness the book survived the frowns of Augustus and, later, the medieval clergy. During the Renaissance, when, like the Augustan smart set, many took it up with relish, such poets as Chaucer, Shakespeare, and Milton became greatly indebted to Ovid's verse.*

The following selection is from a lively prose translation that retains the flavor of the original poem.

Ovid, *The Art of Love,* trans. by Charles D. Young (New York: Liveright Publishing Corporation, 1931), 15–20, 22–24, 50–56, 62–65.

If art and cunning are required for the sailing of ships, for the steering of swift chariots, it will become you well to listen to me and guide yourself by my advice on Love.

• • •

I do not rely upon the help of Clio[1] nor the whispered advice and consolation of Apollo. No bird has secretly imparted important news of stratagems. Naught have I to guide me but my own experience and wisdom. I am no shepherd tending to his herds in the vales of Ascra but a man who truly knows the things he sings.

The love of which I sing does not trespass on the laws. I shall not lead you into shame or treachery. Listen attentively, you who are novices at this game, and it shall go well with you.

First, remember to choose carefully the woman you will set your heart upon; second, you must secure her submission; third, you must perpetuate her attachment to you. This is my entire syllabus and text.

Needless to emphasize, it will take effort to find the woman of your fancy; no passing zephyr will casually deposit her in your lap. You must use your head. The hunter spreads his net for stag and boar, the fowler studies well the habits of his prey, and carefully the fisher baits his hook. You, too, aspiring to a lasting love, study carefully the haunts and promenades of your potential paramour. No great hardships will impose themselves upon you: there are no seas to be crossed and no battles to be fought.

Perseus[2] fetched his bride from torrid Indian climes and Paris[3] sought his precious frail in Sparta. You need not deviate so far in search of beauty, which well abounds in all the streets of Rome. Numberless as the stars in the high heavens, as the grapes in Methymna, as the corn on Gargarus, and as the fish in the sea, are the ravishing faces in Rome. If you prefer the ungainly grace of green

---

[1] The Greek (and Roman) Muse of history.
[2] Perseus, a hero in Greek mythology, married a beautiful, dark-skinned princess, Andromeda. Ovid's verse is full of allusions to Greek myths. For the Romans, in fact, Ovid was the leading authority on the subject.
[3] Son of Priam, the king of Troy. His elopement with Helen, the wife of the king of Sparta, led to the Trojan War.

young striplings, or crave the lush flamboyant charms of fullbodied maturity, or have a weakness for something between these two extremes, you need not be troubled by a lack of choice to glut your appetite. Stroll any evening in the shade of Pompey's portico when the summer sun is just about to set, or pass the wall embossed with foreign marbles, and surely your greedy eyes will have their fill. Also, you will be well repaid if you visit the colonnade which is called the portico of Livia, upon whose walls you will see the Danaides, conspiring the death of their doomed cousins.[4] You must not miss the festival of Adonis[5] nor the weekly celebrations of the Syrian Jews. Mingle freely with the crowds at public gatherings, even if the occasion be a matter of law in the forum, for all places are equally propitious for Love. At the stone basin near the shrine of Venus, where the Appian water flows, many a lawyer has been trapped in Love's snare. Frequently, he who with great circumspection defends his client, makes but a poor attorney for himself; and great orators are at a loss for words in such a pass. There he stands, the great advocate, caught in a snare that will not yield to argument or persuasion, and from the nearby temple there sometimes seems to echo the triumphant laughter of Venus. But the most auspicious place for your researches is undoubtedly the theater. How many women you will find here, for the fancy of a moment, for the entertainment of a night or the love of a lifetime. Like ants that march in legions upon their predatory quest, like bees bearing sweet burdens in swarms from flower to flower, gay throngs of women crowd the theaters, ostensibly to see the play. Sometimes it is difficult to choose in this bewildering galaxy of gay frocks and faces. Surely this is the last place where virtue grows luxuriant.

· · ·

Remember, also, the arena, where well matched steeds strain for the palm of glory. How favorable is this crowded place for Love! Here it is unnecessary to signal by mysterious signs or practice any sort of doubtful mimicry. Sit close beside your loved one; the stalls are narrow, so she cannot prevent that you accidentally brush against her; the closeness of the place makes her acquiescence utterly unnec-

---

[4] The fifty daughters of Danaus married the fifty sons of Aegyptus. On their wedding night, obeying their father, all but one stabbed their cousin-husbands to death.
[5] An annual festival in honor of the legendary hero Adonis, whose beauty made him the beloved of Venus.

essary. There is one thing you must keep steadily in mind: sitting beside her will avail you little unless you know how to start a conversation. Begin, let us say, with the usual banalities reserved for such occasions. A horse has entered the arena, this is your chance to ask the name of its owner. Whichever color she favors in the races becomes automatically your own. When the solemn procession of the gods and goddesses passes your stall, arise and give a cheer for Venus. You must manage poorly indeed if you cannot espy some disfiguring speck of dust upon her bosom. Flick it off with a delicate gesture and an appropriate disclaimer for her gratitude. But if the dust will somehow fail to settle and you descry no blemish, flick it off nevertheless; for any pretext to serve her must be dragged in by the hair if necessary. If the train of her garments drags in the dust, lift it up and caution her. You might by chance be permitted a fleeting gimpse at her leg. Be careful who sits behind you; let no rough knee be digging in her shoulder blades. These seemingly trifles have a cumulative value. Many a conquest has been made by the careful arrangement of a cushion, or the adroit management of a fan. A stool produced at the right moment has achieved miracles. Don't doubt that the circus and the forum are ideal places for the commencement of a love affair. Love comes here for many a trial of strength and many an innocent bystander is wounded. Many a man has asked a fair one for a glimpse of her racing card, has bet his money on the horse of her choice and has been struck by an arrow before he knew who won the race.

· · ·

Other auspicious places that furnish ready access to a woman's favor are dinners and large festivals. Remember that besides the food the wine is frequently a lover's best assistant. When cupid's wings are drenched with wine, he oft grows drowsy and will not stir. But once he's roused, he shakes off the superfluous moisture, sprinkling those around him, and strange is the behavior of those upon whom the dew of Bacchus[6] is thus sprinkled. The pauper fancies that he is rich, bellows at caution and carelessly throws his limbs about. The wrinkled brow unfurls and the calloused heart softens. Truth wells suddenly upon the lips that practise craft and cunning. Love and wine go well together, feeding fuel to the fire, clouding the critical faculties and making all things seem what they are not. If you truly

---

[6] The god of wine.

want to know the why and wherefore of her lips, by all means see her then by daylight and when you are sober. It was thus, beneath a radiant sky, that Paris said to Venus: "You are far lovelier than your two rivals." [7]

The sable mantle of the night covers a multitude of blemishes; in fact, there are no ugly women in the night time. If you examine rare cloths and precious jewels, you choose the sunlight. Let it be thus with women.

It is difficult to make a list of places where the woman hunt can be carried on favorably, for these places are as numerous as the sands in the sea. I suggest Baiae, famed for its hot sulphur springs, with white sails gleaming on the horizon. Many a bather, who has gone there for a cure, comes away saying, "Those precious baths are not so healthy as I thought." Not far outside Rome, there is the temple of Diana, beneath whose trees many a youth and maiden have fought a battle of Love. The chaste Diana has frequently avenged herself for these trespasses—and will frequently avenge herself in the future.

I have been content thus far to advise you where and how to seek your love. Now I am prepared to tell you the means of captivating and holding her. I will insist that this is the most difficult and important of all my teachings. So harken to me, lovers of every land and clime, for I am ready to redeem my promises.

Before all else, make up your mind that there is no woman alive who cannot be won, and then decide quite definitely that you are the man to win her. Only, you must be careful to prepare the soil. It is more likely that the birds would stop singing in the spring, the grasshopper sit sullen and silent in the summer or the hare pursue the hound, than a woman overlook the ardent wooing of a young lover. You may believe she does not want you. You are mistaken. Deep within her heart she wants to yield. Man is naturally a very poor dissembler. Woman, just as naturally, is the very born actress and artificer. If we all should decide not to make advances to women, soon enough the lot of them would be beneath our feet. Out in the dew-drenched meadow the love-sick heifer lows and languishes for the bull and the mare whinnies at sight of the stallion. With us Love is less obvious and passion less unbridled; we keep within the bounds of decorum.

• • •

[7] According to the legendary "Judgment of Paris," Paris had chosen Venus as the most beautiful of goddesses (over Juno and Minerva).

I don't advise you to send poetry. Play safe and venture only on substantial gifts. The most ill-mannered boor, if he is wealthy, has a fair chance to be successful. Remember, you are living in the golden age, for gold will buy you anything you wish. It will purchase Love, esteem and any honors you may set your heart upon. Blind Homer, if he now approached escorted by the nine Muses, could hardly find a willing listener, if once his poverty was well established. But don't be cynical, for there are some cultured women. They are very rare, most of them being content to appear cultured. If you do send poetry, praise them. If you write badly, learn to declaim your verses so effectively that none would notice their weak structure. The best you can hope for is that if they are perfectly written and perfectly recited, they will be considered as a very, very trifling present.

Now, let us assume that you have convinced your mistress that you wish to be in her service. It might chance that you have decided to free one of your slaves—a simple matter. First of all, ask the servant to see your mistress for the purpose of petitioning you for his freedom. If now you let the slave go free, she will think you have done it all for her sake. It costs you nothing and will please her enormously. Quite likely she will feel she can twist you round her finger. There is no harm in letting her think so; there is no surer method of obtaining what you want. Be careful to notice what she wears. If you find her wrapped in Tyrian purple, tell her that nothing becomes her so well; if she is all decked out in cloth of gold, tell her her charms surpass the brilliance of the metal. When it is cold, and you find her wrapped in furs, assure her that you wish for a perpetual winter. If she wears a flimsy shift, tell her that her charms might cause a conflagration and you hope she isn't catching cold. If she parts her hair in the middle of her forehead, insist that you have never seen her looking fairer. If she has it curled and fuzzy, tell her it is the only kind of hair you fancy. When she sings or dances, fall into proper ecstasies of delight and regret that the performance was so soon ended. When you find yourself in bed with her, pay the proper obeisance to the source of all your bliss, and assure her that you think yourself in heaven. Aye, and if she is a very Medusa, you can make her docile with the proper words. Remember that your mimicry must be consistent with your statements, for if hypocrisy is once discovered, it will be rough sailing ever afterwards.

The autumn is a strange season, when the bursting grape and colorful foliage seem to belie the treacherous, nipping cold that steals out from the woods at eventide. It is a dangerous season, and may your mistress be careful of her health. But let us say that she grows languorous and ill. Now, then, is the time for you to show your mettle. Be not discouraged by the peevish, multitudinous demands upon your patience. Render whatever service is required and let her see you weep with worry for her welfare. Tell her you've had a dream filled with a hopeful prophecy. Produce a grandam with withered hands, who, with ointments and herbs, will sweeten and purify the sick chamber. Don't forget sulphur or the eggs of atonement. These kindnesses, item by item, she will treasure in her heart, and many a worthwhile legacy has been bequeathed for such like simple acts of charity. But be cautious, my friend, and don't show too much anxiety. Don't be a busybody; don't fuss too much; above all else, don't prescribe some diet; and in heaven's name, don't bring her ill-tasting medicines to drink. Such things you'd better leave to your rival.

The wind which sails your bark when you first leave the harbor is not the wind that you require on the open sea. Love is frail at birth, but it grows stronger with age if it is properly fed. The roaring bull that frightens you today was the tender calf you stroked not long ago. The tree beneath whose foliage you seek a grateful shade was once a slender sapling. The little rivulet runs on and gathers force and eventually becomes a roaring torrent. Let your mistress become accustomed to you and your curious ways, for the most potent thing in life is habit. Be with her on all occasions until you notice that she is used to you and needs your presence. At this point you can absent yourself for a while, for the soil that is given rest renders with interest the eventual seed that you will sow. . . . At any rate, play safe—don't stay away too long. Time has a way of curing every anguish, and while you are gone, another may take your place. Menelaus left fair Helen to her own devices and she found consolation in the arms of her guest. What a fool he was to depart leaving his wife at home with a stranger! No innocent dove was ever more calmly delivered to the tender mercies of a buzzard. He has nothing to complain of: he merely proved a most accommodating husband.

A boar, when cornered by the huntsman, a frightened lioness beside a litter of cubs, a viper that an innocent traveler has accidentally trod upon are all less dangerous than a woman who finds her husband in another woman's bed. Her fury knows no bounds and she will fling anything that comes to hand. She will dash at her rival like a Maenad driven mad by the Aonian god. Medea murdered her children for the misdeeds of Jason. If you are cautious, you will be careful to avoid all scenes of jealousy and fury.

Don't fear that I shall suddenly begin to preach a set of morals and insist that you pay homage to one mistress only: nothing could be more absurd. But keep your liaisons from becoming notorious and manage your affairs with discretion. Don't brag of your good luck and don't make a gift to some woman that another woman can easily recognize as having originated with you. Make your appointments at divers times and places, and when you write, read carefully what you have written, for many women read between the lines such news and promises as you have never intended.

• • •

A moment ago I cautioned you to be discreet about your love affairs. It may serve you just as well to blazon them abroad. Notice how the sailor slips the ropes through the rings; how well he takes advantage of the changing breeze: all winds are welcome to his cunning hand. Your mistress may be the sort of woman who needs the apprehension of suspecting that she has a rival. A surfeit of happiness renders certain people irresponsible. A small flame must be nursed carefully or grey ashes will smother its feeble light; but if you add a little sulphur, rapidly, fresh flames are kindled. Many a heart grown torpid in its dull routine of safety requires the sting of jealousy. If your mistress is of that sort, then bring new fire into her heart, or let the pallor of uneasiness cover her cheeks. Happy is the lover whose mistress squirms in agony when she hears he is unfaithful! To think that his mistress is raving and tearing her hair, that she pounces upon him and digs her nails into his face, that she drowns him in a flood of tears, while he is certain all the time that she cannot live without him—what happiness for a lover! But when her rage has reached its point of greatest frenzy, hasten to pacify her; press her tear-stained face close to your breast, and ratify your concord on her bed. It is the cradle of forgiveness; and let it cheer you to know that I envy you then.

• • •

Don't discuss with your mistress, even playfully, any of her defects. This is a very profitable axiom to remember. Perseus did not complain that Andromeda had a swarthy skin. The whole of Troy considered Andromache too tall and only Hector believed her of average height. Learn to accustom yourself to the things you don't like. After a while you won't mind them so much. Remember it is only a matter of habit. Love is a frail creature that is easily crushed by trifles. The newly grafted twig can be disturbed by even a slight breeze. In due time, after it has grown strong, it will not mind the blowing of a gale; it will become a sturdy branch richly endowing the alien tree with fruit. Time will accustom you to anything, and even serious physical blemishes that once disturbed you will eventually disappear before your accustomed gaze. Your nostrils are offended by the rutting smell that is emanated by a herd of bulls; eventually you can learn to bear it without discomfort.

Furthermore, miracles can be worked by the proper use of adjectives. If a woman's skin is darker than Illyrian pitch, call her a brunette. If she is red-headed, comment upon her resemblance to Minerva. If she is just skin and bones, and seems to have one foot in the grave, sing praises to her graceful figure. If she is short, tell her how light she is. If she is squat, you can interpret it as an agreeable plumpness. To every defect there is a next-door neighbor that, properly appraised, becomes a quality. It is foolish to demand her age; nor date her birth by asking who was consul[8] at the time. Leave that to the Censor,[9] especially if she is no longer young. Don't be discouraged that she has to pull out her grey hairs, for that age, and even older age than that, can still bestow many pleasures. To you, these are but fields in need of sowing, so that the harvest may be rich for you some day. Labor while you are young and in the prime of your strength, for soon enough a tottering old age will creep upon you. Cleave the water with your valiant oar, or the ground with your ploughshare; wield the battle-ax and the deadly spear; or devote yourself to the service and care of women. This, too, is a sort of military service in which rich trophies may be won. And don't forget that women getting on in years have knowledge apt and curious in many matters denied to youth and inexperience. Cleverly they know how to repair the ravages of time and sometimes do conceal their rightful age quite cunningly. They are well versed in all the mysteries and attitudes of Love, and thereby are able to enhance your

[8] Chief magistrate. Roman chronology was usually related to the tenure-year of individual consuls.
[9] Official responsible for counting the population and collecting the usual information obtained in a periodic census.

pleasure. Being old hands at the game, they can grant you a great many voluptuous liberties. Their appetites do not need to be provoked by wearisome titillations and they will share their pleasures with you equally. It is painful to be involved in such embraces in which only one side truly consumates; that is one of the reasons I have but little pleasure in boys. How hateful is the woman who gives herself out of a sense of duty, who is cold and unresponsive, and who at the height of your excitement, calculates upon her sewing. Dutiful embraces repel me, for nothing can be more pleasing to the ear of a lover than the trembling voice of the beloved when she whispers ecstatically of her joy. What can compare to my happiness when my fair one pleads with me to prolong her rapture? Naught can be sweeter than my beloved, inebriate with ecstasy, holding me at arm's length and pleading with swimming eyes that I slacken my pace.

Such accomplishments one does not readily discover in young virgins. It is the woman over thirty-five who is more likely to be familiar with the intricacies of a real affair. You are welcome to drink the new raw wine that sets your teeth on edge. As for myself, give me the full-scented, rich vintage that dates back to one of our elder consuls. It takes years to equip a tree with sufficient foliage to grant you pleasant shelter, and fields but lately reaped will hurt the naked foot.

· · ·

My task is well-nigh done, and now you have your chance to show your gratitude. Wreathe my brow with fragrant myrtle leaves and present me with the palm of victory. Podalirius was famed for his skill in curing maladies, Pyrrhus for courage, Nestor for his counsel, Calchas for his shrewdness, Achilles for daring, Automedon [10] as a charioteer: so am I worthy to be known among lovers as the best of poets. I have supplied you arms as Vulcan [11] did to Achilles; and when you have successfully conquered your Amazon [12] with the sword I have sharpened for your use, inscribe upon your trophies with a flourish: *"OVID WAS MY MASTER."*

---

[10] All of those named are traditional Greek heroes.
[11] The god of the forge.
[12] The Amazons were a legendary tribe of spirited and proud female warriors, residing in Asia Minor.

18

Lucretius

De Rerum Natura

🔳

Whatever the private opinions of educated Romans during the last century of the Republic (influenced as they were by critical Hellenic thought), publicly they endorsed the cult of the gods. Not only were all citizens morally obliged to uphold the state religion, but its support was recognized by the ruling minority as a prop to their privileged status. Rarely, then, does Roman literature express sentiments subversive of ancestral beliefs.

Titus Lucretius Carus (ca. 96–55 B.C.) was perhaps the most remarkable exception to this Roman conformism. Not that he was an immoral or irreligious man—quite the contrary. He has been described, rather, as "the most sincere religious enthusiast in the whole of Roman literature." Indeed, his attack on superstition puts him in line with the great moral and religious mentors of history.

Of his life we know only that, unlike the typical Roman of good birth, he renounced a public career in favor of philosophy and found the meaning of things in the teachings of Epicurus, the Hellenistic thinker. Hailing Epicurus as "father" and "glory of the Greek race," Lucretius gave himself with missionary fervor to proclaiming Epicurus's liberating gospel; he set it forth in a long philosophic poem, De Rerum Natura *(On the Nature of Things). The following selections present some of Lucretius's views regarding nature, the soul, happiness, and death.*

In all these selections may be seen a single-minded aim: to deliver the human spirit from imaginary fears by presenting a purely naturalistic interpretation of phenomena. True piety, Lucretius held, consisted in permit-

Lucretius, *The Way Things Are*, the *De Rerum Natura* of Titus Lucretius Carus, trans. Rolfe Humphries (Bloomington: Indiana University Press, 1968), 21–22, 24–27, 29–31, 34–36, 52–53, 81–82, 87, 89–93, 110–11, 113–14, 116–17. Copyright © 1968 by Indiana University Press. Reprinted by permission of the publisher.

*ting one to "contemplate all things with a tranquil mind." He believed that
fear of the supernatural and "the dread of something after death" were the
greatest of all terrors. Once released from these by his materialistic philosophy of atomism, men might, as Epicurus said, "go dancing round the world
in unclouded happiness." But authentic Epicureanism did not fit the Roman
temper. Even in antiquity Lucretius's views attracted little notice; throughout
the Middle Ages until the Renaissance, he was scorned as the devil's disciple.
However, with the scientific revolution that began in the seventeenth century, his doctrine of atoms was taken up as never before, and his great poem
gained recognition as a unique expression of the many-sided Roman genius.*

When human life, all too conspicuous,
Lay foully grovelling on earth, weighed down
By grim Religion looming from the skies,
Horribly threatening mortal men, a man,
A Greek,[1] first raised his mortal eyes
Bravely against this menace. No report
Of gods, no lightning-flash, no thunder-peal
Made this man cower, but drove him all the more
With passionate manliness of mind and will
To be the first to spring the tight-barred gates
Of Nature's hold asunder. So his force,
His vital force of mind, a conqueror
Beyond the flaming ramparts of the world
Explored the vast immensities of space
With wit and wisdom, and came back to us
Triumphant, bringing news of what can be
And what cannot, limits and boundaries,
The borderline, the bench mark, set forever.
Religion, so, is trampled underfoot,
And by his victory we reach the stars.

I fear that, in these matters, you may think
You're entering upon a path of crime,
The ABC's of godlessness. Not so.

---

[1] The philosopher Epicurus (342–270 B.C.).

The opposite is true. Too many times
Religion mothers crime and wickedness.
Recall how once at Aulis, when the Greeks,
Those chosen peers, the very first of men,
Defiled, with a girl's blood, the altar-stone
Sacred to Artemis. The princess[2] stood
Wearing the sacred fillets or a veil,
And sensed but could not see the king her father,
Agamemnon, standing sorrowful
Beside the altar, and the priests near-by
Hiding the knife-blade, and the folk in tears
At what they saw. She knelt, she spoke no word,
She was afraid, poor thing. Much good it did her
At such a time to have been the very first
To give the king that other title, *Father!*
Raised by men's hands and trembling she was led
Toward the altar, not to join in song
After the ritual of sacrifice
To the bright god of marriage. No; she fell
A victim by the sacrificing stroke
Her father gave, to shed her virgin blood—
Not the way virgins shed it—but in death,
To bring the fleet a happy exodus!
A mighty counselor, Religion stood
With all that power for wickedness.

• • •

Our terrors and our darknesses of mind
Must be dispelled, not by the sunshine's rays,
Not by those shining arrows of the light,
But by insight into nature, and a scheme
Of systematic contemplation. So
Our starting-point shall be this principle:
Nothing at all is ever born from nothing
By the gods' will. Ah, but men's minds are frightened
Because they see, on earth and in the heaven,

[2] Iphigeneia, a daughter of Agamemnon, the king of Mycenae. Having offended the goddess Artemis, he was required to atone by sacrificing his daughter. Only then would favorable winds be provided for the departure of Agamemnon's fleet from Aulis toward Troy.

Many events whose causes are to them
Impossible to fix; so, they suppose,
The gods' will is the reason. As for us,
Once we have seen that *Nothing comes from nothing,*
We shall perceive with greater clarity
What we are looking for, whence each thing comes,
How things are caused, and no "gods' will" about it.

Now, if things come from nothing, all things could
Produce all kinds of things; nothing would need
Seed of its own. Men would burst out of the sea,
And fish and birds from earth, and, wild or tame,
All kinds of beasts, of dubious origin,
Inhabit deserts and the greener fields,
Nor would the same trees bear, in constancy,
The same fruit always, but, as like as not,
Oranges would appear on apple-boughs.
If things were not produced after their kind,
Each from its own determined particles,
How could we trace the substance to the source?
But now, since all created things have come
From their own definite kinds of seed, they move
From their beginnings toward the shores of light
Out of their primal motes. Impossible
That all things issue everywhence; each kind
Of substance has its own inherent power,
Its own capacity. Does not the rose
Blossom in spring, the wheat come ripe in summer,
The grape burst forth at autumn's urge? There must be
A proper meeting of their seeds in time
For us to see them at maturity
Grown by their season's favor, living earth
Bringing them safely to the shores of light.
But if they came from nothing, they might spring
To birth at any unpropitious time,—
Who could predict?—since there would be no seeds
Whose character rules out untimely union.
Thirdly, if things could come from nothing, time
Would not be of the essence, for their growth,
Their ripening to full maturity.

Babies would be young men, in the blink of an eye,
And full-grown forests come leaping out from the ground.
Ridiculous! We know that all things grow
Little by little, as indeed they must
From their essential nature.

· · ·

Our second axiom is this, that nature
Resolves each object to its basic atoms
But does not ever utterly destroy it.
If anything could perish absolutely,
It might be suddenly taken from our sight,
There would be no need of any force to smash it,
Disrupt and shatter all its fastenings,
But as it is, since everything coheres
Because of its eternal seed,[3] its essence,
Until some force is strong enough to break it
By violent impact, or to penetrate
Its void interstices, and so dissolve it,
Nature permits no visible destruction
Of anything.

Besides, if time destroys
Completely what it banishes from sight
With the procession of the passing years,
Out of what source does Venus bring again
The race of animals, each after its kind,
To the light of life? and how, being restored,
Is each thing fed, sustained and given increase
By our miraculous contriving earth?
And what supplies the seas, the native springs,
The far-off rivers? And what feeds the stars?
By rights, if things can perish, infinite time
And ages past should have consumed them all,
But if, throughout this history, there have been
Renewals, and the sum of things can stay,
Beyond all doubt, there must be things possessed

[3] Atom.

Of an immortal essence. Nothing can
Disintegrate entirely into nothing.

An indiscriminate common violence
Would finish everything, except for this—
Matter is indestructible; it holds
All things together, though the fastenings
Vary in tightness. Otherwise, a touch,
The merest touch, would be a cause of death,
A force sufficient to dissolve in air
Textures of mortal substance. But here's the fact—
The elements are held, are bound together
In different degrees, but the basic stuff
Is indestructible, so things remain
Intact, unharmed, until a force is found
Proportionate to their texture, to effect
Reversion to their primal elements,
But never to complete annihilation.

Finally, when the fathering air has poured
His rainfall into mother earth, the drops
Seem to have gone, but look!—bright harvests rise,
Boughs on the trees bring greenery and growth
And are weighed down by fruit, by which, in turn,
Our race is fed, and so are animals,
And we see happy cities, flowering
With children, and we hear the music rise
As new birds sing all through the leafy woods.
Fat cows lie down to rest their weary sides
In welcome pastures, and the milk drops white
Out of distended udders; and the calves
Romp over the tender grass, or wobble, drunk
On that pure vintage, more than strong enough
For any such experience as theirs.
To sum it up: no visible object dies;
Nature from one thing brings another forth,
And out of death new life is born.

•   •   •

But not all bodily matter is tightly-packed
By nature's law, for there's a void in things.

This knowledge will be useful to you often,
Will keep you from the path of doubt, from asking
Too many questions on the sum of things,
From losing confidence in what I tell you.
By *void* I mean vacant and empty space,
Something you cannot touch. Were this not so,
Things could not move. The property of matter,
Its most outstanding trait, is to stand firm,
Its office to oppose; and everything
Would always be immovable, since matter
Never gives way. But with our eyes we see
Many things moving, in their wondrous ways,
Their marvelous means, through sea and land and sky.
Were there no void, they would not only lack
This restlessness of motion altogether,
But more than that—they never could have been
Quickened to life from that tight-packed quiescence.

Besides, however solid things appear,
Let me show you proof that even these are porous:
In a cave of rocks the seep of moisture trickles
And the whole place weeps its fat blobs of tears.
Food is dispersed all through a creature's body;
Young trees grow tall and yield their fruit in season,
Drawing their sustenance from the lowest roots
Through trunks and branches; voices penetrate
Walls and closed doors; the seep of stiffening cold
Permeates bone. Phenomena like these
Would be impossible but for empty spaces
Where particles can pass. And finally,
Why do we see that some things outweigh others
Which are every bit as large? If a ball of wool
Has the same substance as a ball of lead,
(Assuming the dimensions are the same)
They both should weigh as much, since matter tends
To exercise a constant downward pressure.
But void lacks weight. So, when two objects bulk
The same, but one is obviously lighter,
It clearly states its greater share of void,
And, on the other hand, the heavier thing
Proclaims it has less void and greater substance.

Certainly, therefore, what we're looking for
By logical deduction, does exist,
Is mixed with solid, and we call it *void*.

• • •

Bodies are partly basic elements
Of things, and partly compounds of the same.
The basic elements no force can shatter
Since, being solid, they resist destruction.
Yet it seems difficult to believe that objects
Are ever found to be completely solid.
A thunderbolt goes through the walls of houses,
As noise and voices do, and iron whitens
In fire, and steam at boiling point splits rocks,
Gold's hardnesses are pliant under heat,
The ice of bronze melts in the flame, and silver
Succumbs to warmth or chill, as our senses tell us
With the cup in our hands, and water, hot or cold,
Poured into the wine. No, there is nothing solid
In things, or so it seems; reason, however,
And science are compelling forces—therefore
Stay with me; it will not take many verses
For me to explain that there are things with bodies
Solid and everlasting; these we call
Seeds of things, firstlings, atoms, and in them lies
The sum of all created things.

To start with,
Since it has been established that the nature
Of things is different, dual, one being substance,
The other void, it follows that each one
Must, in its essence, be itself completely.
Where space exists, or what we call the void,
Matter cannot be found; what substance holds
Void cannot occupy. So atoms are
Solid and therefore voidless. Furthermore,
If there is void in things, there has to be
Solid material surrounding this.
Nothing, by logic, can be proved to hold
A void within its mass, unless you grant

It must itself be solid. There can be
Nothing except an organized composure
Of matter, which can hold a void within it.
And matter, therefore, being of solid substance,
Can last forever, while all else is shattered.
Then, were there nothing which we label *void,*
All would be solid substance; and again,
Were there no substance to fill up the spaces,
All would be void and emptiness. These, then,
Must alternate, substance and void, since neither
Exists to the exclusion of the other.
So there is substance, which marks off the limits
Between the full and the empty, and this substance
Cannot be broken if blows are struck against it
From anywhere outside it, not exploded
By dissolution from within, nor weakened
In any other way, as I have shown you.
It must be obvious that, lacking void,
Nothing can possibly be crushed or broken
Or split in two by cutting, or allow
Invasion by water, cold, or fire, those forces
Of dissolution. The more an object holds
Void space within it, the more easily
It weakens under stress and strain; and therefore,
As I have pointed out, when stuff is solid,
Without that void, it must be everlasting.
Were this not true of matter, long ago
Everything would have crumbled into nothing
And things we see today have been restored
From nothing; but remember, I have proved
Nothing can be created out of nothing.
Also, that nothing can be brought to nothing.
So basic elements must be immortal,
Impossible to dissolve in some last moment
Else there would be no matter for renewal.
They must be, then, completely singly solid,
For otherwise they could not through the ages
Be kept intact for restoration's work

• • •

There is no end,
No limit to the cosmos, above, below,
Around, about, stretching on every side.
This I have proven, but the fact itself
Cries loud in proclamation, nature's deep
Is luminous with proof. The universe
Is infinitely wide; its vastness holds
Innumerable seeds, beyond all count,
Beyond all possibility of number,
Flying along their everlasting ways.
So it must be unthinkable that our sky
And our round world are precious and unique
While all those other motes of matter flit
In idleness, achieve, accomplish nothing,
Especially since this world of ours was made
By natural process, as the atoms came
Together, willy-nilly, quite by chance,
Quite casually and quite intentionless
Knocking against each other, massed, or spaced
So as to colander others through, and cause
Such combinations and conglomerates
As form the origin of mighty things,
Earth, sea and sky, and animals and men.
Face up to this, acknowledge it. I tell you
Over and over—out beyond our world
There are, elsewhere, other assemblages
Of matter, making other worlds. Oh, ours
Is not the only one in air's embrace.

• • •

Since I have taught how everything begins,
The nature of those first particles, their shape,
Their differences, their voluntary course,
Their everlasting motion, and the ways
Things are created from them, I must now
Make use of poetry to clarify
The nature of intelligence and spirit,
Of mind and soul.

* * *

First,
The mind—the intellect, we sometimes call it—
The force that gives direction to a life
As well as understanding, is a part
Of a man's make-up, every bit as much
As are his hands and feet and seeing eyes.

* * *

Now pay heed,
I have more to say. To start with, I maintain
That mind and spirit are held close together,
Compose one unity, but the lord and master
Holding dominion over all the body
Is purpose, understanding—in our terms
Mind or intelligence, and this resides
In the region of the heart. Hence we derive
Terror and fear and panic and delight.
Here therefore dwell intelligence and mind.
The rest of spirit is dispersed all through
The entire frame, and it obeys the mind,
Moves, gains momentum, at its nod and beck,
And mind alone is sensible or wise
Or glad all by itself, when body and soul
Are quite unmoved by anything; and as an eye
Or head can hurt us, though we feel no pain
In any other part, so now and then
The mind can suffer or rejoice, while spirit
Is nowhere stirred in any part by strangeness;
But when the mind is deeply moved by fear
We see the spirit share that panic sense
All through the body: sweat breaks out, and pallor comes;
The tongue grows thick, the voice is choked, the eyes
Grow dark, ears ring, the limbs collapse. Men faint,
We have often seen, from a terror in the mind;
From this example all can recognize
That spirit and mind are closely bound together,
And spirit, struck by the impulse of the mind,
Propels and thrusts the body.

                                This same doctrine
Shows that the nature of both mind and spirit
Must be corporeal. We are bound to admit
That spirit and mind are properties of body
When they propel the limbs, arouse from sleep,
Change an expression, turn a man around,
Control him utterly, but none of this
Is possible without contact, nor is touch
Possible without body. Furthermore,
You see that mind can sympathize with body,
Share its emotions. If a weapon drives
Deep into bone and sinew, and yet fails
To shatter life entirely, still it brings
Weakness, collapse, and turbulence of mind
Within the fallen victim, a desire,
Half-hearted and confused, to rise again.
So mind, which suffers under wounds and blows,
Must have a bodily nature.

                                I'll explain,
At this point, what that body's like, what forms it:
First, it is very delicate indeed,
Made of the most diminutive particles.
That this is so requires no argument
Beyond the fact that nothing seems to move
With such velocity as mind intends
Or mind anticipates; mind acts, we know,
Quicker than anything natural we see.
But anything so mobile must consist
Of particles very round and smooth indeed,
And very small indeed, to be so stirred,
So set in motion by the slightest urge.
Water is moved in just this way, and flows
With almost no impulsion, being formed
Of tiny little round motes,[4] adaptable
Most easily for rolling. Honey, though,
Is more cohesive, less disposed to flow,
More sluggish, for its whole supply of matter
Is more condensed; its motes are not as smooth,

---

[4] Atoms.

As round, as delicate. The slightest stir
Of air disturbs a cone of poppy seeds,
Sends the top sliding downward; no such breath
Is adequate to disturb a pile of pebbles
Or even a heap of wheat-ears. Bodies move
With speed proportionate to their size and weight,
If small, then swift. The heavy or the rough
Are the more stable, solid, hard to move.
Now, since the nature of the mind appears
Mobile, extremely so, it must consist
Of particles which are small and smooth and round.
This knowledge, my good scholar, you will find
To your advantage in more ways than one.
Another fact gives evidence how frail,
How delicate spirit is, or soul, or mind,
How almost infinitesimal its compass
Even supposing it were massed together:
When death's calm reassurance takes a man,
And mind and spirit have left him, you perceive
Nothing at all subtracted from the body,
Nothing of weight, of semblance, gone. Death shows
All that was his except the vital sense,
The warming breath. And so the spirit must
Consist throughout of very tiny seeds,
All sown minutely in sinew, flesh, and veins—
So tenuous that when it leaves the body
There seems no difference, no diminution
Of outward contour nor of inward weight.
The same thing happens when the scent of wine,
Or nard's [5] aroma, or any effluence,
Vanishes into air, and still its source
Appears no less substantial to our eyes,
Especially since nothing of its weight
Is lost—so many and such tiny seeds
Imparting scent and flavor in all things.
Let me repeat: infinitesimal motes
Must form both mind and spirit, since we see
No loss of weight when these depart the body.

• • •

[5] An aromatic plant.

How sweet it is, when whirlwinds roil great ocean,
To watch, from land, the danger of another,
Not that to see some other person suffer
Brings great enjoyment, but the sweetness lies
In watching evils you yourself are free from.
How sweet, again, to see the clash of battle
Across the plains, yourself immune to danger.
But nothing is more sweet than full possession
Of those calm heights, well built, well fortified
By wise men's teaching, to look down from here
At others wandering below, men lost,
Confused, in hectic search for the right road,
The strife of wits, the wars for precedence,
The everlasting struggle, night and day,
To win towards heights of wealth and power. O wretched,
O wretched minds of men! O hearts in darkness!
Under what shadows and among what dangers
Your lives are spent, such as they are. But look—
Your nature snarls, yaps, barks for nothing, really,
Except that pain be absent from the body
And mind enjoy delight, with fear dispelled,
Anxiety gone. We do not need so much
For bodily comfort, only loss of pain.
I grant you, luxuries are very pleasant,
But nature does not really care if houses
Lack golden statues in the halls, young men
Holding out fiery torches in their hands
To light the all-night revels. Let the house
Gleam silver and gold, the music waken echoes
In gilded panel and crossbeam—never mind.
Much poorer men are every bit as happy,
Are quite well-off, stretched out in groups together
On the soft grass beside a running brook,
Under a tall tree's shade, in lovely weather,
Where flowers star green meadows. Fever's heat
Departs no sooner if your bodies toss
On crimson sheets, or under figured covers,
Than if you have to lie on a poor blanket.
So, since our bodies find in wealth no profit,
And none in rank or power, it must be mind

Is no more profited. You may see your hosts
Make mimic wars, surging across the drill-ground,
Flanked by their cavalry and well-supported
By strong reserves, high in morale. You may
Behold your fleet churn wide across great seas—
And does all this frighten religious terror
In panic from your heart? does the great fear
Of death depart, and leave you comforted?
What vanity, what nonsense! If men's fears,
Anxieties, pursuing horrors, move,
Indifferent to any clash of arms,
Untroubled among lords and monarchs, bow
Before no gleam of gold, no crimson robe,
Why do you hesitate, why doubt that reason
Alone has absolute power?

               • • •

Men seem to feel some burden on their souls,
Some heavy weariness; could they but know
Its origin, its cause, they'd never live
The way we see most of them do, each one
Ignorant of what he wants, except a change,
Some other place to lay his burden down.
One leaves his house to take a stroll outdoors
Because the household's such a deadly bore,
And then comes back, in six or seven minutes—
The street is every bit as bad. Now what?
He has his horses hitched up for him, drives,
Like a man going to a fire, full-speed,
Off to his country-place, and when he gets there
Is scarcely on the driveway, when he yawns,
Falls heavily asleep, oblivious
To everything, or promptly turns around,
Whips back to town again. So each man flees
Himself, or tries to, but of course that pest
Clings to him all the more ungraciously.
He hates himself because he does not know
The reason for his sickness; if he did,
He would leave all this foolishness behind,
Devote his study to the way things are,

The problem being his lot, not for an hour,
But for all time, the state in which all men
Must dwell forever and ever after death.

· · ·

Death
Is nothing to us, has no relevance
To our condition, seeing that the mind
Is mortal. Just as, long ago, we felt
Not the least touch of trouble when the wars
Were raging all around the shaken earth
And from all sides the Carthaginian hordes[6]
Poured forth to battle, and no man ever knew
Whose subject he would be in life or death,
Which doom, by land or sea, would strike him down,
So, when we cease to be, and body and soul,
Which joined to make us one, have gone their ways,
Their separate ways, nothing at all can shake
Our feelings, not if earth were mixed with sea
Or sea with sky. Perhaps the mind or spirit,
After its separation from our body,
Has some sensation; what is that to us?
Nothing at all, for what we knew of being,
Essence, identity, oneness, was derived
From body's union with spirit, so, if time,
After our death, should some day reunite
All of our present particles, bring them back
To where they now reside, give us once more
The light of life, this still would have no meaning
For us, with our self-recollection gone.
As we are now, we lack all memory
Of what we were before, suffer no wound
From those old days. Look back on all that space
Of time's immensity, consider well
What infinite combinations there have been
In matter's ways and groupings. How easy, then,
For human beings to believe we are

---

[6] The Carthaginians, holding an empire in North Africa, sought to conquer Rome in
the third century B.C.

Compounded of the very selfsame motes,
Arranged exactly in the selfsame ways
As once we were, our long-ago, our now
Being identical. And yet we keep
No memory of that once-upon-a-time,
Nor can we call it back; somewhere between
A break occurred, and all our atoms went
Wandering here and there and far away
From our sensations. If there lies ahead
Tough luck for any man, he must be there,
Himself, to feel its evil, but since death
Removes this chance, and by injunction stops
All rioting of woes against our state,
We may be reassured that in our death
We have no cause for fear, we cannot be
Wretched in nonexistence. Death alone
Has immortality, and takes away
Our mortal life. It does not matter a bit
If we once lived before.

                     So, seeing a man
Feel sorry for himself, that after death
He'll be a rotting corpse, laid in a tomb,
Succumb to fire, or predatory beasts,
You'll know he's insincere, just making noise,
With rancor in his heart, though he believes,
Or tries to make us think so, that death ends all.
And yet, I'd guess, he contradicts himself,
He does not really see himself as gone,
As utter nothingness, but does his best—
Not really understanding what he's doing—
To have himself survive, for, in his life,
He will project a future, a dark day
When beast or bird will lacerate his corpse.
So he feels sorry for himself; he fails
To make the real distinction that exists
Between his castoff body, and the man
Who stands beside it grieving, and imputes
Some of his sentimental feelings to it.

• • •

Hark! The voice of Nature
Is scolding us: "What ails you, little man,
Why this excess of self-indulgent grief,
This sickliness? Why weep and groan at death?
If you have any sense of gratitude
For a good life, if you can't claim her gifts
Were dealt you in some kind of riddled jar
So full of cracks and holes they leaked away
Before you touched them, why not take your leave
As men go from a banquet, fed to the full
On life's good feast, come home, and lie at ease,
Free from anxiety? Alas, poor fool,
If, on the other hand, all of your joys
Are gone, and life is only wretchedness,
Why try to add more to it? Why not make
A decent end? There's nothing, it would seem,
My powers can contrive for your delight.
The same old story, always. If the years
Don't wear your body, don't corrode your limbs
With lassitude, if you keep living on
For centuries, if you never die at all,
What's in it for you but the same old story
Always, and always?"

•   •   •

Such a rebuke from Nature would be right,
For the old order yields before the new,
All things require refashioning from others.
No man goes down to Hell's black pit; we need
Matter for generations yet to come,
Who, in their turn, will follow you, as men
Have died before you and will die hereafter.
So one thing never ceases to arise
Out of another; life's a gift to no man
Only a loan to him. Look back at time—
How meaningless, how unreal!—before our birth.
In this way Nature holds before our eyes
The mirror of our future after death.
Is this so grim, so gloomy? Is it not
A rest more free from care than any sleep?

19

Juvenal

Satires: The Third Satire

🔲

The wealthy aristocracy of the Empire, deprived of any real participation in its government and of any serious public responsibilities, often led a parasitic and meaningless existence. The dangers of such luxurious idleness had been pointed out by others, but it remained for a poet of the early second century to voice a revulsion and disgust unequaled outside the Christian writings of his day.

This poet was Decimus Junius Juvenalis (ca. A.D. 60–ca. 140), born to a middle-class family near Rome. Little is known of his life; but a tentative reconstruction presents him as a man who, failing of advancement in a military career, published a lampoon against the corrupt imperial court and so was exiled to Egypt. Returning to Rome in A.D. 96, with career gone and fortune confiscated, he led the life of an embittered man, sponging upon wealthy patrons. After fifteen years of this wretched existence, he somehow acquired a farm near Tivoli, perhaps at the Emperor Hadrian's bounty. Secure now, but still full of bile, he wrote his poems between 110 and 130.

The theme of the third satire is the age-old fear and hatred of megalopolis, the vast city, with its venality and vice. The keynote is struck in the setting of the poem. In search of quiet, Juvenal meets a friend, Umbricius, another hanger-on, in a once-sacred grove, only to find that it has been "improved" and vulgarized by rapacious foreigners, with whom the city swarms. The poem then takes the form of a tough, frankly spoken monologue by Umbricius, satirizing the bored, selfish, sex-crazy rich in the city he is leaving forever.

The moral chaos depicted helps to explain the growing appeal of Chris-

Juvenal, *The Satires of Juvenal*, trans. Rolfe Humphries (Bloomington: Indiana University Press, 1958), 33–45. Reprinted by permission of the publisher.

*tianity to Romans during the poet's later years. Juvenal offered escape into
the idealized Roman past; Christianity proposed a new way of life.*

🔲

AGAINST THE CITY OF ROME[1]

Troubled because my old friend is going, I still must commend him
For his decision to settle down in the ghost town of Cumae,[2]
Giving the Sibyl one citizen more. That's the gateway to Baiae
There, a pleasant shore, a delightful retreat. I'd prefer
Even a barren rock in that bay to the brawl of Subura.[3]
Where have we ever seen a place so dismal and lonely
We'd not be better off there, than afraid, as we are here, of fires,
Roofs caving in, and the thousand risks of this terrible city
Where the poets recite all through the dog days of August?

While they are loading his goods on one little four-wheeled wagon,
Here he waits, by the old archways which the aqueducts moisten.
This is where Numa,[4] by night, came to visit his goddess.
That once holy grove, its sacred spring, and its temple,
Now are let out to the Jews, if they have some straw and a basket.
Every tree, these days, has to pay rent to the people.
Kick the Muses out; the forest is swarming with beggars.
So we go down to Egeria's vale, with its modern improvements.
How much more close the presence would be, were there lawns by
    the water,
Turf to the curve of the pool, not this unnatural marble!

Umbricius has much on his mind. "Since there's no place in the
    city,"
He says, "For an honest man, and no reward for his labors,

---

[1] It should be noted that while this translation is a modern version, the satire still contains many allusions to conditions of the poet's time and place; but, in general, what
excited Juvenal's anger is what arouses disgust and demonstrations today.
[2] An ancient coastal town south of Rome, founded by the Greeks, the home of a legendary Sibyl, a prophetess.
[3] A slum section of imperial Rome, northeast of the Forum.
[4] The legendary second king of Rome (eighth century B.C.), noted for piety and the inspiration given to him by the nymph Egeria.

Since I have less today than yesterday, since by tomorrow
That will have dwindled still more, I have made my decision. I'm
  going
To the place where, I've heard, Daedalus put off his wings,
While my white hair is still new, my old age in the prime of its
  straightness,
While my fate spinner still has yarn on her spool, while I'm able
Still to support myself on two good legs, without crutches.
Rome, good-bye! Let the rest stay in the town if they want to,
Fellows like A, B, and C, who make black white at their pleasure,
Finding it easy to grab contracts for rivers and harbors,
Putting up temples, or cleaning out sewers, or hauling off corpses,
Or, if it comes to that, auctioning slaves in the market.
Once they used to be hornblowers, working the carneys;
Every wide place in the road knew their puffed-out cheeks and their
  squealing.
Now they give shows of their own. Thumbs up! Thumbs down![5]
  And the killers
Spare or slay, and then go back to concessions for private privies.
Nothing they won't take on. Why not?—since the kindness of For-
  tune
(Fortune is out for laughs) has exalted them out of the gutter.

"What should I do in Rome? I am no good at lying.
If a book's bad, I can't praise it, or go around ordering copies.
I don't know the stars; I can't hire out as assassin
When some young man wants his father knocked off for a price; I
  have never
Studied the guts of frogs, and plenty of others know better
How to convey to a bride the gifts of the first man she cheats with.
I am no lookout for thieves, so I cannot expect a commission
On some governor's staff. I'm a useless corpse, or a cripple.
Who has a pull these days, except your yes men and stooges
With blackmail in their hearts, yet smart enough to keep silent?
No honest man feels in debt to those he admits to his secrets,
But your Verres must love the man who can tattle on Verres
Any old time that he wants. Never let the gold of the Tagus,
Rolling under its shade, become so important, so precious

[5] Signals given by spectators in the amphitheater, indicating mercy or death for defeated gladiators.

You have to lie awake, take bribes that you'll have to surrender,
Tossing in gloom, a threat to your mighty patron forever.

"Now let me speak of the race that our rich men dote on most
   fondly.
These I avoid like the plague, let's have no coyness about it.
Citizens, I can't stand a Greekized Rome. Yet what portion
Of the dregs of our town comes from Achaia only?
Into the Tiber pours the silt, the mud of Orontes,[6]
Bringing its babble and brawl, its dissonant harps and its timbrels,
Bringing also the tarts who display their wares at the Circus.
Here's the place, if your taste is for hat-wearing whores, brightly
   colored!
What have they come to now, the simple souls from the country
Romulus used to know? They put on the *trechedipna*
(That might be called, in our tongue, their running-to-dinner outfit),
Pin on their *niketeria* (medals), and smell *ceromatic*
(Attar of wrestler). They come, trooping from Samos and Tralles,
Andros, wherever that is, Azusa and Cucamonga,
Bound for the Esquiline or the hill we have named for the vineyard,
Termites, into great halls where they hope, some day, to be tyrants.
Desperate nerve, quick wit, as ready in speech as Isaeus,
Also a lot more long-winded. Look over there! See that fellow?
What do you take him for? He can be anybody he chooses,
Doctor of science or letters, a vet or a chiropractor,
Orator, painter, masseur, palmologist, tightrope walker.
If he is hungry enough, your little Greek stops at nothing.
Tell him to fly to the moon and he runs right off for his space ship.
Who flew first? Some Moor, some Turk, some Croat, or some
   Slovene?
Not on your life, but a man from the very center of Athens.

"Should I not run away from these purple-wearing freeloaders?
Must I wait while they sign their names? Must their couches always
   be softer?
Stowaways, that's how they got here, in the plums and figs from
   Damascus.
I was here long before they were: my boyhood drank in the sky

---

[6] That is, the dregs of Syria. Orontes is a river there. Juvenal's ethnocentric bias is
loud and clear.

Over the Aventine hill; I was nourished by Sabine olives.
Agh, what lackeys they are, what sycophants! See how they flatter
Some ignoramus's talk, or the looks of some horrible eyesore,
Saying some Ichabod Crane's long neck reminds them of muscles
Hercules strained when he lifted Antaeus aloft on his shoulders,
Praising some cackling voice that really sounds like a rooster's
When he's pecking a hen. We can praise the same objects that they
    do,
Only, they are believed. Does an actor do any better
Mimicking Thais, Alcestis, Doris without any clothes on?
It seems that a woman speaks, not a mask; the illusion is perfect
Down to the absence of bulge and the little cleft under the belly.
Yet they win no praise at home, for all of their talent.
Why?—Because Greece is a stage, and every Greek is an actor.
Laugh, and he splits his sides; weep, and his tears flow in torrents
Though he's not sad; if you ask for a little more fire in the winter
He will put on his big coat; if you say 'I'm hot,' he starts sweating.
We are not equals at all; he always has the advantage,
Able, by night or day, to assume, from another's expression,
This or that look, prepared to throw up his hands, to cheer loudly
If his friend gives a good loud belch or doesn't piss crooked,
Or if a gurgle comes from his golden cup when inverted
Straight up over his nose—a good deep swig, and no heeltaps!

"Furthermore, nothing is safe from his lust, neither matron nor
    virgin,
Not her affianced spouse, or the boy too young for the razor.
If he can't get at these, he would just as soon lay his friend's
    grandma.
(Anything, so he'll get in to knowing the family secrets!)
Since I'm discussing the Greeks, let's turn to their schools and
    professors,
The crimes of the hood and gown. Old Dr. Egnatius, informant,
Brought about the death of Barea, his friend and his pupil,
Born on that riverbank where the pinion of Pegasus landed.
No room here, none at all, for any respectable Roman
Where a Protogenes rules, or a Diphilus, or a Hermarchus,[7]
Never sharing their friends—a racial characteristic!

[7] Common names of Greeks.

Hands off! he puts a drop of his own, or his countryside's poison
Into his patron's ear, an ear which is only too willing
And I am kicked out of the house, and all my years of long service
Count for nothing. Nowhere does the loss of a client[8] mean less.

"Let's not flatter ourselves. What's the use of our service?
What does a poor man gain by hurrying out in the nighttime,
All dressed up before dawn, when the praetor nags at his troopers
Bidding them hurry along to convey his respects to the ladies,
Barren, of course, like Albina, before any others can get there?
Sons of men freeborn give right of way to a rich man's
Slave; a crack, once or twice, at Calvina or Catiena
Costs an officer's pay, but if you like the face of some floozy
You hardly have money enough to make her climb down from her
    high chair.
Put on the stand, at Rome, a man with a record unblemished,
No more a perjurer than Numa was, or Metellus,[9]
What will they question? His wealth, right away, and possibly, later,
(Only possibly, though) touch on his reputation.
'How many slaves does he feed? What's the extent of his acres?
How big are his platters? How many? What of his goblets and wine
    bowls?'
His word is as good as his bond—if he has enough bonds in his
    strongbox.
But a poor man's oath, even if sworn on all altars
All the way from here to the farthest Dodecanese island,[10]
Has no standing in court. What has he to fear from the lightnings
Of the outraged gods? He has nothing to lose; they'll ignore him.

"If you're poor, you're a joke, on each and every occasion.
What a laugh, if your cloak is dirty or torn, if your toga
Seems a little bit soiled, if your shoe has a crack in the leather,
Or if more than one patch attests to more than one mending!
Poverty's greatest curse, much worse than the fact of it, is that
It makes men objects of mirth, ridiculed, humbled, embarrassed.
'Out of the front-row seats!' they cry when you're out of money,
Yield your place to the sons of some pimp, the spawn of some
    cathouse,

---

[8] A man in the service and pay of a rich patron.
[9] Legendary Romans of heroic virtue.
[10] Islands off the coast of Asia Minor (Turkey).

Some slick auctioneer's brat, or the louts some trainer has fathered
Or the well-groomed boys whose sire is a gladiator.
Such is the law of place, decreed by the nitwitted Otho:
All the best seats are reserved for the classes who have the most money.
Who can marry a girl if he has less money than she does?
What poor man is an heir, or can hope to be? Which of them ever
Rates a political job, even the meanest and lowest?
Long before now, all poor Roman descendants of Romans
Ought to have marched out of town in one determined migration.
Men do not easily rise whose poverty hinders their merit.
Here it is harder than anywhere else: the lodgings are hovels,
Rents out of sight; your slaves take plenty to fill up their bellies
While you make do with a snack. You're ashamed of your earthen-
    ware dishes—
Ah, but that wouldn't be true if you lived content in the country,
Wearing a dark-blue cape, and the hood thrown back on your shoul-
    ders.

"In a great part of this land of Italy, might as well face it,
No one puts on a toga unless he is dead. On festival days
Where the theater rises, cut from green turf, and with great pomp
Old familiar plays are staged again, and a baby,
Safe in his mother's lap, is scared of the grotesque mask,
There you see all dressed alike, the balcony and the front rows,
Even His Honor content with a tunic of simple white.
Here, beyond our means, we have to be smart, and too often
Get our effects with too much, an elaborate wardrobe, on credit!
This is a common vice; we must keep up with neighbors,
Poor as we are. I tell you, everything here costs you something.
How much to give Cossus the time of day, or receive from Veiento
One quick glance, with his mouth buttoned up for fear he might
    greet you?
One shaves his beard, another cuts off the locks of his boy friend,
Offerings fill the house, but these, you find, you will pay for.
Put this in your pipe and smoke it—we have to pay tribute
Giving the slaves a bribe for the prospect of bribing their masters.

"Who, in Praeneste's cool, or the wooded Volsinian uplands,
Who, on Tivoli's heights, or a small town like Gabii, say,
Fears the collapse of his house? But Rome is supported on pipestems,
Matchsticks; it's cheaper, so, for the landlord to shore up his ruins,
Patch up the old cracked walls, and notify all the tenants

They can sleep secure, though the beams are in ruins above them.
No, the place to live is out there, where no cry of *Fire!*
Sounds the alarm of the night, with a neighbor yelling for water,
Moving his chattels and goods, and the whole third story is smok-
    ing.
This you'll never know: for if the ground floor is scared first,
You are the last to burn, up there where the eaves of the attic
Keep off the rain, and the doves are brooding over their nest eggs.

Codrus owned one bed, too small for a midget to sleep on,
Six little jugs he had, and a tankard adorning his sideboard,
Under whose marble (clay), a bust or a statue of Chiron,
Busted, lay on its side; an old locker held Greek books
Whose divinest lines were gnawed by the mice, those vandals.
Codrus had nothing, no doubt, and yet he succeeded, poor fellow,
Losing that nothing, his all. And this is the very last straw—
No one will help him out with a meal or lodging or shelter.
Stripped to the bone, begging for crusts, he still receives nothing.
"Yet if Asturicus' mansion burns down, what a frenzy of sorrow!
Mothers dishevel themselves, the leaders dress up in black,
Courts are adjourned. We groan at the fall of the city, we hate
The fire, and the fire still burns, and while it is burning,
Somebody rushes up to replace the loss of the marble,
Some one chips in toward a building fund, another gives statues,
Naked and shining white, some masterpiece of Euphranor
Or Polyclitus'[11] chef d'oeuvre; and here's a fellow with bronzes
Sacred to Asian gods. Books, chests, a bust of Minerva,
A bushel of silver coins. *To him that hath shall be given!*
This Persian, childless, of course, the richest man in the smart set,
Now has better things, and more, than before the disaster.
How can we help but think he started the fire on purpose?

"Tear yourself from the games, and get a place in the country!
One little Latian town, like Sora, say, or Frusino,
Offers a choice of homes, at a price you pay here, in one year,
Renting some hole in the wall. Nice houses, too, with a garden,
Springs bubbling up from the grass, no need for a windlass or
    bucket,
Plenty to water your flowers, if they need it, without any trouble.

---

[11] Polyclitus was a famous Greek sculptor of the fifth century B.C.

Live there, fond of your hoe, an independent producer,
Willing and able to feed a hundred good vegetarians.
Isn't it something, to feel, wherever you are, how far off,
You are a monarch? At least, lord of a single lizard.

"Here in town the sick die from insomnia mostly.
Undigested food, on a stomach burning with ulcers,
Brings on listlessness, but who can sleep in a flophouse?
Who but the rich can afford sleep and a garden apartment?
That's the source of infection. The wheels crack by on the narrow
Streets of the wards, the drivers squabble and brawl when they're
   stopped.
More than enough to frustrate the drowsiest son of a sea cow.
When his business calls, the crowd makes way, as the rich man,
Carried high in his car, rides over them, reading or writing,
Even taking a snooze, perhaps, for the motion's composing.
Still, he gets where he wants before we do; for all of our hurry
Traffic gets in our way, in front, around and behind us.
Somebody gives me a shove with an elbow, or two-by-four scant-
   ling.
One clunks my head with a beam, another cracks down with a beer
   keg.
Mud is thick on my shins, I am trampled by somebody's big feet.
Now what?—a soldier grinds his hobnails into my toes.

"Don't you see the mob rushing along to the handout?
There are a hundred guests, each one with his kitchen servant.
Even Samson himself could hardly carry those burdens,
Pots and pans some poor little slave tries to keep on his head, while
   he hurries
Hoping to keep the fire alive by the wind of his running.
Tunics, new-darned, are ripped to shreds; there's the flash of a fir
   beam
Huge on some great dray, and another carries a pine tree,
Nodding above our heads and threatening death to the people.
What will be left of the mob, if that cart of Ligurian marble
Breaks its axle down and dumps its load on these swarms?
Who will identify limbs or bones? The poor man's cadaver,
Crushed, disappears like his breath. And meanwhile, at home, his
   household
Washes the dishes, and puffs up the fire, with all kinds of a clatter

Over the smeared flesh-scrapers, the flasks of oil, and the towels.
So the boys rush around, while their late master is sitting,
Newly come to the bank of the Styx,[12] afraid of the filthy
Ferryman there, since he has no fare, not even a copper
In his dead mouth to pay for the ride through that muddy whirlpool.

"Look at other things, the various dangers of nighttime.
How high it is to the cornice that breaks, and a chunk beats my
   brains out,
Or some slob heaves a jar, broken or cracked, from a window.
Bang! It comes down with a crash and proves its weight on the side-
   walk.
You are a thoughtless fool, unmindful of sudden disaster,
If you don't make your will before you go out to have dinner.
There are as many deaths in the night as there are open windows
Where you pass by; if you're wise, you will pray, in your wretched
   devotions,
People may be content with no more than emptying slop jars.
"There your hell-raising drunk, who has had the bad luck to kill no
   one,
Tosses in restless rage, like Achilles mourning Patroclus,[13]
Turns from his face to his back, can't sleep, for only a fracas
Gives him the proper sedation. But any of these young hoodlums,
All steamed up on wine, watches his step when the crimson
Cloak goes by, a lord, with a long, long line of attendants,
Torches and brazen lamps, warning him, *Keep your distance!*
Me, however, whose torch is the moon, or the feeblest candle
Fed by a sputtering wick, he absolutely despises.
Here is how it all starts, the fight, if you think it is fighting
When he throws all the punches, and all I do is absorb them.
He stops. He tells me to stop. I stop. I have to obey him.
What can you do when he's mad and bigger and stronger than you
   are?
'Where do you come from?' he cries, 'you wino, you bean-bloated
   bastard?

[12] A river flowing around the border of the underworld (Hades). The dead souls were
   ferried across it.
[13] Achilles' best friend. His death before the gates of Troy at the hands of the Trojan
   champion Hector caused Achilles, who had been sulking in his tent, to return to
   combat.

Off what shoemaker's dish have you fed on chopped leeks and boiled
    lamb-lip?
What? No answer? Speak up, or take a swift kick in the rear.
Tell me where you hang out—in some praying-house with the Jew-
    boys?'
If you try to talk back, or sneak away without speaking,
All the same thing: you're assaulted, and then put under a bail bond
For commiting assault. This is a poor man's freedom.
Beaten, cut up by fists, he begs and implores his assailant,
Please, for a chance to go home with a few teeth left in his mouth.

"This is not all you must fear. Shut up your house or your store,
Bolts and padlocks and bars will never keep out all the burglars,
Or a holdup man will do you in with a switch blade.
If the guards are strong over Pontine marshes and pinewoods
Near Volturno,[14] the scum of the swamps and the filth of the forest
Swirl into Rome, the great sewer, their sanctuary, their haven.
Furnaces blast and anvils groan with the chains we are forging:
What other use have we for iron and steel? There is danger
We will have little left for hoes and mattocks and ploughshares.
Happy the men of old, those primitive generations
Under the tribunes and kings, when Rome had only one jailhouse!

"There is more I could say, I could give you more of my reasons,
But the sun slants down, my oxen seem to be calling,
My man with the whip is impatient, I must be on my way.
So long! Don't forget me. Whenever you come to Aquino [15]
Seeking relief from Rome, send for me. I'll come over
From my bay to your hills, hiking along in my thick boots
Toward your chilly fields. What's more, I promise to listen
If your satirical verse esteems me worthy the honor."

[14] Areas close to Rome.
[15] A town near Cumae, the rustic destination of Umbricius. (Aquino may have been
    the birthplace of Juvenal.)

20

Marcus Aurelius

Thoughts

🔲

Plato had dreamed of the possibility of wisdom and political authority meeting in the same man, and the early Stoics taught the idea of a cosmopolis or "universal city" of gods and men. Although the Roman Empire fell far short of these ideals, the reigning philosophy, Stoicism, did provide its autocrats with moral justification, and its thinkers with the concept of natural law. The second century of the Empire may not have been "the period in the history of the world in which the condition of the human race was most happy and prosperous," as the historian Edward Gibbon thought; but for a portion of that century supreme power rested in the hands of the Stoics, and Marcus Aurelius Antoninus (A.D. 121–180) personified Plato's ideal of the philosopher-king.

Born and reared in Rome, Marcus so impressed Emperor Antoninus that he legally adopted him, named him his successor, and in 145 began to share with him the government of the Empire. After Marcus became sole ruler (A.D. 161–180) there was hard fighting on the northern frontier against the barbarians; finally, a plague carried off Marcus Aurelius together with a quarter of his subjects. Marcus Aurelius was the last of the "good emperors," and his reign was the end of an epoch. "At heart," wrote the nineteenth-century French historian, Ernest Renan, "all of us mourn Marcus Aurelius as if he had died yesterday."

The following selection is no Stoic tract in which an individual appeals for the improvement of others; rather it is the unaffected private diary of a man communing with his own soul, recording at the end of each busy day as soldier and administrator his innermost thoughts and feelings. As such, it is

Marcus Aurelius, *The Thoughts of the Emperor Marcus Aurelius*, trans. George Long (Boston: Little, Brown, 1892), 97–231, passim, adapted.

unique, and its very survival remains a mystery. For centuries at a time it disappeared from view, and only during the Renaissance was it recognized for what it is: one of the priceless treasures of humanity.

Written when the emperor was somewhat past fifty, Thoughts *reveals a man not brilliant but modest, unselfish, high-minded, and imbued with the highest sense of duty. The selected passages (here rearranged in a topical order) reveal the principles of Roman Stoicism: a religion without revelation, a lofty ethic without hope of reward or fear of punishment to come—one of the last and finest products of the classical mind.*

ON NATURE

All things are implicated with one another, and the bond is holy; and there is hardly anything unconnected with any other thing. For things have been co-ordinated, and they combine to form the same universe. For there is one universe made up of all things, one god who pervades all things, one substance, one law, one reason common to all intelligent beings, and one truth. . . .

ON LIVING IN HARMONY WITH NATURE

Everything harmonizes with me, which is harmonious to you, O Universe. Nothing for me is too early nor too late, which is in due time for you. Everything is fruit to me which your seasons bring, O Nature: from you are all things, in you are all things, to you all things return. The poet says, Dear city of Cecrops; [1] and will you not say, Dear city of Zeus?

• • •

Judge every word and deed which are according to nature to be fit for you; and be not diverted by the blame which follows from any people nor by their words, but if a thing is good to be done or said,

---

[1] The legendary first king of Athens. Here the distinction made by Marcus is, of course, between devotion to a mere city-state (Athens) and devotion to the order of nature.

do not consider it unworthy of you. For those persons have their peculiar leading principle and follow their peculiar movement; which things you must not regard, but go straight on, following your own nature and the common nature; and the way of both is one.

ON REASON

A man should always have these two rules in readiness; the one to do only whatever the reason of the ruling and legislating faculty may suggest for the use of men; the other, to change your opinion, if there is any one at hand who sets you right and moves you from any opinion. But this change of opinion must proceed only from a certain persuasion, as of what is just or of common advantage, and the like, not because it appears pleasant or brings reputation.

Have you reason? I have.—Why then not use it? For if this does its own work, what else do you wish?

• • •

Remember that the ruling faculty is invincible, when self-collected it is satisfied with itself, if it does nothing which it does not choose to do, even if it resist from mere obstinacy. What then will it be when it forms a judgment about anything aided by reason and deliberately? Therefore the mind which is free from passions is a citadel, for man has nothing more secure to which he can fly for refuge and for the future be invincible. He then who has not seen this is an ignorant man; but he who has seen it and does not fly to this refuge is unhappy.

ON DUTY AND RESPONSIBILITY

Every moment think steadily as a Roman and a man to do what you have in hand with perfect and simple dignity, and feeling of affection, and freedom, and justice, and to give yourself relief from all other thoughts. And you will give yourself relief if you do every act of your life as it if were the last, laying aside all carelessness and passionate aversion from the commands of reason, and all hypocrisy, and self-love, and discontent with the portion which has been given to you. You see how few the things are, which, if a man lays hold of, he is able to live a life which flows in quiet, and is like the existence of the gods; for the gods on their part will require nothing more from him who observes these things.

• • •

Do not disturb yourself by thinking of the whole of your life. Let not your thoughts at once embrace all the various troubles which you may expect to come; but on every occasion ask yourself, What is there in this which is intolerable and past bearing? for you will be ashamed to confess. In the next place remember that neither the future nor the past pains you, but only the present. But this is reduced to a very little, if you only circumscribe it, and chide your mind if it is unable to hold out against even this.

• • •

If you work at that which is before you, following right reason seriously, vigorously, calmly, without allowing anything else to distract you, but keeping your divine part pure, as if you should be bound to give it back immediately; if you hold to this, expecting nothing, fearing nothing, but satisfied with your present activity according to nature, and with heroic truth in every word and sound which you utter, you will live happy. And there is no man who is able to prevent this.

ON THE MORAL LIFE

If you find in human life anything better than justice, truth, temperance, fortitude, and, in a word, anything better than your own mind's self-satisfaction in the things which it enables you to do according to right reason; if, I say, you see anything better than this, turn to it with all your soul, and enjoy that which you have found to be the best. But if nothing appears to be better than the Deity which is planted in you, which has subjected to itself all your appetites, and carefully examines all the impressions, and, as Socrates said, has detached itself from the persuasions of sense, and has submitted itself to the gods, and cares for mankind; if you find everything else smaller and of less value than this, give place to nothing else, for if you once diverge and incline to it, you will no longer without distraction be able to give the preference to that good thing which is your proper possession and your own; for it is not right that anything of any other kind, such as praise from the many, or power, or enjoyment of pleasure, should come into competition with that which is rationally and politically [or, practically] good. . . . I say, do simply and freely choose the better, and hold to it. . . .

Never value anything as profitable to you which shall compel you to break your promise, to lose your self-respect, to hate any man, to suspect, to curse, to act the hypocrite, to desire anything which needs walls and curtains. For he who has preferred to everything else his own intelligence and daemon[2] and the worship of its excellence, acts no tragic part, does not groan, will not need either solitude or much company; and, what is chief of all, he will live without either pursuing or flying from death, but whether for a longer or a shorter time he shall have the soul enclosed in the body, he cares not at all. For even if he must depart immediately, he will go as readily as if he were going to do anything else which can be done with decency and order; taking care of this alone all through life, that his thoughts turn not away from anything which belongs to an intelligent animal and a member of a civil community.

ON HUMILITY AND FORBEARANCE

When you are offended with any man's shameless conduct, immediately ask yourself, Is it possible, then, that shameless men should not be in the world? It is not possible. Do not, then, require what is impossible. For this man also is one of those shameless men who must of necessity be in the world. Let the same considerations be present to your mind in the case of the knave, and the faithless man, and of every man who does wrong in any way. For at the same time that you remind yourself that it is impossible that such kind of men should not exist, you will become more kindly disposed towards every one individually. It is useful to perceive this, too, immediately when the occasion arises, what virtue nature has given to man to oppose to every wrongful act. For she has given to man, as an antidote against the stupid man, mildness, and against another kind of man some other power. And in all cases it is possible for you to correct by teaching the man who is gone astray; for every man who errs

[2] Inner spirit, or conscience.

misses his object and is gone astray. Besides, wherein have you been injured? For you will find that no one among those against whom you are irritated has done anything by which your mind could be made worse; but that which is evil to you and harmful has its foundation only in the mind. And what harm is done or what is there strange, if the man who has not been instructed does the acts of an uninstructed man? Consider whether you should not rather blame yourself because you did not expect such a man to err in such a way. For you had means given you by your reason to suppose that it was likely that he would commit this error, and yet you have forgotten and are amazed that he has erred. But most of all when you blame a man as faithless or ungrateful, turn to yourself. For the fault is manifestly your own, whether you did trust that a man who had such a disposition would keep his promise, or when conferring your kindness you did not confer it absolutely, nor yet in such way as to have received from your very act all the profit. For what more do you want when you have done a man a service? Are you not content that you have done something conformable to your nature, and do you seek to be paid for it? just as if the eye demanded a recompense for seeing, or the feet for walking. For as these members are formed for a particular purpose, and by working according to their several constitutions obtain what is their own; so also a man is formed by nature to acts of benevolence. When he has done anything benevolent or in any other way conducive to the common interest, he has acted conformably to his constitution, and he gets what is his own.

ON EQUANIMITY AND IMPERTURBABILITY

Hippocrates, after curing many diseases, himself fell sick and died. The Chaldaei[3] foretold the deaths of many, and then fate caught them too. Alexander and Pompey and Caius Caesar, after so often completely destroying whole cities, and in battle cutting to pieces many ten thousands of cavalry and infantry, themselves too at last departed from life. Heraclitus,[4] after so many speculations on the conflagration of the universe, was filled with water internally and

---

[3] The ancient Chaldeans (of Mesopotamia) enjoyed a high reputation as astrologers and sorcerers—thus, the scriptural phrase "Wise Men of the East."

[4] A famous Greek "nature" philosopher of the sixth century B.C.

died smeared all over with mud. And lice destroyed Democritus;[5] and other lice[6] killed Socrates. What means all this? You have embarked, you have made the voyage, you have come to shore; get out. If indeed to another life, there is no want of gods, not even there; but if to a state without sensation, you will cease to be held by pains and pleasures, and to be a slave to the body, which is as much inferior as that which serves it is superior: for the one is intelligence and deity; the other is earth and corruption.

• • •

This is the chief thing: Be not perturbed, for all things are according to the nature of the universal; and in a little time you will be nobody and nowhere, like Hadrian and Augustus.[7] In the next place, having fixed your eyes steadily on your business, look at it; and at the same time remembering that it is your duty to be a good man, and what man's nature demands, do that without turning aside; and speak as it seems to you most just, only let it be with a good disposition and with modesty and without hypocrisy.

ON RETIREMENT INTO ONE'S SELF

Men seek retreats for themselves, houses in the country, seashores, and mountains; and you too are accustomed to desire such things very much. But this is altogether a mark of the most common sort of men, for it is in your power whenever you choose to retire into yourself. For nowhere either with more quiet or more freedom from trouble does a man retire than into his own soul, particularly when he has within him such thoughts that by looking into them he is immediately in perfect tranquillity; and I affirm that tranquillity is nothing else than the good ordering of the mind. Constantly then give yourself this retreat, and renew yourself; and let your principles be brief and fundamental, which, as soon as you recur to them, will be sufficient to cleanse the soul completely, and to send you back free from all discontent with the things to which you return. For with what are you discontented? With the badness of men? Recall to your

---

[5] A Greek thinker who devised the "atomic" theory of matter, in the fifth century B.C.
[6] A play on words; Marcus here refers to the mean-spirited men who convicted Socrates on charges of subversion.
[7] Deceased Roman emperors.

mind this conclusion, that rational animals exist for one another, and that to endure is a part of justice, and that men do wrong involuntarily; and consider how many already, after mutual enmity, suspicion, hatred, and fighting, have been stretched dead, reduced to ashes; and be quiet at last. But perhaps you are dissatisfied with that which is assigned to you out of the universe.—Recall to your recollection this alternative: either there is providence or atoms [fortuitous concurrence of things]; or remember the arguments by which it has been proved that the world is a kind of political community. But perhaps corporeal things will still fasten upon you.—Consider then further that the mind mingles not with the breath, whether moving gently or violently, when it has once drawn itself apart and discovered its own power, and think also of all that you have heard and assented to about pain and pleasure.—But perhaps the desire of the thing called fame will torment you.—See how soon everything is forgotten, and look at the chaos of infinite time on each side of the present and the emptiness of applause, and the changeableness and want of judgment in those who pretend to give praise, and the narrowness of the space within which it is circumscribed. For the whole earth is a point, and how small a nook in it is this your dwelling, and how few are there in it, and what kind of people are they who will praise you.

This then remains: Remember to retire into this little territory of your own, and above all do not distract or strain yourself, but be free, and look at things as a man, as a human being, as a citizen, as a mortal. But among the things readiest to your hand to which you will turn, let there be these, which are two. One is that *things* do not touch the soul, for they are external and remain outside the soul; but our perturbations come only from our perception, which is within. The other is that all these things, which you see, change immediately and will no longer be; and constantly bear in mind how many of these changes you have already witnessed. The universe is change; life is your perception of it.

21

Old Testament

The Old Testament, as the Jewish sacred books are called by Christians, is venerated as the divinely inspired account of God's dealings with his chosen witnesses, the Jews. In a wider sense it is accepted by believers as the revelation of the mind and purpose of God to all mankind. Dating from much earlier times, the Old Testament is presented here at this point because it was accepted from the first by Christians as the prologue of their own evangel, and only through them did it come to be known widely outside Jewish circles in the early days of the Roman Empire. The following selections represent the Jewish account of certain crises in the tremendous encounter between the human and the divine, and the developing human comprehension of God's presence and designs.

The drama begins in a garden, typifying the world as God had planned it—a world full of good things, where man and woman enjoy the intimacy of their creator. This right relationship is ruptured by their mutinous self-will, the primordial sin, followed by the first murder. Evil, then, is inherent in human nature, and judgment falls upon mankind in the Flood, from which only Noah and his family are rescued. Thus the themes that run all through the Judeo-Christian epic are prefigured: a recurring pattern of sin, divine judgment, and—because of the merits of one only, or of a few—divine mercy.

The Jewish people are then selected as the instrument of the divine purposes. They pledge obedience to God and through Moses are given the Law. But once more humans prove unequal to the divine challenge. Exposed to the contaminating influences of their neighbors, the Jews follow strange gods and adopt a life of self-indulgence. God's anger is expressed through his spokesmen, the prophets, who warn and threaten in his name. Gradually they give *shape and direction to the religious experience of the Jews. The books named for the prophets constitute no fewer than a third of those in the Old Testament. The first of these prophets—figures peculiar to the Semitic religions—was Amos, who, in the eighth century* B.C., *denounced the luxury and social injustice of the Jews and predicted the judgment to come.*

First the northern kingdom, Israel, was wiped out by the Assyrians in 722 B.C. *Later the southern kingdom, Judah, fell to the Babylonians, and its leading citizens were carried into captivity. Reflecting upon these disasters and guided by the insights of the "Second Isaiah," a prophet who wrote about 540* B.C., *the Jews acquired a clearer understanding of God's nature and of their role in history. This ultimate awareness marked the acme of their religious experience and, so Christians believe, prepared the way for God's further revelation (through Jesus and the New Testament).*

GENESIS

The Beginnings of History

2:4–4:16

These are the generations of the heavens and the earth when they were created.

In the day that the Lord God made the earth and the heavens, when no plant of the field was yet in the earth and no herb of the field had yet sprung up—for the Lord God had not caused it to rain upon the earth, and there was no man to till the ground; but a mist went up from the earth and watered the whole face of the ground—then the Lord God formed man of dust from the ground, and breathed into his nostrils the breath of life; and man became a living being. And the Lord God planted a garden in Eden, in the east; and there he put the man whom he had formed. And out of the ground the Lord God made to grow every tree that is pleasant to the sight and good for food, the tree of life also in the midst of the garden, and the tree of the knowledge of good and evil.

A river flowed out of Eden to water the garden, and there it divided and became four rivers. The name of the first is Pishon; it is the one which flows around the whole land of Hav′ilah, where there is gold; and the gold of that land is good; bdellium and onyx stone are there. The name of the second river is Gihon; it is the one which flows around the whole land of Cush. And the name of the third river is Tigris, which flows east of Assyria. And the fourth river is the Eu-phra'tes.

The Lord God took the man and put him in the garden of Eden to till it and keep it. And the Lord God commanded the man, saying, "You may freely eat of every tree of the garden; but of the tree of the knowledge of good and evil you shall not eat, for in the day that you eat of it you shall die."

Then the Lord God said, "It is not good that the man should be alone; I will make him a helper fit for him. So out of the ground the Lord God formed every beast of the field and every bird of the air, and brought them to the man to see what he would call them; and whatever the man called every living creature, that was its name. The man gave names to all cattle, and to the birds of the air, and to every beast of the field; but for the man there was not found a helper fit for him. So the Lord God caused a deep sleep to fall upon the man, and while he slept took one of his ribs and closed up its place with flesh; and the rib which the Lord God had taken from the man he made into a woman and brought her to the man. Then the man said,

> "This at last is bone of my bones
>   and flesh of my flesh;
> she shall be called Woman,
>   because she was taken out of Man."

Therefore a man leaves his father and his mother and cleaves to his wife, and they become one flesh. And the man and his wife were both naked, and were not ashamed.

Now the serpent was more subtle than any other wild creature that the Lord God had made. He said to the woman, "Did God say, 'You shall not eat of any tree of the garden'?" And the woman said to the serpent, "We may eat of the fruit of the trees of the garden; but God said, 'You shall not eat of the fruit of the tree which is in the midst of the garden, neither shall you touch it, lest you die.' " But the serpent said to the woman, "You will not die. For God knows that when you eat of it your eyes will be opened, and you will be like God, knowing good and evil." So when the woman saw that the tree was good for food, and that it was a delight to the eyes, and that the tree was to be desired to make one wise, she took of its fruit and ate; and she also gave some to her husband, and he ate. Then the eyes of both were opened, and they knew that they were naked; and they sewed fig leaves together and made themselves aprons.

And they heard the sound of the Lord God walking in the garden in the cool of the day, and the man and his wife hid themselves from the presence of the Lord God among the trees of the garden. But the Lord God called to the man, and said to him, "Where are you?" And he said, "I heard the sound of thee in the garden, and I was afraid, because I was naked; and I hid myself." He said, "Who told you that you were naked? Have you eaten of the tree of which I commanded you not to eat?" The man said, "The woman whom thou gavest to be with me, she gave me the fruit of the tree, and I ate." Then the Lord God said to the woman, "What is this that you have done?" The woman said, "The serpent beguiled me, and I ate." The Lord God said to the serpent,

> "Because you have done this,
>   cursed are you above all cattle,
>   and above all wild animals;
> upon your belly you shall go,
>   and dust you shall eat
>   all the days of your life.
> I will put enmity between you and the woman,
>   and between your seed and her seed;
> he shall bruise your head,
>   and you shall bruise his heel."

To the woman he said,

> "I will greatly multiply your pain in childbearing;
>   in pain you shall bring forth children,
> yet your desire shall be for your husband,
>   and he shall rule over you."

And to Adam he said,

> "Because you have listened to the voice of your wife,
>   and have eaten of the tree
> of which I commanded you,
>   'You shall not eat of it,'
> cursed is the ground because of you;
>   in toil you shall eat of it all the days of your life;
> thorns and thistles it shall bring forth to you;
>   and you shall eat the plants of the field.

> In the sweat of your face
>> you shall eat bread
> till you return to the ground,
>> for out of it you were taken;
> you are dust,
>> and to dust you shall return."

The man called his wife's name Eve, because she was the mother of all living. And the Lord God made for Adam and for his wife garments of skins, and clothed them.

Then the Lord God said, "Behold, the man has become like one of us, knowing good and evil; and now, lest he put forth his hand and take also of the tree of life, and eat, and live for ever"—therefore the Lord God sent him forth from the garden of Eden, to till the ground from which he was taken. He drove out the man; and at the east of the garden of Eden he placed the cherubim, and a flaming sword which turned every way, to guard the way to the tree of life.

Now Adam knew Eve his wife, and she conceived and bore Cain, saying, "I have gotten a man with the help of the Lord." And again, she bore his brother Abel. Now Abel was a keeper of sheep, and Cain a tiller of the ground. In the course of time Cain brought to the Lord an offering of the fruit of the ground, and Abel brought of the firstlings of his flock and of their fat portions. And the Lord had regard for Abel and his offering, but for Cain and his offering he had no regard. So Cain was very angry, and his countenance fell. The Lord said to Cain "Why are you angry, and why has your countenance fallen? If you do well, will you not be accepted? And if you do not do well, sin is couching at the door; its desire is for you, but you must master it."

Cain said to Abel his brother, "Let us go out to the field." And when they were in the field, Cain rose up against his brother Abel, and killed him. Then the Lord said to Cain, "Where is Abel your brother?" He said, "I do not know; am I my brother's keeper?" And the Lord said, "What have you done? The voice of your brother's blood is crying to me from the ground. And now you are cursed from the ground, which has opened its mouth to receive your brother's blood from your hand. When you till the ground, it shall no longer yield to you its strength; you shall be a fugitive and a wanderer on the earth." Cain said to the Lord, "My punishment is greater than I can bear. Behold, thou hast driven me this day away from the ground; and from thy face I shall be hidden; and I shall be a fugitive and a wanderer on the earth, and whoever finds me will slay me." Then the Lord said to him, "Not so! If anyone slays Cain, vengence shall be taken on him sevenfold." And the Lord put a mark on Cain, lest any who came upon him should kill him. Then Cain went away from the presence of the Lord, and dwelt in the land of Nod, east of Eden.

The Flood

6:1–22

When men began to multiply on the face of the ground, and daughters were born to them, the sons of God saw that the daughters of men were fair; and they took to wife such of them as they chose. Then the Lord said, "My spirit shall not abide in man for ever, for he is flesh, but his days shall be a hundred and twenty years." The Nephilim were on the earth in those days, and also afterward, when the sons of God came in to the daughters of men, and they bore children to them. These were the mighty men that were of old, the men of renown.

The Lord saw that the wickedness of man was great in the earth, and that every imagination of the thoughts of his heart was only evil continually. And the Lord was sorry that he had made man on the earth, and it grieved him to his heart. So the Lord said, "I will blot out man whom I have created from the face of the ground, man and beast and creeping things and birds of the air, for I am sorry that I have made them." But Noah found favor in the eyes of the Lord.

These are the generations of Noah. Noah was a righteous man, blameless in his generation; Noah walked with God. And Noah had three sons, Shem, Ham, and Japheth.

Now the earth was corrupt in God's sight, and the earth was filled with violence. And God saw the earth, and behold, it was corrupt; for all flesh had corrupted their way upon the earth. And God said to Noah, "I have determined to make an end of all flesh; for the earth is filled with violence through them; behold, I will destroy them with the earth. Make yourself an ark of gopher wood; make rooms in the ark, and cover it inside and out with pitch. This is how you are to make it: the length of the ark three hundred cubits, its breadth fifty cubits, and its height thirty cubits. Make a roof for the ark, and finish it to a cubit above; and set the door of the ark in its side; make it with lower, second, and third decks. For behold, I will bring a flood of waters upon the earth, to destroy all flesh in which is the breath of life from under heaven; everything that is on the earth shall die. But I will establish my covenant with you; and you shall come into the ark, you, your sons, your wife, and your sons' wives with you. And of every living thing of all flesh, you shall bring two of every sort into the ark, to keep them alive with you; they shall be male and female. Of the birds according to their kinds, and of the animals according to their kinds, of every creeping thing of the ground according to its kind, two of every sort shall come in to you, to keep them alive. Also take with you every sort of food that is eaten, and store it up; and it shall serve as food for you and for them." Noah did this; he did all that God commanded him.

EXODUS

The Covenant

19:1–20:21

On the third new moon after the people of Israel had gone forth out of the land of Egypt, on that day they came into the wilderness of Sinai. And when they set out from Reph'idim and came into the wilderness of Sinai, they encamped in the wilderness; and there Israel encamped before the mountain. And Moses went up to God, and the Lord called to him out of the mountain, saying, "Thus you shall say to the house of Jacob, and tell the people of Israel: You have seen what I did to the Egyptians, and how I bore you on eagles' wings and brought you to myself. Now therefore, if you will obey my voice and keep my covenant, you shall be my own possession among all peoples; for all the earth is mine, and you shall be to me a kingdom of priests and a holy nation. These are the words which you shall speak to the children of Israel."

So Moses came and called the elders of the people, and set before them all these words which the Lord had commanded him. And all the people answered together and said, "All that the Lord has spoken we will do." And Moses reported the words of the people to the Lord. And the Lord said to Moses, "Lo, I am coming to you in a thick cloud, that the people may hear when I speak with you, and may also believe you for ever."

Then Moses told the words of the people to the Lord. And the Lord said to Moses, "Go to the people and consecrate them today and tomorrow, and let them wash their garments, and be ready by the third day; for on the third day the Lord will come down upon Mount Sinai in the sight of all the people. And you shall set bounds for the people round about saying, 'Take heed that you do not go up into the mountain or touch the border of it; whoever touches the mountain shall be put to death; no hand shall touch him, but he shall be stoned or shot; whether beast or man, he shall not live.' When the trumpet sounds a long blast, they shall come up to the mountain." So Moses went down from the mountain to the people, and consecrated the people; and they washed their garments. And he said to the people, "Be ready by the third day; do not go near a woman."

On the morning of the third day there were thunders and lightnings, and a thick cloud upon the mountain, and a very loud trumpet blast, so that all the people who were in the camp trembled. Then Moses brought the people out of the camp to meet God; and they took their stand at the foot of the mountain. And Mount Sinai was wrapped in smoke, because the Lord descended upon it in fire; and the smoke of it went up like the smoke of a kiln, and the whole mountain quaked greatly. And as the sound of the trumpet grew louder and louder, Moses spoke, and God answered him in thunder. And the Lord came down upon Mount Sinai, to the top of the mountain; and the Lord called Moses to the top of the mountain, and Moses went up. And the Lord said to Moses, "Go down and warn the people, lest they break through to the Lord to gaze and many of them perish. And also let the priests who come near to the Lord consecrate themselves, lest the Lord break out upon them." And Moses said to the Lord, "The people cannot come up to Mount Sinai; for thou thyself didst charge us, saying, 'Set bounds about the mountain, and consecrate it.' " And the Lord said to him, "Go down, and come up bringing Aaron with you; but do not let the priests and the people break through to come up to the Lord, lest he break out against them." So Moses went down to the people and told them.

And God spoke all these words, saying,

> "I am the Lord your God, who brought you out of the land of Egypt, out of the house of bondage.
> "You shall have no other gods before me.
> "You shall not make for yourself a graven image, or any likeness of anything that is in heaven above, or that is in the earth beneath, or that

is in the water under the earth; you shall not bow down to them or serve them; for I the Lord your God am a jealous God, visiting the iniquity of the fathers upon the children to the third and the fourth generation of those who hate me, but showing steadfast love to thousands of those who love me and keep my commandments.

"You shall not take the name of the Lord your God in vain; for the Lord will not hold him guiltless who takes his name in vain.

"Remember the sabbath day, to keep it holy. Six days you shall labor, and do all your work; but the seventh day is a sabbath to the Lord your God; in it you shall not do any work, you, or your son, or your daughter, your manservant, or your maidservant, or your cattle, or the sojourner who is within your gates; for in six days the Lord made heaven and earth, the sea, and all that is in them, and rested the seventh day; therefore the Lord blessed the sabbath day and hallowed it.

"Honor your father and your mother, that your days may be long in the land which the Lord your God gives you.

"You shall not kill.

"You shall not commit adultery.

"You shall not steal.

"You shall not bear false witness against your neighbor.

"You shall not covet your neighbor's house; you shall not covet your neighbor's wife, or his manservant, or his maidservant, or his ox, or his ass, or anything that is your neighbor's."

Now when all the people perceived the thunderings and the lightnings and the sound of the trumpet and the mountain smoking, the people were afraid and trembled; and they stood afar off, and said to Moses, "You speak to us, and we will hear; but let not God speak to us, lest we die." And Moses said to the people, "Do not fear; for God has come to prove you, and that the fear of him may be before your eyes, that you may not sin."

And the people stood afar off, while Moses drew near to the thick darkness where God was.

The Torah, or Law

20:22–23:33

And the Lord said to Moses, "Thus you shall say to the people of Israel: 'You have seen for yourselves that I have talked with you from heaven. You shall not make gods of silver to be with me, nor shall you make yourselves gods of gold. An altar of earth you shall make for me and sacrifice on it your burnt offerings and your peace offerings, your sheep and your oxen; in every place where I cause my name to be remembered I will come to you and bless you. And if you make me an altar of stone, you shall not build it of hewn stones; for if you wield your tool upon it you profane it. And you shall not go up by steps to my altar, that your nakedness be not exposed on it.'

"Now these are the ordinances which you shall set before them. When you buy a Hebrew slave, he shall serve six years, and in the seventh he shall go out free, for nothing. If he comes in single, he shall go out single; if he comes in married, then his wife shall go out with him. If his master gives him a wife and she bears him sons or daughters, the wife and her children shall be her master's and he shall go out alone. But if the slave plainly says, 'I love my master, my wife, and my children; I will not go out free,' then his master shall bring him to God, and he shall bring him to the door or the door-post; and his master shall bore his ear through with an awl; and he shall serve him for life.

"When a man sells his daughter as a slave, she shall not go out as the male slaves do. If she does not please her master, who has designated her for himself, then he shall let her be redeemed; he shall have no right to sell her to a foreign people, since he has dealt faithlessly with her. If he designates her for his son, he shall deal with her as with a daughter. If he takes another wife to himself, he shall not diminish her food, her clothing, or her marital rights. And if he does not do these three things for her, she shall go out for nothing, without payment of money.

"Whoever strikes a man so that he dies shall be put to death. But if he did not lie in wait for him, but God let him fall into his hand, then I will appoint for you a place to which he may flee. But if a man willfully attacks another to kill him treacherously, you shall take him from my altar, that he may die.

"Whoever strikes his father or his mother shall be put to death.

"Whoever steals a man, whether he sells him or is found in possession of him, shall be put to death.

"Whoever curses his father or his mother shall be put to death.

"When men quarrel and one strikes the other with a stone or with his fist and the man does not die but keeps his bed, then if the man rises again and walks abroad with his staff, he that struck him shall be clear; only he shall pay for the loss of his time, and shall have him thoroughly healed.

"When a man strikes his slave, male or female, with a rod and the slave dies under his hand, he shall be punished. But if the slave survives a day or two, he is not to be punished; for the slave is his money.

"When men strive together, and hurt a woman with child, so that there is a miscarriage, and yet no harm follows, the one who hurt her shall be fined, according as the woman's husband shall lay upon him; and he shall pay as the judges determine. If any harm follows, then you shall give life for life, eye for eye, tooth for tooth, hand for hand, foot for foot, burn for burn, wound for wound, stripe for stripe.

"When a man strikes the eye of his slave, male or female, and destroys it, he shall let the slave go free for the eye's sake. If he knocks out the tooth of his slave, male or female, he shall let the slave go free for the tooth's sake.

"When an ox gores a man or woman to death, the ox shall be stoned, and its flesh shall not be eaten; but the owner of the ox shall be clear. But if the ox has been accustomed to gore in the past, and its owner has been warned but has not kept it in, and it kills a man or a woman, the ox shall be stoned, and its owner also shall be put to death. If a ransom is laid on him, then he shall give for the redemption of his life whatever is laid upon him. If it gores a man's son or daughter, he shall be dealt with according to this same rule. If the ox gores a slave, male or female, the owner shall give to their master thirty shekels of silver, and the ox shall be stoned.

"When a man leaves a pit open, or when a man digs a pit and does not cover it, and an ox or an ass falls into it, the owner of the pit shall make it good; he shall give money to its owner, and the dead beast shall be his.

"When one man's ox hurts another's, so that it dies, then they shall sell the live ox and divide the price of it; and the dead beast also they shall divide. Or if it is known that the ox has been accustomed to gore in the past, and its owner has not kept it in, he shall pay ox for ox, and the dead beast shall be his.

"If a man steals an ox or a sheep, and kills it or sells it, he shall pay five oxen for an ox, and four sheep for a sheep. He shall make restitution; if he has nothing, then he shall be sold for his theft. If the stolen beast is found alive in his possession, whether it is an ox or an ass or a sheep, he shall pay double.

"If a thief is found breaking in, and is struck so that he dies, there shall be no bloodguilt for him; but if the sun has risen upon him, there shall be bloodguilt for him.

"When a man causes a field or vineyard to be grazed over, or lets his beast loose and it feeds in another man's field, he shall make restitution from the best in his own field and in his own vineyard.

"When fire breaks out and catches in thorns so that the stacked grain or the standing grain or the field is consumed, he that kindled the fire shall make full restitution.

"If a man delivers to his neighbor money or goods to keep, and it is stolen out of the man's house, then, if the thief is found, he shall pay double. If the thief is not found, the owner of the house shall come near to God, to show whether or not he has put his hand to his neighbor's goods.

"For every breach of trust, whether it is for ox, for ass, for sheep, for clothing, or for any kind of lost thing, of which one says, 'This is it,' the case of both parties shall come before God; he whom God shall condemn shall pay double to his neighbor.

"If a man delivers to his neighbor an ass or an ox or a sheep or any beast to keep, and it dies or is hurt or is driven away, without any one seeing it, an oath by the Lord shall be between them both to see whether he has not put his hand to his neighbor's property; and the owner shall accept the oath, and he shall not make restitution. But if it is stolen from him, he shall make restitution to its owner. If it is torn by beasts, let him bring it as evidence; he shall not make restitution for what has been torn.

"If a man borrows anything of his neighbor, and it is hurt or dies, the owner not being with it, he shall make full restitution. If the owner was with it, he shall not make restitution; if it was hired, it came for its hire.

"If a man seduces a virgin who is not bethrothed, and lies with her, he shall give the marriage present for her, and make her his wife. If her father utterly refuses to give her to him, he shall pay money equivalent to the marriage present for virgins.

"You shall not permit a sorceress to live.

"Whoever lies with a beast shall be put to death.

"Whoever sacrifices to any god, save to the Lord only, shall be utterly destroyed.

"You shall not wrong a stranger or oppress him, for you were strangers in the land of Egypt. You shall not afflict any widow or orphan. If you do afflict them, and they cry out to me, I will surely hear their cry; and my wrath will burn, and I will kill you with the sword, and your wives shall become widows and your children fatherless.

"If you lend money to any of my people with you who is poor, you shall not be to him as a creditor, and you shall not exact interest from him. If ever you take your neighbor's garment in pledge, you shall restore it to him before the sun goes down; for that is his only covering, it is his mantle for his body; in what else shall he sleep? And if he cries to me, I will hear, for I am compassionate.

"You shall not revile God, nor curse a ruler of your people.

"You shall not delay to offer from the fulness of your harvest and from the outflow of your presses.

"The first-born of your sons you shall give to me. "You shall do likewise with your oxen and with your sheep: seven days it shall be with its dam; on the eighth day you shall give it to me.

"You shall be men consecrated to me; therefore you shall not eat any flesh that is torn by beasts in the field; you shall cast it to the dogs.

"You shall not utter a false report. You shall not join hands with a wicked man, to be a malicious witness. You shall not follow a multitude to do evil; nor shall you bear witness in a suit, turning aside after a multitude, so as to pervert justice; nor shall you be partial to a poor man in his suit.

"If you meet your enemy's ox or his ass going astray, you shall bring it back to him. If you see the ass of one who hates you lying under its burden, you shall refrain from leaving him with it, you shall help him to lift it up.

"You shall not pervert the justice due to your poor in his suit. Keep far from a false charge, and do not slay the innocent and righteous, for I will not acquit the wicked. And you shall take no bribe, for a bribe blinds the officials, and subverts the cause of those who are in the right.

"You shall not oppress a stranger; you know the heart of a stranger, for you were strangers in the land of Egypt.

"For six years you shall sow your land and gather in its yield; but the seventh year you shall let it rest and lie fallow, that the poor of your people may eat; and what they leave the wild beasts may eat. You shall do likewise with your vineyard, and with your olive orchard.

"Six days you shall do your work, but on the seventh day you shall rest; that your ox and your ass may have rest, and the son of your bondmaid, and the alien, may be refreshed. Take heed to all that I have said to you; and make no mention of the names of other gods, nor let such be heard out of your mouth.

"Three times in the year you shall keep a feast to me. You shall keep the feast of unleavened bread; as I commanded you, you shall eat unleavened bread for seven days at the appointed time in the month of Abib, for in it you came out of Egypt. None shall appear before me empty-handed. You shall keep the feast of harvest, of the first fruits of your labor, of what you sow in the field. You shall keep the feast of ingathering at the end of the year, when you gather in from the field the fruit of your labor. Three times in the year shall all your males appear before the Lord God.

"You shall not offer the blood of my sacrifice with leavened bread, or let the fat of my feast remain until the morning.

"The first of the first fruits of your ground you shall bring into the house of the Lord your God.

"You shall not boil a kid in its mother's milk.

"Behold, I send an angel before you, to guard you on the way and to bring you to the place which I have prepared. Give heed to him and hearken to his voice, do not rebel against him, for he will not pardon your transgression; for my name is in him.

"But if you hearken attentively to his voice and do all that I say, then I will be an enemy to your enemies and an adversary to your adversaries.

"When my angel goes before you, and brings you in to the Amorites, and the Hittites, and the Per'izzites, and the Canaanites, the Hivites, and the Jeb'usites, and I blot them out, you shall not bow down to their gods, nor serve them, nor do according to their works, but you shall utterly overthrow them and break their pillars in pieces. You shall serve the Lord your God, and I will bless your bread and your water; and I will take sickness away from the midst of you. None shall cast her young or be barren in your land; I will fulfil the number of your days. I will send my terror before you, and will throw into confusion all the people against whom you shall come, and I will make all your enemies turn their backs to you. And I will send hornets before you, which shall drive out Hivite, Canaanite, and Hittite from before you. I will not drive them out from before you in one year, lest the land become desolate and the wild beasts multiply against you. Little by little I will drive them out from before you, until you are increased and possess the land. And I will set your bounds from the Red Sea to the sea of the Philistines, and from the wilderness to the Eu-phra'tes; for I will deliver the inhabitants of the land into your hand, and you shall drive them out before you. You shall make no covenant with them or with their gods.

They shall not dwell in your land lest they make you sin against me; for if you serve their gods, it will surely be a snare to you."

AMOS

The Prophecy

1:1–2;   2:4–3:8;   5:1–27;   8:1–10

The words of Amos, who was among the shepherds of Teko'a, which he saw concerning Israel in the days of Uzzi'ah king of Judah and in the days of Jerobo'am the son of Jo'ash, king of Israel, two years before the earthquake. And he said:

"The Lord roars from Zion,
  and utters his voice from Jerusalem;
the pastures of the shepherds mourn,
  and the top of Carmel withers.

• • •

Thus says the Lord:
"For three transgressions of Judah,
  and for four, I will not revoke the punishment;
because they have rejected the law of the Lord,
  and have not kept his statutes,
but their lies have led them astray,
  after which their fathers walked.
So I will send a fire upon Judah,
  and it shall devour the strongholds of Jerusalem."

Thus says the Lord:
"For three transgressions of Israel,
  and for four, I will not revoke the punishment;
because they sell the righteous for silver,
  and the needy for a pair of shoes—
they that trample the head of the poor into the dust of the earth,
  and turn aside the way of the afflicted;
a man and his father go in to the same maiden,
  so that my holy name is profaned;
they lay themselves down beside every altar
  upon garments taken in pledge;

and in the house of their God they drink
 the wine of those who have been fined.
"Yet I destroyed the Amorite before them,
 whose height was like the height of the cedars,
 and who was as strong as the oaks;
I destroyed his fruit above,
 and his roots beneath.
Also I brought you up out of the land of Egypt,
 and led you forty years in the wilderness,
 to possess the land of the Amorite.
And I raised up some of your sons for prophets,
 and some of your young men for Nazirites.
 Is it not indeed so, O people of Israel?"
        says the Lord.

"But you made the Nazirites drink wine,
 and commanded the prophets,
 saying, 'You shall not prophesy.'
"Behold, I will press you down in your place,
 as a cart full of sheaves presses down.
Flight shall perish from the swift,
 and the strong shall not retain his strength,
 nor shall the mighty save his life;
he who handles the bow shall not stand,
 and he who is swift of foot shall not save himself,
 nor shall he who rides the horse save his life;
and he who is stout of heart among the mighty
 shall flee away naked in that day,"
        says the Lord.

Hear this word that the Lord has spoken against you, O people of
Israel, against the whole family which I brought up out of the land of
Egypt:

"You only have I known
 of all the families of the earth
therefore I will punish you
 for all your iniquities.

"Do two walk together,
 unless they have made an appointment?

Does a lion roar in the forest,
    when he has no prey?
Does a young lion cry out from his den,
    if he has taken nothing?
Does a bird fall in a snare on the earth,
    when there is no trap for it?
Does a snare spring up from the ground,
    when it has taken nothing?
Is a trumpet blown in a city,
    and the people are not afraid?
Does evil befall a city,
    unless the LORD has done it?
Surely the Lord GOD does nothing,
    without revealing his secret
    to his servants the prophets.
The lion has roared;
    who will not fear?
The Lord GOD has spoken;
    who can but prophesy?"

•   •   •

Hear this word which I take up over you in lamentation, O house
of Israel:

"Fallen, no more to rise,
    is the virgin Israel;
forsaken on her land,
    with none to raise her up."

For thus says the Lord GOD:
"The city that went forth a thousand
    shall have a hundred left,
and that which went forth a hundred
    shall have ten left
    to the house of Israel."

For thus says the LORD to the house of Israel:
"Seek me and live;
    but do not seek Bethel,
and do not enter into Gilgal
    or cross over to Beer-sheba;

for Gilgal shall surely go into exile,
  and Bethel shall come to nought."

Seek the LORD and live,
  lest he break out like fire in the house of Joseph,
  and it devour, with none to quench it for Bethel,
O you who turn justice to wormwood,
  and cast down righteousness to the earth!

He who made the Plei'ades and Orion,
  and turns deep darkness into the morning,
  and darkens the day into night,
who calls for the waters of the sea,
  and pours them out upon the surface of the earth,
the LORD is his name,
who makes destruction flash forth against the strong,
  so that destruction comes upon the fortress.

They hate him who reproves in the gate,
  and they abhor him who speaks the truth.
Therefore because you trample upon the poor
  and take from him exactions of wheat,
you have built houses of hewn stone,
  but you shall not dwell in them;
you have planted pleasant vineyards,
  but you shall not drink their wine.
For I know how many are your transgressions,
  and how great are your sins—
you who afflict the righteous, who take a bribe,
  and turn aside the needy in the gate.
Therefore he who is prudent will keep silent in such a time;
  for it is an evil time.

Seek good, and not evil,
  that you may live;
and so the LORD, the God of hosts, will be with you,
  as you have said.
Hate evil, and love good,
  and establish justice in the gate;
it may be that the LORD, the God of hosts,
  will be gracious to the remnant of Joseph.

Therefore thus says the LORD, the God of hosts, the Lord:
"In all the squares there shall be wailing;
    and in all the streets they shall say, 'Alas! alas!'
They shall call the farmers to mourning
    and to wailing those who are skilled in lamentation,
and in all vineyards there shall be wailing,
    for I will pass through the midst of you,"
                                        says the LORD.

Woe to you who desire the day of the LORD!
    Why would you have the day of the LORD?
It is darkness, and not light;
    as if a man fled from a lion,
    and a bear met him;
or went into the house and leaned with his hand against the wall,
    and a serpent bit him.
Is not the day of the LORD darkness, and not light,
    and gloom with no brightness in it?

"I hate, I despise your feasts,
    and I take no delight in your solemn assemblies.
Even though you offer me your burnt offerings and cereal offerings,
    I will not accept them,
and the peace offerings of your fatted beasts
    I will not look upon.
Take away from me the noise of your songs;
    to the melody of your harps I will not listen.
But let justice roll down like waters,
    and righteousness like an ever-flowing stream.

"Did you bring to me sacrifices and offerings the forty years in the
wilderness, O house of Israel? You shall take up Sakkuth your king,
and Kaiwan your star-god, your images, which you made for yourselves; therefore I will take you into exile beyond Damascus," says
the LORD, whose name is the God of hosts.

• • •

Thus the Lord GOD showed me: behold, a basket of summer fruit.
And he said, "Amos, what do you see?" And I said, "A basket of
summer fruit." Then the LORD said to me,

"The end has come upon my people Israel;
I will never again pass by them.

The songs of the temple shall become wailings in that day,"
> says the Lord GOD;
"the dead bodies shall be many;
> in every place they shall be cast out in silence."

Hear this, you who trample upon the needy,
> and bring the poor of the land to an end,
saying, "When will the new moon be over,
> that we may sell grain?
And the sabbath,
> that we may offer wheat for sale,
that we may make the ephah small and the shekel great,
> and deal deceitfully with false balances,
that we may buy the poor for silver
> and the needy for a pair of sandals,
> and sell the refuse of the wheat?"

The LORD has sworn by the pride of Jacob:
> "Surely I will never forget any of their deeds.
Shall not the land tremble on this account,
> and every one mourn who dwells in it,
and all of it rise like the Nile,
> and be tossed about and sink again, like the Nile of Egypt?"

"And on that day," says the Lord GOD,
> "I will make the sun go down at noon,
> and darken the earth in broad daylight.
I will turn your feasts into mourning,
> and all your songs into lamentation;
I will bring sackcloth upon all loins
> and baldness on every head;
I will make it like the mourning for an only son,
> and the end of it like a bitter day.

ISAIAH

The Prophecy

40:1–41:14;   45:8–25;   52:13–53:12

> Comfort, comfort my people,
> > says your God.
> Speak tenderly to Jerusalem,
> > and cry to her

that her warfare is ended,
   that her iniquity is pardoned,
that she has received from the Lord's hand
   double for all her sins.

A voice cries:
"In the wilderness prepare the way of the Lord,
   make straight in the desert a highway for our God.
Every valley shall be lifted up,
   and every mountain and hill be made low;
the uneven ground shall become level,
   and the rough places a plain.
And the glory of the Lord shall be revealed,
   and all flesh shall see it together,
   for the mouth of the Lord has spoken."

A voice says, "Cry!"
   And I said, "What shall I cry?"
All flesh is grass,
   and all its beauty is like the flower of the field.
The grass withers, the flower fades,
   when the breath of the Lord blows upon it;
   surely the people is grass.
The grass withers, the flower fades;
   but the word of our God will stand for ever.

Get you up to a high mountain,
   O Zion, herald of good tidings;
lift up your voice with strength,
   O Jerusalem, herald of good tidings,
   lift it up, fear not;
say to the cities of Judah,
   "Behold your God!"
Behold, the Lord God comes with might,
   and his arm rules for him;
behold, his reward is with him,
   and his recompense before him.
He will feed his flock like a shepherd,
   he will gather the lambs in his arms,
he will carry them in his bosom,
   and gently lead those that are with young.

Who has measured the waters in the hollow of his hand
  and marked off the heavens with a span,
enclosed the dust of the earth in a measure
  and weighed the mountains in scales
  and the hills in a balance?
Who has directed the Spirit of the Lord,
  or as his counselor has instructed him?
Whom did he consult for his enlightenment,
  and who taught him the path of justice,
and taught him knowledge,
  and showed him the way of understanding?
Behold, the nations are like a drop from a bucket,
  and are accounted as the dust on the scales;
  behold, he takes up the isles like fine dust.
Lebanon would not suffice for fuel,
  nor are its beasts enough for a burnt offering.
All the nations are as nothing before him,
  they are accounted by him as less than nothing and emptiness.

To whom then will you liken God,
  or what likeness compare with him?
The idol! a workman casts it,
  and a goldsmith overlays it with gold,
  and casts for it silver chains.
He who is impoverished chooses for an offering
  wood that will not rot;
he seeks out a skilful craftsman
  to set up an image that will not move.

Have you not known? Have you not heard?
  Has it not been told you from the beginning?
  Have you not understood from the foundations of the earth?
It is he who sits above the circle of the earth,
  and its inhabitants are like grasshoppers;
who stretches out the heavens like a curtain,
  and spreads them like a tent to dwell in;
who brings princes to nought,
  and makes the rulers of the earth as nothing.

Scarcely are they planted, scarcely sown,
  scarcely has their stem taken root in the earth,

when he blows upon them, and they wither,
   and the tempest carries them off like stubble.
To whom then will you compare me,
   that I should be like him? says the Holy One.
Lift up your eyes on high and see:
   who created these?
He who brings out their host by number,
   calling them all by name;
by the greatness of his might,
   and because he is strong in power
   not one is missing.

Why do you say, O Jacob,
   and speak, O Israel,
"My way is hid from the Lord,
   and my right is disregarded by my God"?
Have you not known? Have you not heard?
The Lord is the everlasting God,
   the Creator of the ends of the earth.
He does not faint or grow weary,
   his understanding is unsearchable.
He gives power to the faint,
   and to him who has no might he increases strength.
Even youths shall faint and be weary,
   and young men shall fall exhausted;
but they who wait for the Lord shall renew their strength,
   they shall mount up with wings like eagles,
they shall run and not be weary,
   they shall walk and not faint.

Listen to me in silence, O coastlands;
   let the peoples renew their strength;
let them approach, then let them speak;
   let us together draw near for judgment.

Who stirred up one from the east
   whom victory meets at every step?
He gives up nations before him,
   so that he tramples kings under foot;
he makes them like dust with his sword,
   like driven stubble with his bow.

He pursues them and passes on safely,
  by paths his feet have not trod.
Who has performed and done this,
  calling the generations from the beginning?
I, the Lord, the first,
  and with the last; I am He.

The coastlands have seen and are afraid,
  the ends of the earth tremble;
  they have drawn near and come.
Every one helps his neighbor,
  and says to his brother, "Take courage!"
The craftsman encourages the goldsmith,
  and he who smooths with the hammer him who strikes the anvil,
saying of the soldering, "It is good";
  and they fasten it with nails so that it cannot be moved.

But you, Israel, my servant,
  Jacob, whom I have chosen,
  the offspring of Abraham, my friend;
you whom I took from the ends of the earth,
  and called from its farthest corners,
saying to you, "You are my servant,
  I have chosen you and not cast you off";
fear not, for I am with you,
  be not dismayed, for I am your God;
I will strengthen you, I will help you,
  I will uphold you with my victorious right hand.

Behold, all who are incensed against you
  shall be put to shame and confounded;
those who strive against you
  shall be as nothing and shall perish.
You shall seek those who contend with you,
  but you shall not find them;
those who war against you
  shall be as nothing at all.
For I, the Lord your God,
  hold your right hand;
it is I who say to you, "Fear not,
  I will help you."

Fear not, you worm Jacob,
  you men of Israel!
I will help you, says the Lord;
  your Redeemer is the Holy One of Israel.

• • •

"Shower, O heavens, from above,
  and let the skies rain down righteousness;
let the earth open, that salvation may sprout forth,
  and let it cause righteousness to spring up also;
  I the Lord have created it.

"Woe to him who strives with his Maker,
  an earthen vessel with the potter!"
Does the clay say to him who fashions it, 'What are you making'?
  or 'Your work has no handles'?
Woe to him who says to a father, 'What are you begetting?'
  or to a woman, 'With what are you in travail?' "
Thus says the Lord,
  the Holy One of Israel, and his Maker:
"Will you question me about my children,
  or command me concerning the work of my hands?
I made the earth,
  and created man upon it;
it was my hands that stretched out the heavens,
  and I commanded all their host.
I have aroused him in righteousness,
  and I will make straight all his ways;
he shall build my city
  and set my exiles free,
not for price or reward,"
  says the Lord of hosts.

Thus says the Lord:
"The wealth of Egypt and the merchandise of Ethiopia,
  and the Sabe'ans, men of stature,
shall come over to you and be yours,
  they shall follow you;
  they shall come over in chains and bow down to you.
They will make supplication to you, saying:
  'God is with you only, and there is no other,
  no god besides him.' "

Truly, thou art a God who hidest thyself,
 O God of Israel, the Savior.
All of them are put to shame and confounded,
 the makers of idols go in confusion together.
But Israel is saved by the Lord
 with everlasting salvation;
you shall not be put to shame or confounded
 to all eternity.

For thus says the Lord,
who created the heavens
 (he is God!),
who formed the earth and made it
 (he established it;
he did not create it a chaos,
 he formed it to be inhabited!):
"I am the Lord, and there is no other.
I did not speak in secret,
 in a land of darkness;
I did not say to the offspring of Jacob,
 'Seek me in chaos.'
I the Lord speak the truth,
 I declare what is right.

"Assemble yourselves and come,
 draw near together,
 you survivors of the nations!
They have no knowledge
 who carry about their wooden idols,
and keep on praying to a god
 that cannot save.
Declare and present your case;
 let them take counsel together!
Who told this long ago?
 Who declared it of old?
Was it not I, the Lord?
 And there is no other god besides me,
a righteous God and a Savior;
 there is none besides me.

"Turn to me and be saved,
 all the ends of the earth!

For I am God, and there is no other.
By myself I have sworn,
    from my mouth has gone forth in righteousness
    a word that shall not return:
'To me every knee shall bow,
    every tongue shall swear.'

"Only in the Lord, it shall be said of me,
    are righteousness and strength;
to him shall come and be ashamed,
    all who were incensed against him.
In the Lord all the offspring of Israel
    shall triumph and glory."

               •   •   •

Behold, my servant shall prosper,
    he shall be exalted and lifted up,
    and shall be very high.
As many were astonished at him—
    his appearance was so marred, beyond human semblance,
    and his form beyond that of the sons of men—
so shall he startle many nations;
    kings shall shut their mouths because of him;
for that which has not been told them they shall see,
    and that which they have not heard they shall understand.

Who has believed what we have heard?
    And to whom has the arm of the Lord been revealed?
For he grew up before him like a young plant,
    and like a root out of dry ground;
he had no form or comeliness that we should look at him,
    and no beauty that we should desire him.
He was despised and rejected by men;
    a man of sorrows, and acquainted with grief;
and as one from whom men hide their faces
    he was despised, and we esteemed him not.

Surely he has borne our griefs
    and carried our sorrows;
yet we esteemed him stricken,
    smitten by God, and afflicted.

But he was wounded for our transgressions,
   he was bruised for our iniquities;
upon him was the chastisement that made us whole,
   and with his stripes we are healed.
All we like sheep have gone astray;
   we have turned every one to his own way;
and the Lord has laid on him
   the iniquity of us all.

He was oppressed, and he was afflicted,
   yet he opened not his mouth;
like a lamb that is led to the slaughter,
   and like a sheep that before its shearers is dumb,
   so he opened not his mouth.
By oppression and judgment he was taken away;
   and as for his generation, who considered
that he was cut off out of the land of the living,
   stricken for the transgression of my people?
And they made his grave with the wicked
   and with a rich man in his death,
although he had done no violence,
   and there was no deceit in his mouth.

Yet it was the will of the LORD to bruise him;
   he has put him to grief;
when he makes himself an offering for sin,
   he shall see his offspring, he shall prolong his days;
the will of the LORD shall prosper in his hand;
   he shall see the fruit of the travail of his soul and be satisfied;
by his knowledge shall the righteous one, my servant,
   make many to be accounted righteous;
   and he shall bear their iniquities.
Therefore I will divide him a portion with the great,
   and he shall divide the spoil with the strong;
because he poured out his soul to death,
   and was numbered with the transgressors;
yet he bore the sin of many,
   and made intercession for the transgressors.

22

New Testament

The New Testament is so called because the Christians claim that the message of Jesus represents a new covenant or testament (the words are the same in Greek), superseding the old one entered into between God and the Jews. The twenty-seven books that make up the New Testament were not written as a unified work but on a piecemeal basis, during the second half of the first century, in each case to meet a particular practical requirement. Moreover, they were not regarded as sacred, as were the scriptures of the Jews, until the second century or later, and it was not until 367 that the contents, as we know them now, were authoritatively promulgated. The New Testament is the result of a slow winnowing-out process from an extensive body of early Christian writings, some of which still survive as the Apocrypha (writings of disputed authority). Although, as with the Jewish scriptures, the New Testament was not a product of the Western mind, it has pervaded it through and through, so that the Judeo-Christian tradition and Western culture are now inseparable.

The following selections deal with some of the most fundamental matters of Christian faith—convictions arrived at not by reasoning, as in the philosophies, but by an intuitive response to the life and teachings of a unique personality. As such, they are highly colored by the prescientific thought-forms and terminology of the first century of our era.

These influences themselves underwent alteration from the outset. The gospel was first preached in a Jewish atmosphere in Palestine, where ideas of a "Messiah," a "Kingdom of God," and a "Son of Man" were current. As the Christian movement became more and more identified with the gentiles (non-Jews), its message was restated in a form intelligible to Greek-speaking peoples. Such different terms as "Savior," "Son of God," and "Body of

Christ" then appeared. This development is to be seen especially in the Gospel according to St. John (dating ca. 100), where Jesus appears not merely as a human teacher and prophet favored by God, but as a divine being.

The Sermon on the Mount, from the Gospel according to St. Matthew (dating ca. 90), represents another aspect of Christian tradition—the ethical aspect. Jesus's words go beyond the Law of Moses and summon men to an inwardness of religious life in place of the Jewish externalism of that day. The three chapters from St. Matthew included here are probably the best known in the Bible, and the most popular despite the demands they make upon those who have chosen to commit themselves to God rather than to self.

The crucifixion of Jesus had appeared to his friends and enemies as the termination of an ill-fated religious mission. But his disciples soon became convinced of his resurrection from death and awaited Jesus's promised power to carry his gospel to the ends of the earth. Seven weeks after the reported resurrection, on the day of Pentecost in the Christian calendar, the disciples were "filled with the Holy Spirit." Thus, the Christian Church was born, and the disciples proceeded upon the work of converting Jews and other non-believers. The remarkable story of these missionary beginnings is told in the fifth book of the New Testament, the Acts of the Apostles (ca. 50).

Probably the most influential of the apostles was St. Paul, an ardent convert to the faith. He proved to be a fearless preacher and organizer, founding and guiding new congregations in Asia Minor and Greece and giving instruction through numerous personal visits and letters. One of the most significant of these letters is excerpted here—St. Paul's first letter to the Corinthians (I Corinthians), which was written about the year 55. In a style characteristic of his letters it answers questions from the congregation at Corinth and gives authoritative advice on such matters as Christian sexual morality, the conduct of Church services, and the differing roles of men and women. The letter also explains to the Corinthians the proper way of partaking of the Lord's Supper (the earliest sacrament), the supreme value of Christian love, and the nature of the resurrection of bodies after death. Later incorporated into Holy Scripture, these words of St. Paul were to exercise enormous influence on the thinking and practices of Christians for centuries to come.

ST. MATTHEW

The Sermon on the Mount

4:23–7:29

And he went about all Galilee, teaching in their synagogues and preaching the gospel of the kingdom and healing every disease and every infirmity among the people. So his fame spread throughout all Syria, and they brought him all the sick, those afflicted with various diseases and pains, demoniacs, epileptics, and paralytics, and he healed them. And great crowds followed him from Galilee and the Decap'olis and Jerusalem and Judea and from beyond the Jordan.

Seeing the crowds, he went up on the mountain, and when he sat down his disciples came to him. And he opened his mouth and taught them, saying:

"Blessed are the poor in spirit, for theirs is the kingdom of heaven.

"Blessed are those who mourn, for they shall be comforted.

"Blessed are the meek, for they shall inherit the earth.

"Blessed are those who hunger and thirst for righteousness, for they shall be satisfied.

"Blessed are the merciful, for they shall obtain mercy.

"Blessed are the pure in heart, for they shall see God.

"Blessed are the peacemakers, for they shall be called sons of God.

"Blessed are those who are persecuted for righteousness' sake, for theirs is the kingdom of heaven.

"Blessed are you when men revile you and persecute you and utter all kinds of evil against you falsely on my account. Rejoice and be glad, for your reward is great in heaven, for so men persecuted the prophets who were before you.

"You are the salt of the earth; but if salt has lost its taste, how shall its saltness be restored? It is no longer good for anything except to be thrown out and trodden under foot by men.

"You are the light of the world. A city set on a hill cannot be hid. Nor do men light a lamp and put it under a bushel, but on a stand, and it gives light to all in the house. Let your light so shine before men, that they may see your good works and give glory to your Father who is in heaven.

"Think not that I have come to abolish the law and the prophets; I have come not to abolish them but to fulfil them. For truly, I say to you, till heaven and earth pass away, not an iota, not a dot, will pass from the law until all is accomplished. Whoever then relaxes one of the least of these commandments and teaches men so, shall be called least in the kingdom of heaven; but he who does them and teaches them shall be called great in the kingdom of heaven. For I tell you, unless your righteousness exceeds that of the scribes and Pharisees, you will never enter the kingdom of heaven.

"You have heard that it was said to the men of old, 'You shall not kill; and whoever kills shall be liable to judgment.' But I say to you that every one who is angry with his brother shall be liable to judgment; whoever insults his brother shall be liable to the council, and whoever says, 'You fool!' shall be liable to the hell of fire. So if you are offering your gift at the altar, and there remember that your brother has something against you, leave your gift there before the altar and go; first be reconciled to your brother, and then come and offer your gift. Make friends quickly with your accuser, while you are going with him to court, lest your accuser hand you over to the judge, and the judge to the guard, and you be put in prison; truly, I say to you, you will never get out till you have paid the last penny.

"You have heard that it was said, 'You shall not commit adultery.' But I say to you that every one who looks at a woman lustfully has already committed adultery with her in his heart. If your right eye causes you to sin, pluck it out and throw it away; it is better that you lose one of your members than that your whole body be thrown into hell. And if your right hand causes you to sin, cut it off and throw it away; it is better that you lose one of your members than that your whole body go into hell.

"It was also said, 'Whoever divorces his wife, let him give her a certificate of divorce.' But I say to you that every one who divorces his wife, except on the ground of unchastity, makes her an adulteress; and whoever marries a divorced woman commits adultery.

"Again you have heard that it was said to the men of old, 'You shall not swear falsely, but shall perform to the Lord what you have sworn.' But I say to you, Do not swear at all, either by heaven, for it is the throne of God, or by the earth, for it is his footstool, or by Jerusalem, for it is the city of the great King. And do not swear by your head, for you cannot make one hair white or black. Let what you say be simply 'Yes' or 'No'; anything more than this comes from evil.

"You have heard that it was said, 'An eye for an eye and a tooth for a tooth.' But I say to you, Do not resist one who is evil. But if any one strikes you on the right cheek, turn to him the other also; and if any one would sue you and take your coat, let him have your cloak as well; and if any one forces you to go one mile, go with him two miles. Give to him who begs from you, and do not refuse him who would borrow from you.

"You have heard that it was said, 'You shall love your neighbor and hate your enemy.' But I say to you, Love your enemies and pray for those who persecute you, so that you may be sons of your Father who is in heaven; for he makes his sun rise on the evil and on the good, and sends rain on the just and on the unjust. For if you love those who love you, what reward have you? Do not even the tax collectors do the same? And if you salute only your brethren, what more are you doing than others? Do not even the Gentiles do the same? You, therefore, must be perfect, as your heavenly Father is perfect.

"Beware of practicing your piety before men in order to be seen by them; for then you will have no reward from your Father who is in heaven.

"Thus, when you give alms, sound no trumpet before you, as the hypocrites do in the synagogues and in the streets, that they may be praised by men. Truly, I say to you, they have received their reward. But when you give alms, do not let your left hand know what your right hand is doing, so that your alms may be in secret; and your Father who sees in secret will reward you.

"And when you pray, you must not be like the hypocrites; for they love to stand and pray in the synagogues and at the street corners, that they may be seen by men. Truly, I say to you, they have received their reward. But when you pray, go into your room and shut the door and pray to your Father who is in secret; and your Father who sees in secret will reward you.

"And in praying do not heap up empty phrases as the Gentiles do; for they think that they will be heard for their many words. Do not be like them, for your Father knows what you need before you ask him. Pray then like this:

> Our Father who art in heaven,
> Hallowed be thy name.
> Thy kingdom come,
> Thy will be done,
>   On earth as it is in heaven.
> Give us this day our daily bread;

And forgive us our debts,
>   As we also have forgiven our debtors;
And lead us not into temptation,
>   But deliver us from evil.

For if you forgive men their trespasses, your heavenly Father also will forgive you; but if you do not forgive men their trespasses, neither will your Father forgive your trespasses.

"And when you fast, do not look dismal, like the hypocrites, for they disfigure their faces that their fasting may be seen by men. Truly, I say to you, they have received their reward. But when you fast, anoint your head and wash your face, that your fasting may not be seen by men but by your Father who is in secret; and your Father who sees in secret will reward you.

"Do not lay up for yourselves treasures on earth, where moth and rust consume and where thieves break in and steal, but lay up for yourselves treasure in heaven, where neither moth nor rust consumes and where thieves do not break in and steal. For where your treasure is, there will your heart be also.

"The eye is the lamp of the body. So, if your eye is sound, your whole body will be full of light; but if your eye is not sound, your whole body will be full of darkness. If then the light in you is darkness, how great is the darkness!

"No one can serve two masters; for either he will hate the one and love the other, or he will be devoted to the one and despise the other. You cannot serve God and mammon.

"Therefore I tell you, do not be anxious about your life, what you shall eat or what you shall drink, nor about your body, what you shall put on. Is not life more than food, and the body more than clothing? Look at the birds of the air: they neither sow nor reap nor gather into barns, and yet your heavenly Father feeds them. Are you not of more value than they? And which of you by being anxious can add one cubit to his span of life? And why are you anxious about clothing? Consider the lilies of the field, how they grow; they neither toil nor spin; yet I tell you, even Solomon in all his glory was not arrayed like one of these. But if God so clothes the grass of the field, which today is alive and tomorrow is thrown into the oven, will he not much more clothe you, O men of little faith? Therefore do not be anxious, saying, 'What shall we eat?' or 'What shall we drink?' or 'What shall we wear?' For the Gentiles seek all these things; and your heavenly Father knows that you need them all. But seek first his kingdom and his righteousness, and all these things shall be yours as well.

"Therefore do not be anxious about tomorrow, for tomorrow will be anxious for itself. Let the day's own trouble be sufficient for the day.

"Judge not, that you be not judged. For with the judgment you pronounce you will be judged, and the measure you give will be the measure you get. Why do you see the speck that is in your brother's eye, but do not notice the log that is in your own eye? Or how can you say to your brother, 'Let me take the speck out of your eye,' when there is the log in your own eye? You hypocrite, first take the log out of your own eye, and then you will see clearly to take the speck out of your brother's eye.

"Do not give dogs what is holy; and do not throw your pearls before swine, lest they trample them under foot and turn to attack you.

Ask, and it will be given you; seek, and you will find; knock, and it will be opened to you. For every one who asks receives, and he who seeks finds, and to him who knocks it will be opened. Or what man of you, if his son asks him for bread, will give him a stone? Or if he asks for a fish, will give him a serpent? If you then, who are evil, know how to give good gifts to your children, how much more will your Father who is in heaven give good things to those who ask him! So whatever you wish that men would do to you, do so to them; for this is the law and the prophets.

"Enter by the narrow gate; for the gate is wide and the way is easy, that leads to destruction, and those who enter by it are many. For the gate is narrow and the way is hard, that leads to life, and those who find it are few.

"Beware of false prophets, who come to you in sheep's clothing but inwardly are ravenous wolves. You will know them by their fruits. Are grapes gathered from thorns, or figs from thistles? So, every sound tree bears good fruit, but the bad tree bears evil fruit. A sound tree cannot bear evil fruit, nor can a bad tree bear good fruit. Every tree that does not bear good fruit is cut down and thrown into the fire. Thus you will know them by their fruits.

"Not every one who says to me, 'Lord, Lord,' shall enter the kingdom of heaven, but he who does the will of my Father who is in heaven. On that day many will say to me, 'Lord, Lord, did we not prophesy in your name, and cast out demons in your name, and do many mighty works in your name?' And then will I declare to them, 'I never knew you; depart from me, you evildoers.'

"Every one then who hears these words of mine and does them will be like a wise man who built his house upon the rock; and the rain fell, and the floods came, and the winds blew and beat upon that house, but it did not fall, because it had been founded on the rock. And every one who hears these words of mine and does not do them will be like a foolish man who built his house upon the sand; and the rain fell, and the floods came, and the winds blew and beat against that house, and it fell; and great was the fall of it."

And when Jesus finished these sayings, the crowds were astonished at his teaching, for he taught them as one who had authority, and not as their scribes.

ST. JOHN

Jesus, the Divine Being

1:1–18;   6:30–59;   13:36–14:11

In the beginning was the Word, and the Word was with God, and the Word was God. He was in the beginning with God; all things were made through him, and without him was not anything made that was made. In him was life, and the life was the light of men. The light shines in the darkness, and the darkness has not overcome it.

There was a man sent from God, whose name was John. He came for testimony, to bear witness to the light, that all might believe through him. He was not the light, but came to bear witness to the light.

The true light that enlightens every man was coming into the world. He was in the world, and the world was made through him, yet the world knew him not. He came to his own home, and his own people received him not. But to all who received him, who believed in his name, he gave power to become children of God; who were born, not of blood nor of the will of the flesh nor of the will of man, but of God.

And the Word became flesh and dwelt among us, full of grace and truth; we have beheld his glory, glory as of the only Son from the

Father. (John bore witness to him, and cried, "This was he of whom I said, 'He who comes after me ranks before me, for he was before me.' ") And from his fulness have we all received, grace upon grace. For the law was given through Moses; grace and truth came through Jesus Christ. No one has ever seen God; the only Son who is in the bosom of the Father, he has made him known.

. . .

So they said to him, "Then what sign do you do, that we may see, and believe you? What work do you perform? Our fathers ate the manna in the wilderness; as it is written, 'He gave them bread from heaven to eat.' " Jesus then said to them, "Truly, truly, I say to you, it was not Moses who gave you the bread from heaven; my Father gives you the true bread from heaven. For the bread of God is that which comes down from heaven, and gives life to the world." They said to him, "Lord, give us this bread always."

Jesus said to them, "I am the bread of life; he who comes to me shall not hunger, and he who believes in me shall never thirst. But I said to you that you have seen me and yet do not believe. All that the Father gives me will come to me; and him who comes to me I will not cast out. For I have come down from heaven, not to do my own will, but the will of him who sent me; and this is the will of him who sent me, that I should lose nothing of all that he has given me, but raise it up at the last day. For this is the will of my Father, that every one who sees the Son and believes in him should have eternal life; and I will raise him up at the last day."

The Jews then murmured at him, because he said, "I am the bread which came down from heaven." They said, "Is not this Jesus, the son of Joseph, whose father and mother we know? How does he now say, 'I have come down from heaven'?" Jesus answered them, "Do not murmur among yourselves. No one can come to me unless the Father who sent me draws him; and I will raise him up at the last day. It is written in the prophets, 'And they shall all be taught by God.' Every one who has heard and learned from the Father comes to me. Not that any one has seen the Father except him who is from God; he has seen the Father. Truly, truly, I say to you, he who believes has eternal life. I am the bread of life. Your fathers ate the manna in the wilderness, and they died. This is the bread which comes down from heaven, that a man may eat of it and not die. I am the living bread which came down from heaven; if any one eats of this bread, he will live for ever; and the bread which I shall give for the life of the world is my flesh."

The Jews then disputed among themselves, saying, "How can this man give us his flesh to eat?" So Jesus said to them, "Truly, truly, I say to you, unless you eat the flesh of the Son of man and drink his blood, you have no life in you; he who eats my flesh and drinks my blood has eternal life, and I will raise him up at the last day. For my flesh is food indeed, and my blood is drink indeed. He who eats my flesh and drinks my blood abides in me, and I in him. As the living Father sent me, and I live because of the Father, so he who eats me will live because of me. This is the bread which came down from heaven, not such as the fathers ate and died; he who eats this bread will live for ever." This he said in the synagogue, as he taught at Ca-per′na-um.

• • •

Simon Peter said to him, "Lord, where are you going?" Jesus answered, "Where I am going you cannot follow me now; but you shall follow afterward." Peter said to him, "Lord, why cannot I follow you now? I will lay down my life for you." Jesus answered, "Will you lay down your life for me? Truly, truly, I say to you, the cock will not crow, till you have denied me three times.

"Let not your hearts be troubled; believe in God, believe also in me. In my Father's house are many rooms; if it were not so, would I have told you that I go to prepare a place for you? And when I go and prepare a place for you, I will come again and will take you to myself, that where I am you may be also. And you know the way where I am going." Thomas said to him, "Lord, we do not know where you are going; how can we know the way?" Jesus said to him, "I am the way, and the truth, and the life; no one comes to the Father, but by me. If you had known me, you would have known my Father also; henceforth you know him and have seen him."

Philip said to him, "Lord, show us the Father, and we shall be satisfied." Jesus said to him, "Have I been with you so long, and yet you do not know me, Philip? He who has seen me has seen the Father; how can you say, 'Show us the Father'? Do you not believe that I am in the Father and the Father in me? The words that I say to you I do not speak on my own authority, but the Father, who dwells in me does his works. Believe me that I am in the Father and the Father in me; or else believe me for the sake of the works themselves.

THE ACTS OF THE APOSTLES

The Beginnings of the Church

1:1–2:47

In the first book, O The-oph'ilus, I have dealt with all that Jesus began to do and teach, until the day when he was taken up, after he had given commandment through the Holy Spirit to the apostles whom he had chosen. To them he presented himself alive after his passion by many proofs, appearing to them during forty days, and speaking of the kingdom of God. And while staying with them he charged them not to depart from Jerusalem, but to wait for the promise of the Father, which, he said, "you heard from me, for John baptized with water, but before many days you shall be baptized with the Holy Spirit."

So when they had come together, they asked him, "Lord will you at this time restore the kingdom to Israel?" He said to them, "It is not for you to know times or seasons which the Father has fixed by his own authority. But you shall receive power when the Holy Spirit has come upon you; and you shall be my witnesses in Jerusalem and in all Judea and Samar'ia and to the end of the earth." And when he had said this, as they were looking on, he was lifted up, and a cloud took him out of their sight. And while they were gazing into heaven as he went, behold, two men stood by them in white robes, and said, "Men of Galilee, why do you stand looking into heaven? This Jesus, who was taken up from you into heaven, will come in the same way as you saw him go into heaven."

Then they returned to Jerusalem from the mount called Olivet, which is near Jerusalem, a sabbath day's journey away; and when they had entered, they went up to the upper room, where they were staying, Peter and John and James and Andrew, Philip and Thomas, Bartholomew and Matthew, James the son of Alphaeus and Simon the Zealot and Judas the son of James. All these with one accord devoted themselves to prayer, together with the women and Mary the mother of Jesus, and with his brothers.

In those days Peter stood up among the brethren (the company of persons was in all about a hundred and twenty), and said, "Brethren, the scripture had to be fulfilled, which the Holy Spirit spoke before-hand by the mouth of David, concerning Judas who was guide to those who arrested Jesus. For he was numbered among us, and was allotted his share in this ministry. (Now this man bought a field with the reward of his wickedness; and falling headlong he burst open in the middle and all his bowels gushed out. And it became known to all the inhabitants of Jerusalem, so that the field was called in their language Akel'dama, that is, Field of Blood.) For it is written in the book of Psalms,

'Let his habitation become desolate, and let there be no one to live in it';

and

'His office let another take.'

So one of the men who have accompanied us during all the time that the Lord Jesus went in and out among us, beginning from the baptism of John until the day when he was taken up from us—one of these men must become with us a witness to his resurrection." And they put forward two, Joseph called Barsabbas, who was surnamed Justus, and Matthi'as. And they prayed and said, "Lord, who knowest the hearts of all men, show which one of these two thou hast chosen to take the place in this ministry and apostleship from which Judas turned aside, to go to his own place." And they cast lots for them, and the lot fell on Matthi'as; and he was enrolled with the eleven apostles.

When the day of Pentecost had come, they were all together in one place. And suddenly a sound came from heaven like the rush of a mighty wind, and it filled all the house where they were sitting. And there appeared to them tongues as of fire, distributed and resting on each one of them. And they were all filled with the Holy Spirit and began to speak in other tongues, as the Spirit gave them utterance.

Now there were dwelling in Jerusalem Jews, devout men from every nation under heaven. And at this sound the multitude came together, and they were bewildered, because each one heard them speaking in his own language. And they were amazed and wondered, saying, "Are not all these who are speaking Galileans? And how is it that we hear, each of us in his own native language? Par'thians and Medes and Elamites and residents of Mesopota'mia, Judea and Cappado'cia, Pontus and Asia, Phryg'ia and Pamphyl'ia, Egypt and the parts of Libya belonging to Cyre'ne, and visitors from Rome, both Jews and proselytes, Cretans and Arabians, we hear them telling in our own tongues the mighty works of God." And all were amazed and perplexed, saying to one another, "What does this mean?" But others mocking said, "They are filled with new wine."

But Peter, standing with the eleven, lifted up his voice and addressed them, "Men of Judea and all who dwell in Jerusalem, let this be known to you, and give ear to my words. For these men are not drunk, as you suppose, since it is only the third hour of the day; but this is what was spoken by the prophet Jo'el:

> 'And in the last days it shall be, God declares,
> that I will pour out my Spirit upon all flesh,
> and your sons and your daughters shall prophesy,
> and your young men shall see visions,
> and your old men shall dream dreams;
> yea, and on my menservants and my maidservants in those days
> I will pour out my Spirit; and they shall prophesy.
> And I will show wonders in the heaven above
> and signs on the earth beneath,
> blood, and fire, and vapor of smoke;
> the sun shall be turned into darkness
> and the moon into blood,
> before the day of the Lord comes, the great and manifest day.
> And it shall be that whoever calls on the name of the Lord shall be
>   saved.'

"Men of Israel, hear these words: Jesus of Nazareth, a man attested to you by God with mighty works and wonders and signs which God did through him in your midst, as you yourselves know—this Jesus, delivered up according to the definite plan and foreknowledge of God, you crucified and killed by the hands of lawless men. But God raised him up, having loosed the pangs of death, because it was not possible for him to be held by it. For David says concerning him,

> 'I saw the Lord always before me,
> for he is at my right hand that I may not be shaken;
> therefore my heart was glad, and my tongue rejoiced;
> moreover my flesh will dwell in hope.
> For thou wilt not abandon my soul to Hades,
> nor let thy Holy One see corruption.
> Thou hast made known to me the ways of life;
> thou wilt make me full of gladness with thy presence.'

"Brethren, I may say to you confidently of the patriarch David that he both died and was buried, and his tomb is with us to this day. Being therefore a prophet, and knowing that God had sworn with an oath to him that he would set one of his descendants upon his throne, he foresaw and spoke of the resurrection of the Christ, that he was not abandoned to Hades, nor did his flesh see corruption. This Jesus God raised up, and of that we all are witnesses. Being therefore exalted at the right hand of God, and having received from the Father the promise of the Holy Spirit, he has poured out this which you see and hear. For David did not ascend into the heavens; but he himself says,

'The Lord said to my Lord, Sit at my right hand,
till I make [of] thy enemies a stool for thy feet.'

Let all the house of Israel therefore know assuredly that God has made him both Lord and Christ, this Jesus whom you crucified.''

Now when they heard this they were cut to the heart, and said to Peter and the rest of the apostles, "Brethren, what shall we do?" And Peter said to them, "Repent, and be baptized every one of you in the name of Jesus Christ for the forgiveness of your sins; and you shall receive the gift of the Holy Spirit. For the promise is to you and to your children and to all that are far off, every one whom the Lord our God calls to him." And he testified with many other words and exhorted them, saying, "Save yourselves from this crooked generation." So those who received his word were baptized, and there were added that day about three thousand souls. And they devoted themselves to the apostles' teaching and fellowship, to the breaking of bread and the prayers.

And fear came upon every soul; and many wonders and signs were done through the apostles. And all who believed were together and had all things in common; and they sold their possessions and goods and distributed them to all, as any had need. And day by day, attending the temple together and breaking bread in their homes, they partook of food with glad and generous hearts, praising God and having favor with all the people. And the Lord added to their number day by day those who were being saved.

THE FIRST LETTER OF PAUL TO THE CORINTHIANS

Salutation

1:1–3

Paul, called by the will of God to be an apostle of Christ Jesus, and our brother Sos'thenes,

To the church of God which is at Corinth, to those sanctified in Christ Jesus, called to be saints together with all those who in every place call on the name of our Lord Jesus Christ, both their Lord and ours:

Grace to you and peace from God our Father and the Lord Jesus Christ.

On Sexual Morality and Marriage

5:1–2;   7:1–11

It is actually reported that there is immorality among you, and of a kind that is not found even among pagans; for a man is living with his father's wife. And you are arrogant! Ought you not rather to mourn? Let him who has done this be removed from among you.

• • •

Now concerning the matters about which you wrote. It is well for a man not to touch a woman. But because of the temptation to immorality, each man should have his own wife and each woman her own husband. The husband should give to his wife her conjugal rights, and likewise the wife to her husband. For the wife does not rule over her own body, but the husband does; likewise the husband does not rule over his own body, but the wife does. Do not refuse one another except perhaps by agreement for a season, that you may devote yourselves to prayer; but then come together again, lest Satan tempt you through lack of self-control. I say this by way of concession, not of command. I wish that all were as I myself am. But each has his own special gift from God, one of one kind and one of another.

To the unmarried and the widows I say that it is well for them to remain single as I do. But if they cannot exercise self-control, they should marry. For it is better to marry than to be aflame with passion.

To the married I give charge, not I but the Lord, that the wife should not separate from her husband (but if she does, let her remain single or else be reconciled to her husband)—and that the husband should not divorce his wife.

On Roles of Men and Women

11:2–12;   14:34–35

I commend you because you remember me in everything and maintain the traditions even as I have delivered them to you. But I want you to understand that the head of every man is Christ, the head of a woman is her husband, and the head of Christ is God. Any man who prays or prophesies with his head covered dishonors his head, but any woman who prays or prophesies with her head unveiled dishonors her head—it is the same as if her head were shaven. For if a woman will not veil herself, then she should cut off her hair; but if it is disgraceful for a woman to be shorn or shaven, let her wear a veil. For a man ought not to cover his head, since he is the image and glory of God; but woman is the glory of man. (For man was not made from woman, but woman from man. Neither was man created for woman, but woman for man.) That is why a woman ought to have a veil on her head, because of the angels. (Nevertheless, in the Lord woman is not independent of man nor man of woman; for as woman was made from man, so man is now born of woman. And all things are from God.)

•   •   •

As in all the churches of the saints, the women should keep silence in the churches. For they are not permitted to speak, but should be subordinate, as even the law says. If there is anything they desire to know, let them ask their husbands at home. For it is shameful for a woman to speak in church.

The Lord's Supper

10:1–4,15–22;   11:17–27

I want you to know, brethren, that our fathers were all under the cloud, and all passed through the sea, and all were baptized into Moses in the cloud and in the sea, and all ate the same supernatural food and all drank the same supernatural drink. For they drank from the supernatural Rock which followed them, and the Rock was Christ. . . . I speak as to sensible men; judge for yourselves what I say. The cup of blessing which we bless, is it not a participation in the blood of Christ? The bread which we break, is it not a participation in the body of Christ? Because there is one bread, we who are many are one body, for we all partake of the one bread. Consider the people of Israel; are not those who eat the sacrifices partners in the altar? What do I imply then? That food offered to idols is anything, or that an idol is anything? No, I imply that what pagans sacrifice they offer to demons and not to God. I do not want you to be partners with demons. You cannot drink the cup of the Lord and the cup of demons. You cannot partake of the table of the Lord and the table of demons. Shall we provoke the Lord to jealousy? Are we stronger than he?

• • •

But in the following instructions I do not commend you, because when you come together it is not for the better but for the worse. For, in the first place, when you assemble as a church, I hear that there are divisions among you; and I partly believe it, for there must be factions among you in order that those who are genuine among you may be recognized. When you meet together, it is not the Lord's supper that you eat. For in eating, each one goes ahead with his own meal, and one is hungry and another is drunk. What! Do you not have houses to eat and drink in? Or do you despise the church of God and humiliate those who have nothing? What shall I say to you? Shall I commend you in this? No, I will not.

For I received from the Lord what I also delivered to you, that the Lord Jesus on the night when he was betrayed took bread, and when he had given thanks, he broke it, and said, "This is my body which is for you. Do this in remembrance of me." In the same way also the cup, after supper, saying, "This cup is the new covenant in my blood. Do this, as often as you drink it, in remembrance of me." For as often as you eat this bread and drink the cup, you proclaim the Lord's death until he comes.

Whoever, therefore, eats the bread or drinks the cup of the Lord in an unworthy manner will be guilty of profaning the body and blood of the Lord.

On Love

13:1–13

If I speak in the tongues of men and of angels, but have not love, I am a noisy gong or a clanging cymbal. And if I have prophetic powers, and understand all mysteries and all knowledge, and if I have all faith, so as to remove mountains, but have not love, I am nothing. If I give away all I have, and if I deliver my body to be burned, but have not love, I gain nothing.

Love is patient and kind; love is not jealous or boastful; it is not arrogant or rude. Love does not insist on its own way; it is not irritable or resentful; it does not rejoice at wrong, but rejoices in the right. Love bears all things, believes all things, hopes all things, endures all things.

Love never ends; as for prophecies, they will pass away; as for tongues, they will cease; as for knowledge, it will pass away. For our knowledge is imperfect and our prophecy is imperfect; but when the perfect comes, the imperfect will pass away. When I was a child, I spoke like a child, I thought like a child, I reasoned like a child; when I became a man, I gave up childish ways. For now we see in a mirror dimly, but then face to face. Now I know in part; then I shall understand fully, even as I have been fully understood. So faith, hope, love abide, these three; but the greatest of these is love.

Life After Death

15:1–58

Now I would remind you, brethren, in what terms I preached to you the gospel, which you received, in which you stand, by which you are saved, if you hold it fast—unless you believed in vain.

For I delivered to you as of first importance what I also received, that Christ died for our sins in accordance with the scriptures, that he was buried, that he was raised on the third day in accordance with the scriptures, and that he appeared to Cephas, then to the twelve. Then he appeared to more than five hundred brethren at one time, most of whom are still alive, though some have fallen asleep. Then he appeared to James, then to all the apostles. Last of all, as to one untimely born, he appeared also to me. For I am the least of the apostles, unfit to be called an apostle, because I persecuted the church of God. But by the grace of God I am what I am, and his grace toward me was not in vain. On the contrary, I worked harder than any of them, though it was not I, but the grace of God which is with me. Whether then it was I or they, so we preach and so you believed.

Now if Christ is preached as raised from the dead, how can some of you say that there is no resurrection of the dead? But if there is no resurrection of the dead, then Christ has not been raised; if Christ has not been raised, then our preaching is in vain and your faith is in vain. We are even found to be misrepresenting God, because we testified of God that he raised Christ, whom he did not raise if it is true that the dead are not raised. For if the dead are not raised, then Christ has not been raised. If Christ has not been raised, your faith is futile and you are still in your sins. Then those also who have fallen asleep in Christ have perished. If for this life only we have hoped in Christ, we are of all men most to be pitied.

But in fact Christ has been raised from the dead, the first fruits of those who have fallen asleep. For as by a man came death, by a man has come also the resurrection of the dead. For as in Adam all die, so also in Christ shall all be made alive. But each in his own order: Christ the first fruits, then at his coming those who belong to Christ. Then comes the end, when he delivers the kingdom to God the Father after destroying every rule and every authority and power. For he must reign until he has put all his enemies under his feet. The last enemy to be destroyed is death. "For God has put all things in subjection under his feet." But when it says, "All things are put in subjection under him," it is plain that he is excepted who put all things under him. When all things are subjected to him, then the Son himself will also be subjected to him who put all things under him, that God may be everything to every one.

Otherwise, what do people mean by being baptized on behalf of the dead? If the dead are not raised at all, why are people baptized on their behalf? Why am I in peril every hour? I protest, brethren, by my pride in you which I have in Christ Jesus our Lord, I die every day! What do I gain if, humanly speaking, I fought with beasts at Ephesus? If the dead are not raised, "Let us eat and drink, for tomorrow we die." Do not be deceived: "Bad company ruins good morals." Come to your right mind, and sin no more. For some have no knowledge of God. I say this to your shame.

But some one will ask, "How are the dead raised? With what kind of body do they come?" You foolish man! What you sow does not come to life unless it dies. And what you sow is not the body which is to be, but a bare kernel, perhaps of wheat or of some other grain. But God gives it a body as he has chosen, and to each kind of seed its own body. For not all flesh is alike, but there is one kind for men, another for animals, another for birds, and another for fish. There are celestial bodies and there are terrestrial bodies; but the glory of the celestial is one, and the glory of the terrestrial is another. There is one glory of the sun, and another glory of the moon, and another glory of the stars; for star differs from star in glory.

So is it with the resurrection of the dead. What is sown is perishable, what is raised is imperishable. It is sown in dishonor, it is raised in glory. It is sown in weakness, it is raised in power. It is sown a physical body, it is raised a spiritual body. If there is a physical body, there is also a spiritual body. Thus it is written, "The first man Adam became a living being"; the last Adam became a life-giving spirit. But it is not the spiritual which is first but the physical, and then the spiritual. The first man was from the earth, a man of dust; the second man is from heaven. As was the man of dust, so are those who are of the dust; and as is the man of heaven, so are those who are of heaven. Just as we have borne the image of the man of dust, we shall also bear the image of the man of heaven. I tell you this, brethren: flesh and blood cannot inherit the kingdom of God, nor does the perishable inherit the imperishable.

Lo! I tell you a mystery. We shall not all sleep, but we shall all be changed, in a moment, in the twinkling of an eye, at the last trumpet. For the trumpet will sound, and the dead will be raised imperishable, and we shall be changed. For this perishable nature must put on the imperishable, and this mortal nature must put on immortality. When the perishable puts on the imperishable, and the mortal puts on immortality, then shall come to pass the saying that is written:

> "Death is swallowed up in victory."
> "O death, where is thy victory?
> O death, where is thy sting?"

The sting of death is sin, and the power of sin is the law. But thanks be to God, who gives us the victory through our Lord Jesus Christ.

Therefore, my beloved brethren, be steadfast, immovable, always abounding in the work of the Lord, knowing that in the Lord your labor is not in vain.

23

St. Jerome

Letter CXXV

🔲

By the fourth century Christianity was making further inroads upon classical culture. Many devout Christian men and women of rank and fashion were abandoning civilized life in the cities and the civic and social responsibilities traditional to it—the supreme achievement of the ancient world—for a withdrawn life of solitude. The aspiration to pursue the "ascetic ideal," often in waste places, was fast becoming the greatest force in the life of the Church.

One of the most famous and influential of these ascetics was St. Jerome (Eusebius Hieronymus, ca. 340–420), born of Christian parents in the Roman province of Pannonia. Although a scholar and "intellectual," at twenty-eight St. Jerome retired to the Syrian desert near Antioch, sharing for five years the austerities of other Christian hermits there. In 382, he moved temporarily to Rome and became the fervid leader of a protest movement, not only against the secular world but against the increasing involvement of churchmen therein. When he left the metropolis, a pious group of aristocratic women accompanied him to Bethlehem, where he spent the remainder of his days in a monastery built with funds they provided. Devoted as ever to study and writing, he produced there (among other works) the famous Latin translation of the Bible known as the Vulgate.

Over 150 of his letters survive. The one reprinted here in part was written in 411 and represents a moderate expression of his asceticism. It furnishes the standard arguments for monasticism. Rusticus, whom St. Jerome addressed in the letter, took his advice, entered a monastery, and afterward became a bishop. The letter is notable also for revealing the decay of the

St. Jerome, *Select Letters*, trans. F. A. Wright (Loeb Classical Library—London: Heinemann and New York: Putnam, 1933), 407–19, 423–29, 435–39. Reprinted by permission of Harvard University Press.

classical spirit—that of Socrates and Plato, Cato and Cicero—and for illustrating the preoccupation of the kind of men who, in the pre-Christian era, would have served the state as generals and magistrates.

If you wish to be, and not merely seem, a monk, have regard not for your property—you began your vows by renouncing it—but for your soul. Let a squalid garb be the evidence of a clean heart: let a coarse tunic prove that you despise the world; provided only that you do not pride yourself on such things nor let your dress and language be at variance. Avoid hot baths: your aim is to quench the heat of the body by the help of chilling fasts. But let your fasts be moderate, since if they are carried to excess they weaken the stomach, and by making more food necessary to make up for it lead to indigestion, which is the parent of lust. A frugal, temperate diet is good both for body and soul.

See your mother often, but do not be forced to see other women when you visit her. Their faces may dwell in your heart and so

'A secret wound may fester in your breast.'

You must remember too that the maids who wait upon her are an especial snare; the lower they are in rank, the easier it is to ruin them. John the Baptist had a saintly mother and his father was a priest; but neither his mother's love nor his father's wealth could prevail upon him to live in his parents' house at the risk of his chastity. He took up his abode in the desert, and desiring only to see Christ refused to look at anything else. His rough garb, his skin girdle, his diet of locusts and wild honey were all alike meant to ensure virtue and self-restraint. The sons of the prophets, who are the monks of the Old Testament, built huts for themselves by the stream of Jordan, and leaving the crowded cities lived on porridge and wild herbs.

As long as you stay in your native city, regard your cell as Paradise, gather in it the varied fruits of the Scriptures, make them your delight, and rejoice in their embrace. If your eye or your foot or your hand offend you, cast it off. Spare nothing, provided that you spare your soul. 'Whosoever looketh on a woman to lust after her hath committed adultery with her already in his heart.' 'Who can boast "I have made my heart clean"?' The stars are not pure in God's sight: how much less are men, whose life is one long temptation! Woe to us, who commit fornication whenever we have lustful thoughts! 'My sword,' says the Scripture, 'hath drunk its fill in heaven': much more than will it on earth, which produces thorns and thistles. The chosen vessel, from whose mouth we hear Christ's own words, keeps his body under and brings it into subjection; but still he perceives that the natural heat of the body fights against his fixed purpose, and he is compelled to do what he will not. Like a man suffering violence he cries aloud and says: 'O wretched man that I am, who shall deliver me from the body of his death?' And do *you* think then that you can pass through life without a fall and without a wound, if you do not keep your heart with all diligence and say with the Saviour: 'My mother and my brethren are these which hear the word of God and do it'? Such cruelty as this is really love. Nay, what greater love can there be than to guard a holy son for a holy mother? She desires your eternal life: she is content not to see you for the moment, provided that she may see you for ever with Christ. She is like Hannah, who brought forth Samuel,[1] not for her own comfort, but for the service of the tabernacle.

The sons of Jonadab drank no wine nor strong drink and lived in tents which they pitched whenever night came on. Of them the psalm says that they were the first to undergo captivity, for when the Chaldean host was devastating Judaea they were compelled to enter cities. Let others think as they will—every one follows his own bent—but to me a town is a prison, and the wilderness a paradise. What do we monks want with crowded cities, we whose very name bespeaks loneliness? Moses was trained for forty years in the desert to fit him for the task of leading the Jewish people, and from being a shepherd of sheep he became a shepherd of men. The apostles left their fishing on Lake Gennesaret to fish for human souls. Then they had a father, nets, and a little boat: but they followed the Lord straightway and abandoned everything, carrying their cross every day, without so much as a stick in their hands.

I say this, so that if you are tickled by a desire to become a clergyman, you may learn now what you will then be able to teach others, offering a reasonable sacrifice to Christ. You must not think yourself an old soldier while you are still a recruit, a master while you are still a pupil. It would not become my lowly rank to pass judgment on

---

[1] A prophet and leader of the Hebrews in the Old Testament.

others, or to say anything unfavourable about those who serve in churches. Let them keep their proper place and station, and if you ever join them, my treatise written for Nepotian will show you how you ought to live in that position. For the moment I am discussing a monk's early training and character, a monk, moreover, who after a liberal education in his early manhood placed upon his neck the yoke of Christ.

The first point with which I must deal is whether you ought to live alone or in a monastery with others. I would prefer you to have the society of holy men and not to be your own teacher. If you set out on a strange road without a guide you may easily at the start take a wrong turning and make a mistake, going too far or not far enough, running till you weary yourself or delaying your journey for a sleep. In solitude pride quickly creeps in, and when a man has fasted for a little while and has seen no one, he thinks himself a person of some account. He forgets who he is, whence he comes, and where he is going, and lets his body run riot within, his tongue abroad. Contrary to the apostle's wishes, he judges another man's servants; he stretches out his hand for anything that his gullet craves; he does what he pleases and sleeps as long as he pleases; he fears no one, he thinks all men his inferiors, spends more time in cities than in his cell, and though among the brethren he makes a pretence of modesty, in the crowded squares he ruffles it with the best. What then, you will say? Do I disapprove of the solitary life? Not at all: I have often commended it. But I wish to see the soldiers who march out from a monastery-school men who have not been frightened by their early training, who have given proof of a holy life for many months, who have made themselves last that they might be first, who have not been overcome by hunger or satiety, who take pleasure in poverty, whose garb, conversation, looks and gait all teach virtue, and who have no skill—as some foolish fellows have—in inventing monstrous stories of their struggles with demons, tales invented to excite the admiration of the ignorant mob and to extract money from their pockets.

Just lately, to my sorrow, I saw the fortune of a Croesus[2] brought to light at one man's death, and beheld a city's alms collected ostensibly for the poor's benefit left by will to his sons and their descen-

---

[2] A king of Lydia in the sixth century B.C., proverbial for his vast wealth. (See the selection from Herodotus, pp. 76–88.)

dants. Then the iron which was hidden in the depths floated upon the surface, and amid the palm trees the bitter waters of Marah were seen. Nor need we wonder at his avarice: his partner and teacher was a man who turned the hunger of the needy into a source of wealth for himself, and to his own wretchedness kept back the legacies that were left to the wretched. But at last their cries reached heaven and were too much for God's patient ears, so that he sent an angel to say to this villainous Nabal the Carmelite: 'Thou fool, this night thy soul shall be required of thee: then whose shall those things be which thou has provided?'

For the reasons then which I have given above, I wish you not to live with your mother. And there are some further considerations. If she offers you a dainty dish, you would grieve her by refusing it, while if you take it you would be throwing oil on fire. Moreover, in a house that is full of girls you would see things in the day-time that you would think about in the night. Always have a book in your hand and before your eyes; learn the psalms word by word, pray without ceasing, keep your senses on the alert and closed against vain imaginings. Let your mind and body both strain towards the Lord, overcome wrath by patience; love the knowledge of the Scriptures and you will not love the sins of the flesh.

Do not let your mind offer a lodging to disturbing thoughts, for if they once find a home in your breast they will become your masters and lead you on into fatal sin. Engage in some occupation, so that the devil may always find you busy. If the apostles who had the power to make the Gospel their livelihood still worked with their hands that they might not be a burden on any man, and gave relief to others whose carnal possessions they had a right to enjoy in return for their spiritual benefits, why should you not provide for your own future wants? Make creels of reeds or weave baskets of pliant osiers. Hoe the ground and mark it out into equal plots, and when you have sown cabbage seed or set out plants in rows, bring water down in channels and stand by like the onlooker in the lovely lines:

> 'Lo, from the channelled slope he brings the stream,
> Which falls hoarse murmuring o'er the polished stones
> And with its bubbling flood allays the heat
> Of sun-scorched fields,'

Graft barren trees with buds or slips, so that you may, after a little time, pluck sweet fruit as a reward for your labours. Make hives for bees, for to them the Proverbs of Solomon send you, and by watching the tiny creatures learn the ordinance of a monastery and the discipline of a kingdom. Twist lines too for catching fish, and copy out manuscripts, so that your hand may earn you food and your soul be satisfied with reading. 'Every one that is idle is a prey to vain desires.' Monasteries in Egypt make it a rule not to take any one who will not work, thinking not so much of the necessities of life as of the safety of men's souls, lest they should be led astray by dangerous imaginings, and be like Jerusalem in her whoredoms, who opened her feet to every chance comer.

• • •

No art is learned without a master. Even dumb animals and herds of wild beasts follow leaders of their own. Bees have rulers, and cranes fly behind one of their number in the shape of the letter Y. There is one emperor, and one judge for each province. When Rome was founded it could not have two brothers reigning together, and so it was inaugurated by an act of fratricide. Esau and Jacob warred against one another in Rebecca's womb. Each church has but one bishop, one arch-presbyter, one archdeacon; every ecclesiastical order is subjected to its own rulers. There is one pilot in a ship, one master in a house; and however large an army may be, the soldiers await one man's signal.

I will not weary my reader with further repetition, for the purpose of all these examples is simply this. I want to show you that you had better not be left to your own discretion, but should rather live in a monastery under the control of one father and with many companions. From one of them you may learn humility, from another patience; this one will teach you silence, that one meekness. You will not do what you yourself wish; you will eat what you are ordered; you will take what you are given; you will wear the dress allotted to you; you will perform a set amount of work; you will be subordinate to some one you do not like; you will come to bed worn out with weariness and fall asleep as you walk about. Before you have had your fill of rest, you will be forced to get out of bed and take your turn in psalm-singing, a task where real emotion is a greater requisite than a sweet voice.

The apostle says: 'I will pray with the spirit and I will pray with the understanding also,' and, again: 'Make melody in your hearts.' He had read the precept: 'Sing ye praises with understanding.' You

will serve the brethren; you will wash the feet of guests; if you suffer
wrong you will say nothing; the superior of the monastery you will
fear as a master and love as a father. Whatever precepts he gives you
will believe to be wholesome for you. You will not pass judgment
upon your elder's decisions, for it is your duty to be obedient and
carry out orders, according to the words of Moses: 'Keep silence and
hearken, O Israel.' You will be so busy with all these tasks that you
will have no time for vain imaginings, and while you pass from one
occupation to the next you will only have in mind the work that you
are being forced to do.

I myself have seen some men who after they had renounced the
world—in garb, at least, and in verbal professions, but not in reality—changed nothing of their former mode of life. Their household
has increased rather than diminished; they have the same number of
servants to wait upon them and keep the same elaborate table;
though they drink from glass and eat from plates of earthenware, it
is gold they swallow, and amidst crowds of servants swarming
round them they claim the name of hermit. Others, who are poor
and of slender means and think themselves full of wisdom, pass
through the streets like the pageants in a procession, to practise a
cynical eloquence. Others shrug their shoulders and croak indistinctly
to themselves, and with glassy eyes fixed upon the earth they balance
swelling words upon their tongues, so that if you add a crier, you
might think it was his excellency the governor who was coming
along. Some, too, by reason of damp cells and immoderate fasts,
added to the weariness of solitude and excessive study, have a singing in their ears day and night, and turning melancholy mad need
Hippocrates'[3] medications more than any advice of mine.

Very many cannot forgo their previous trades and occupations,
and though they change its name carry on the same pedlar's traffic as
before, seeking for themselves not food and raiment, as the apostle
directs, but greater profits than men of the world expect. In the past
the mad greed of sellers was checked by the aediles, or as the Greeks
call them, market-inspectors, and men could not cheat with impunity: to-day under the cloak of religion such men hoard up unjust
gains, and the good name of Christianity does more wrong than it
suffers. I am ashamed to say it, but I must—at least we ought to
blush at our disgrace—we hold out our hands in public for alms

---

[3] Hippocrates was a famous physician of ancient Greece.

while we have gold hidden under our rags, and to every one's surprise after living as poor men we die rich with purses well filled.

In your case, since you will be in a monastery, such conduct will not be allowed; habits will gradually grow on you, and finally you will do of your own accord what was at first a matter of compulsion; you will take pleasure in your labours, and forgetting what is behind you will reach out to that which is before; you will not think at all of the evil that others do, but only of the good which it is your duty to perform.

Do not be influenced by the number of those that sin, or disturbed by the host of the perishing, so as to have the unspoken thought: 'What? Shall all then perish who live in cities? Behold, they enjoy their property, they serve in the churches, they frequent the baths, they do not disdain unguents, and yet they flourish and are universally respected.' To such reasonings I have replied before, and will now do so briefly again, merely remarking that in this present short treatise I am not discussing the behaviour of the clergy, but laying down rules for a monk. The clergy are holy men, and in every case their life is worthy of praise. Go then and so live in your monastery that you may deserve to be a clergyman, that you may keep your youth free from all stain of defilement, and that you may come forth to Christ's altar as a virgin steps from her bower; that you may be well spoken of abroad, and that women may know your reputation but not your looks. When you come to ripe years, that is, if life be granted you, and have been appointed as a clergyman either by the people or by the bishop of the city, then act as becomes a cleric, and among your colleagues choose the better men as your models. In every rank and condition of life the very bad is mingled with the very good.

• • •

Truth does not love corners nor does she seek out whisperers. To Timothy[4] it is said: 'Against an elder receive not an accusation suddenly; but him that sinneth rebuke before all, that others also may fear.' When a man is of ripe years you should not readily believe evil of him; his past life is a defence and so is the honourable title of elder. Still, as we are but men and sometimes in spite of our mature

---

[4] An associate of St. Paul. The quotation is from Paul's letter to Timothy on church discipline (I Timothy 5:19–20).

age fall into the sins of youth, if I do wrong and you wish to correct me, rebuke me openly and do not indulge in secret backbiting. 'Let the righteous smite me, it shall be a kindness, and let him reprove me; but let not the oil of the sinner enrich my head.' 'Whom the Lord loveth, he chasteneth, and scourgeth every son whom he receiveth.' By the mouth of Isaiah God makes proclamation: 'O my people, they who call you happy cause you to err and destroy the way of your paths.' What benefit is it to me if you tell other people of my misdeeds, if without my knowledge you hurt another by the story of my sins or rather by your slanders, if while really eager to tell your tale to all you speak to each individual as though he were your only confidant? Such conduct seeks not my improvement but the satisfaction of your own vice. The Lord gave commandment that those who sin against us should be arraigned privately or else in the presence of a witness, and that if they refuse to listen they should be brought before the Church, and those who persist in wickedness should be regarded as heathens and publicans.

I have spoken thus definitely because I wish to free a young friend of mine from an itching tongue and itching ears, so that I may present him born again in Christ without spot or roughness as a chaste virgin, holy both in body and in mind. I would not have him boast in name alone, or be shut out by the Bridegroom because his lamp has gone out for want of the oil of good works. You have in your town a saintly and most learned prelate, Proculus, and he by the living sound of his voice can do more for you than any pages I can write. By daily homilies he will keep you in the straight path and not suffer you to turn right or left and leave the king's highway, whereby Israel undertakes to pass on its hasty journey to the promised land. May the voice of the Church's supplication be heard: 'Lord, ordain peace for us, for thou also hast wrought all our works for us.' May our renunciation of the world be a matter of free will and not of necessity! May we seek poverty as a glorious thing, not have it forced upon us as a punishment!

However, in our present miseries, with swords raging fiercely all around us, he is rich enough who is not in actual want of bread, he is more powerful than he needs be who is not reduced to slavery. Exuperius, the saintly bishop of Toulouse, like the widow of Zarephath[5] feeds others and goes hungry himself. His face is pale with

---

[5] An Old Testament figure.

fasting, but it is the craving of others that torments him, and he has spent all his substance on those that are Christ's flesh. Yet none is richer than he; for in his wicker basket he carries the body of the Lord and in his glass cup His blood. He has driven greed from the temple; without scourge of ropes or chiding words he has overthrown the tables of mammon of those that sell doves, that is, the gifts of the Holy Spirit; he has scattered the money of the moneychangers, so that the house of God might be called a house of prayer and not a den of robbers.

Follow closely in his steps and in those of others like him in virtue, men whom their holy office only makes more humble and more poor. Or else, if you desire perfection, go out like Abraham from your native city and your kin, and travel whither you know not. If you have substance, sell it and give it to the poor. If you have none, you are free from a great burden. Naked yourself follow a naked Christ. The task is hard and great and difficult; but great also are the rewards.

24

St. Augustine

The City of God

⊡

As the heirs of Greco-Roman civilization, imbued with its forms of thought
and expression, fourth-century Christians for the most part were unable to
conceive of themselves outside its fold. Instead of turning their backs upon
this civilization, Christian thinkers generally sought by mutual understanding to give it new moral and spiritual direction, thus achieving a kind of
synthesis of Christianity and classicism. The most important of these, the
greatest of the Latin Fathers, was Aurelius Augustinus (354–430).

Born near Carthage, St. Augustine received the best education his pagan
father, a man of modest standing, could afford; afterward, he became a
professor of rhetoric at Carthage, then Rome, and then Milan. There, about
387, he was converted to Christianity. A few years after his return to his
birthplace, he was made bishop of Hippo, a minor coastal town in North
Africa. But his personality and writings spread his fame far and wide so that
he became the outstanding figure in the whole Western Church, and St.
Jerome hailed him as the "second founder of the ancient faith."

St. Augustine's most important writing, The City of God, undertaken
between 413 and 426, was meant to "combat the blasphemies and errors" of
those who, bewildered by the collapse of their old security, laid the blame for
the capture of Rome by the Goths upon men's defection from the old gods.
Deeply versed in the mind of the pagan world himself and admiring much of
it, St. Augustine answered with the argument of the "two cities." This,
"the most famous of all philosophic meditations on history," as it has been
called, is set forth in the selection. Nothing illustrates better the process

St. Augustine, *The City of God.* From Volume II of *Basic Writings of Saint Augustine,*
edited by Whitney J. Oates. Copyright 1948 by Random House, Inc. Reprinted by
permission. [Pp. 38–40, 143, 257, 274–76, 278–79, 474–75, 493–94.]

whereby a Semitic religion, and the Christian movement to which it gave rise, became domesticated in Greco-Roman culture.

The vast historical importance of this saint and doctor of the Church is suggested by the words of the historian, Terrot R. Glover:

> *He gave to Christian thought . . . an impulse and direction the force of which is still unspent. He shaped the Catholic theory of the Church; he gave the great popes the idea of the City of God . . . he was the father of the mystics; the founder of the scholastic philosophy of the Middle Ages; and above all the hero and master of the Renaissance and the Reformation.* *

THAT THE OVERTHROW OF ROME HAS NOT CORRECTED THE VICES OF THE ROMANS

Oh infatuated men, what is this blindness, or rather madness, which possesses you? How is it that while, as we hear, even the eastern nations are bewailing your ruin, and while powerful states in the most remote parts of the earth are mourning your fall as a public calamity, ye yourselves should be crowding to the theatres, should be pouring into them and filling them; and, in short, be playing a madder part now than ever before? This was the foul plague-spot, this the wreck of virtue and honor that Scipio [1] sought to preserve you from when he prohibited the construction of theatres; this was his reason for desiring that you might still have an enemy to fear, seeing as he did how easily prosperity would corrupt and destroy you. He did not consider that republic flourishing whose walls stand, but whose morals are in ruins. But the seductions of evil-minded devils had more influence with you than the precautions of prudent men. Hence the injuries you do, you will not permit to be imputed to you; but the injuries you suffer, you impute to Christianity. Depraved by good fortune, and not chastened by adversity, what you desire in the restoration of a peaceful and secure state, is not the tranquillity of the commonwealth, but the impunity of your own vicious luxury. Scipio wished you to be hard pressed by an enemy, that you might not abandon yourselves to luxurious manners; but so abandoned are you,

---

* *Life and Letters in the Fourth Century* (New York: G. E. Stechert & Co., 1924), 194.
[1] A Roman consul and general of the republican era.

that not even when crushed by the enemy is your luxury repressed. You have missed the profit of your calamity; you have been made most wretched, and have remained most profligate.

OF GOD'S CLEMENCY IN MODERATING THE RUIN OF THE CITY

And that you are yet alive is due to God, who spares you that you may be admonished to repent and reform your lives. It is He who has permitted you, ungrateful as you are, to escape the sword of the enemy, by calling yourselves His servants, or by finding asylum in the sacred places of the martyrs.

It is said that Romulus and Remus,[2] in order to increase the population of the city they founded, opened a sanctuary in which every man might find asylum and absolution of all crime—a remarkable foreshadowing of what has recently occurred in honor of Christ. The destroyers of Rome followed the example of its founders. But it was not greatly to their credit that the latter, for the sake of increasing the number of their citizens, did that which the former have done, lest the number of their enemies should be diminished.

OF THE SONS OF THE CHURCH WHO ARE HIDDEN AMONG THE WICKED, AND OF FALSE CHRISTIANS WITHIN THE CHURCH

Let these and similar answers (if any fuller and fitter answers can be found) be given to their enemies by the redeemed family of the Lord Christ, and by the pilgrim city of King Christ. But let this city bear in mind, that among her enemies lie hid those who are destined to be fellow-citizens, that she may not think it a fruitless labor to bear what they inflict as enemies until they become confessors of the faith. So, too, as long as she is a stranger in the world, the city of God has in her communion, and bound to her by the sacraments, some who shall not eternally dwell in the lot of the saints. Of these, some are not now recognized; others declare themselves, and do not hesitate to make common cause with our enemies in murmuring

[2] The legendary twin founders of Rome.

against God, whose sacramental badge they wear. These men you may to-day see thronging the churches with us, to-morrow crowding the theatres with the godless. But we have the less reason to despair of the reclamation even of such persons, if among our most declared enemies there are now some, unknown to themselves, who are destined to become our friends. In truth, these two cities are entangled together in this world, and intermixed until the last judgment effects their separation. I now proceed to speak, as God shall help me, of the rise, progress, and end of these two cities; and what I write, I write for the glory of the city of God, that, being placed in comparison with the other, it may shine with a brighter lustre.

WHAT SUBJECTS ARE TO BE HANDLED IN THE FOLLOWING DISCOURSE

But I have still some things to say in confutation of those who refer the disasters of the Roman republic to our religion, because it prohibits the offering of sacrifices to the gods. For this end I must recount all, or as many as may seem sufficient, of the disasters which befell that city and its subject provinces, before these sacrifices were prohibited; for all these disasters they would doubtless have attributed to us, if at that time our religion had shed its light upon them, and had prohibited their sacrifices. I must then go on to show what social well-being the true God, in whose hand are all kingdoms, vouchsafed to grant to them that their empire might increase. I must show why He did so, and how their false gods, instead of at all aiding them, greatly injured them by guile and deceit. And, lastly, I must meet those who, when on this point convinced and confuted by irrefragable proofs, endeavor to maintain that they worship the gods, not hoping for the present advantages of this life, but for those which are to be enjoyed after death. And this, if I am not mistaken, will be the most difficult part of my task, and will be worthy of the loftiest argument; for we must then enter the lists with the philosophers, not the mere common herd of philosophers, but the most renowned, who in many points agree with ourselves, as regarding the immortality of the soul, and that the true God created the world, and by His providence rules all He has created. But as they differ from us on other points, we must not shrink from the task of exposing their errors, that, having refuted the gainsaying of the wicked with such ability as God may vouchsafe, we may assert the city of God, and true piety, and the worship of God, to which alone the promise of true and everlasting felicity is attached. Here, then, let us conclude, that we may enter on these subjects in a fresh book.

. . .

OF THIS PART OF THE WORK, WHEREIN WE BEGIN TO EXPLAIN THE ORIGIN AND END OF THE TWO CITIES

The city of God we speak of is the same to which testimony is borne by that Scripture, which excels all the writings of all nations by its divine authority, and has brought under its influence all kinds of minds, and this not by a casual intellectual movement, but obviously by an express providential arrangement. For there it is written, "Glorious things are spoken of thee, O city of God." And in another psalm we read, "Great is the Lord, and greatly to be praised in the city of our God, in the mountain of His holiness, increasing the joy of the whole earth." And, a little after, in the same psalm, "As we have heard, so have we seen in the city of the Lord of hosts, in the city of our God. God has established it for ever." And in another, "There is a river the streams whereof shall make glad the city of our God, the holy place of the tabernacles of the Most High. God is in the midst of her, she shall not be moved." From these and similar testimonies, all of which it were tedious to cite, we have learned that there is a city of God, and its Founder has inspired us with a love which makes us covet its citizenship. To this Founder of the holy city the citizens of the earthly city prefer their own gods, not knowing that He is the God of gods, not of false, *i.e.,* of impious and proud gods, who, being deprived of His unchangeable and freely communicated light, and so reduced to a kind of poverty-stricken power, eagerly grasp at their own private privileges, and seek divine honors from their deluded subjects; but of the pious and holy gods, who are better pleased to submit themselves to one, than to subject many to themselves, and who would rather worship God than be worshipped as God.

. . .

OF THE NATURE OF MAN'S FIRST SIN

If any one finds a difficulty in understanding why other sins do not alter human nature as it was altered by the transgression of those first human beings, so that on account of it this nature is subject to the great corruption we feel and see, and to death, and is distracted and tossed with so many furious and contending emotions, and is certainly far different from what it was before sin, even though it were then lodged in an animal body—if, I say, any one is moved by this, he ought not to think that that sin was a small and light one because it was committed about food, and that not bad nor noxious, except because it was forbidden; for in that spot of singular felicity God could not have created and planted any evil thing. But by the precept He gave, God commended obedience, which is, in a sort, the mother and guardian of all the virtues in the reasonable creature, which was so created that submission is advantageous to it, while the fulfillment of its own will in preference to the Creator's is destruction. And as this commandment enjoining abstinence from one kind of food in the midst of great abundance of other kinds was so easy to keep—so light a burden to the memory—and, above all, found no resistance to its observance in lust, which only afterwards sprung up as the penal consequence of sin, the iniquity of violating it was all the greater in proportion to the ease with which it might have been kept.

THAT IN ADAM'S SIN AN EVIL WILL PRECEDED THE EVIL ACT

Our first parents fell into open disobedience because already they were secretly corrupted; for the evil act had never been done had not an evil will preceded it. And what is the origin of our evil will but pride? For "pride is the beginning of sin." And what is pride but the craving for undue exaltation? And this is undue exaltation, when the soul abandons Him to whom it ought to cleave as its end, and becomes a kind of end to itself. This happens when it becomes its own satisfaction, and it does so when it falls away from that unchangeable good which ought to satisfy it more than itself. This falling away is spontaneous; for if the will had remained steadfast in the love of that higher and changeless good by which it was illumined to intelligence and kindled into love, it would not have turned away to find satisfaction in itself, and so become frigid and benighted. The woman would not have believed the serpent spoke the truth, nor would the man have preferred the request of his wife to the command of God, nor have supposed that it was a venial transgression to cleave to the partner of his life, even in a partnership of sin. The wicked deed,

then,—that is to say the transgression of eating the forbidden fruit,—
was committed by persons who were already wicked.

•   •   •

OF THE NATURE OF THE TWO CITIES, THE EARTHLY AND THE HEAVENLY

Accordingly, two cities have been formed by two loves: the
earthly by the love of self, even to the contempt of God; the heavenly by the love of God, even to the contempt of self. The former, in
a word, glories in itself, the latter in the Lord. For the one seeks
glory from men; but the greatest glory of the other is God, the
witness of conscience. The one lifts up its head in its own glory; the
other says to its God, "Thou art my glory, and the lifter up of mine
head." In the one, the princes and the nations it subdues are ruled by
the love of ruling; in the other, the princes and the subjects serve one
another in love, the latter obeying, while the former take thought for
all. The one delights in its own strength, represented in the persons
of its rulers; the other says to its God, "I will love Thee, O Lord, my
strength." And therefore the wise men of the one city, living according to man, have sought for profit to their own bodies or souls, or
both, and those who have known God "glorified Him not as God,
neither were thankful, but became vain in their imaginations, and
their foolish heart was darkened; professing themselves to be
wise"—that is, glorying in their own wisdom; and being possessed
by pride—"they became fools, and changed the glory of the incor-
ruptible God into an image made like to corruptible man, and to
birds, and four-footed beasts, and creeping things." For they were
either leaders or followers of the people in adoring images, "and
worshipped and served the creature more than the Creator, who is
blessed for ever." But in the other city there is no human wisdom,
but only godliness, which offers due worship to the true God, and
looks for its reward in the society of the saints, of holy angels as well
as holy men, that God may be all in all.

OF THE TWO LINES OF THE HUMAN RACE WHICH FROM FIRST TO LAST DIVIDE IT

Of the bliss of Paradise, of Paradise itself, and of the life of our
first parents there, and of their sin and punishment, many have

thought much, spoken much, written much. We ourselves, too, have spoken to these things in the foregoing books, and have written either what we read in the Holy Scriptures, or what we could reasonably deduce from them. And were we to enter into a more detailed investigation of these matters, an endless number of endless questions would arise, which would involve us in a larger work than the present occasion admits. We cannot be expected to find room for replying to every question that may be started by unoccupied and captious men, who are ever more ready to ask questions than capable of understanding the answer. Yet I trust we have already done justice to these great and difficult questions regarding the beginning of the world, or of the soul, or of the human race itself.

This race we have distributed into two parts, the one consisting of those who live according to man, the other of those who live according to God. And these we also mystically call the two cities, or the two communities of men, of which the one is predestined to reign eternally with God, and the other to suffer eternal punishment with the devil. This, however, is their end, and of it we are to speak afterwards. At present, as we have said enough about their origin, whether among the angels, whose numbers we know not, or in the two first human beings, it seems suitable to attempt an account of their career, from the time when our two first parents began to propagate the race until all human generation shall cease. For this whole time or world-age, in which the dying give place and those who are born succeed, is the career of these two cities concerning which we treat.

Of these two first parents of the human race,[3] then, Cain was the first-born, and he belonged to the city of men; after him was born Abel, who belonged to the city of God. For as in the individual the truth of the apostle's statement is discerned, "that is not first which is spiritual, but that which is natural, and afterward that which is spiritual," whence it comes to pass that each man, being derived from a condemned stock, is first of all born of Adam evil and carnal, and becomes good and spiritual only afterwards, when he is grafted into Christ by regeneration: so was it in the human race as a whole.

When these two cities began to run their course by a series of deaths and births, the citizen of this world was the first-born, and after him the stranger in this world, the citizen of the city of God, predestinated by grace, elected by grace, by grace a stranger below,

---

[3] Adam and Eve.

and by grace a citizen above. By grace—for so far as regards himself he is sprung from the same mass, all of which is condemned in its origin: but God, like a potter (for his comparison is introduced by the apostle judiciously, and not without thought) of the same lump made one vessel to honor, another to dishonor. But first the vessel to dishonor was made, and after it another to honor. For in each individual, as I have already said, there is first of all that which is reprobate, that form which we must begin, but in which we need not necessarily remain; afterwards is that which is well-approved, to which we may by advancing attain, and in which, when we have reached it, we may abide. Not, indeed, that every wicked man shall be good, but that no one will be good who was not first of all wicked; but the sooner any one becomes a good man, the more speedily does he receive this title, and abolish the old name in the new. Accordingly, it is recorded of Cain that he built a city, but Abel, being a sojourner, built none. For the city of the saints is above, although here below it begets citizens, in whom it sojourns till the time of its reign arrives, when it shall gather together all in the day of the resurrection; and then shall the promised kingdom be given to them, in which they shall reign with their Prince, the King of the ages, time without end.

• • •

OF THE CONFLICT AND PEACE OF THE EARTHLY CITY

But the earthly city, which shall not be everlasting (for it will no longer be a city when it has been committed to the extreme penalty), has its good in this world, and rejoices in it with such joy as such things can afford. But as this is not a good which can discharge its devotees of all distresses, this city is often divided against itself by litigations, wars, quarrels, and such victories as are either life-destroying or short-lived. For each part of it that arms against another part of it seeks to triumph over the nations though itself in bondage to vice. If, when it has conquered, it is inflated with pride, its victory is life-destroying; but if it turns its thoughts upon the common casualties of our mortal condition, and is rather anxious concerning the disasters that may befall it than elated with the successes already achieved, this victory, though of a higher kind, is still only short-lived; for it cannot abidingly rule over those whom it has victoriously subjugated.

But the things which this city desires cannot justly be said to be evil, for it is itself, in its own kind, better than all other human good. For it desires earthly peace for the sake of enjoying earthly goods, and it makes war in order to attain to this peace; since, if it has conquered, and there remains no one to resist it, it enjoys a peace which it had not while there were opposing parties who contested for the enjoyment of those things which were too small to satisfy both. This peace is purchased by toilsome wars; it is obtained by what they style a glorious victory. Now, when victory remains with the party which had the juster cause, who hesitates to congratulate the victor, and style it is desirable peace? These things, then, are good things, and without doubt the gifts of God. But, if they neglect the better things of the heavenly city, which are secured by eternal victory and peace never-ending, and so inordinately covet these present good things that they believe them to be the only desirable things, or love them better than those things which are believed to be better—if this be so, then it is necessary that misery follow and ever increase.

• • •

WHAT THE CHRISTIANS BELIEVE REGARDING THE SUPREME GOOD AND EVIL, IN OPPOSITION TO THE PHILOSOPHERS, WHO HAVE MAINTAINED THAT THE SUPREME GOOD IS IN THEMSELVES

If, then, we be asked what the city of God has to say upon these points, and, in the first place, what its opinion regarding the supreme good and evil is, it will reply that life eternal is the supreme good, death eternal the supreme evil, and that to obtain the one and escape the other we must live rightly. And thus it is written, "The just lives by faith," [4] for we do not as yet see our good, and must therefore live by faith; neither have we in ourselves power to live rightly, but can do so only if He who has given us faith to believe in His help do help us when we believe and pray. As for those who have supposed that the sovereign good and evil are to be found in this life and have placed it either in the soul or the body, or in both, or, to speak more explicitly, either in pleasure or in virtue, or in both; in repose or in virtue, or in both; in pleasure and repose, or in virtue, or in all com-

---

[4] A quotation from St. Paul (Romans 1:17).

bined; in the primary objects of nature, or in virtue, or in both—all these have, with a marvelous shallowness, sought to find their blessedness in this life and in themselves. Contempt has been poured upon such ideas by the Truth, saying by the prophet, "The Lord knoweth the thoughts of men" (or, as the Apostle Paul cites the passage, "The Lord knoweth the thoughts of the *wise*") "that they are vain."

. . .

WHAT PRODUCES PEACE, AND WHAT DISCORD, BETWEEN THE HEAVENLY AND EARTHLY CITIES

But the families which do not live by faith seek their peace in the earthly advantages of this life; while the families which live by faith look for those eternal blessings which are promised, and use as pilgrims such advantages of time and of earth as do not fascinate and divert them from God, but rather aid them to endure with greater ease, and to keep down the number of those burdens of the corruptible body which weigh upon the soul. Thus the things necessary for this mortal life are used by both kinds of men and families alike, but each has its own peculiar and widely different aim in using them.

The earthly city, which does not live by faith, seeks an earthly peace, and the end it proposes, in the well-ordered concord of civic obedience and rule, is the combination of men's wills to attain the things which are helpful to this life. The heavenly city, or rather the part of it which sojourns on earth and lives by faith, makes use of this peace only because it must, until this mortal condition which necessitates it shall pass away. Consequently, so long as it lives like a captive and a stranger in the earthly city, though it has already received the promise of redemption, and the gift of the Spirit as the earnest of it, it makes no scruple to obey the laws of the earthly city, whereby the things necessary for the maintenance of this mortal life are administered; and thus, as this life is common to both cities, so there is a harmony between them in regard to what belongs to it.

But, as the earthly city has had some philosophers whose doctrine is condemned by the divine teaching, who, being deceived either by their own conjectures or by demons, supposed that many gods must be invited to take an interest in human affairs, and assigned to each a separate function and a separate department—to one the body, to another the soul; and in the body itself, to one the head, to another the neck, and each of the other members to one of the gods; and in like manner, in the soul, to one god the natural capacity was assigned, to another education, to another anger, to another lust; so the various affairs of life were assigned—cattle to one, corn to another, wine to another, oil to another, the woods to another, money to another, navigation to another, wars and victories to another, marriages to another, births and fecundity to another, and other things to other gods.

The celestial city, on the other hand, knew that one God only was to be worshipped, and that to Him alone was due that service which the Greeks call Latria, and which can be given only to a god, so it has come to pass that the two cities could not have common laws of religion, and that the heavenly city has been compelled in this matter to dissent, and to become obnoxious to those who think differently, and to stand the brunt of their anger and hatred and persecutions, except in so far as the minds of their enemies have been alarmed by the multitude of the Christians and quelled by the manifest protection of God accorded to them.

This heavenly city, then, while it sojourns on earth, calls citizens out of all nations, and gathers together a society of pilgrims of all languages, not scrupling about diversities in the manners, laws, and institutions whereby earthly peace is secured and maintained, but recognizing that, however various these are, they all tend to one and the same end of earthly peace. It therefore is so far from rescinding and abolishing these diversities, that it even preserves and adopts them, so long only as no hindrance to the worship of the one supreme and true God is thus introduced. Even the heavenly city, therefore, while in its state of pilgrimage, avails itself of the peace of earth, and, so far as it can without injuring faith and godliness, desires and maintains a common agreement among men regarding the acquisition of the necessaries of life, and makes this earthly peace bear upon the peace of heaven; for this alone can be truly called and esteemed the peace of the reasonable creatures, consisting as it does in the perfectly ordered and harmonious enjoyment of God and of one another in God. When we shall have reached that peace, this mortal life shall give place to one that is eternal, and our body shall be no more this animal body which by its corruption weighs down the soul, but a spiritual body feeling no want, and in all its members subjected to the will. In its pilgrim state the heavenly city possesses this peace by faith; and by this faith it lives righteously when it refers to the attainment of that peace every good action towards God and man; for the life of the city is a social life.